Vietnam's Communist Revolution

By tracing the evolving worldview of Vietnamese communists over eighty years as they led Vietnam through wars, social revolution, and peaceful development, this book shows the depth and resilience of their commitment to the communist utopia in their foreign policy. Unearthing new material from Vietnamese archives and publications, this book challenges the conventional scholarship and the popular image of the Vietnamese revolution and the Vietnam War as being driven solely by patriotic inspirations. The revolution saw not only successes in defeating foreign intervention, but also failures in bringing peace and development to Vietnam. This was, and is, the real Vietnam Tragedy. Spanning the entire history of the Vietnamese revolution and its aftermath, this book examines its leaders' early rise to power, the tumult of three decades of war with France, the United States, and China, and the dismal legacies left behind, which still influence Vietnam's foreign policy today.

Tuong Vu is Director of Asian Studies and Professor of Political Science at the University of Oregon. A native of Vietnam, he has published extensively on Vietnamese politics and history, Cold War history, and East Asian politics. Vu served on the editorial board of the *Journal of Vietnamese Studies* during 2006–2014. His first book, *Paths to Development in Asia: South Korea, Vietnam, China, and Indonesia*, received a 2011 Bernard Schwartz Award Honorable Mention.

Cambridge Studies in US Foreign Relations

Edited by

Paul Thomas Chamberlin, *Columbia University*
Lien-Hang T. Nguyen, *Columbia University*

This series showcases cutting-edge scholarship in US foreign relations that employs dynamic new methodological approaches and archives from the colonial era to the present. The series is guided by the ethos of transnationalism, focusing on the history of American foreign relations in a global context rather than privileging the United States as the dominant actor on the world stage.

Also in the Series

Michael Neagle, *America's Forgotten Colony: Cuba's Isle of Pines*

Elisabeth Leake, *The Defiant Border: The Afghan-Pakistan Borderlands in the Era of Decolonization, 1936–1965*

Renata Keller, *Mexico's Cold War: Cuba, the United States, and the Legacy of the Mexican Revolution*

Vietnam's Communist Revolution

The Power and Limits of Ideology

TUONG VU
University of Oregon

CAMBRIDGE
UNIVERSITY PRESS

One Liberty Plaza, 20th Floor, New York, NY 10006, USA

Cambridge University Press is part of the University of Cambridge.

It furthers the University's mission by disseminating knowledge in the pursuit of education, learning, and research at the highest international levels of excellence.

www.cambridge.org
Information on this title: www.cambridge.org/9781316607909

© Tuong Vu 2017

This publication is in copyright. Subject to statutory exception and to the provisions of relevant collective licensing agreements, no reproduction of any part may take place without the written permission of Cambridge University Press.

First published 2017

Printed in the United Kingdom by Clays, St Ives plc

A catalogue record for this publication is available from the British Library.

ISBN 978-1-107-15402-5 Hardback
ISBN 978-1-316-60790-9 Paperback

Cambridge University Press has no responsibility for the persistence or accuracy of URLS for external or third-party Internet Web sites referred to in this publication and does not guarantee that any content on such Web sites is, or will remain, accurate or appropriate.

Contents

Acknowledgments

This is not a book I intended to write; fortuitous circumstances and generous support from colleagues and institutions came together to nudge me along, chapter by chapter, over ten years. Three scholars who have influenced this project the most are Peter Zinoman, Keith Taylor, and Chris Goscha. Peter Zinoman taught me to write as a historian and offered valuable comments on many chapters. Keith Taylor's scholarship is a great source of inspiration. Chris Goscha's invitation to participate in a Euroseas conference in Paris in 2004 had me put my thoughts on the topic together for the first time. I'm indebted to Chris for giving me so many helpful suggestions besides the chance to start the project. I'm also grateful to the encouragement from many fellow panelists at that conference, including Christian Ostermann, the late Ilya Gaiduk, Chen Jian, and Nayan Chanda. This Euroseas paper eventually became Chapter 3 of this book.

In the same spirit, I greatly appreciate historian Sergey Glebov who encouraged me to write an article for the journal *Ab Imperio: Studies of New Imperial History and Nationalism in the Post-Soviet Space*. Parts of this article were included in Chapter 1 and Chapter 2 of this book. Smith College deserves thanks for offering me generous support through a Mendenhall Fellowship, which contributed greatly to my research for this book.

Two other institutions awarded year-long fellowships that enabled me to complete the bulk of the project. The Asia Research Institute (ARI), National University of Singapore, provided substantial funding and a collegial working environment during 2007–2008. ARI's directors, Anthony Reid, John Gavin, and Lily Kong, deserve credit for their support of this project. Jamie Davidson, Karl Hack, Huang Jianli, SR Joey Long, Anthony Reid, Nicolai Volland, Geoff Wade, Wasana Wongsurawat, Leong Yew, and other colleagues offered insightful comments on papers that would be included in this study. David Koh and Pham Nhu Quynh made Singapore feel like home.

I'm indebted to Princeton Institute of International and Regional Studies (PIIRS), Princeton University, for offering me a Development and Democracy Fellowship during 2011–2012. Atul Kohli deserves special thanks for suggesting the fellowship, arranging a talk on the project, reading chapters of the manuscript, and giving me meticulous feedback. Deborah Yashar and Mark Beissinger also were very kind and generous with their time and advice. I'm also thankful to my former Princeton professors Lynn T. White III and Miguel Centeno for discussing this project with me.

The Naval Postgraduate School and the University of Oregon deserve great thanks for having provided substantial funding that enabled me to make many research trips to Vietnam. I'm grateful to Mr. Ed Colligan, an alumnus of the Department of Political Science at the University of Oregon, for supporting a department award of which I was a recipient. I'm indebted to colleagues in Oregon, especially Deborah Baumgold, Erin Beck, Gerry Berk, Dan HoSang, Karrie Koesel, Joe Lowndes, Craig Parsons, Priscilla Southwell, Dan Tichenor, and Priscilla Yamin for their enthusiasm about the project.

Lien-Hang Nguyen was a firm supporter from early on. Ed Miller read the entire manuscript and made numerous excellent suggestions on structure and arguments in a truly comradely spirit. Jacques Hymans was enthusiastic and gave valuable advice for framing the main arguments. Ben Kerkvliet is the best mentor one can ever hope for. Pierre Asselin's very helpful advice on the project is greatly appreciated. Sophie Quinn-Judge and Kosal Path kindly provided important archival and other materials. In the process of revising, I received very helpful comments from Kosal Path, Zachary Shore, and Lewis Stern that significantly improved the arguments. At the University of Oregon, I benefited greatly from Glenn May's wise advice and unfailing support. Other friends and colleagues who helped sustain my interest in Vietnamese studies were Haydon Cherry, Olga Dror, Erik Harms, Tuan Hoang, Alec Holcombe, Charles Keith, Liam Kelley, Ben Kerkvliet, Christian Lentz, Martin Loicano, Ken MacLean, Shawn McHale, Martina Nguyen, Phan Nhien Hao, Gerard Sasges, Balasz Szalontai, Keith Taylor, Philip Taylor, Alex Thai-Vo, Nu-Anh Tran, and Alex Vuving.

In Vietnam, I want to express my gratitude to Lai Nguyen An, Nguyen Hue Chi, Duong Danh Dy, Le Tien Hoan, Vu The Khoi, Pham Quang Minh, Tran Phu Thuyet, Vu Ngoc Tien, and numerous others who have talked to me or given me advice on the project but who cannot be named here. Lai Nguyen An translated a key document from the Russian archive that shed light on the relationship between Tran Phu and Nguyen Ai Quoc. I'm grateful to Nguyen Dai Co Viet and Nguyen Nguyet Cam for assisting with contacts.

I owe a great debt to many librarians and archivists in the United States, Singapore, and Vietnam without whose help this book would not have been completed. In the same way, this book benefited so much from the brave efforts of many individuals to circulate and publish online materials deemed sensitive or subversive by the Vietnamese government. The memoirs, analyses and other documents published by the websites Talawas. org, Boxitvn.net, Viet-studies.info, Basam.info, diendan.org, and danluan. org were particularly useful. Two individuals who deserve special mention are Pham Thi Hoai, the founder and editor of Talawas, and Nguyen Huu Vinh, the founder and editor of Basam. Others include Nguyen Hue Chi, Pham Viet Dao, Nguyen Cong Huan, Nguyen Quang Lap, Truong Duy Nhat, Pham Toan, and Pham Doan Trang. Many of these bloggers have been harassed and imprisoned. At the time of writing, Nguyen Huu Vinh and his assistant Nguyen Thi Minh Thuy have just been sentenced to five years in prison. The courage and perseverance of these individuals have contributed tremendously to the study of Vietnamese modern history and politics in general, and to this book in particular.

As editors of the series, Lien-Hang Nguyen and Paul Chamberlin, guided the manuscript efficiently through rounds of review and offered wise advice along the way. At Cambridge, I was fortunate to have Deborah Gershenowitz as editor, who was very enthusiastic and supportive of the project from the beginning. Kristina Deusch deserves thanks for her patient assistance.

I wish to thank the Woodrow Wilson Center, Stanford University Press, Palgrave Macmillan, and *Ab Imperio: Studies of New Imperial History and Nationalism in the Post-Soviet Space* for their permission to include materials that form parts of Chapters 1, 2, 3, and 4 in this book. I'm thankful to Dang Thi Van Chi, Le Viet Khoa, Vu Khoa, Nguyen Quoc Phong, and Martin Rathie, and Andrew Walker for assisting with images (although they were not published in the book for technical reasons). Mary Moore and Kate Vu offered very useful editing advice.

I dedicate this book to my family.

Abbreviations

ARVN	The Armed Forces of Vietnam (RVN military)
ASEAN	Association of Southeast Asian Nations
CCP	Chinese Communist Party
Comintern	The Third Communist International
COSVN	Central Office of the Party in South Vietnam [Trung Uong Cuc Mien Nam]
CPSU	Communist Party of the Soviet Union
DRV	Democratic Republic of Vietnam (official name of Vietnam from 1945 to 1976; referring to the regime in power in the northern part of Vietnam above the 17th parallel during 1954–1975)
GMD	Guomindang, the Chinese Nationalist Party
ICP	Indochinese Communist Party (name of the Vietnamese Communist Party during 1930–1945)
PAVN	People's Army of Vietnam (communist military)
RVN	Republic of Vietnam (referring only to the regime in power in the southern part of Vietnam below the 17th parallel during 1954–1975)
SRV	Socialist Republic of Vietnam (official name of Vietnam since 1976)
TCCS	*Tap Chi Cong San* [Review of Communism]
TCQPTD	*Tap Chi Quoc Phong Toan Dan* [All-People Defense Review]
VCP	Vietnamese Communist Party
VWP	Vietnamese Workers' Party (name of the Vietnamese Communist Party during 1951–1976)

Map 1. Vietnam since 1976.

Map 2. Vietnam during the Civil War (1959–1975).

Introduction

The Vietnamese Revolution in World History

The odds are stacked against revolutionaries in any society. Most have never had a chance to wield state power because even weak governments command sufficient forces to defeat them. Even if revolutions successfully overthrow the *ancien régime*, young revolutionary states from France to Russia have often faced powerful foreign enemies that make their survival even more remarkable. This book focuses on Vietnam as one of those rare exceptions in modern world history when revolution succeeded and endured.

In this study, I trace the worldview of Vietnamese revolutionaries over an eighty-year period, starting from the 1920s when they were a band of outlaws who dreamed of building a communist paradise; through the decades in between, when they struggled to seize power, build a new society, and defeat foreign interventions; and to the late 1980s when they attempted in vain to save socialism at home and abroad. The revolution effectively ended then, but its legacies are surprisingly resilient: the communist regime is under tremendous pressure for change but has stubbornly refused to abandon its widely discredited ideology. Thus, this book places ideology at the center of nearly a century of modern Vietnamese history. I argue that ideology helped Vietnamese communists persevere against great odds, but did not lead them to success and left behind dismal legacies.

In the popular image, Vietnamese revolutionaries appear as pragmatic nationalists who inherited strong patriotic traditions and whose heroism deserves great admiration. By closely examining their vision, this book shows them in a very different (yet not necessarily negative) light – as radicals who dedicated their careers to utopia. The story the reader encounters here is less sanguine than that told in numerous accounts of this revolution: the deeply held belief of Vietnamese revolutionaries was the source of not only glorious triumphs but also colossal tragedies.

This book serves three goals. First, it aims to be a historical study of communist thought in Vietnam with a special focus on the world-view of revolutionaries. I am interested in how these Vietnamese imagined the world surrounding them and how Marxist-Leninist concepts inspired them. Few previous studies of this kind exist. Scholars of the Vietnam War and the Vietnamese revolution have commonly dismissed Vietnamese communism as ideologically shallow.

Second, this book hopes to offer explanations for the foreign relations of the Vietnamese communist state. Unlike most existing accounts, the explanations I provide here are centered on the Marxist-Leninist ideology of state leaders. My central claim is that ideology was a primary factor shaping Vietnam's external relations. Because Vietnam is a country of growing importance in Southeast Asia, scholars, students, and policy makers must be aware of the robust legacies of ideology in Vietnamese politics today.

Third and finally, this book can serve as a case study about the significance of revolution in world politics. At one point, the Vietnamese revolution had a critical impact on the global order and became a beacon in the eyes of millions around the world. The light from that beacon ultimately led to nowhere, yet that fact reflected the inherent limits of radical politics in solving human problems, not the limits of Vietnamese leaders' revolutionary commitments. This book is the first study that traces those commitments over the entire length of the revolution, showing how they once turned Vietnam into the vanguard of world revolution.

For all that this book attempts to accomplish, I do not claim to offer a comprehensive history of the Vietnamese revolution.[1] Nor is this book

---

[1] For notable studies of particular periods or events, see Christopher Goscha, *Vietnam: A State Born of War, 1945–1954* (unpublished manuscript); Stein Tønnesson, *The Vietnamese Revolution of 1945* (Newbury Park, CA: SAGE Publications, 1991); Stein Tønnesson, *Vietnam 1946: How the War Began* (Berkeley: University of California Press, 2010); David G. Marr, *Vietnam 1945: The Quest for Power* (Berkeley: University of California Press, 1995); David G. Marr, *Vietnam: State, War, and Revolution, 1945–1946* (Berkeley: University of California Press, 2013); David Elliott, *The Vietnamese War: Revolution and Social Change in the Mekong Delta 1930–1975* (New York: Armonk, 2003). For a rare comparative study that stresses the role of the communist ideology in the Vietnamese revolution, see Clive Christie, *Ideology and Revolution in Southeast Asia 1900–1980: Political Ideas of the Anti-Colonial Era* (Richmond, Surrey: Curzon Press, 2001).

aimed to be a diplomatic history of communist Vietnam.[2] My primary objects of analysis are not particular events and policies but the evolving thoughts of revolutionaries about Vietnam's relations with the world. Major policies and historical events are discussed only if they were relevant to or reflected significantly in the worldview of revolutionaries. This Introduction will first present the puzzle about the Vietnamese revolution and the comparative scholarship on the role of radical revolutions in world politics. I will then discuss the Marxist-Leninist worldview of Vietnamese communists and its role in their revolution.

THE PUZZLE ABOUT A MISUNDERSTOOD REVOLUTION

During much of the twentieth century, many anti-Western revolutions swept throughout Eastern Europe, Asia, Africa, and Latin America.[3] Embracing ideologies from communism to Islamism, those revolutions sought to overthrow or roll back Western domination. Revolutionary states, whether large (Russia and China) or small (Cuba and Nicaragua), might have deterred but were never able to defeat the West. Many have collapsed, including the once mighty Soviet Union. Most survivors have in fact made peace with their former Western enemies. Nevertheless, even small revolutionary states had tremendous impact on world politics in their heydays. For example, we now know that the attacks in June 1950 that started the Korean War were launched at the initiative of Kim Il-sung, who persuaded Stalin and Mao to go along.[4] Kim failed in his goal to conquer South Korea, but the war drew the United States back to mainland East Asia and escalated tensions between Washington and Moscow. The Cold War might have been confined to Europe if Kim had not made the move. China's participation in the Korean War accelerated

[2] Major studies that have been published in recent years include: Ang Cheng Guan, *Ending the Vietnam War: The Vietnamese Communists' Perspective* (New York: RoutledgeCurzon, 2003); Lien-Hang Nguyen, *Hanoi's War: An International History of the War for Peace in Vietnam* (Chapel Hill: University of North Carolina Press, 2012); Pierre Asselin, *Hanoi's Road to the Vietnam War, 1954–1965* (Berkeley: University of California Press, 2013); and David Elliott, *Changing Worlds: Vietnam's Transition from Cold War to Globalization* (New York: Oxford University Press, 2012).

[3] Of course, there were other revolutions that were not against the West such as the Chinese revolution of 1911. The term "the West" here can be understood broadly as the countries in the Western European-American bloc that are economically capitalist and culturally secular.

[4] Kathryn Weathersby, "Soviet Aims in Korea and the Origins of the Korean War, 1945–1950: New Evidence from Russian Archives," in Christian Ostermann ed., *Cold War International History Project Working Paper 8* (Washington, DC: Woodrow Wilson Center for Scholars, 1993).

its own domestic social revolution, forced the indefinite delay of its plan to invade Taiwan, and deepened its conflict with the West.

In an endeavor even bolder than North Korea's, communist North Vietnam decided to orchestrate an insurgency in South Vietnam in 1959 against the wishes of not only the United States but also the Soviet Union and China, eventually drawing all three into the conflict. Despite committing about half a million troops to the conflict at one point, Washington failed to achieve its goal of defending its South Vietnamese ally. The conflict in Vietnam profoundly divided American elites, seriously damaged American credibility around the world, and lent moral support to many radical movements in Africa and Latin America. Some observers credit the conflict for inspiring "antisystemic movements" in the 1960s and 1970s in North America, Europe, Japan, and Latin America.[5] One source counts at least fourteen revolutions that ensued in the seven years following US withdrawal of troops from South Vietnam in 1973.[6]

Scholars of international politics have made the case that the great French Revolution introduced the mass conscripted armies and the practice of foreign interference into weaker states.[7] By contrast, the conflict in Vietnam contributed to the American move to abandon conscription and revert to the paid volunteer military of the eighteenth century (with some modifications). American failure in Vietnam led to its retreat from nation-building missions abroad in the subsequent two decades. This self-restraint was partially lifted only with the Al-Qaeda attacks of September 11, 2001, which, for the first time since 1814, brought war to continental United States.[8] Al-Qaeda was hosted by the Taliban state in Afghanistan, another revolutionary state that had earlier battled Soviet forces and accelerated the collapse of the Soviet Union.[9] The Taliban state not only waged war on the United States indirectly through its support for Al-Qaeda but also drew Washington and its allies into a costly war that now stands as the longest in American history.

---

[5] Giovanni Arrighi, Terence Hopkins, and Immanuel Wallerstein, *Antisystemic Movements* (London: Verso, 1989), 35–36.

[6] Fred Halliday, *Revolution and World Politics: The Rise and Fall of the Sixth Great Power* (Durham, NC: Duke University Press, 1999), 178.

[7] Richard Rosecrance, *Action and Reaction in World Politics; International Systems in Perspective* (Boston: Little, Brown, 1963), 45–46.

[8] George Herring, "The War that Never Seems to Go Away," in David Anderson and John Ernst, eds. *The War That Never Ends: New Perspectives on the Vietnam War* (Lexington: University Press of Kentucky, 2007), 346.

[9] For discussions of the Taliban's ideology as a fundamentalist movement, see William Maley, "Interpreting the Taliban," in William Maley, ed. *Fundamentalism Reborn? Afghanistan and the Taliban* (New York: New York University Press, 1998), 1–28.

Given their limited military and economic capabilities, the ability and determination of small but radical states like North Vietnam and Afghanistan to inflict such humiliation on the superpowers pose a significant analytical puzzle. Their risky behaviors did not conform to the normal notion of rationality. The death of some states (Cambodia's Khmer Rouge, Afghanistan's Taliban) and the dire poverty of survivors (Cuba, North Korea, Vietnam until recently) suggested the steep price they paid for standing up against powerful external enemies. The puzzle is: What were the thoughts of revolutionary leaders in those states? How could they even think of challenging those much more powerful than they were?

These questions must be asked for all revolutions, but they hold special importance in the Vietnamese case because the nature of this revolution has been widely misunderstood.[10] During the Vietnam War, Vietnamese revolutionaries were commonly portrayed either as pawns in the game of great powers or as nationalists who inherited a tradition of patriotism and were motivated simply by national independence. The image of Vietnamese revolutionaries as minions for Moscow or Beijing was frequently put forward by US leaders as a reason for intervention. In this image, Vietnamese communists neither possessed their own belief nor were they capable of independent action. The then-Assistant Secretary of State Dean Rusk testified before a Congressional committee in 1951 that Vietnamese communists were "strongly directed from Moscow and could be counted upon ... to tie Indochina into the world communist program."[11] A decade later, when he sent American troops to Vietnam, President Lyndon Johnson pointed to Beijing as the real culprit:

Over this war – and all of Asia – is another reality: the deepening shadow of Communist China. The rulers in Hanoi are urged on by Peking. This is a regime which has destroyed freedom in Tibet, which has attacked India and has been condemned by the United Nations for aggression in Korea. It is a nation which is helping the forces of violence in almost every continent. The contest in Vietnam is part of a wider pattern of aggressive purposes.[12]

---

[10] For a full treatment of all perspectives in the debate over Vietnam in the United States, see David W. Levy, *The Debate over Vietnam*, 2nd ed. (Baltimore: The Johns Hopkins University Press, 1995).

[11] Ibid., 97. For a recent analysis of early American arguments for intervention, see Andrew Rotter, "Chronicle of a War Foretold: The United States and Vietnam, 1945–1954," in Mark Lawrence and Fredrik Logevall, eds. *The First Vietnam War: Colonial Conflict and Cold War Crisis* (Cambridge, MA: Harvard University Press, 2007), 282–308.

[12] Lyndon Johnson, "Lyndon B. Johnson Explains Why Americans Fight in Vietnam, 1965," in Robert McMahon, ed. *Major Problems in the History of the Vietnam War: Documents and Essays*, 2nd ed. (Lexington, MA: D. C. Heath, 1995), 210–211.

Whether Moscow or Beijing was behind Hanoi, the domino theory justified US intervention, as then-Senator Hubert Humphrey spoke in 1951, "We cannot afford to see southeast [sic] Asia fall prey to the Communist onslaught ... If Indochina were lost, it would be as severe a blow as if we were to lose Korea. The loss of Indochina would mean the loss of Malaya, the loss of Burma and Thailand, and ultimately the conquest of all the south and southeast Asiatic area."[13]

Not all Americans were persuaded by Rusk, Johnson, and Humphrey. In opposing American intervention, early critics harped on the nationalist myth about traditional animosity between China and Vietnam as if it were truth.[14] Senator William Fulbright claimed that

> Ho Chi Minh is not a mere agent of Communist China ... He is a bona fide nationalist revolutionary, the leader of his country's rebellion against French colonialism. He is also ... a dedicated communist but always a Vietnamese communist ... For our purposes, the significance of Ho Chi Minh's nationalism is that it is associated with what Bernard Fall has called "the 2,000-year-old distrust in Vietnam of everything Chinese." Vietnamese communism is therefore a potential bulwark – perhaps the only potential bulwark – against Chinese domination of Vietnam.[15]

Although admitting that "it is not meaningful to speak of the Viet Minh as more nationalist than communist or as more communist than nationalist," Fulbright believed that their belief in communism would not be sufficient to overcome Ho and his comrades' instinctive fear of China.[16] In his 1989 memoir, Fulbright disclosed that he had believed as early as 1965 that Ho "was a true patriot, like Tito of Yugoslavia."[17]

---

[13] William Gibbons, *The U.S. Government and the Vietnam War: Executive and Legislative Roles and Relationships: Part I: 1945–1960* (Princeton, NJ: Princeton University Press, 1986), 96.

[14] Premodern relationship between China and Vietnam was fundamentally peaceful and periods of war were rare. In fact, the Vietnamese have historically fought against other Vietnamese or against other states on China's southern frontier far more often than against Chinese. See Keith Taylor, "The Vietnamese Civil War of 1955–1975 in Historical Perspective," in Andrew Wiest and Michael Doidge, eds. *Triumph Revisited: Historians Battle for the Vietnam War* (Hoboken, NJ: Taylor & Francis, 2010), 18–22. Also, Tuong Vu, "State Formation on China's Southern Frontier: Vietnam as a Shadow Empire and Hegemon," *HumaNetten* (forthcoming).

[15] J. William Fulbright, *The Arrogance of Power* (New York: Random House, 1966), 112, 114.

[16] Fulbright approvingly quoted Bernard Fall who speculated that "Ho is probably equipped with an instinctive Vietnamese fear of Chinese domination ..." Ibid., 112.

[17] J. William Fulbright with Seth Tilman, *The Price of Empire* (New York: Pantheon Books, 1989), 110.

In an influential book that has been touted as "the bible for opponents to the war in the 1970s,"[18] scholars George Kahin and John Lewis echoed Fulbright and claimed that "American support of France [in the early 1950s] forced Ho Chi Minh's Vietminh into an unwelcome dependence upon China and denied the movement the freedom to act in accordance with the historically conditioned, anti-Chinese proclivity of Vietnamese nationalism."[19]

Some war critics did notice, and in fact admire, certain revolutionary policies that went beyond traditional Vietnamese nationalism. In his famous address in 1967, Martin Luther King, Jr. took issue with the US government for rejecting

a revolutionary [Vietnamese] government seeking self-determination, and a government that had been established not by China (for whom the Vietnamese have no great love) but by clearly indigenous forces that included some communists. For the peasants, this new government meant real land reform, one of the most important needs in their lives.[20]

Although both sides in the debate had a point, this book suggests that many arguments by the antiwar camp do not stand up to scrutiny. The Vietnamese revolution was, at heart, a communist revolution, and Vietnamese revolutionaries as a group were internationalists no less than their comrades in the Soviet Union or China. Although Dr. King was correct that the government in Hanoi was led by indigenous forces, he underestimated its commitments to world revolution. While giving priority to their revolution, Ho and his comrades did not ignore revolutions elsewhere. As a Comintern representative for Southeast Asia, Ho presided over the formation of the Indochinese, Siamese, and Malay

[18] George Herring, "America and Vietnam: The Debate Continues," *The American Historical Review* 92: 2 (April 1987), 354.

[19] George Kahin and John Lewis, *The United States in Vietnam*, 2nd ed. (New York: Delta, 1969), 326–327. Kahin and Lewis's arguments were later repeated by many American diplomatic historians and prominent journalists whose works have profoundly shaped the popular perception of the Vietnamese revolution. For example, see George Herring, *America's Longest War*, 4th ed. (New York: McGraw-Hill, 2002), 3–4; Marilyn Young, *The Vietnam Wars, 1945–1990* (New York: HarperPerennial, 1990), 2; Frances FitzGerald, *Fire in the Lake: The Vietnamese and the Americans in Vietnam* (Boston: Little, Brown, 1972), esp. 8; Stanley Karnow, *Vietnam, a History* (New York: Viking Press, 1983), esp. 110; Neil Sheehan, *A Bright Shining Light: John Paul Vann and America in Vietnam* (New York: Random House, 1988), 159–162.

[20] Martin Luther King, Jr., "Declaration of Independence from the War in Vietnam," April 1967 in Marvin Gettleman, Jane Franklin, Marilyn Young, et al., eds. *Vietnam and America: The Most Comprehensive Documented History of the Vietnam War*, 2nd ed. (New York: Grove Press, 1995), 313.

communist parties in the 1930s. In mid-1949, he ordered Vietnamese
units into southern China to assist Mao's army in defending its base from
attacks by Chiang Kai-shek's forces.[21] Vietnamese troops helped establish
communist regimes in Laos and Cambodia in 1975, and until the 1980s
Vietnam directly supported communist parties in other Southeast Asian
countries. Postwar Vietnam trained sappers for, and sent surplus weapons to Algeria, Chile, and El Salvador in service of revolutions there.[22]
Significantly, the internationalist spirit of the Vietnamese Communist
Party (VCP) is still alive today, a quarter century after the collapse of
world communism. As recently as 2012, Party chief Nguyen Phu Trong
journeyed across the globe to Cuba, where he preached about the merits
of socialism and the evils of capitalism.[23] If not because of internationalist commitments, why would the Vietnamese leader want to thumb his
nose at Washington? Why did he risk alienating the US government and
American corporations on whose aid and investment poor Vietnam was
dependent?

   Dr. King's characterization that the Vietnamese had "no great love"
for China cannot explain the awe and veneration Vietnamese communists showered on Chinese leaders in the 1950s and the slavish deference
the Vietnamese leadership today expresses toward China.[24] It is true that
North Vietnamese leaders implemented a "real land reform" by redistrib-
uting large amounts of land to landless peasants, but they also executed

[21] Nguyen Thi Mai Hoa, *Cac nuoc Xa hoi chu nghia ung ho Viet Nam khang chien chong My, cuu nuoc* [Socialist countries' assistance to Vietnam's resistance against America to save the country] (Hanoi: Chinh tri Quoc gia, 2013), 53–55.

[22] Merle Pribbenow, "Vietnam Covertly Supplied Weapons to Revolutionaries in Algeria and Latin America." Cold War History Project e-Dossier No. 25, n.d. Available at www.wilsoncenter.org/publication/e-dossier-no-25-vietnam-covertly-supplied-weapons-to-revolutionaries-algeria-and-latin; Merle Pribbenow, "Vietnam Trained Commando Forces in Southeast Asia and Latin America." Cold War History Project E-Dossier no. 27, January 2012. Available at www.wilsoncenter.org/publication/e-dossier-no-27-vietnam-trained-commando-forces-southeast-asia-and-latin-america. Pribbenow collected the information from the PAVN history blog www.vnmilitaryhistory.net/index.php, where veterans posted comments, personal documents, and sometimes internal official documents.

[23] The text of the speech of General Secretary Nguyen Phu Trong in Cuba in November 2012 is available at http://vov.vn/Home/Bai-noi-chuyen-ve-Chu-nghia-Xa-hoi-cua-Tong-Bi-thu-tai-Cuba/20124/205986.vov

[24] For the popularity and influence of Maoism from the late 1940s through the 1950s, see Kim Ninh, *A World Transformed: The Politics of Culture in Revolutionary Vietnam, 1945–1965* (Ann Arbor: University of Michigan Press, 2002), esp. 39–41; for the enormous influence of China on Vietnamese politics today, see Alexander Vuving, "Vietnam: A Tale of Four Players," *Southeast Asian Affairs* 1 (2010), 366–391.

about 15,000 landlords and rich peasants in the process.[25] For all that bloodshed and fanfare, barely five years later most peasants had been coerced into giving up their lands and joining Maoist-style cooperatives. By the time Dr. King made his speech, most farmland in North Vietnam had been collectivized for nearly a decade.[26] Forced to stay in cooperatives and denied any escape by a strict household registration system in the cities, the free farmer of North Vietnam was reduced to a modern serf. He and his family were chronically hungry and occasionally threatened by famines.

Antiwar activists misunderstood the nature of the Vietnamese revolution, but proponents of intervention fared no better, as Vietnamese communists were no stooges of Moscow or Beijing. At the height of the war, Hanoi leaders scorned both their Soviet and Chinese comrades for not daring to stand up against US imperialism.[27] After their victory in 1975, they thought of themselves as the vanguard of world revolution and snubbed not only the United States but also China and the Soviet Union.[28] Hanoi attempted to defend the international communist camp even when its big brothers had abandoned it. In 1989, when Eastern European communist regimes were about to fall, the general secretary of the VCP prodded Soviet leader Mikhail Gorbachev to convene a conference of all communist and workers parties to discuss strategies for saving the socialist camp from the coming collapse.[29] When Gorbachev turned a deaf ear to the request, Vietnam asked China to create an anti-imperialist alliance (Beijing also said no).[30]

In the end, Vietnamese communism stopped short of exporting revolution beyond Indochina because its radical character had created enemies

[25] Vo Nhan Tri, *Vietnam's Economic Policy Since 1975* (Singapore: ASEAN Economic Research Unit, Institute of Southeast Asian Studies, 1990), 3.

[26] See Benedict J. Kerkvliet, *The Power of Everyday Politics: How Vietnamese Peasants Transformed National Policy* (Ithaca, NY: Cornell University Press, 2005); Andrew Vickerman, *The Fate of the Peasantry: Premature "Transition to Socialism" in the Democratic Republic of Vietnam* (New Haven, CT: Yale University Southeast Asia Studies, Yale Center for International and Area Studies, 1986).

[27] On their criticism of Khrushchev in 1963–1964, see R. B. Smith, *An International History of the Vietnam War*, v. 2 (New York: St. Martin's Press, 1983), chap. 13, esp. 227; for their criticism of China in 1971–1972, see Qiang Zhai, *China and the Vietnam Wars, 1950–1975* (Chapel Hill: University of North Carolina Press, 2000), 197–202.

[28] Nayan Chanda, *Brother Enemy: The War after the War* (San Diego: Harcourt Brace Jovanovich, 1986).

[29] Huy Duc, *Ben Thang Cuoc* [The Winners], v. 2 (Los Angeles: Osinbook, 2012), 63–67.

[30] Tran Quang Co, *Hoi uc va suy nghi* [Memories and Thoughts] (July 2005). Published online; available at www.diendan.org/tai-lieu/ho-so/hoi-ky-tran-quang-co

everywhere around it, from Vietnamese peasants who resisted collectivization, to Chinese and Cambodian leaders who resented Vietnam's claims to be the vanguard of world revolution. The prointervention camp widely exaggerated the security threat of the Vietnamese revolution to the United States. Yet that threat never materialized, not because Vietnamese communists were not real communists as the antiwar camp claimed, but because their fanaticism was self-destructive and engineered their own demise. With all due respects for their intellect and conscience, both sides in the Vietnam War debate misunderstood the Vietnamese revolution because they failed to grasp its communist nature. As this debate continues today, the same misunderstanding is frequently found in scholarship.[31]

REVOLUTIONS AND WORLD POLITICS

A study of ideology in the Vietnamese revolution is valuable not only for the enduring Vietnam War debate but also for the comparative study of revolutions. The voluminous comparative literature on revolutions has privileged factors such as social classes, state structure, and economic and political crises.[32] However, ideology tends to be neglected. Revolutions are generally treated as domestic events: although they may be influenced by international factors, their bearing on international politics lies outside the scope of most works.

A handful of studies that do address the international dimensions of revolutions nonetheless indicate their enormous impacts on world politics.[33] As Robert Jervis recently observes, "Revolutionaries rarely

[31] For recent reviews of the Vietnam War debate, see Andrew Wiest, ed. *America and the Vietnam War* (London and New York: Taylor & Francis, 2009); David Anderson and John Ernst, eds. *The War That Never Ends: New Perspectives on the Vietnam War* (Lexington: University Press of Kentucky, 2007).

[32] For reviews, see Jeff Goodwin, "Revolutions and Revolutionary Movements," in Thomas Janoski, Robert Alford, Alexander Hicks et al., *The Handbook of Political Sociology* (New York: Cambridge University Press, 2005), esp. 421; Jack Goldstone, "Comparative Historical Analysis and Knowledge Accumulation in the Study of Revolutions," in James Mahoney and Dietrich Rueschemeyer, eds. *Comparative Historical Analysis in the Social Sciences* (New York: Cambridge University Press, 2003), esp. 70.

[33] See Halliday, *Revolution and World Politics*; Mark Katz, *Revolutions and Revolutionary Waves* (London: Macmillan, 1997); Robert S. Snyder, "The U.S. and Third World Revolutionary States: Understanding the Breakdown in Relations," *International Studies Quarterly* 43: 2 (1999): 265–290; Stephen Walt, *Revolution and War* (Ithaca, NY: Cornell University Press, 1996); Patrick Conge, *From Revolution to War: State Relations in a World of Change* (Ann Arbor: University of Michigan Press, 1996); J. D. Armstrong,

have small ideas, and big ones are almost always disruptive internation-ally."[34] Martin Wight is more specific:

A revolutionary power is morally and psychologically at war with its neighbours all the time, even if legally peace prevails, because it believes it has a mission to transform international society by conversion or coercion, and cannot admit that its neighbours have the same right to continue existence which it assumes for itself.[35]

With their messianic beliefs, revolutions not only brew tension and breed war with neighbors but also bring about fundamental changes in the international system.[36] Analyzing the evolution of the "international society" since the French revolution, J. D. Armstrong argues that the rela-tionship between revolutionary states and the international society has typically been tense.[37] The main source of tension is ideological: "The belief system on which revolution was founded and which legitimized the assumption of state power by the revolutionary elite is certain to run counter to the prevailing political doctrines of most other states, many of which may represent the 'old regime' values against which the revolu-tion was aimed." From the United States in 1776 to the Soviet Union in 1917, for survival reasons young revolutionary states have been forced to eschew part of their ideological beliefs to accommodate the Westphalian state system. At the same time, Armstrong shows that they have sought to change that system to make it suit their visions.

Revolution and World Order: The Revolutionary State in International Society (Oxford: Clarendon Press, 1993); Theda Skocpol, "Revolutions and Mass Military Mobilization," *World Politics* 40: 2 (1988), 147–168; Peter Calvert, *Politics, Power, and Revolution: An Introduction to Comparative Politics* (Brighton, Sussex: Wheatsheaf Books, 1983); and Kyung-won Kim, *Revolution and the International System* (New York: New York University Press, 1970). Earlier works, such as Martin Wight, *Power Politics*, eds. Hedley Bull and Carsten Holbraad (New York: Holmes & Meier, 1978), 81–94; Rosecrance, *Action and Reaction in World Politics*; and James Rosenau, *International Aspects of Civil Strife* (Princeton, NJ: Princeton University Press, 1964) discussed but not focused solely on the issue. For a list of studies on particular revolu-tions, see Halliday, *Revolution and World Politics*, 378–395. For a recent study of "ren-egade regimes" that include many revolutionary states, see Miroslav Nincic, *Renegade Regimes: Confronting Deviant Behavior in World Politics* (New York: Columbia University Press, 2005).

[34] Robert Jervis, "Socialization, Revolutionary States and Domestic Politics," *International Politics* 52: 5 (2015), 609–616.

[35] Wight, *Power Politics*, 90.

[36] Of course, misperception and uncertainty can lead to war involving revolutionary states. See Walt, *Revolution and War*; and Conge, *From Revolution to War*.

[37] Armstrong, *Revolution and World Order*, 9.

For example, the challenge from the French revolutionary state generated acceptance for nationality and popular support as new principles of
legitimacy for states in the interstate system.[38] The Soviet state succeeded
in making self-determination an international norm and in placing social
issues such as labor and racial discrimination on the international agenda.
Revolutionary states often provoked change indirectly, that is, through
the reactions of their opponents and supporters. "Third World" revolutionary communist states encouraged the United States to undertake
a hegemonic role in the postwar world. Although revolutionary states
were often forced to accept certain international laws they despised, their
challenges compelled established states to defend and show greater commitment to those laws than they would have otherwise.

In theory, Fred Halliday tells us, we should expect revolutions to
impact world politics just by examining the beliefs of revolutionaries.
Halliday points out that no clear separation exists between the domestic
and the international spheres for revolutionary thoughts; whatever their
particular national or internal origins, all past revolutionary ideologies
not only called for a new domestic order but also claimed the salience of
their vision for the international sphere.[39] Claims of global relevance by
revolutionaries were not made arbitrarily but were based on a coherent
logic. Revolutions legitimized themselves by appealing to abstract and
universal principles such as freedom, independence, dignity of the people,
and proletarian justice. These principles were obviously not limited by
national boundaries. From the American to the Iranian Revolution, part
of revolutionary discourses also evoked the fraternity and peace between
nations and peoples. Enemies of revolutions were perceived not within
national boundaries but on the global scale, whether as imperialists or
infidels.

Given their definition of enemy, one should expect revolutionary states
to export revolution abroad if they had the opportunity to do so. As
Halliday argues, "much as revolutionary states may deny it and [their]
liberal friends downplay it, the commitment to the export of revolution,
i.e. to the use of the resources of the revolutionary state to promote radical change in other societies, is a constant of radical regimes."[40] Not
only did revolutionary states provide substantial material assistance to

---

[38] Ibid., 111, 156, 198, 243.
[39] Halliday, *Revolution and World Politics*, 58–59.
[40] Ibid., 99.

their comrades abroad but also the creation of international organizations, such as the Soviet Union's Communist International (Comintern) or Cuba's short-lived Organization of Solidarity with the People of Asia, Africa, and Latin America (OSPAAAL), were examples of revolutionary states' deep commitment to international solidarity.

John Owen calls organizations such as the Comintern and OSPAAAL "transnational ideological networks," and argues that those networks have been a salient feature of world politics for centuries.[41] Such networks involve ideologues across states who share beliefs and interests in promoting their ideologies, whether it is Calvinism or democracy, communism or Islamism. Networks are independent from states, but they can offer incentives for rulers to intervene abroad to promote their ideologies during times of transnational ideological polarization. When rulers do so, they frequently do not separate self-interest or national security from ideology. As Owen explains, "state rulers who are members of an ideological movement will tend to see the interests of the ideology and of their particular state as complementary, such that in protecting the state they are advancing the ideology and vice versa."[42] For Owen, ideology and interests are mutually constituted, and ideologies are no less important than interests in explaining war and international alliance.

If the nature of the Vietnamese revolution was defined by the communist ideology, as I claim, Vietnam adds another case to the comparative literature, demonstrating the salience of revolutionary ideology in world politics. In this case, the size or the material capabilities of the country did not predict the potential impact of a domestic revolution on world affairs. Explaining that mismatch between domestic capabilities and international influence requires an appreciation for the radical worldview of Vietnamese revolutionaries to be discussed next.

THE VIETNAMESE REVOLUTIONARY WORLDVIEW

Ideology and worldview are the most important concepts in this study. Ideology can be defined broadly as a set of systematic beliefs and assumptions about the nature and dynamics of politics, while worldviews are beliefs and assumptions more specifically about the nature and dynamics

---

[41] John M. Owen, *The Clash of Ideas in World Politics: Transnational Networks, States, and Regime Change, 1510–2010* (Princeton, NJ: Princeton University Press, 2010).

[42] Ibid., 36.

of world politics.[43] Although ideology can be influenced by material interests, it often defines what those interests are.[44]

The Vietnamese communist movement emerged in the 1920s as an offshoot of Vietnamese nationalism. Modern national consciousness emerged in colonized Vietnam around the beginning of the twentieth century.[45] Anticolonial nationalism was not a uniquely Vietnamese phenomenon but a global trend across Asia at that time.[46] Most Vietnamese communists began their political careers being motivated simply by the desire to liberate Vietnam from French colonial rule, just like any other anticolonial activists. Over time, they became communists by joining these networks abroad or inside Vietnam. Karl Marx, Vladimir Lenin, Josef

[43] For other definitions, see Alexander L. George, "The "Operational Code": A Neglected Approach to the Study of Political Leaders and Decision-Making," *International Studies Quarterly* 13: 2 (1969): 190–222; Giovanni Sartori, "Politics, Ideology, and Belief Systems, *The American Political Science Review* 63, no. 2 (1969): 398–411; Michael Hunt, *Ideology and US Foreign Policy* (New Haven, CT: Yale University Press, 1987); John Gerring, "Ideology: a Definitional Analysis," *Political Research Quarterly* 50, no. 4 (1997): 957–994. In the field of Foreign Policy Analysis, worldview and ideology are often studied from psychological perspectives under the concept of "belief system," or more narrowly, "operational code." For a brief review of recent scholarship on belief systems and operational code, see Jonathan Renshon, "Stability and Change in Belief Systems: the Operational Code of George W. Bush," *The Journal of Conflict Resolution* 52, no.6 (2008): 821–828. For an earlier but more substantial overview of the literature, see Richard Little and Steve Smith, *Belief Systems and International Relations* (Oxford, UK: Blackwell, 1988). In contrast, the literature in International Relations (IR) tends to avoid the concept of ideology and focuses instead on the broader concept of "ideas," defined in one version as "beliefs held by individuals." "World views" are regarded as ideas that "define the universe of possibilities for action" at the most fundamental level. Other, less important types of ideas are "principled beliefs" and "causal beliefs." Judith Goldstein and Robert O. Keohane, *Ideas and Foreign Policy: Beliefs, Institutions, and Political Change* (Ithaca, NY: Cornell University Press, 1993), 3–11.
[44] Nigel Gould-Davies, "Rethinking the Role of Ideology in International Politics During the Cold War," *Journal of Cold War Studies* 1: 1 (1999): 97–99; Nina Tannenwald, "Ideas and Explanation: Advancing the Theoretical Agenda," *Journal of Cold War Studies* 7: 2 (2005): 20–22. The notion that ideas and interests are mutually constituted is of course the basic premise of the constructivist school in International Relations. See Emanuel Adler, "Constructivism in International Relations: Sources, Contributions, and Debates," in Walter Carlsnaes, Thomas Risse, and Beth Simmons, eds. *Handbook of International Relations*, 2nd ed. (New York: Sage, 2013), 112–144.
[45] Unlike most scholars, David Marr and Huynh Kim Khanh avoid the term "nationalism" and do not distinguish between Vietnam's modern nationalism and traditional patriotism. See David Marr, *Vietnamese Anticolonialism, 1885–1925* (Berkeley: University of California Press, 1971); Huynh Kim Khanh, *Vietnamese Communism 1925–1945* (Ithaca, NY: Cornell University Press, 1982).
[46] For a broad discussion of the trend, see Odd Arne Westad, *The Global Cold War: Third World Interventions and the Making of Our Times* (Cambridge, UK: Cambridge University Press, 2005), ch. 3.

Stalin, and Mao Zedong exerted the greatest influence on the Vietnamese communist worldview. In its essence, this worldview portrayed international politics as essentially a life-and-death struggle of the oppressed proletariat against their capitalist oppressors regardless of nationalities. The proletariat was to triumph in this historic struggle because they were standing at the pinnacle of a historical trend. This trend would deliver to the human race the most materially advanced and ethically progressive society that it could ever have hoped for.

In the 1920s, Marxism-Leninism was not a dogma as it would later become. Back then, the theory was still basking in the aura generated by its scientific claims and progressive vision. That vision was still a new and unfolding reality in the young Soviet Union that held so much promise for communists worldwide. As Odd Arne Westad describes in the case of China, "[t]he European, pre-Soviet ideal of socialism had appealed to some Chinese because of its opposition to imperialism, but it was the practice of socialism in the Soviet Union that set their minds on fire."[47] One can get a flavor of the same excitement in the words of Truong Chinh, a leader and major theoretician of Vietnamese communism, who described what Marxism-Leninism meant to him as follows:

Marxism-Leninism arms us with a revolutionary worldview, enlightens our hearts and minds, and helps us find our lives' mission and meaning. It helps us grasp the developmental laws of nature, or society, and of thought. It places us right at the center of the struggle between the antagonisms so that we can see all aspects of things and find truth. It helps us grasp the most essential, important, and significant things in this complex world.... It helps us understand not only the present but also the future, making us aware of our responsibilities to life. Thus, Marxism-Leninism does not make our hearts barren and unresponsive to the good and beautiful things in life as some people think; on the contrary, it makes us love life and humankind more passionately. It lifts our souls and gives us our dreams. It fires up our hearts with great communist ideals.[48]

Truong Chinh, whose pseudonym meant "Long March" in Vietnamese, exemplified the background and career of many Vietnamese communist leaders. He was born Dang Xuan Khu in 1906 into a local gentry family in northern Vietnam, was expelled from a vocational high school for

[47] Westad, *The Global Cold War*, 374. For the popularity of communist ideas in China in the 1920s, see Michael Hunt, *The Genesis of Chinese Communist Foreign Policy* (New York: Columbia University Press, 1996); for Indonesia, see Ruth McVey, *The Rise of Indonesian Communism* (Ithaca, NY: Cornell University Press, 1965).

[48] Truong Chinh, "Bai noi chuyen tai Dai Hoi Van Nghe Toan Quoc lan thu III" [Speech at the Third National Conference of Artists and Writers], December 1962. *Hoc Tap* 12 (1962), 26–27.

joining a demonstration to honor the death of the nationalist intellectual
Phan Chau Trinh, and became a communist in his early twenties while in
colonial prison.

As Truong Chinh's biography suggested, Marxism-Leninism built on
nationalist frustrations when it entered Vietnam. Unlike the common
myth about the necessarily antagonistic relationship between nationalism and communism, Marxism-Leninism as a theory did not oppose
nationalities.[49] Marx and Engels argued that the proletariat "must rise
to be the leading class of the nation and constituting itself the nation."[50]
In the same vein, Lenin asked, "Is the sense of national pride alien to us,
Great-Russian, class-conscious proletarians? Certainly not! We love our
language and our country, we are doing our utmost to raise *its* toiling
masses (i.e., nine-tenths of *its* population) to democratic and socialist
consciousness."[51]

Moscow's pledge of support for anticolonial movements certainly
helped to convert young Ho Chi Minh and many other Vietnamese to
communism. Their conversion in turn started a thought process that was
long, muddled, and fraught with tensions for each individual and for the
movement as a whole. A key question that the Vietnamese grappled with
early on concerned the relationship between their and world revolution.
Eventually, they settled on a worldview in which the Vietnamese revolution was imagined as an integral part of world revolution. A successful
proletarian revolution in Vietnam was a step forward for world revolution, which was to occur country by country, region by region.

As a component of world revolution against capitalism and imperialism, the Vietnamese revolution was no longer concerned only with
national independence. Vietnamese communists did not sacrifice national
interests as their opponents accused, but identified such interests with

---

[49] As Martin Mevius argues, "From Cuba to Korea, all communist parties attempted to
gain national legitimacy. This was not incidental or a deviation from Marxist ortho-
doxy, but ingrained in the theory and practice of the communist movement since its
inception." Martin Mevius, "Reappraising Communism and Nationalism," *Nationalities
Papers* 37: 4 (2009). See also David Brandenberger, *National Bolshevism: Stalinist
Mass Culture and the Formation of Modern Russian National Identity, 1931–1956*
(Cambridge, MA: Harvard University Press, 2002); S. A. Smith, *Revolution and the
People in Russia and China: A Comparative History* (New York: Cambridge University
Press, 2008), ch. 4.

[50] Quoted from Karl Marx and Friedrich Engels, "The Manifesto of the Communist Party."
Martin Mevius, "Reappraising Communism and Nationalism," 382–383.

[51] V. I. Lenin, "The National Pride of the Great Russians," in V. I. Lenin, *The National-
Liberation Movement in the East*, 2nd impression, transl. by M. Levin (Moscow: Foreign
Languages Publishing House, 1962), 86. Italics in original.

those of working classes in Vietnam and elsewhere. To them, national liberation was important but would mean little if class oppression and exploitation continued. Vietnamese communists claimed that their revolution could advance *both* sets of interests, and it was *the only approach* capable of doing so. The main question that confronted them throughout the revolution was not to sacrifice one set of interests for the other, but how to divide the revolutionary mission into smaller goals to gain tactical advantages at any particular point in time.

The term "national" to Vietnamese communists thus acquired an additional, specific content. Their definition of the nation was based on shared class interests as well as on shared language or ethnicity. In their view of national history, for example, Vietnamese communists were not proud of everything Vietnamese; rather, they embraced those traditions that could be claimed as created and sustained by "working classes" (such as "peasant uprisings"), and disowned those that were attributable to "ruling classes" (such as Confucian culture and the oppression of women).

In politics, Vietnamese communists viewed fellow Vietnamese of "exploitative classes" as a small minority in the Vietnamese national community. These classes did not represent the nation and ought to be eliminated even though they were ethnically Vietnamese. At the same time, even though French workers were French nationals, they shared the same interests with the Vietnamese masses as both were exploited and oppressed by French colonialists and imperialists. To Vietnamese communists, those who saw only the French-Vietnamese ethnic division but not the cross-national solidarity between French and Vietnamese working classes fell victim to a form of nationalism that was "bourgeois" and "narrow."

On becoming communists, Vietnamese revolutionaries did not have to give up their nationality while acquiring membership in the international brotherhood of fellow communist activists, parties, and movements. In their view, the brotherhood was much more than a security or economic alliance, although that was an important part of it.[52] Conceptually the camaraderie was understood to be the material form of a historical phenomenon called "the Age of the [Russian] October Revolution." Its

---

[52] Without the Soviet bloc, especially China, as their vast rear base, communists would not have been able to dominate Vietnam. Nowhere in Southeast Asia was any communist party able to take power even though Malayan and Philippine communist movements were stronger than their Vietnamese counterpart at the end of World War II. See Jeff Goodwin for an insightful comparison, *No Other Way Out: States and Revolutionary Movements, 1945–1991* (New York: Cambridge University Press, 2001), 66–133.

moral foundation was proletarian internationalism [tinh than quoc te vo san] defined as the solidarity among working class parties across many national communities. In its ideal condition, members of the brotherhood shared a proletarian spirit and working class interests unencumbered by geographical barriers and unpolluted by narrow national sentiments.

Relationship with other socialist brothers has been the cornerstone of Vietnamese foreign policy throughout and beyond the revolution. Until the late 1950s, Vietnamese communists imagined the brotherhood in its ideal condition and displayed deep admiration and full trust in the Soviet Union. They viewed Soviet leadership of world revolution as a given historical condition, not as a contradiction to the principles of equality embodied in the brotherhood. Soviet leadership did not mandate the submission of smaller nations to Moscow, nor did it imply any inherent inferiority on their part. However, the attitude of key Vietnamese communist leaders toward Moscow changed in the wake of the Sino-Soviet conflict in the early 1960s. They rallied to Mao and condemned Khrushchev's policy of peaceful coexistence as deviating from the mission of world revolution. Yet they also disapproved of Mao's attempts to create a new Communist International that would signal a formal split in the Soviet bloc. From idealistic they became more realistic in their attitude while still loyal to internationalism.

By the late 1960s, the outpouring of world support elevated the Vietnamese revolutionary spirit to the extent that Hanoi leaders began to imagine themselves being the vanguard of world revolution. Their attitude is best captured by the term "vanguard internationalism," which was a mixture of fervent national pride and fiery revolutionary ambitions. Their national pride sprang less from any patriotic traditions than from an exaggerated estimation of their lifetime revolutionary experience that had been gained in the particular context of Vietnam. That pride in their revolutionary achievements fuelled grand ambitions to shape the future of Southeast Asia and to lead the "tidal waves" of world revolution. After Hanoi's victory in the civil war, vanguard internationalism contributed to Vietnam's tensions with its brothers and wars with Cambodia and China in 1979. As their postwar foreign policy encountered colossal failures, Hanoi leaders abandoned their conceit of being vanguard while remaining committed to internationalism.

Although the relationship between communist Vietnam and its brothers was far from ideal, the remarkable thing was its steadfast loyalty to internationalism. Whether being idealistic, realistic, or self-centered, throughout the entire course of the revolution Vietnamese communists never imagined breaking away from the brotherhood. Although they expected to be assisted by their brothers, to say they joined the brotherhood just for material aid would be an insult to them.

The depth of their commitment to the brotherhood is clear if it is contrasted to their attitude toward noncommunist developing countries. On the one hand, Vietnamese revolutionaries expressed solidarity and maintained ties with peoples and movements in other colonized and dependent countries. In their thought, the struggle against European colonialism and American imperialism in Asia, Africa, and Latin America constituted a major front of world revolution. They adamantly advocated decolonization and cultivated friendly and mutually supportive relations with former colonies, including those such as India where a "bourgeois" nationalist movement led decolonization. In turn, support for their revolution from other oppressed peoples around the world greatly emboldened the Vietnamese.

On the other hand, relations of revolutionary Vietnam with so-called "Third World" countries were neither as deep nor as wide-ranging as those with its communist brothers. The Vietnamese saw little benefit to learn from countries that were less revolutionary than theirs. China and the Soviet bloc, not other Third World states, were where they sent thousands of officials and students to study. In the first decade after their rise to power, Hanoi leaders copied quite faithfully Soviet and Chinese political institutions and models of economic development – from Stalin's 1936 Constitution to his cult of personality, from land reform to collectivization, and from central planning to the preoccupation with building heavy industry – down to the names of particular institutions such as *Su That* [Soviet *Pravda* or Truth], *Nhan Dan* [Chinese *Renmin Ribao* or People's Daily], *Doan Thanh Nien Cong San* [Soviet *Komsomol* or Young Communist League], and *ho khau* [Chinese *hukou* or household registration]. These borrowings should not be interpreted as indicating Vietnamese inability of independent and original thought. Rather, they conveyed their enthusiasm about the most advanced revolutionary ideas at the time and their ambition to realize those ideas in a historical context far less conducive to those ideas than was either the Soviet Union or China.

Without acknowledging full Vietnamese agency, it would be difficult to appreciate the richness of their thought and imagination which encompassed the meaning of life, the history of human society, new concepts of the nation and the world, and Vietnam's place in the global revolutionary struggle. The worldview of Vietnamese communist leaders did not come

as a package but evolved over time as their ideals encountered harsh
realities. Individually, they were neither uniformly well versed in Marxist-
Leninist theory, nor did they always achieve consensus over the interpretations of particular revolutionary concepts. As a group, their systematic
and radical worldview profoundly distinguished them from others in the
anticolonial movement, as well as powerfully shaped the trajectory of the
Vietnamese revolution.

ROLE OF IDEOLOGY IN THE VIETNAMESE REVOLUTION

Ideology played three broad roles in the Vietnamese revolution. Its first
role was to serve as a guide or a compass. Ideology defined the mission of the revolution, which was not just national independence but also
social changes and contributions to world revolution. Ideology offered
Vietnamese revolutionaries a tangible vision of the future in the form of
a society modeled after the Soviet system. That vision helped them keep
a long-term perspective and survive short-term challenges. Ideology provided a set of lenses for them to interpret and explain world events thousands of miles away with little direct impact on Vietnam. Throughout
their revolution, ideology informed Vietnamese communists' assumptions
about the nature and trends of world politics and about the behavior of
foreign states such as the Soviet Union, China, or the United States. In
addition, the Leninist ideology viewed war as an extension of revolution.
In some situations, this suggested particular war strategies that placed as
much emphasis on mass mobilization as on the deployment of main force
units. Without the Leninist concept of correlation of forces, Hanoi might
well have been deterred by massive American firepower.

Ideology did not always point Vietnamese revolutionaries in the right
direction, and one can even argue that it frequently caused them to
make wrong interpretations of world events. Their interpretations of US
behavior, for example, were often too dogmatic and negative. Their use
of Leninist concepts in devising war strategies caused gross miscalcula-
tions and grave losses of revolutionary forces during the *Tet* Offensive.
In the post-1975 period, they completely misread the world situation.
Ideological loyalty unnecessarily created enemies for them left and right.
Their belief in the Stalinist model had disastrous consequences for the
Vietnamese economy. The regime today has lost its legitimacy because
the Party clings to an outdated doctrine. The point is: Ideology influenced
and explained many decisions made by Vietnamese revolutionaries but
did not determine their success or failure in any particular endeavor. The

intense ideological belief that history and justice were on their side simply gave revolutionaries the courage (or foolhardiness, from another perspective) to stand up to powerful – real or imagined – domestic and external enemies, whereas ideological concepts offered them some tools to operate, but the outcome was decided by numerous other factors.

The second role of ideology was to serve as the bond linking members in the communist movement domestically and internationally. Domestically it was the glue that kept the Party together most clearly during the prepower phase. As long as they truly believed in it, the ideological mission enthralled Party members and helped them to persevere in the face of extreme hardship and danger. Ideological principles deeply informed the organization of the Party, its membership policy, its standard operating procedures, and its communication to the masses (propaganda). Externally, ideology linked Vietnamese revolutionaries to a transnational network of states and movements sharing belief in the same ideology. In the prepower phase this network provided information, training, support, and sanctuaries from French police. This network rescued the Vietnamese movement after it had been nearly destroyed by colonial suppression in 1931 and in 1940. This network gave incentives to revolutionaries to coordinate their strategies with the world communist and worker movement to take advantage of the available resources.

Again, ideology was not always helpful, and created problems for the Vietnamese revolution as much as it helped. Throughout the 1940s, Vietnamese communists received little or no support from the transnational network of worker and communist movements. The network simply ignored Indochina and left it at the mercy of imperialism. If the Soviet Union had lost to Germany, the Vietnamese revolution would have been doomed to fail. In the same vein, it would have faced tremendous challenges if Chinese communists had lost the civil war on mainland China. The collapse of the network in the late 1980s contributed to the effective end of the Vietnamese revolution.

During the 1960s, ideology was a source of bitter factional conflict in Hanoi and between North Vietnam and its allies. Ideology fostered factionalism because Marxism-Leninism was broad enough to be interpreted in more than one way. Ideological disagreement with Moscow and Beijing created a significant headache for Hanoi, which felt that the revolution needed support from both brothers. Brutal ideological discord within the Vietnamese communist leadership in the 1960s could have destroyed the revolution. Again, the larger point is: Ideology embedded in the organization of the Communist Party and in the transnational network was useful to Vietnamese revolutionaries in some aspects, but eventually did not help them succeed.

The third role of ideology in the Vietnamese revolution was to be a crucial tool for building a cohesive state. "The dictatorship of the proletariat" justified the concentration of power within state organs and the relentless and systematic violence carried out against counterrevolutionaries. Ideological principles were deployed to restructure society according to the Stalinist vision that Vietnamese revolutionaries cherished. The land reform, for example, used ideological principles to categorize the rural population and turn villagers against each other; in the process the Party was able to extend its control down to the village level. Ideology offered justifications for *complete* state control of the economy. Robust or creative ideological arguments, whether produced locally or borrowed from the transnational network of communist and worker movements, provided the content for effective state propaganda. Ideological indoctrination was a *systematic* tool for creating long-term loyalty to the state.

However, ideology assisted state building at the expense of the economy, society, and culture. As the state expanded its bureaucratic control, the economy suffered. Each wave of radical agrarian and capitalist reform (1953–1956, 1958–1960, 1976–1978) was followed by a grave economic crisis. The systematic and persistent efforts by revolutionary authorities to promote and enforce a dogmatic belief in Marxism-Leninism severely inhibited the development of science, thought, and culture. When the leadership reluctantly abandoned central planning and rural cooperatives in the late 1980s, Vietnam was the third poorest and one of the most oppressive countries in Southeast Asia.

In terms of Vietnam's particular foreign policies and general orientations of external relations, ideology played a central role in the Democratic Republic of Vietnam (DRV)'s decision to join the Soviet bloc in 1948. If Vietnamese revolutionaries had not been communists, they would not have made that decision. Ideological considerations subsequently contributed to the DRV's decision to accept the Geneva Agreements. Ideological reasons further explained why the DRV sided with China in the Sino-Soviet dispute, but did not support Beijing's bid to form a new Communist International during 1963–1964, despite Beijing's offer of substantial aid. Ideological belief in the unity of the socialist camp led Hanoi to denounce efforts by Yugoslavia, Poland, Hungary, and Czechoslovakia at various times to pursue their own paths to socialism. The same belief motivated Hanoi in its attempts to save the Soviet bloc on its deathbed. Ideology was a key factor in Vietnam's normalization of relations with China in 1990 and its deference to China since then. Inductively derived evidence thus indicates that ideology was critical throughout the Vietnamese revolution and is indispensable for explaining key foreign policies and the general orientation of Vietnam's external relations. Those policies could have been far-sighted or mistaken, and those external relations could have benefited or harmed Vietnam's national interests, but the influence of ideology is undeniable.

Of course, that influence waxed and waned. In the entire course of the revolution, the 1940s and the 1980s were two periods when that influence ebbed. During both periods, the revolution was fragile domestically and isolated internationally. In the 1940s, the Party disintegrated following its failed revolt in 1940. In that decade, it was for the most part isolated from the world revolution. In the 1980s, Vietnam experienced a protracted and severe economic crisis, and was economically embargoed by the West and diplomatically isolated by most countries in the United Nations. If international and domestic events gave the impetus for pragmatism, leadership changes facilitated ideological moderation in both periods. A new central leadership of the Party was formed in northern Vietnam in 1941, with the return of Ho Chi Minh. The 1980s similarly saw a gradual transition from Le Duan and Le Duc Tho to Truong Chinh and Nguyen Van Linh. In both periods, it should be noted, the Vietnamese revolution by no means veered away from doctrinal orthodoxy directed from Moscow. In the 1940s, Ho and Truong Chinh were following standing Comintern policy that communists cooperated with nationalists to struggle against fascism. In the 1980s, Vietnamese reformers like Truong Chinh and Nguyen Van Linh were following the lead of Gorbachev up to 1988. Nevertheless, when they realized that Gorbachev had deviated from orthodoxy, they labeled him a traitor and supported the (failed) coup against him.

PLAN OF THE BOOK

In Chapter 1, I show how communism arrived in Vietnam and how early Vietnamese communists developed their understanding of the concept of revolution. Chapter 2 traces developments of Vietnam's communist movement through the 1930s, at the end of which a revolutionary vision crystalized. The achievement of unity over that radical vision within the leadership of the movement indicates that ideological conflict, especially between Nguyen Ai Quoc and his comrades, has been much exaggerated in existing scholarship.

The 1940s was a critical period when Vietnamese communists seized power, organized a state, and became a member of the Soviet bloc. Chapter 3 will show that, even while pursuing diplomatic recognition from the United States and negotiating for peace with France, they tried desperately to attract the attention and support of their initially uninterested Chinese and Soviet comrades. The evidence presented in this chapter specifically refutes the "missed opportunity" hypothesis popular in the Vietnam War literature.

In Chapter 4, I turn to the 1950s and discuss how ideological loyalty might have shaped key decisions of the Party. Chapter 5 focuses on the ideological debate among Vietnamese leaders in the late 1950s and early 1960s in response to the Sino-Soviet split. The events of the late 1960s to the end of the Vietnam War are analyzed in Chapter 6. In this period, Vietnamese thoughts and policies began to reflect what I call "vanguard internationalism." Hanoi leaders remained deeply committed to internationalism while becoming more self-centered and displaying an unabashed national pride in Vietnam as the vanguard of world revolution.

During the postwar period, triumphs faded and tragedies accumulated. In Chapter 7, I argue that vanguard internationalism was responsible for Vietnam's failure to take advantage of the favorable postwar world order after the communist victory in 1975. Chapter 8 examines the 1980s, which witnessed the growth in Soviet-Vietnamese ties. Gorbachev's rise to power in the Soviet Union in the mid-1980s helped a faction led by Truong Chinh to galvanize support for economic reform. Yet the Tiananmen protests and the imminent collapse of Eastern European communist regimes in 1989 frightened Vietnamese leaders. They denounced Gorbachev and sought an alliance with China to save world socialism.

The Vietnamese revolution effectively ended in the late 1980s when the Stalinist model was abandoned at home, the Soviet bloc crumbled, and several top leaders of the Party died within a few years. Nevertheless, the legacies of ideology have proved quite durable. As discussed in Chapter 9, the two-camp view of world politics remains powerful in Vietnamese politics today despite the emergence of other worldviews. The central role of ideology throughout the Vietnamese revolution conveys many implications for scholarly debates that will be discussed in the epilogue. These debates concern the Vietnam War, and revolutionary and postrevolutionary politics.

NOTE ON METHODOLOGY AND SOURCES

In this book I used the inductive method and discursive analysis to interpret the worldview of Vietnamese revolutionaries. The main task I set out to do was to trace their thoughts over time through various sources, with particular attention to how key concepts were employed to explain reality and assert foreign policy positions. Throughout this study I link ideology to specific policies, but the focus is really on broad external relations. Not all foreign policies can be explained directly by ideological loyalty, nor can they be linked to ideological debates.[53] Where possible, I sought to demonstrate what ideological issues were at stake and how they were debated before policies were made. Over time, it was possible to observe a clear pattern suggesting that Vietnamese communists were not only loyal to Marxism-Leninism but were also acting under its guidance despite and besides their concerns for other factors.

I lived in socialist Vietnam during 1975–1990 and was heavily exposed to state propaganda from middle school through college. Propaganda penetrated the lives of Vietnamese young and old not only at school and in the workplace but also through the ubiquitous public address system which blasted out revolutionary news and songs everyday from dawn to dusk. Although I did not have a choice back then, this exposure immersed me in Vietnamese political discourse at the height of the revolution, taught me its codes and structures, and trained my ears to be sensitive to subtle shifts in it. The experience also was valuable in the sense that I *lived* the discourse *in current use* together with millions of other Vietnamese, as opposed to merely accessing it through archived texts. If the discourse today may sound archaic to most Vietnamese speakers, it was live at the time, still bubbling with raw passions and vigorous authority. Living, or one might even say breathing, the revolutionary discourse everyday through its ebbs and flows for fifteen years gave me confidence in my ability to appreciate its power as well as its limits in Vietnamese politics.

Of course, the experience cannot substitute for documented evidence. As my interest in the subject grew over the last decade, I have made numerous visits to Vietnam, a few weeks at a time, to carry out interviews and collect materials for this project. More specifically, I conducted research at the National Archive III in Hanoi over the course of a year in 2002–2003 and again in 2013. I also read a broad range of newspapers published from the 1920s to 2000s at the Revolutionary Museum and the National Library in Hanoi.

[53] For a nice review of an earlier literature that employed decision-making models to explain Vietnamese foreign policy, see Carlyle Thayer, "Vietnamese perspectives on international security: Three revolutionary currents," in Donald McMillen, ed. *Asian Perspectives on International Security* (London: Macmillan, 1984), 57–76.

Without the new sources emerging from Vietnam since the 1990s, this study would not have been possible. The most important source for this book was the fifty-four volumes of *Van Kien Dang Toan Tap* [Collected Party Documents] published by the Vietnamese Communist Party during 1998–2007. This source includes about 40,000 pages of documents produced by central and local Party organs and covering seventy years of Party history, from 1924 to 1995. Although some documents in these volumes had been released before in less complete forms, most became available to researchers for the first time. A major strength of this source is the broad scope and wide variety of the documents, which covered not only central Party policies and analyses but also local implementation, and not only politics but also economy, propaganda, and culture. Another key strength of the collection is the length of its coverage; earlier collections typically covered a particular period of the revolution. The resolutions and political reports of almost every Central Committee plenums prior to the 1980s were included, allowing me to trace the thoughts of Party leaders through time without breaks. For the colonial period when the Party operated in secret, the collection included many documents acquired from Russian and French archives.

The collection undoubtedly represents only a small portion of the Party archive, which remains off-limits to most researchers. Another limit of this source is the formal character of the documents it contains. In general, it is not a place to look for information on informal interaction within the top leadership, nor does it say much about the differences in the viewpoints of individual leaders on particular policies. However, my intention was not to write an event-driven history of the Vietnamese revolution. To the extent that we were interested mostly in Party leaders' collective and formal thoughts about the world, including their self-images and their images of other countries, this limitation was not debilitating.

There is no question that the documents in the collection had been edited before publication. The level of editing varied: pre-1975 documents appeared to have been edited only lightly; those before 1945 were hardly edited at all. As I have explained elsewhere, the publication of these volumes was unprecedented in the history of communist Vietnam.[54] The decision to publish them reflected the fears and anxieties among the second generation of Vietnamese leaders who did not participate much

[54] Tuong Vu, "Van Kien Dang Toan Tap: The Regime's Gamble and Researchers' Gains," *Journal of Vietnamese Studies* 5:2 (Summer 2010), 183–194.

in the revolution and who needed to borrow the legitimacy of their predecessors by disclosing, as much as possible, the seven decades of Party
records for public view. The publication of the volumes, as the Politburo
explained in its decision, was to demonstrate not only the revolutionary
past of the Party but also its contributions to the nation, not only the
Party's successes but also (some of) its failures. The volume for 1940–
1945, for example, included a special section with numerous documents
issued by the Viet Minh front to mobilize national solidarity, not to
launch class struggle. The volume for 1948 contained a document that,
for the first time, showed that the Politburo authorized a quota of landlords to be executed (one per 1,000 people) for the land rent reduction
campaign.[55] This document is significant because it makes clear that the
mass killings were premeditated. Top Party leaders knew what was going
on, and the excesses on the whole cannot be blamed on zealous local
peasants. These examples suggest that, to some extent at least, editors of
the volumes were committed to the multiple goals of the project and did
not edit them merely to exaggerate the communist beliefs and credentials
of Party leadership.

The second kind of source that directly informed this study includes
a very wide range of Vietnamese newspapers, journals, books, personal
diaries, and memoirs published over the last seven decades in Vietnam.[56]
These publications are rich in all kinds of information, from high politics to everyday life. The newspapers published in the 1930s or earlier
were useful for gaining a sense of how communism was portrayed and
received in French Indochina. From 1945 to 1946, the communists did
not yet control the media and I was able to access a dozen newspapers published by groups of various political affiliations. Scholars have
scarcely used some communist newspapers, such as *Viet Nam Doc Lap*
(Independent Vietnam) and *Su That* (Truth), even though these were the
primary newspapers for the crucial decade of 1942–1950. During this
decade when the central purposes of communist policy were to support

[55] See Dang Lao Dong Viet Nam [Vietnamese Workers' Party], "Politburo's Directive Issued
on May 4, 1953, on Some Special Issues regarding Mass Mobilization," transl. by Tuong
Vu. *Journal of Vietnamese Studies* 5:2 (Summer 2010), 243–247.
[56] The most notable among these are Le Van Hien, *Nhat ky cua mot Bo truong* [Diary of
a minister], 2 vols. (Da Nang: Da Nang Publishing House, 1995); Nguyen Huy Tuong,
Nhat Ky [Diary] (preserved by Trinh Thi Uyen and edited by Nguyen Huy Thang), 3 vols.
(Hanoi: Thanh Nien, 2006); Bui Tin, *Following Ho Chi Minh* (Honolulu: University of
Hawaii Press, 1995); Tran Quang Co, *Hoi uc va suy nghi*; and Huy Duc, *Ben Thang
Cuoc*. Some valuable memoirs or documents are posted by PAVN veterans on the blog
"Quan Su Viet Nam" <www.vnmilitaryhistory.net/index.php>.

the Allies (1942–1945) and to mobilize for national unity and independence (the entire period), the promotion of communist ideals found in these newspapers in both subtle and overt forms was telling evidence of deep commitments.

Many personal diaries of contemporaries, from communist leaders to writers and soldiers, have been published posthumously within the last decade and are particularly revealing about the thinking of people at the time. Diaries of dead communist soldiers in South Vietnam spoke to their ideological commitments beyond patriotism.[57] Remarkably, some authors of these diaries such as Dang Thuy Tram and Nguyen Van Thac came from suspect class backgrounds in communist North Vietnam, and their ideological belief and personal sacrifice for a regime that frequently belittled their service stood as unquestionably authentic testaments to the power of ideology in society.[58] Their diaries did not discuss any foreign policy decisions, but the external relations of communist Vietnam were not created simply by its top leaders. On a broader level, those relations that involved savage wars over decades were built on the sweat and blood of millions.

Memoirs by participants in major events were another important source for this study. Some memoirs of high-level officials such as those by Tran Quynh and Tran Quang Co have hardly been used by scholars before, even though they have been around for years in online form. These memoirs offer valuable information about particular policies although they require a careful assessment to discount authors' possible justifications of past policies. The majority of the memoirs that informed this study are of a different kind: they belonged to mid-level officials and former revolutionaries who never held power or have long fallen out of favor in the regime. Examples of these include Tran Dinh Long, Dao Duy

---

[57] See, for example, Dang Kim Tram, ed., *Nhat ky Dang Thuy Tram* [Diary of Dang Thuy Tram] (Hanoi: Nha Nam, 2005), 39, 68, 256; Dang Vuong Hung, ed., *Tro ve trong giac mo: Nhat ky cua liet si Tran Minh Tien* [Return in a dream: Diary of martyr Tran Minh Tien] (Hanoi: Hoi Nha Van, 2005), esp. 233–234; Dang Vuong Hung, ed., *Mai mai tuoi hai muoi: Nhat ky cua liet si Nguyen Van Thac* [Forever twenty: Diary of martyr Nguyen Van Thac] (Hanoi: Thanh Nien, 2005), esp. 198–199; Tran Van Thuy, *Nhat ky Thanh Nien Xung Phong Truong Son, 1965–1969* [Diary of a Youth Assault Brigade Cadre in Truong Son] (Ho Chi Minh City: Van Hoa Van Nghe, 2011); Do Ha Thai and Nguyen Tien Hai, eds. *Nhat Ky Vu Xuan* [Diary of Vu Xuan] (Hanoi: Quan Doi Nhan Dan, 2005).

[58] For a similar argument in a recent study of diaries written by Soviet citizens, see Jochen Hellbeck, *Revolution on My Mind: Writing a Diary under Stalin* (Cambridge, MA: Harvard University Press, 2006).

Anh, Tran Van Giau, Nguyen Kien Giang, Tran Dinh, Nguyen Van Tran, Tran Thu, Bui Tin, Hoang Huu Yen, and others. Again, the main purpose was not to search for information about particular foreign policy decisions although some memoirs did contain such information. Rather, the memoirs were useful to gain a sense of how others besides the top leaders thought and talked informally about ideology and politics.

Although not directly useful for this book, a significant new source from Vietnam deserves mention. This is the millions of pages of archival documents from government agencies of the DRV for the period of 1945 to 1975 that are housed in National Archive III in Hanoi. Documents specifically on foreign policy are generally not available from this archive, although documents on foreign relations are. Nevertheless, the available collection reveals beyond dispute the commitments of Vietnamese leaders to developing socialism at home despite repeated setbacks.[59] This collection alone shows that they were *bona fide* revolutionaries dedicated to building utopia no less than were Stalin and Mao. This archival resource on the whole validated and reinforced what I found in other sources.

Most arguments in this study were crafted by juxtaposing various sources. An example is useful here to show how the combined sources help to assess certain controversial statements or issues. In 1958, the DRV Prime Minister Pham Van Dong sent a diplomatic note to his Chinese counterpart Zhou Enlai in which Dong essentially concurred with China's sweeping territorial claims in the South China Sea. It is not clear from the note that Dong was acting out of his own will and not under Chinese pressure.[60] Nevertheless, Dong's true intent can be probed by cross-checking three other sources. First, *Nhan Dan*, the Party's newspaper, translated and published in full Zhou Enlai's announcement on China's claims two days after it was made, whereas Dong's note was published eight days later, together with news of huge mass rallies in Hanoi

---

[59] Examples of works that exploit this source are Nguyen, *Hanoi's War*; Benoît de Tréglodé, *Heroes and Revolution in Vietnam*, transl. Claire Duiker (Singapore: NUS Press in association with IRASEC, 2012); Tuong Vu, *Paths to Development in Asia: South Korea, Vietnam, China, and Indonesia* (New York: Cambridge University Press, 2010); Kerkvliet, *The Power of Everyday Politics*; Ninh, *A World Transformed*.

[60] For opposing views on this note by Vietnamese scholars, see Pham Quang Tuan, "Co can phai thong cam cho ong Pham Van Dong?" [Should we have sympathy for Mr. Pham Van Dong?], *Bauxite Vietnam*, June 15, 2014, http://boxitvn.blogspot.com/2014/06/co-can-phai-thong-cam-cho-ong-pham-van.html; Cao Huy Thuan, "Cong ham Pham Van Dong: Gop y ve viec giai thich" [Pham Van Dong's Diplomatic Note: How to Interpret it], *Thời Đại Mới* [New Era], July 31, 2014), www.tapchithoidai.org/ThoiDai31/201431_CaoHuyThuan.pdf.

in support of China.[61] It would be difficult to argue that these prompt
and public gestures were made under pressure. The second source that
offered useful context to Dong's note was the recently published personal
diary of Le Van Hien, the Minister of Finance and a high-ranking leader
of the Party until the 1950s. In his diary, Hien expressed joy on hearing
that Chinese communist forces seized parts of the Paracel Islands in the
South China Sea from the French in May 1950 (the Paracels were also
claimed by China). Hien thought that the Chinese takeover would help
the Vietnamese revolution advance in central and southern Vietnam; he
did not raise any sovereignty issues.[62] Still another source: the *World
Geography* textbook used in the DRV in the 1950s was translated ver-
batim from a Chinese textbook that included maps showing in full a
nine-dashed line of China's sovereignty claim over most of the South
China Sea.[63] The three sources did not completely rule out the possibility
that Dong acted merely out of solidarity or that some subtle diplomatic
pressure was exerted. Still, *together* they pointed to the greater likelihood
of Dong and his colleagues trustfully viewing Chinese as brothers and
accepting Chinese claims without any reservation.

[61] T.T.X.V.N. [Vietnam News Service], "Chinh phu nuoc Cong hoa Nhan dan Trung hoa
    ra tuyen bo quy dinh hai phan cua Trung quoc," *Nhan Dan* [The People], September
    6, 1958.
[62] See the entry dated May 14, 1950 in Le Van Hien, *Nhat Ky Mot Bo Truong*, v. 2, 318.
[63] See Nhan Dich Khanh and Chu Quang Ky, *Dia ly the gioi* [World Geography], transl.
    Nguyen Duoc and Nguyen An (Hanoi: Bo Giao Duc, 1955), 202–203.

I

Revolutionary Paths through the Mind, 1917–1930

Ho Chi Minh, the man who came to symbolize Vietnamese nationalism and communism, was one of the first Vietnamese to convert to Leninism. As he later reminisced,

At first, patriotism, not yet communism, led me to believe in Lenin, in the Third International. Step by step, along the struggle, by studying Marxism-Leninism parallel with participation in practical activities, I gradually came upon the fact that only socialism and communism can liberate the oppressed nations and the working people throughout the world from slavery. There is a legend, in our country as well as in China, of the miraculous "Book of the Wise." When facing great difficulties, one opens it and finds a way out. Leninism is not only a miraculous "Book of the Wise... " it is also the radiant sun illuminating our path to final victory, to socialism and communism.[1]

Born Nguyen Sinh Cung (or Con) around 1890, Ho received limited formal education as a child and became a political activist by the end of World War I while living in France.[2] His path from patriotism to Leninism was a common experience shared by many Vietnamese communists, as in the case of Truong Chinh. As Ho admitted, acquiring a belief in Leninism was not the end but just the beginning of a new path. It took time and

---

[1] Ho Chi Minh, "The Path That Led Me to Leninism," in Prasenjit Duara, ed. *Decolonization: Perspectives from Now and Then* (New York: Routledge, 2004), 31.

[2] Ho studied Chinese classics at home and may have attended a Vietnamese-Franco elementary school. His formal education was disrupted many times and appeared limited. See Pierre Brocheux, *Ho Chi Minh: A Biography*, transl. Claire Duiker (New York: Cambridge University Press, 2007), 2–7; Thuy Khue, *Nhan Van Giai Pham va Van de Nguyen Ai Quoc* (Online publication, 2011), 595–597; available at http://thuykhue.free.fr/stt/n/nhanvan15-2.html

effort for him to fully grasp communist ideas. The revolutionary path was an intellectual as much as a physical struggle for Nguyen Ai Quoc (or Quac or Kwak in some versions), the name Ho was using at the time. It is possible to observe this mental struggle through his writings: he first expressed a simplistic and mechanical understanding of the concept of world revolution, but gradually showed a more sophisticated knowledge.

By the early 1930s, the Communist Party that Quoc helped found under Comintern guidance had settled on a clear and firm vision of their revolution as a component of world revolution. In this vision, the Vietnamese revolution was to pass through two phases: the "bourgeois democratic" phase and the "proletarian" phase. The first phase involved the overthrow of French rule, a land revolution, and the formation of a state based on a triple alliance of workers, peasants, and soldiers, but led solely by workers. The second phase would take Vietnam to socialism.

The Marxist-Leninist worldview united, rather than divided, Quoc and his comrades. They all shared a deep love of the Soviet Union as a laboratory of revolution. They did not see eye to eye on some issues, but their disagreement reflected not a difference in their worldview or their loyalty to the Comintern, but the timing of their induction into the movement, their formal education and personal theoretical aptitude, and timely access to information from the Comintern.

"FIRST MAKE A NATIONAL REVOLUTION, THEN MAKE A WORLD REVOLUTION"

By the turn of the twentieth century, the French colonial system in Vietnam had been consolidated and was about to experience rapid expansion.[3] In the following three decades, colonial administration continued to penetrate deeply into Vietnamese villages to enforce control and exploit resources for a growing capitalist economy. In many parts of the colony, landlessness became more widespread, and state extraction through taxes, forced labor, and conscription became more effective.

Against that backdrop of colonial development were the establishment of a formal school system that taught French and other subjects, the broad adoption of the Vietnamese vernacular language *Quoc Ngu*, and

[3] The best account of French colonialism in Indochina is Pierre Brocheux and Daniel Hémery, *Indochina: An Ambiguous Colonization, 1858–1954*, transl. Ly-Lan Dill-Klein, Eric Jennings, Nora A. Taylor, and Noémi Tousignant (Berkeley, CA: University of California Press, 2009).

the emergence of a reading public.[4] Similar to other colonies, these trends fuelled the rise of modern Vietnamese nationalism.[5] Prior to the turn of the century, the universe for most Vietnamese was the East Asian cultural sphere anchored in China. Ideas from outside that sphere were mostly absorbed through the medium of the Chinese language and worldview. Knowledge of French opened up a whole new world for Vietnamese youth who came of age in the 1920s and afterward. It brought not only new concepts but also direct contacts with European social and political movements of the time.

The Vietnamized term "cach mang" (revolution) in its modern sense was imported into Vietnam by way of Japan and China around the turn of the century,[6] but there was no evidence of Vietnamese knowledge of Marx and Lenin before the Russian Revolution in 1917.[7] Reports in the Vietnamese-language press on that revolution likely drew from French and Chinese sources and were generally unfavorable. For example, *Nam Phong* [Southern Wind], a prominent Vietnamese/Chinese journal, praised the Kerensky government and described its opponents, including Lenin, as "corrupt" and "selling their country" to Germany for money [bai liet o hanh, phan nuoc].[8] The term "Bolshevik" was translated into Vietnamese as "*qua kich*" [extremist].[9] Subsequently, in an extended analysis of Russian politics, *Nam Phong* reported that Lenin's party favored the use of violence to force the "powerful capitalists" to cede more rights to the people.[10] At the same time, the Bolsheviks were against

---

[4] Ibid.

[5] Benedict Anderson, *Imagined Communities* (London, UK: Verso, 1991). For Vietnam, see William Duiker, *The Rise of Nationalism in Vietnam, 1900–1941* (Ithaca, NY: Cornell University Press, 1976); and Christopher Goscha, *Going Indochinese: Contesting Concepts of Space and Place in French Indochina* (Copenhagen: NIAS, 2012).

[6] For a detailed discussion of the origins of this term in the Vietnamese political discourse, see George Dutton, "Cach Mang, Révolution: The Early History of 'Revolution' in Vietnam," *Journal of Southeast Asian Studies* 46: 1 (2015), 4–31. According to this source, the French term "révolution" appeared in French Cochinchina much earlier, perhaps in the 1870s. The Vietnamese term first appeared around 1910 but was hardly used by any anticolonialists prior to 1920.

[7] Some Vietnamese official historians argued that French censorship prevented information about the Russian revolution from reaching Vietnam. See, for example, Minh Tranh, *Chung run so truoc anh huong cua Cach mang Thang Muoi toi Viet Nam* [They trembled at the influence of the October Revolution in Vietnam] (Hanoi: Su That, 1958).

[8] "Talk of the Day" [*Thoi Dam*], *Nam Phong* 2, August 1917, 132–133.

[9] Ibid. The French word "maximalistes" accompanied the Vietnamese term in original. The contemporary spelling of this Vietnamese term is "qua khich."

[10] "Talk of the Day" [*Thoi Dam*], *Nam Phong* no. 7, January 1918, 53.

war, believing that it would only benefit capitalists. *Nam Phong* criticized the Bolsheviks' penchant for violence and for "betraying the Allies"
and "disgracing the (Russian) nation" by signing a peace agreement with
Germany-Austria."[11]

In contrast, exiled Vietnamese revolutionaries in France and southern
China welcomed the Russian revolution. Yet they did so for different reasons. Older Vietnamese revolutionaries, in particular, either hoped to secure
Soviet military support or to draw practical lessons from the Russian revolution. Phan Boi Chau, who was the most prominent revolutionary at the
time and who had earlier sought Japan's assistance in fighting France, went
to meet Soviet officials in Peiping (Beijing) in 1920 to inquire about possible
assistance for sending Vietnamese students to study in the Soviet Union. He
described the attitude of Soviet officials as "friendly and honest."[12] They
promised to cover all expenses of interested students on the condition that
those students believe in communism and be committed to carrying out
the revolution in Vietnam after graduation. Phan Boi Chau did not reveal
his reactions to this offer but no further contacts followed. A year later, he
wrote an article published in a Chinese military journal praising Lenin as
a superb revolutionary strategist.[13] Although he credited the Soviet government with establishing the first ever government of workers and peasants
[*chinh phu Lao Nong*], he was mostly impressed, not with communism, but
with the Bolsheviks' success in seizing power. Phan Chau Trinh, another vet-
eran revolutionary of Phan Boi Chau's generation, reacted in the same manner. In his letter to Nguyen Ai Quoc in 1922, Phan Chau Trinh expressed
general admiration for the 1917 revolution, but for him the main lesson
from this revolution was that revolutionaries could succeed only if they
operated inside the country (rather than from abroad).[14]

Like Phan Boi Chau, Nguyen Ai Quoc's interest in the Bolshevik revolution stemmed from Lenin's support for colonial independence. Unlike
Phan, Quoc strived to understand communism by studying the theory

[11] "Talk of the Day" [*Thoi Dam*], *Nam Phong* no. 9, March 1918, 186.
[12] Phan Boi Chau, "Phan Boi Chau Nien Bieu" [The Timeline of Phan Boi Chau's Career] in Chuong Thau, ed., *Phan Boi Chau Toan Tap* [Complete works by Phan Boi Chau] (Hanoi: Trung Tam Van Hoa Ngon Ngu Dong Tay, 2001), v. 6, 251–252.
[13] Phan Boi Chau, "Luoc truyen Liet Ninh, vi nhan cua nuoc Nga Do" [A brief story about Lenin, the great man of Red Russia] in Chuong Thau, ed., *Phan Boi Chau Toan Tap*, v. 5, 317–323.
[14] Phan Chau Trinh, "Thu gui Nguyen Ai Quoc," February 18, 1922 in Chuong Thau, Duong Trung Quoc, Le Thi Kinh et al., eds., *Phan Chau Trinh Toan Tap* [Complete works by Phan Chau Trinh] (Da Nang: Da Nang Publishing House, 2005), v. 3, 99–104.

and by being involved in the communist movement.[15] This process of radicalization is traceable in his writings. Quoc left the socialists to join the communists in France in 1920, after having read and being convinced by Lenin's thesis on the colonial question. Throughout his writings in the early 1920s, Quoc was obsessed with colonialism and its crimes against his people. But his perspective became increasingly internationalized and influenced by Leninist concepts.[16]

In an article published in 1921, for example, Quoc cited Chinese thinkers such as Confucius and Mencius to argue that it would be easier to realize communism in Asia than in Europe.[17] According to him, labor mobilization and the public ownership of land had been common in Asian societies since ancient times, which would make them more receptive to communist ideas and institutions. This article was perhaps written simply to raise support from the European left for revolutions in the colonies, but it betrayed Quoc's shallow understanding of Marxism.

By the following year, however, Quoc showed a better grasp of the doctrine. He was now able to understand the social basis of communism and to distinguish communism from nationalism. In the colonies, he complained that

ordinary people have no idea what class struggle is, as there is no industry and commerce as well as workers' organizations there. To indigenous people, Bolshevism means either the destruction of everything or the liberation from foreign rule. The first interpretation makes the uneducated and timid masses avoid us. The second interpretation leads them to nationalism. Both are dangerous.[18]

The process of intellectual radicalization accelerated after Nguyen Ai Quoc arrived in the Soviet Union in June 1923 at the invitation of the Comintern.[19] His writings were now dominated by themes of class struggle. Among his favorite topics were workers movements around

---

[15] See Sophie Quinn-Judge, *Ho Chi Minh: The Missing Years 1919–1941* (Berkeley, CA: University of California Press, 2002), esp. 31–32.

[16] See William Duiker, *Ho Chi Minh: A Life* (New York: Hyperion, 2000), 123 for a similar observation.

[17] Nguyen Ai Quoc, "Phong trao Cong san quoc te" [The international Communist movement], published in *La Revue Communiste* no. 15 (May 1921) and reprinted in Ho Chi Minh, *Ho Chi Minh Toan Tap* [Collected works by Ho Chi Minh, hereafter *HCMTT*], 2nd ed., v. 1 (Hanoi: Chinh tri Quoc gia, 1995), 33–36.

[18] Nguyen Ai Quoc, "May y nghi ve van de thuoc dia" [Some thoughts about the colonial problem], published in *L'Humanite*, May 25, 1922. *HCMTT*, 2nd ed., v. 1, 63.

[19] Brocheux, *Ho Chi Minh*, 23–29.

the world.[20] He also paid attention to gender and racial issues across national boundaries.[21] He went from denouncing colonialism to launching broad attacks on French and American "civilizations."[22] In an article titled "Lynching: A Little Known Aspect of American Civilization," for example, Quoc blamed capitalism for slavery and expressed solidarity with American blacks. The article included graphic descriptions of several lynching cases, some apparently translated from American newspapers. The paragraph below, which described the climax of a lynching case, showcased Quoc's sharp writing skills and his intense feelings about the injustice toward blacks:

The black man could no longer scream; his tongue had swollen after a hot iron bar was thrust into his mouth. His whole body twisted like a beaten snake – half-alive, half-dead. A knife was raised, and an ear fell off. Oh my god, how black it was! How disgusting! Then the [white] women ripped his face apart .... [After they had burned the black man's body,] the ground was dirty with [burned] fat and [the air filled with] smoke. [Left behind] was a blackened, burned, and crushed skull that horrifyingly grimaced at the setting sun with the question: "is that a civilized [act]?"[23]

While writing for newspapers and participating in Comintern activities, Quoc also received some training at the University of the Toilers of the East.[24] The Soviet government created this university in 1921 to train foreign youths in communism and revolutionary science. Quoc was particularly impressed with the school's diverse student body, the majority of whom came from working-class backgrounds.[25] In the classroom, he described, "young people of 62 nations sat side by side like brothers." They did not just study but also helped with work on farms. They lived

[20] For example, see his articles on the workers' movement in China, Japan, and Turkey, respectively, in *HCMTT*, 2nd ed., v. 1, 215–220, 224–226.

[21] Nguyen Ai Quoc, "Phu nu phuong Dong" [Women of the East], May 1924, in *HCMTT*, 2nd ed., v. 1, 267–268; "Dang Ku Klux Klan" [Ku Klux Klan Party], *Inprekorr* no. 74 (1924), in *HCMTT*, 2nd ed., v. 1, 336–341.

[22] For example, see Nguyen Ai Quoc, "Giao duc quoc dan" [National education], *Le Paria* no. 29 (September 1924), in *HCMTT*, 2nd ed., v. 1, 313–314.

[23] "Hanh hinh kieu lynso" [Lynching], *Inprekorr* no. 59 (1924), in *HCMTT*, 2nd ed., v. 1, 306–312.

[24] There is no formal record of his registration at the school although several sources suggest he attended some training there. See Quinn-Judge, *Ho Chi Minh*, 54–55.

[25] Nguyen Ai Quoc, "Cach mang Nga voi cac dan toc thuoc dia" [The Russian revolution and the colonized nations], published in 1925 in *Ban an che do thuc dan Phap* [Verdict on the French colonial regime] and reprinted in Ho Chi Minh, *Ket hop chat che long yeu nuoc voi tinh than quoc te vo san* [Unity of patriotism and proletarian internationalism] (Hanoi: Su That, 1976), 57–62.

comfortably as the school paid for their room, board, clothes, and even gave them some pocket money. They enjoyed a rich intellectual life with free access to libraries and cinema theaters. Although they were denied political freedoms in their own countries, they were invited to participate in school management and even to vote in local elections, just like Soviet citizens. Quoc passionately called on his "brothers in colonized countries" to compare "bourgeois democracy" with "proletarian democracy."[26]

Yet it would be a mistake to think that life in the Soviet Union was always pleasant for Quoc. The Comintern archive in Moscow still keeps a letter he wrote to the Secretary of the Eastern Department of the Comintern after having lived for nine months in Moscow.[27] The letter asked for help in dealing with the housing department, which threatened to take him to court if he failed to pay an amount of 40 roubles and 35 kopecks he allegedly owed. Quoc explained that he was not negligent but had paid only 5 roubles per month for rent (instead of the full rent, perhaps as a gesture of protest?) because the house he lived in was too noisy with four or five renters and the bed was full of bedbugs that caused him to lose many nights of sleep.

Irritating pests, overcrowded apartments, and red tape, however, did not dampen Quoc's admiration for the Soviet Union. As he reminisced some 20 years later:

Some thought Russia was hell. Others said Russia was a paradise. To [me], Russia was certainly not hell, but at the same time not yet a paradise. It was a transforming country with many admirable aspects, but still it had not eliminated all defects. Occasionally one could still see the wounds left by wars such as orphaned children, the shortage of housing and food, etc. But these wounds were healing. Everywhere people were working enthusiastically... [I] did not forget that this was a country that had just experienced four years of World War and one year of civil war . . . [I] did not forget comparing Russia where a revolution was advancing with Vietnam that had been a colony for decades.[28]

[26] Ibid., 61.
[27] "Gui dong chi Pe to rop, chu tich Ban Phuong dong" [To Comrade Petrov, Chair of the Eastern Department] (c. March 1924). Reprinted in *HCMTT*, 2nd ed., v. 1, 248.
[28] Tran Dan Tien (a pseudonym), *Nhung mau chuyen ve doi hoat dong cua Ho Chu tich* [Stories about the life and career of Chairman Ho] (Hanoi: Su That, 1976), 59; Olga Dror, "Establishing Ho Chi Minh's Cult: Vietnamese Traditions and Their Transformations," *Journal of Asian Studies*, 75: 2 (2016), 433–466. According to Olga Dror's meticulous research, the first versions of this book were published in 1949 in Paris (in Vietnamese with Tran Ngoc Danh named as author), and in Shanghai (in Chinese with Tran Dan Tien, a pseudonym, as author) in 1949. It was published for the first time in Vietnam in 1955 with Tran Dan Tien as author, and has since served as a central tool in creating the cult of Ho Chi Minh. The book was either written by Ho himself or by his subordinates

If we can believe him, Quoc was impressed neither by Soviet level of wealth nor by its social conditions. Rather, it was the enthusiasm of Soviet people and the promises of the revolution that enchanted him.

By the time Quoc arrived in southern China in late 1924 to work as a Comintern agent for Southeast Asia, his theoretical understanding had improved but remained limited. For the next three years, Quoc led *Hoi Viet Nam Cach Mang Thanh Nien* (Vietnamese Revolutionary Youth League, hereafter Thanh Nien), a revolutionary group that he helped found. Working closely with leaders of the Chinese Communist Party (CCP), Thanh Nien recruited its first members among exiled Vietnamese and organized the smuggling of youth from inside Vietnam to Guangzhou for revolutionary training.

As the trainer, Quoc edited the journal *Thanh Nien* and authored a pamphlet titled "The Revolutionary Path" [Duong Kach Menh]. The pamphlet was Quoc's first and most elaborate theoretical analysis to date. It opened with Lenin's famous dictum that "without a revolutionary theory, there can be no revolutionary movement."[29] Quoc explained what "revolution" meant and called on Vietnamese to follow the model of the Russian revolution.[30] An analysis of how Quoc explained the concept of revolution in this pamphlet is key to understanding his emerging Leninist worldview.

Quoc employed Marxist-Leninist theory – as he understood it – to propose a taxonomy that included three kinds of revolutions – namely, "capitalist," "national," and "class-based" revolutions.[31] According to

based on what he told them. The tone in the quoted paragraph is consistent with his view expressed in other texts.

[29] Nguyen Ai Quoc, "Duong Kach Menh" [The Revolutionary Path], originally published in 1927 and reprinted in *Van Kien Dang Toan Tap* [Collected Party documents], hereafter *VKDTT*, v. 1, 15.

[30] By mistranslating key quotes from the pamphlet and misinterpreting Quoc's argument, Mark Bradley incorrectly argues that Quoc wanted Vietnamese to study the American revolution and that he had little interest in the Stalinist model. For example, the Vietnamese phrase "hoc My" that Quoc used is translated by Bradley as "study the American revolution," whereas it should be translated as "imitate the Americans to launch a revolution." Quoc's statement "The moi khoi hy sinh nhieu lan, the dan chung moi duoc hanh phuc" is mistranslated by Bradley as "Only by struggling many times over can all the people have happiness." The correct translation is: "Only [by a radical revolution unlike the one in America] would we not have to sacrifice again and again and would [our] people achieve happiness." "Duong Kach Menh," 26–27; Mark Bradley, *Imagining Vietnam & America: The Making of Postcolonial Vietnam 1919–1950* (Chapel Hill: University of North Carolina Press, 2000), 34–35.

[31] An earlier taxonomy of revolutions found in *Thanh Nien* (July 26, 1925) distinguished political, social, and world revolutions, with political revolutions apparently similar to

Quoc, capitalist revolutions were caused by conflicts between capitalists and landlords; national revolutions were caused by conflicts between an oppressed nation and the oppressor nation; and class-based revolutions were caused by conflicts between capitalists and worker-peasants. Having juxtaposed capitalist, national, and class-based revolutions, Quoc further distinguished between national and world revolutions. "World revolution" was defined as the unity of peasants and workers of all nations and races in the world "to overthrow capitalist rule, to make all nations happy, [and] to create a harmonious world."[32] National and world revolutions were different because all the social classes uniting against the national authorities made the former event, whereas the proletariat of all nations led the latter. Quoc went on to say,

> But the two revolutions are interconnected. For example, the success of the Annamese national revolution will weaken French capitalists, making it easier for French peasants and workers to launch a class-based revolution. And [vice versa, if] the revolution of French peasants and workers succeeds, the Annamese nation will be liberated. Thus Annamese and French [revolutionaries] must maintain contact.[33]

Some articles written earlier by Quoc in the journal *Thanh Nien* mechanically considered making national revolution as the first mission of the Vietnamese communist movement and making world revolution as its second mission distinct from the first.[34] In "The Revolutionary Path," hints emerged of a more dynamic and sophisticated view that fused together the national revolution with class-based revolution and with world revolution. The thinking was still fluid; at one point Quoc still tried to distinguish national from class-based from world revolution, but at other points world revolution was thought of as a complex process that involved many components both substantively (national and class issues) and geographically (Annamese and French).

This evolutionary thought process is significant because initially Quoc had been concerned only with the colonial relationship between Vietnam

---

national revolutions and social revolutions similar to class-based revolutions. See Huynh, *Vietnamese Communism* 87–88.

[32] Nguyen Ai Quoc, "Duong Kach Menh," 22. The concept of a harmonious world [thien ha dai dong] is a Confucian one. The context of the entire article suggests that Nguyen Ai Quoc's use of this concept here does not suggest his belief in Confucianism but rather his attempt to make the Marxist vision of classless society easier to be imagined for his fellow Vietnamese.

[33] Ibid.

[34] See Huynh, *Vietnamese Communism*, 85–88, for a discussion in *Thanh Nien* on this topic.

and France, but now had moved much closer to a worldview in which that relationship was part of other, more fundamental relationships. The separation or compartmentalization of different kinds of revolutions in his mind was evidence of the incomplete or superficial acceptance of the Marxist-Leninist worldview, whereas the fusion of those revolutions marked a conceptual leap in consciousness toward complete mental submission to that worldview. In the 1940s, Quoc would still advocate for the primacy of national revolution relative to class-based revolution for Vietnam, but that argument was conceived only in *tactical* terms. Conceptually Quoc no longer compartmentalized them. As will be seen in the next section, younger and better-educated revolutionaries would take further steps to articulate that conceptual fusion more forcefully.

"THE VIETNAMESE REVOLUTION WAS A COMPONENT OF WORLD REVOLUTION"

Nguyen Ai Quoc arrived in southern China at an auspicious time. A series of events had deeply radicalized Vietnamese politics and readied it for the acceptance of communism. A few years earlier, the colonial government had released many prominent political prisoners such as Huynh Thuc Khang and Ngo Duc Ke who had led the 1908 antitax revolt in central Vietnam. These older leaders quickly revived their dormant anticolonial network, and their return inspired many youths toward political activism.[35] Opportunities for such activism expanded with the rapid growth of the press in Saigon in the early 1920s and with the elections organized for the Chambers of People's Deputies [Vien Dan Bieu]. The reform carried out by the new Indochinese Governor-General Alexander Varenne (1925–1928), however limited, also contributed to a more open political context.[36] A leader of the French Socialist Party, Varenne sought to rein in the excesses of colonial rule in Indochina.

Just as the political environment was heating up, it was jolted by two particular events: one was the capture of Phan Boi Chau in China and his trial in Hanoi in 1925, and the other was Phan Chau Trinh's return to Vietnam from France and his subsequent death in 1926. These two events aroused great popular resentment and triggered many spontaneous

[35] Dao Duy Anh, *Nho nghi chieu hom* [Memoirs and thoughts] (Ho Chi Minh City: Tre Publishers, 1989), 8–26.
[36] Philippe Peycam, *The Birth of Vietnamese Political Journalism: Saigon, 1916–1930* (New York: Columbia University Press, 2012); Brocheux and Hémery, *Indochina: An Ambiguous Colonization*, 308.

student protests against the colonial regime. Hundreds of students were expelled from school for their participation in the protests; many would soon join clandestine political groups.[37]

Thanks to such an auspicious environment Thanh Nien gained many followers inside Vietnam, either through the spread of propaganda into Vietnam or through direct training offered to youths smuggled out of Vietnam. But Thanh Nien was not the only source of radical ideas for Vietnamese youths. As Sun Yat-sen reorganized the Chinese Nationalist Party (Guomindang or GMD) and prepared to launch a military campaign to reunify China, his Three People's Principles (which were themselves influenced in part by communist ideas) were also popular in Vietnam. Books and newspapers imported from France and China or published in Saigon offered those Vietnamese with foreign language skills much more systematic discussions of Marx and Lenin than did Thanh Nien's materials.[38]

The final source of radicalization came from China and the Soviet Union. In April 1927, Chiang Kai-shek ordered the massacre of Chinese communists in Shanghai, ending the United Front between the GMD and the CCP. Chiang's "betrayal" contributed to the new, radical policy decided at the Sixth World Congress and the Tenth Plenum of the Executive Committee of the Comintern in Moscow in 1928 and 1929, respectively. At these events, Comintern leaders issued calls for communists worldwide to strengthen the proletarian character of their parties and to engage in class struggle against the bourgeoisie.[39] Chiang's turn against Chinese communists also made it unsafe for Thanh Nien members in southern China. By mid-1928, Nguyen Ai Quoc had fled China while Thanh Nien withered in Guangzhou.

The conditions described earlier in Vietnam and abroad combined to shift the center of radicalism from southern China into Vietnam. By late 1928, there had emerged small revolutionary groups in all three regions of Vietnam. A major group was the Vietnamese Nationalist Party (VNP) that embraced Three People's Principles as its ideological foundation. Thanh Nien trainees created other groups who were eager to take the movement to a new radical height. This shift can be observed in the contrast between the Tan Viet group based mainly in central Vietnam and the Dong Duong group in northern Vietnam.

[37] Many were future leaders of the VCP, including Pham Van Dong, Vo Nguyen Giap, and Truong Chinh.
[38] See Dao Duy Anh, *Nho nghi chieu hom*, 27, 31–34.
[39] Quinn-Judge, *Ho Chi Minh*, 121–130; Huynh, *Vietnamese Communism*, 105–109.

Tan Viet Revolutionary Party (hereafter Tan Viet) originated from Phuc Viet Hoi (Party for Restoring Vietnam), which had been organized several years earlier by political prisoners released from Poulo Condore. Younger leaders of Phuc Viet received training from Thanh Nien but also were influenced by Sun Yat-sen's ideas.[40] According to Tan Viet's manifesto drafted in 1928, its mission was "to unite comrades inside and outside [Vietnam], domestically leading peasants, workers, and soldiers, and externally linking with other oppressed nations to overthrow imperialism and build a new equal and benevolent society."[41] Once achieving power, the party pledged to implement the dictatorship of the proletariat, equal human rights for all citizens, provision of welfare for children, the invalids, and the elderly, and the public ownership of land and other means of production. Significantly, the manifesto did not mention communism as a revolutionary goal. Newly admitted party members were required to swear their loyalty "under the sacred spirit of the Vietnamese land and the revered law of world revolution."[42] Clearly Tan Viet's program was communist in spirit but its language was not fully purged of nationalist concepts, as was the case with Thanh Nien.

The Dong Duong group based in northern Vietnam provided an interesting contrast with Tan Viet. Trained by Thanh Nien, Dong Duong men such as Ngo Gia Tu and Trinh Dinh Cuu quickly grew dissatisfied with Thanh Nien's leadership and political program.[43] At the First National Congress of Thanh Nien in Hong Kong in 1929, these men walked out of the meeting when the majority of those present refused their request to dissolve Thanh Nien to create a new communist party.[44] Upon their return from Hong Kong, Dong Duong leaders founded the Dong Duong Communist Party (hereafter Dong Duong).[45]

[40] Dinh Tran Duong, *Tan Viet Cach Mang Dang trong cuoc van dong thanh lap Dang Cong San Viet Nam* [Tan Viet Revolutionary Party's role in the formation of the Vietnamese Communist Party] (Hanoi: Chinh tri Quoc gia, 2006).
[41] "Dang Chuong" [Party Manifesto], *VKDTT*, v. 1,143.
[42] Ibid., 148.
[43] Quinn-Judge speculates that Dong Duong leaders were influenced by the southern branch of the Chinese Communist Party based in Saigon at the time. See Quinn-Judge, *Ho Chi Minh*, 132.
[44] See an account by Tran Cung and Trinh Dinh Cuu, "Mot vai net ve chi bo dau tien cua Dang va ve Dong Duong Cong San Dang" [On the first Party cell and the Indochinese Communist Party] in *Hoi Ky Cach Mang tuyen chon* [Selected memoirs about the revolution] (Hanoi: Hoi Nha Van, 1995), 55–64.
[45] Dong Duong means Indochina or Indochinese. Here I do not translate the word to avoid confusion with the name of the Vietnamese Communist Party during 1930–1945.

The manifesto of Dong Duong authored by Trinh Dinh Cuu suggested its leaders were more radical and theoretically more ambitious than their counterparts in Tan Viet.[46] The document began with a lengthy chapter on the theory of Marxism-Leninism, which it claimed "not to be a mysterious doctrine or the product of anyone's imagination, but a *scientific* ideology based on facts."[47] After analyzing class conflicts in capitalist societies, the authors of the manifesto argued that "the gap between capitalist and proletarian classes today is so wide that the struggle between them must be brutal: one class must win and survive whereas the other lose and die."[48] Who would win? It was said, "the imperialist countries are in conflict and will soon fight each other in a war that will be many times more destructive than the recent one" (i.e., World War I). In opposition to imperialism was the "proletarian camp comprising millions of proletarian brothers in capitalist countries who are poised to seize power, hundreds of millions of colonized people who are clamoring for revolution, as well as millions of Soviet proletarian brothers – all are aligned on a front led by the [Soviet] Communist Party and the Comintern." Given the existing balance of forces, the manifesto concluded, the days of capitalist societies were numbered.

In the same manifesto, Dong Duong leaders took Thanh Nien and Tan Viet to task on two counts. First, Thanh Nien and Tan Viet's membership was "open to all Vietnamese." Dong Duong leaders found such a nation- and race-based membership policy "uncommunist." They believed that a "communist" membership policy should be based only on class. Second, recall that the motto of Thanh Nien was first to make a national revolution, then to make a world revolution. That was wrong, Dong Duong argued, because "national revolution was [necessarily] a component of world revolution."[49] Making a national revolution required a national alliance of all classes without distinguishing capitalists from proletarians, and landlords from peasants. Not only incorrect, that motto was also "uncommunist."

Dong Duong leaders also believed that the Indochinese revolution had to go through two phases, but they defined the phases differently, showing

---

46 Tran Cung and Trinh Dinh Cuu, "Mot vai net ve chi bo dau tien cua Dang va ve Dong Duong Cong San Dang," 60.

47 "Tuyen ngon cua Dang Cong San Dong Duong" [Manifesto of the Dong Duong Communist Party], *VKDTT*, v. 1, 179. Italics in original. It does not appear that this manifesto was informed of the new Comintern policy decided at the Sixth World Congress. See Quinn-Judge, *Ho Chi Minh*, 132.

48 "Tuyen ngon cua Dang Cong San Dong Duong," *VKDTT*, v. 1, 185.

49 Ibid., 208–209.

their greater familiarity with Leninist concepts. Because capitalism was not well developed and feudal forces remained strong in Indochina, those phases included a "bourgeois democratic revolution" led by proletarians and peasants to overthrow imperialism and feudalism, and a subsequent "social revolution" to eliminate capitalism and build communism.[50] This two-phase formula came from Lenin and fused national, class-based, and world revolutions in one single dynamic framework.[51] The thinking was sharper and the language of Dong Duong's manifesto more lucid relative to that in Nguyen Ai Quoc's "Revolutionary Path." The commitment to communism was firm and explicit, unlike that of Tan Viet.

Although Dong Duong leaders were theoretically sophisticated, it would be a mistake to assume that they were dogmatic in their tactics. During the "bourgeois democratic" phase, they believed that the appropriate slogan should be limited to the redistribution of lands to peasants, but not yet public ownership of all lands.[52] This was apparently to maximize peasants' interests in the revolution. Although Dong Duong leaders wanted Thanh Nien and Tan Viet to dissolve immediately to pave the way for a new communist party, they were willing to work with the Vietnamese Nationalist Party during the first phase of the revolution.[53] Despite their sharp criticism of Thanh Nien, Dong Duong leaders still held some respect for Nguyen Ai Quoc.[54]

After leaving China in mid-1927, Quoc spent about a year in the Soviet Union and Europe before traveling to Siam to organize a communist movement there.[55] While in Siam, he received the news from a Thanh Nien leader informing him of the disputes between Thanh Nien and Dong Duong.[56] Claiming to represent the Comintern, Quoc traveled

[50] Ibid., 192.
[51] The idea appeared to come from Lenin's so-called "April Theses" of 1917, titled "The Tasks of the Proletariat in the Present Revolution," April 7, 1917. V. I. Lenin, *Selected Works* (Moscow: Foreign Languages Publishing House, 1952), v.2, book 2, 13–17.
[52] "Nhiem vu can kip cua nhung nguoi cong san Dong Duong" [Urgent tasks for Indochinese communists], *VKDTT*, v. 1, 268.
[53] "Tuyen ngon cua Dang Cong san Dong duong," *VKDTT*, v. 1, 230–231.
[54] "Trung uong Dang Cong san Dong duong gui cho nhung nguoi Cong san An nam o Tau" [from the Central leadership of the Dong Duong Communist Party to Annamese communists in China], *VKDTT*, v. 1, 231. My interpretation is based on the fact that Nguyen Ai Quoc was not personally criticized in the document and that Dong Duong leaders proposed to discuss any disagreements they might have with him. See a different interpretation by Quinn-Judge in *Ho Chi Minh*, 150.
[55] Much of Quoc's time was spent waiting for money and instructions from the Comintern for his return to Asia. Quinn-Judge, *Ho Chi Minh*, 116–120.
[56] Quinn-Judge, *Ho Chi Minh*, 150.

to Hong Kong in late 1929 and immediately convened a meeting to facilitate the unification of all Vietnamese communist groups based in China and Vietnam. At that meeting, which took place in early 1930, representatives of Dong Duong, Tan Viet, Annamese Communist Party (Thanh Nien branch in southern Vietnam), and Thanh Nien in southern China agreed to form the Vietnamese Communist Party (VCP).

Although this "unification meeting" has been treated as a historical landmark of Vietnamese communism in official historiography,[57] it achieved little beyond an agreement among the groups to join a new organization, the VCP. The documents produced at this meeting were untypically brief: the minutes of the meeting, the Party's program, the Party code, and the strategy statement were about 10 pages total, compared to Dong Duong's "Manifesto," which was forty-two pages. This brevity likely reflected the huge gap among the groups on many issues. The meeting also failed to elect new leadership, agreeing only on the process to nominate a Central Committee to be formed later.

A question that historians have not asked is why Quoc did not make himself the head of the VCP at this meeting. With his authority as the Comintern representative and with his ability to convene the meeting and force Dong Duong representatives to admit their mistakes (see later), he must have been able to assume the top post if he so wished. It is not clear why he did not do so, but Quoc was an official in the Comintern bureaucracy responsible for entire Southeast Asia and he most likely did not want to assume personal responsibility for the Vietnamese Party unless being appointed to the position by the Comintern.[58] Regardless of his motives, the point is that Quoc did not seek to take personal control of the VCP even though he was in a position to do so.[59] Without leadership, however, the VCP existed only on paper.

[57] This is the term commonly used by Vietnamese official history.

[58] This was, in fact, the reason given by Quoc when he declined the offer to be the Party's general secretary in 1941 (see Chapter 3). According to Truong Chinh who made the offer, Quoc said he did not want the job because he worked for the Comintern, which might later send him to work elsewhere.

[59] Alternatively, Quoc may have wished to maintain his Comintern position that he would have to give up if assuming personal leadership of the new VCP. Given the bitter quarrel among various Vietnamese factions over strategy and their shared loyalty to Comintern authority, he may have felt that he would have greater influence on the future of Vietnamese communism as a Comintern official. Another possible explanation is that, as the top leader of the VCP he would have to return to Vietnam where a death sentence (issued *in absentia*) awaited him. The danger was real because Quoc had been away from Vietnam for nineteen years and did not have any experience organizing inside Vietnam when he left.

The VCP program tersely pledged to "make a bourgeois democratic revolution and land revolution to achieve communism," without further elaboration.[60] This new formula was brief and crude but it fundamentally did not contradict the concept of the two-phase revolution Dong Duong had advocated earlier. According to the minutes of the meeting, Dong Duong was criticized for being too restrictive in its membership policy, for being organized "like a clique aloof from the masses," and for causing the dissolution of Thanh Nien and Tan Viet against Comintern policy.[61] Significantly, those criticisms were based on Comintern policy and were mostly directed at Dong Duong's organizational business, not at its ideological vision.[62]

In correcting Dong Duong's errors, the VCP defined the main enemies of the revolution more narrowly to involve only the imperialists and the big landlords. This move indicated a flexible strategy but not a change in worldview, as the VCP's strategy statement produced at the same meeting made clear.[63] In this document, the VCP vowed to make the best efforts to establish links with other classes, including the petit bourgeoisie, intellectuals, and middle peasants, to attract their support for the proletariat. The VCP would also try to "take advantage of" [loi dung] rich peasants, middle and small landlords, and Vietnamese capitalists who had not yet showed "counterrevolutionary tendencies." But there were clear limits to any class coalitions despite the new flexibility:

While making coalitions with other classes, [we] must be careful not to compromise on any interests of workers and peasants; while advocating the independence of Annam, [we need to] simultaneously advocate and maintain links with other oppressed nations and with the world's proletarian class, especially the French proletariat.[64]

In other words, the new VCP maintained doctrinal loyalty while being more flexible and pragmatic with respect to the strategy of class coalition. Cooperation with other classes beyond workers and poor peasants was purely a political expediency, not suggesting solidarity based on a shared

---

[60] "Chanh cuong van tat cua Dang" [Brief Program of the Party], *VKDTT*, v. 2, 2.

[61] "Bao cao tom tat Hoi nghi" [Brief Minutes of meeting], *VKDTT*, v. 2, 11.

[62] The memoir by Tran Cung and Trinh Dinh Cuu does not reveal how Cuu and Nguyen Duc Canh, the other Dong Duong representative at the meeting, reacted to such criticisms. Tran Cung and Trinh Dinh Cuu, "Mot vai net ve chi bo dau tien cua Dang va ve Dong Duong Cong San Dang," 63–64.

[63] "Sach luoc van tat cua Dang" [Brief Statement on Strategy of the Party], *VKDTT*, v. 2, 4–5.

[64] Ibid.

Vietnamese identity. The VCP Program did not deviate from the resolution of the Sixth World Congress of the Comintern of 1928, and Nguyen Ai Quoc was acting as an agent who faithfully carried out Comintern policy at this point, even without specific Comintern authorization and without knowing that Comintern leaders had moved further to the left in July 1929 with the Tenth Plenum of its executive committee.[65] With a very brief program and no leadership, the VCP appeared to have been devised as a temporary truce whose details were left to further negotiations among stakeholders.

The news of the disputes between Dong Duong and Thanh Nien likely reached Moscow at the same time it got to Quoc in Siam. In late 1929, while Quoc was on his way from Siam to Hong Kong, a meeting of Comintern officials in Moscow discussed and issued an order for rival Indochinese communist groups to form a communist party.[66] Quoc had no knowledge of this meeting. In the archived notes from the meeting, Moscow praised Thanh Nien for keeping up with the new Comintern policy but also criticized it for making many mistakes in strategy and organization.[67] The praise and criticism were directed at the policy made by Thanh Nien leaders in May 1929.[68] No specific criticisms were made of Nguyen Ai Quoc who had not been at the helm of Thanh Nien since mid-1928. This is important evidence that Quoc had not lost his status at the Comintern.

Two Vietnamese students attended the Comintern meeting in Moscow. They were Tran Phu and Ngo Duc Tri, two former Thanh Nien members trained by Quoc and sent to study in Moscow in 1927. After the meeting, Phu and Tri left Moscow for Indochina with instructions for unifying Vietnamese communist groups there. By the time they arrived in Hong Kong, the unification meeting that Quoc convened had occurred.[69] Yet Phu and Tri appeared not to have been authorized by the Comintern to replace Quoc. When they finally met in Hong Kong in March 1930, Quoc had enough authority to send Tran Phu to work in Hanoi and Ngo Duc

[65] Quinn-Judge, *Ho Chi Minh*, 157–158.

[66] "Ban dua ra thao luan tai phien hop cua Hoi dong Ban Bi thu Phuong Dong" [Draft for discussion at the meeting of the Eastern Bureau Secretariat], October 18, 1929. *VKDTT*, v. 1, 593–612; "Ve viec thanh lap mot Dang Cong san o Dong duong" [On establishing a communist party in Indochina], October 27, 1930. *VKDTT*, v. 1, 613–620.

[67] "Ban dua ra thao luan tai phien hop cua Hoi dong Ban Bi thu Phuong Dong." *VKDTT*, v. 1, 594–596.

[68] This referred to the First National Congress of Thanh Nien. See the Congress's Manifesto, Minimum Program, and Resolutions in *VKDTT*, v. 1, 90–133.

[69] See Quinn-Judge in *Ho Chi Minh*, 150–153.

Tri to travel to Saigon.[70] Then in March-April 1930, Quoc was authorized by the Shanghai-based Far Eastern Bureau of the Comintern to preside over the formation of the Siamese Communist Party in Bangkok and the Malayan Communist Party conference in Singapore. In the conventional view, Phu is portrayed as posing a challenge to Quoc's leadership of Vietnamese communism. This would not make sense if Quoc only saw his role as a Comintern representative but not leader of the VCP. These events suggested that Phu and Tri accepted Quoc's authority as a Comintern representative, while Quoc recognized them as Comintern-mandated leaders of the VCP. In other words, no power rivalry existed between them, only a mutually accepted division of roles and duties.

Together, Quoc, Phu, and Tri convened a meeting that would later be called the Party's First Plenum in Hong Kong in October 1930. This meeting, which was also attended by a few representatives from Vietnam, took place against the backdrop of an extremely volatile situation in Vietnam. In February 1930, just after the unification meeting, the Yen Bai rebellion broke out in northern Vietnam, led by the Vietnamese Nationalist Party (VNP). The rebels attempted to seize control of several French garrisons in the Red River Delta, and they were briefly successful in the town of Yen Bai, before being brutally crushed. Thirteen VNP leaders were guillotined in June 1930 and thousands of their followers were imprisoned. By then, unrest had spread to Nghe An and Ha Tinh in central Vietnam – this time led in part by members of local Thanh Nien or Dong Duong. The movement there started with a strike by workers in the city of Vinh on May 1st and soon engulfed nearby rural areas and provinces.[71] Thousands of peasants marched, attacked government buildings, and in some cases executed local notables and French officials. In some districts and villages, peasants even formed "Soviet governments" that killed landlords and expropriated their lands. The colonial government responded with force, but it would take nearly a year for the movement to die out.

Even though the VCP did not yet have a central leadership and played no direct role in the Nghe-Tinh movement, the events appeared to confirm the new Comintern analysis of the world situation since 1928. Tran Phu's "Political Thesis" presented at the First Plenum in October 1930 fully adopted that analysis. The world was believed to have entered a new period in 1928 with an economic crisis in the capitalist system, looming threats of imperialist warfare, and brightening prospects of worker

[70] Ibid., 162–163, 169.
[71] Huynh, *Vietnamese Communism*, 151–171.

movements worldwide.[72] To Phu, the massive unrest in Indochina during the previous eight months was a clear sign of how revolution there was "marching to the same vigorous tune" [*ram ro*] with world revolution.[73] Phu took delight in the fact that the worker and peasant movement in Vietnam had now gained its own momentum and was no longer motivated by nationalism as before.

Phu presented an updated and most elaborate exposition of the two-phase concept of revolution to date. Indochina's backwardness would not permit the construction of socialism right away, so revolution there had to begin with the bourgeois democratic phase. The success of this phase would foster the growth and power of the proletariat, preparing Indochina to advance to the next phase of "proletarian revolution." As Phu imagined, the proletarian revolution would be possible then because "[t]his age is the age of worldwide proletarian revolution and the age of socialist construction in the Soviet Union. Indochina will receive assistance from proletarian governments in other countries to develop socialism without the need to go through the capitalist stage first."[74]

To Phu, the bourgeois democratic phase had two mutually dependent tasks of antifeudalism and anti-imperialism. One task could not be fulfilled without the other. On land policy, Phu's program took a sharper class line than Nguyen Ai Quoc's earlier program. The latter promised the redistribution of land taken from French owners to "poor peasants."[75] Phu's thesis proposed to take land not only from foreign landlords but also from indigenous landlords and from the church, to redistribute to "middle and poor peasants, with ownership rights retained by the government."[76] The difference here was on the strategy of mobilization: Quoc had wanted to mobilize small indigenous landlords and indigenous capitalists, whereas Phu considered them enemies of the revolution even in the bourgeois democratic phase.[77] Phu also made clear for the first time that land must be publicly owned.

[72] "Luan cuong chanh tri cua Dang Cong san Dong duong" [Political Thesis of the Indochinese Communist Party], *VKDTT*, v. 2, 88–89.
[73] Phu did not mention the stock market crash in the United States in late 1929 and the economic crisis that followed.
[74] "Luan cuong chanh tri," *VKDTT*, v. 2, 94.
[75] "Chanh cuong van tat cua Dang," *VKDTT*, v. 2, 3.
[76] "Luan cuong chanh tri," *VKDTT*, v. 2, 95. Also, "An nghi quyet cua Trung uong toan the dai hoi noi ve tinh hinh hien tai o Dong duong va nhiem vu can kip cua Dang" [Resolution of the Central Committee meeting on the current situation in Indochina and the urgent tasks of the Party], *VKDTT*, v. 2, 110.
[77] "Luan cuong chanh tri," *VKDTT*, v. 2, 98.

The resolution of this Plenum announced the annulment of the VCP's Program, Strategy Statement, and Party Code drafted by the unification meeting convened by Nguyen Ai Quoc eight months earlier.[78] The Plenum also changed the Party's name from Vietnamese Communist Party to Indochinese Communist Party, and made Phu its general secretary. Significantly, although Phu's thesis proposed a new program more in line with the latest Comintern policy, it did not directly criticize the VCP program. Such criticisms were raised only in the resolution issued after the meeting. This resolution delved at length on the strategic and organizational mistakes made in that program. According to the resolution, those mistakes indicated that the VCP was "too preoccupied with the anti-imperialist task but neglected class interests."[79] A letter sent by the new Central Committee to Party members in December 1930 explained that the mistakes in the VCP program had occurred because

the comrade who convened the unification meeting was sent [to Hong Kong] with a broad assignment but did not receive any specific plans from the Comintern [for unification]. When he arrived and learned about the disputes ..., he acted on his own. Many mistakes were made and the policy did not follow the Comintern's plan. He has since admitted those mistakes and agreed with the Central Committee [of the Party] to correct them.[80]

The preceding quotation appeared less a criticism than an explanation aimed at confused members who were not present at the Plenum. Quoc was not named, and it did not seem that he was forced to correct his "mistakes." Tran Phu's rise to becoming general secretary also did not mean Quoc had lost power over Vietnamese communism or "authority to interpret Comintern policy for Vietnam" as Huynh Kim Khanh and Quinn-Judge argue.[81] It is a fact that Quoc did not try to make himself the head of the Party at the unification meeting; no power rivalry was involved, nor had Quoc lost his status at the Comintern. We do not know what he really thought about the new Comintern policy, but Quoc had always, including at the unification meeting, willingly followed Comintern guidance, and there is no reason to expect him not to have

---

[78] "An nghi quyet," *VKDTT*, v. 2, 112–113.

[79] Ibid., 110.

[80] "Thu cua Trung uong gui cho cac cap Dang bo" [Letter from the Central Committee to the Party's rank and file], *VKDTT*, v. 2, 238.

[81] Quinn-Judge makes her argument based on the simple fact that the program of the VCP was replaced by Tran Phu's "Political Thesis," which was "in tune with current Comintern policy." She provides no evidence that Quoc disagreed with the new Comintern policy. See Quinn-Judge, *Ho Chi Minh*, 180.

done so in this circumstance. As the preceding quotation implied, his comrades well understood the situation in which "mistakes" were made. Specifically, they were made because Quoc had been out of contact with Moscow, not because he did not obey the new Comintern policy that had not yet reached him.

Tran Phu's "Political Thesis" would have a lasting impact on the thinking of Vietnamese communists, even though he would soon die while under arrest. In the Thesis, Lenin's concept of revolution was fully developed and expressed *in Vietnamese* for the first time, with the "bourgeois democratic" phase structurally connected to the "proletarian" phase, and both phases intertwined organically with the worldwide proletarian movement in an "age of proletarian revolutions." The revolutionary character of the age and the proletarian leadership of the revolution would allow Vietnamese communists to bypass capitalism and build a socialist country from scratch on the foundation of a still backward economy.

Yet it was not simply the thought process that offered Phu and his comrades a deep sense of the age in which they were living. For some of them their personal experience of being in the Soviet Union and participating in the Stalinist revolution contributed as much to that sense. From the accounts left behind, it is possible to understand what it was about the Soviet Union that impassioned them. Such personal experiences were crucial not only for their direct impacts on particular individuals but also for their informative and symbolic values to the communist movement as a whole.[82] To communists of Phu's generation, the Soviet Union was seen as a symbol and model of the future. Most Vietnamese communists, including those who later led the communist regime such as Truong Chinh, Le Duan, Pham Van Dong, Hoang Quoc Viet, and Le Duc Tho, never set foot in the Soviet Union before rising to leadership positions. What they knew about Lenin's homeland was through the accounts of those who had been there such as Tran Dinh Long whose story is described next.

A TASTE OF PARADISE

By the late 1920s, many Vietnamese youths had followed Nguyen Ai Quoc to study in the Soviet Union. One of these was Tran Dinh Long,

---

[82] See Hoang Quoc Viet, "Tinh than Pham Hong Thai" [The spirit of Pham Hong Thai] in *Hoi Ky Cach Mang tuyen chon* [Selected memoirs about the revolution] (Hanoi: Hoi Nha Van, 1995), 165.

whose time at the same university during 1928–1931 partially overlapped with that of Tran Phu and Ngo Duc Tri. Long was also enlisted for four months in the Soviet Red Army. After his return to Indochina he became a journalist. During 1936–1939 when Indochina enjoyed greater freedom of press, thanks to the government of the Popular Front in France, Long published serially a long memoir in two newspapers recounting his experience in the Soviet Union.[83] Apparently the first half of this memoir has been lost, but the remaining half of nearly 200 pages is sufficient to offer an example of the particular ways the Soviet Union might have been alluring to Vietnamese youth at the time.[84] Although it is possible that Tran Dinh Long exaggerated his feelings for the Soviet Union in his memoir, in fact numerous Soviet citizens at the time shared his enthusiasm.[85]

Unlike Nguyen Ai Quoc, Tran Dinh Long was in the Soviet Union at a high tide of revolution: 1928–1933 were the first and formative years of the Stalin era. These years roughly coincided with the first Five-Year Plan (1929–1933), which involved an all-out drive for industrialization and rural collectivization.[86] In the cultural realm, a cultural revolution sponsored by Stalin took on a life of its own, becoming a mass movement directed against the old intelligentsia as class enemies. As Sheila Fitzpatrick has described it, this revolution had many facets. "It was a worker-promotion movement linked to a political campaign to discredit the 'Right Opposition' within the Party. It was an iconoclastic youth movement directed against 'bureaucratic' authority. It was a process by which militant Communist groups in the professions established

[83] The colonial Vietnamese-language press sometimes published positive news and stories about the Soviet Union, but these accounts were brief. See, for example, C. P., "Nghe chieu bong tai nuoc Nga" [Russian cinema], *Ngo Bao*, February 15, 1933; Chuyet Phu, "Van de huan luyen quan su cua To Nga" [On military training in Russia], *Ngo Bao*, March 25, 1933; L. V. Hoe, "Tho chu nghia duy vat la ngu dai u?" [Is it stupid to believe in materialism?], *Cong Luan*, March 28, 1936; No author, "Nga So Viet lap dao nu binh" [Soviet Russia formed a female army], *Cong Luan*, January 06, 1937.

[84] Le Thanh Hien, ed. *Tuyen Tap Tran Dinh Long* [Tran Dinh Long's selected works] (Hanoi: Van Hoc, 2000). The memoir was published during 1938–1939 under the title "Ba nam o nuoc Nga Xo Viet" [My three years in the Soviet Union]. Tran Dinh Long would be arrested in the early 1940s and became an official in the Viet Minh government in late 1945. He was allegedly abducted and killed in late 1945 by agents of the Vietnamese Nationalist Party.

[85] See, for example, Stephen Kotkin, *Magnetic Mountain: Stalinism as a Civilization* (Berkeley, CA: University of California Press, 1995); Jochen Hellbeck, *Revolution on My Mind: Writing a Diary under Stalin* (Cambridge, MA: Harvard University Press, 2006).

[86] M. Levin, "Society, State, and Ideology during the First Five-Year Plan" in Sheila Fitzpatrick, ed. *Cultural Revolution in Russia, 1928–1931* (Bloomington: Indiana University Press, 1978), 41–77.

local dictatorships and attempted to revolutionize their disciplines."[87] Although Long mentioned none of these events in the remaining part of his memoir, one can sense a far more radical political environment in the background of his account compared to earlier ones.

Long's topics ranged from life in the Soviet Red Army; gender and sexual relationships; political and social institutions including the courts, prisons, youth organizations, child care, and the "hygiene police"; cultural activities such as arts, sports, dance, and cinema; and social and cultural "vices" such as prostitution, drugs, drinking, and religion. Long's often-defensive tone indicated his effort to counter negative views of the Soviet Union that emerged from reports of Stalin's show trials published in the colonial press at the same time.[88] Yet his lively images and frank discussions of personal feelings displayed a genuine sense of excitement and earnest belief in the Soviet revolution.

Two central threads ran throughout his account. The first thread was the contrast between the "proletarian" society in the Soviet Union on the one hand, and the "capitalist," "imperialist," and "feudal" societies on the other. The Soviet Red Army, Tran Dinh Long told us from his own experience, was very different from "capitalist armies." Although it had an iron discipline that made it a "powerful army," Red Army soldiers followed discipline not because they were forced to, as in "capitalist armies," but because they were conscious of the fact that "discipline was necessary to protect their interests as well as their class interests in the national and international arenas."[89] Long believed that this class consciousness helped maintain true equality between officers and soldiers. Although soldiers must obey officers during office hours, in regular "town-hall" meetings [*hoi dong*] of the entire unit, soldiers were free to criticize officers who gave wrong orders or who displayed inappropriate attitudes to them. If the whole unit expressed disapproval of an officer, he could be reprimanded and transferred. Long admitted that most soldiers came from peasant backgrounds and were still deferent [*rut re e so*] to officers, and some officers still displayed upper-class [*truong gia*] mentality in their behavior and treated soldiers with arrogance [*venh vao*]. Yet

---

[87] Sheila Fitzpatrick, "Cultural Revolution as Class War" in Sheila Fitzpatrick, ed. *Cultural Revolution in Russia, 1928–1931*, 11.

[88] For an excellent analysis of Vietnamese press coverage of the show trials, see Alex Holcombe, "Stalin, the Moscow Show Trials, and Contesting Visions of Vietnamese Communism in the late 1930s: A Reappraisal," paper presented at the Workshop on the Vietnamese Revolution, University of California, Berkeley, November 11–12, 2011.

[89] Le Thanh Hien, ed. *Tuyen Tap Tran Dinh Long*, 35–38.

he believed that the Red Army was the "most democratic" and "most equal" army of the world.

Another sharp contrast Tran Dinh Long found between the Red Army and its capitalist counterparts was the projustice character of the former. "Every Red Army soldier I asked," he recalled, "told me directly that he was enlisted to defend the Soviet Union and serve the world's proletariat when needed."[90] Unlike capitalist armies created to suppress labor strikes and people's protests and to conquer colonies, the Red Army was involved in building a classless society in the Soviet Union and to assist the world's proletariat in their struggle with the capitalist class. Rephrasing a statement by Soviet leader Voroshilov, Long clarified that the Red Army was ready to help the world's proletariat to overthrow capitalism, but this did not mean that the Red Army would seek to invade other countries. It only made itself available to the world's proletariat when they needed it. It was involved in Outer Mongolia, Spain, and China to help those weak nations resist foreign invaders. "The Red Army [was] the only army in the world that [fought] sincerely for justice" [*cong ly*].[91]

The contrast between the socialist system and its predecessors was described most lively in gender relations in the Soviet Union. Tran Dinh Long foreshadowed his discussion with a criticism of the caricatures of communists in Vietnam at the time. In the negative version of these caricatures, communists shared everything, including their wives. In the positive version, communists were depicted as monks who were so devoted to their ideology that they never knew romance [*tinh ai*].[92] Long contended that communists were only human beings with normal feelings. Although their feelings for justice were stronger than in ordinary people, they were capable of being moved by natural beauty and by "romantic feelings that are honest and free." In capitalist societies, "love" resulted from family oppression and desire for power, social status, and money. In the Soviet Union, love was genuine without any intention of taking advantage of each other. This was possible because the Soviet woman was financially independent, whereas her counterpart in capitalist societies was not. One was truly liberated and could enjoy true love, whereas the other was only a slave of her husband and had to cling to him.

Spending vacations in the Crimea and "Ughennana" (Ukraine?), Tran Dinh Long described physical contacts between men and women in the

[90] Ibid., 44.
[91] Ibid., 45–46.
[92] Ibid., 56.

Soviet Union as open and "natural" [*tu nhien*] – even "intimate" [*suong sa*], but at the same time, as maintaining clear boundaries between love and friendship.[93] His two female art teachers who were young college students were not shy about touching and hugging him while playing with him. In the vacation house for workers in the Crimea, he made friends with hundreds of Russian girls. One asked him once to sit on her lap; another lifted him up on her arms to demonstrate her strength; still another went out with him at 3:00 A.M. on an empty beach. Long confessed he was at first tempted by these girls but then quickly discovered that such physical intimacy meant neither love nor lust. Recalling gender relations in Vietnam, he chastised Confucius for teaching that women must keep a physical distance from men. Soviet gender relations indicated that restrictions on physical intimacy only increased people's curiosity about sex and their desire for it. Suppressed curiosity and desire in turn would lead to illicit relationships. Long credited the Russian revolution for "having enlightened Russian women and placed them equal to men in all respects." He eloquently declared, "Russian women have demolished the wall between men and women – the wall built by the self-serving morality of feudalists and capitalists that split society into two halves and that blocked the evolutionary path [*con duong tien hoa*] of humankind."[94]

As Tran Dinh Long went from one topic to the next, the sharp contrast between capitalism and socialism appeared again and again. Soviet family laws allowed easy marriages and divorces based simply on the will of couples, which differed from "capitalist laws" that often prevented loving couples from marrying each other and abused women from getting a divorce.[95] Soviet courts held trials (especially for counterrevolutionaries) in courthouses infrequently compared to courts in capitalist countries. These events were instead held in much larger public venues such as theaters so that ordinary people could attend and yell at the accused to express their anger. Soviet courts often came down to factories, offices, schools, and collective farms to hold trials on site, unlike "capitalist courts" that were aloof [*quan dang, be ve*] from the people.[96] Soviet sports did not cultivate professional players who were in effect commodities for sale in capitalist countries.[97] Sports in the Soviet Union

93 Ibid., 58–61.
94 Ibid., 58.
95 Ibid., 66–67.
96 Ibid., 73–78.
97 Ibid., 125.

were to improve people's health so that they could fight to end the exploitation of men by men. Soviet arts similarly were oriented to serving the whole society, especially the working people, whereas capitalist arts were mainly created for money and served only a wealthy minority. Under declining economies and decadent political systems, capitalist arts necessarily took the forms of "pornographic literature [*khieu dam, phong dang*], obscene dances [*uon eo, tho tuc*], and movies full of naked women, lust, and crimes."[98]

As an example of how the Soviet system fostered the development of arts in service of the masses, Tran Dinh Long discussed Soviet policy to protect and promote the cultures of ethnic minorities.[99] Before the revolution, he noted that 90 percent of minorities in northeastern Russia were illiterate. These peoples used to have their own literatures but their cultures had been gradually destroyed after being colonized by Tsarist Russia for two hundred years. Since the rise of "proletarian rule," the Soviet government had tried hard to collect and preserve the folk songs and folk dances of all ethnic groups to protect their best traditions.[100] It also did its best to improve education and develop ethnic literatures based on the language of each group, "bringing bright literary light to shine on the most remote areas" where Mongolians, Turks, and Eskimos lived.[101] The "proletarian approach to literary development" specifically aimed to nurture "literary concepts and spirits" for each ethnic group, based on their native tongue and aided by Russian if necessary. The promotion of native tongues to be foundations for ethnic literatures and arts allowed these to "develop freely according to their natural characteristics."[102] Thanks to efforts by the Soviet government, "all ethnic groups in the USSR today possess their own print media to develop their own talents and to gather the refined knowledge [*tri thuc cao sieu*] of all the masses that has long been trampled and wasted under capitalism."

Long's account of Soviet "affirmative-action" policies to protect ethnic cultures clearly implied where he placed his loyalties. Although such policies were unprecedented in world history,[103] Long did not treat them in a separate section but subsumed them under Soviet literary policies.

---

[98] Ibid., 127.

[99] Ibid., 134–137 and 143–144.

[100] Ibid., 143.

[101] Ibid., 135.

[102] Ibid., 136.

[103] Terry Martin, *The Affirmative-Action Empire: Nations and Nationalisms in the Soviet Union, 1923–1939* (Ithaca, NY: Cornell University Press, 2001).

The central tenet of these policies, to Long, was to serve the masses as opposed to the elites. The dominant theme throughout his description remained the contrast between communism and capitalism, not the distinction between Russians and the ethnic minorities – even though the topic was essentially about ethnic policies. Ethnic minorities were viewed more as part of "the masses" than as those with distinctive identities. Nowhere in his memoir (at least the available part) did he mention issues such as national or ethnic independence or autonomy. What excited him was the liberation of *the masses* from *capitalist* and *feudal* exploitation rather than the liberation of oppressed *nations* from imperial Russia.

The second thread in Tran Dinh Long's description of the Soviet Union was the intrusive yet "humane" methods of social reform that were transforming Soviet society. Similar to Nguyen Ai Quoc, Long was unapologetic about the social problems he found in the Soviet Union. He frankly admitted that in the Soviet Union there were still thieves, robbers, murderers, and of course, counterrevolutionaries.[104] Among the majority of "ideologically conscious" [*giac ngo*] Soviet people, there were still many alcohol addicts, bandits who used to be white soldiers, and kulaks who extorted money. These bad people represented the legacies of feudal and capitalist systems over "two-three thousand years." On prostitution, for example, he believed that this social vice began when the exploitation of men by men emerged in human society. Kings and nobilities had time to burn and forced women to serve them. "Under capitalist society which was like a putrid, bleeding, and filthy corpse, prostitution grew just like abscesses on the skin."[105]

Blaming social vices (including religion) on classed societies, Long was fascinated with the "humane" methods used by the Soviet government for reform. On drinking, he noted that the government did not force people to quit, but educated them so that they themselves decided to do so. "This method [maintained] respect, protected individual freedom, and avoided resistance from those who [were] still addicted … The method of the proletarian government [was] not to stop producing alcohols but to have no one get drunk."[106] This was accomplished by gradually reducing the alcohol level in the drinks produced and by launching antialcohol educational campaigns using both science and humor. Body organs taken from (dead?) drunkards were on display together with murder cases involving

---

[104] Le Thanh Hien, ed. *Tuyen Tap Tran Dinh* Long, 68–69.
[105] Ibid., 78–79.
[106] Ibid., 88–90.

alcohol. Humorous plays were staged and humorous pamphlets published to make fun of drunkenness.[107]

A similar approach was used to weaken the influence of religions. Quoting Karl Marx, Long argued that religions were even worse than opium. Although the latter destroyed individuals, religions destroyed entire communities. Religions exploited people; stole [*rut tia*] their lands, money, and houses; caused their minds to become feeble, slow, muddled [*ngan ngo, ngay dai*], and melancholic [*u am*].[108] Religions made people lose their sense of autonomy and willingness to struggle in this life. The Soviet government could have closed all churches, imprisoned all priests, and banned people from following religions in one decree, but it did not. The problem was only the priests who were a kind of parasites. Their followers (except capitalists) were, after all, "brothers of the proletariat who were exploited both materially and mentally and were duped by the priests." The humane method was not to ban, but to educate people with scientific evidence about the origins of humankind and with historical evidence about the close relationship between priests and the Tsar and about past crimes committed by the clergy. Besides plays and pamphlets, two special tools were antireligion museums and antireligion associations established in all the big cities in the Soviet Union.

Tran Dinh Long believed that the method had been effective, as evidenced in the empty and quiet churches he saw that had to use candles because they ran out of money to pay for electricity. Another piece of evidence was the priests he met on Moscow streets who were begging or selling newspapers to make a living. Long was glad that most urban churches had closed down. Rural churches still survived in greater numbers because priests there were supported by the kulaks. He predicted that, after collectivization when the kulaks were liquidated [*tieu diet*], the countryside would catch up with the cities. The days of religion in the Soviet Union were numbered.[109]

Campaigns for social reform sometimes took coercive forms, as in the case of "hygiene teams." These special teams wore all white like nurses and were all smiling while swooping down on selected neighborhoods.[110] Unlike the tax collecting cops in his native town in Vietnam who generated fear and hatred, Long noted that the hygiene police did not carry

---

[107] Ibid., 90–92.
[108] Ibid., 93–95.
[109] Ibid., 95–103.
[110] Ibid., 83–85.

weapons or beat up people. They were teams of volunteers organized by the unions of doctors and nurses who went house to house in certain neighborhoods on holidays and weekends to check on household hygiene. Tidy and clean families were praised publicly, whereas those untidy and dirty were ordered [*bat*] to help with cleaning up the house, furniture, clothes, and children. Men who wore long hair and beards were made fun of [*che*] and forced to sit down [*keo co*, literally, had their necks held down] for a haircut. Long argued that printing a thousand books was not equal to one hands-on demonstration of hygienic lifestyle provided by the teams. This method was easy to understand, even for the less intelligent [*toi da*].[111] The hygiene teams not only eliminated backwardness [*toi tam*][112] and uncleanness but also taught people how to live cleanly and hygienically. They served as the link between workers and peasants, bringing light and cleanness to the latter.

The hygiene police reflected the raging Cultural Revolution in the Soviet Union during the First Five-Year Plan.[113] Tran Dinh Long appeared thoroughly mesmerized by this revolution. He marveled not only at the imagined or real contrasts between socialist and capitalist systems but also at the coercive methods and the far-reaching goals of social and cultural reform in the Soviet Union. Like Nguyen Ai Quoc before him, Long was enthusiastic about the Soviet Union not because he found it a perfect country or system. Rather, it was the transformative vision, the radical methods, and the profound promises embodied in the Stalinist revolution that captivated him.

CONCLUSION

Communism was completely foreign to Vietnam. When Vietnamese revolutionaries came upon Marx and Lenin's teachings, it took them some time, if they were interested, to reconcile radical communist ideas with their existing worldview. In the first transition from Phan Boi Chau to Nguyen Ai Quoc, interest in the Russian revolution slowly developed into limited knowledge of the Marxist-Leninist worldview. It took time and effort for new adherents to that worldview among Vietnamese

---

[111] Ibid., 86–87. In original, "toi da" in the sense of "at most" was perhaps a typo.
[112] Literally means "darkness."
[113] During the First Five-Year Plan, Soviet cities grew by 44 percent while their salaried labor force increased by about 12 million. Moscow and Leningrad each received 3.5 million peasant migrants during this period. See Lewin, "Society, State, and Ideology during the First Five-Year Plan," 53–54.

revolutionaries to understand the concept of world revolution in its connection with the Vietnamese revolution. This process of radicalization was filled with confusion for some and with excitement for others. It created tension within the movement because some activists were quicker than others to absorb new ideas and concepts. The rate of absorption naturally depended on personal aptitude, linguistic ability, level of formal education, and international exposure. It varied among those who participated in socialist circles in Paris, those who studied in Moscow, those who had not been abroad but who were sufficiently educated to read and understand Marxist and Leninist texts in French, and those who had little formal education and who received their ideological training second-hand from other Vietnamese communists. Frictions among them were further amplified by changing Comintern policy and by communication problems.

Through the documents produced by Thanh Nien, a gradual process could be observed by which the worldview of Vietnamese revolutionaries became internationalized but still was mostly compartmentalized. Nguyen Ai Quoc's thinking indicated that he was simply an internationalist in evolution. From "Revolutionary Path" to his program for the VCP, he sought to translate internationalist concepts into the Vietnamese language and closely followed the most recent Comintern line of thinking as it was communicated to him.

In the second transition, from Tan Viet to Dong Duong to the Indochinese Communist Party that involved many of Quoc's younger and better-educated comrades, the Marxist-Leninist worldview acquired a dynamic and organic quality thanks to the fusion of aspects specific to Vietnam and those of global politics. The upshot was the clarity and firmness of vision and strategy, with vision fully separated from and deeply influencing strategy. To be sure, both vision and strategy would be continually adjusted to reflect changing reality, but we will see in the next chapters how the core aspects would remain consistent for the next half century as men of Tran Phu's generation stood at the helm of the revolution.

Existing scholarship points to the change in class coalition policy from Nguyen Ai Quoc to Tran Phu as evidence of an "internationalist" and "dogmatic" faction trained by Moscow defeating the "nationalist" and "pragmatic" factions, which were primarily concerned about national independence. Yet the available records suggest that they were all loyal to Comintern leadership and policy. The conflict among various groups and personalities in the movement during 1928–1930 was primarily about leadership, organization, and strategy, not about revolutionary belief. That belief did not divide these factions; it united them. To them, Marxism-Leninism was not an abstract dogma but a dynamic and successful scientific theory. The evidence was right there in the Soviet Union, where they found a compelling vision of radical change despite the imperfections of Soviet society. Stalinist coercive methods won their admiration, and they showed little sympathy and toleration for the traditional culture and society where they came from.

In this period, ideology served Vietnamese revolutionaries in three ways. First, it redefined their mission, which was not only the liberation of Vietnam from French rule but also the creation of a new revolutionary society and contributions to world revolution. Ideology offered them a vision and blueprint for change, in this case the Soviet model, which would guide their revolution through ebbs and flows. Second, ideology provided the glue for like-minded young men and women such as Phu and Long to create an organization with a mission, the Indochinese Communist Party. Finally, ideology linked Vietnamese revolutionaries to a transnational network of states (the Soviet Union) and movements (French and Chinese communism) that provided funds, training, and sanctuaries from French repression.

Ideology would continue to serve the Vietnamese revolution in the next decade. Next, Chapter 2 will discuss how Tran Phu's vision of the Vietnamese revolution persisted through the 1930s despite two complete turnovers of leadership. To the extent that it was effective, colonial suppression destroyed only the messengers but not the message.

2

The Consolidation of a Leninist Vision, 1931–1940

In November 1931, Tran Dinh Long received the order to return to Indochina together with Le Hong Phong, his classmate in Moscow. Long and Phong brought with them $400 from the Comintern and were instructed to join the leadership of the Indochinese Communist Party (ICP). We do not know how Long returned, but Phong later sent a report to the Comintern about his meandering and treacherous journey. The pair parted ways in Paris, and Phong chose to return to Vietnam through Siam because he had contacts there who could brief him about the situation in Indochina.[1] Upon arriving in Bangkok, however, he learned that Siamese policy had changed and now required a passport for entry. Unable to enter Siam, Phong waited for ten days in a hotel before boarding a ship to Hong Kong. Unfortunately, all his money (including the $400) was stolen when he arrived. Usually he kept his money in small amounts in different places in his suitcases and pockets, but on that particular day when the thief struck him, he unexplainably had all his money in one place. Phong had to sell his jacket for $5 (Hong Kong currency) to buy a ticket to Guangzhou.

There he applied to a local university, claiming that he was a Vietnamese nationalist who wanted to study Sun Yatsen-ism. He was invited to meet the Rector of the university who put him in touch with Vietnamese Nationalist Party (VNP) members in town. One day, four VNP members came to speak to Phong in his hotel, and he learned from them about the feud between Vietnamese nationalist and communist

[1] "Ve cong tac trong ba nam qua va tinh hinh Dang Cong san Dong duong" [Our work in the last three years and the current situation of the ICP], signed Hai An (one of Phong's pseudonyms), January 15, 1935. *VKDTT*, v. 5, 391–404.

groups in Guangzhou. Fearing his identity might have been revealed, that night he sold his suitcase and some clothes for 30 *yuan* and moved to a different hotel. He did the right thing, because, as he would learn a few months later from a friend, the police came to search for him the next day. He would later find work as a mechanist in Guangxi, and within a year reconnected with Indochinese Communist Party (ICP) members in southern China and Siam.

The brief recount of Phong's journey in his own words offers a sense of the dangerous environment in which clandestine communists operated. Phong's experience was common among Vietnamese revolutionaries. The exciting years studying in Moscow were followed by months spent on merchant ships, weeks in cheap hotels, and temporary jobs and residence in foreign countries taken under false identities, with missteps, bad fortunes, and arrests often waiting just around the corner. Numerous comrades of Phong left the movement to live a quiet life or, worse, betrayed the cause to spy for French police.[2] Those who remained committed like Phong must have possessed a deeper belief in the cause, even though faith was certainly not the only factor.

Phong returned to Asia at a crucial time. The 1930s opened auspiciously but turned out to be the most brutal decade for the movement. Six months before Phong left Moscow, Tran Phu and Ngo Duc Tri had been captured by French police in Saigon. Nguyen Ai Quoc and many key collaborators in southern China and Hong Kong were arrested shortly afterward.[3] But as Phong's journey implied, there were glimmers of hope despite the narrow escapes.

"COMMUNISM AND NATIONALISM ARE LIKE HEAVEN AND EARTH"

The 1930s opened with profound events in world affairs, including the Great Depression, the industrialization of the Soviet Union, and the emergence of fascism. When Tran Phu convened a meeting of ICP leaders in March 1931 (later known as the Second Plenum), the capitalist world was tumbling down.[4] Trade had stopped, banks collapsed, and

---

[2] See the names of some of these in "Thu cua Ban Chi huy o ngoai gui Dong Phuong Bo Quoc te Cong san" [Letter from the Overseas Bureau to the Eastern Bureau of the Comintern], December 20, 1934. *VKDTT*, v. 4, 196–201.

[3] Sophie Quinn-Judge, *Ho Chi Minh: The Missing Years 1919–1941* (Berkeley, CA: University of California Press , 2002), 191–192.

[4] "An nghi quyet cua Trung uong toan the hoi nghi lan thu hai" [Resolution of the Second Plenum], March 1931. *VKDTT*, v. 3, 83–86.

production was massively scaled back. In Europe and America, the meeting noted, more than 50 million workers became unemployed. If their families were counted, the total number affected amounted to 150 to 180 million people, or one-tenth of the world population. In the Soviet Union, by contrast, "the development of socialism was advancing rapidly [*len vun vut*] and had far exceeded the plan." Industrial production now accounted for 70 percent of the Soviet economy. Collective farms covered nearly half of total cultivated areas. Not only did unemployment disappear but there was a shortage of workers. ICP leaders hoped that the "working masses of the world" could now see the stark contrast between Soviet and capitalist systems. One witnessed economic growth and the elimination of unemployment and deprivation [*thong kho*]. The other was in decay and workers were suffering.

The Plenum resolution observed that problems in the capitalist world and progress in the Soviet Union had boosted revolutionary movements everywhere.[5] In Germany, the United States., France, and Spain, recent strikes had involved millions of workers. These strikes now connected workers in many countries and had an international character; they were no ordinary strikes but protests against the entire capitalist system. In Burma, Morocco, Peru, Argentina, India, China, and Indochina, liberation movements had also expanded despite state repression. In Indochina, although the Nghe-Tinh movement had receded, ICP leaders felt encouraged by the fact that peasant struggles had taken on more advanced organizational forms and a clearer class character; they were now directed not only against imperialism but also against landlords and local notables.[6]

Party leaders believed that economic reforms could no longer save imperialism. The only path available to imperialist countries was to use force, but they could not do so without first suppressing revolutionary movements and defeating the Soviet Union, "the fortress of world revolution." Evidence of this trend was found in capitalist states' adoption of "fascist" tactics in crushing domestic opposition and in their busy preparations for war. Their joint charges against "Soviet dumping" smacked of a conspiracy against the Soviet Union.[7]

Although the leaders appreciated the favorable international climate, they expressed deep frustration with their Party. A year after the bickering

[5] Ibid., 85–86.
[6] Ibid., 87.
[7] Ibid., 86.

communist groups had been united, and five months had passed since the new leadership under Tran Phu was established, the reality was that the Party still had very few members with working-class backgrounds. Its rural cells were expanding rapidly; intellectuals and peasants now accounted for 90 percent of members.[8] The regional committees in northern and central Vietnam were yet to work collectively as a group. Party discipline was lax in some units, and was based only on command and intimidation tactics in others. To central leaders, the aforementioned phenomena reflected the "petit bourgeois mode" of thinking and behavior, such as the "fear of struggle" and the "lack of trust in the masses." The decision by some regional committees not to organize strikes during the economic crisis for fear of weak support from workers suggested that fear of struggle. Another "petit bourgeois" error was found in the demands that employers not punish workers by subtracting more than one-third of their daily wage, or that employers not make workers stay home on Sundays. Those demands appeared too timid.[9]

To rectify the situation, the resolution of the Plenum called for adding more workers to regional committees while removing "opportunistic intellectuals."[10] In addition, every Party member was called on to eliminate opportunistic tendencies in their thoughts and behavior. The Party as a whole must attract more workers, organize more cells, and focus on developing worker unions and communist youth unions (rather than peasant unions). Clearly, the resolution was seeking to implement the class struggle policy of the Comintern in 1928–1929 as approved at the First Plenum of the Party in October 1930.

In her biography of Ho Chi Minh, Quinn-Judge argues that he continued to be criticized by Tran Phu at this point. Her evidence is a letter in which Phu, according to Quinn-Judge, "held Ho largely responsible for the legacy of the 'old revolutionary organizations' [such as Thanh Nien] within the Vietnamese party."[11] Although Phu did mention that legacy in his letter, he in fact stated explicitly that "we draw your [i.e., Comintern officials'] attention to the issue *not to criticize Kok* [sic], but only to remind you how the united Indochinese Party was born and how

---

[8] Ibid., 90–91.
[9] Presumably to reduce their wage bills, employers let workers stay home on Sunday without pay. According to central leaders, the correct demands ought to be the abolition of all punishments and a six-day work week with workers receiving wages despite having Sundays off. Ibid., 92–96.
[10] Ibid., 97.
[11] Quinn-Judge, *Ho Chi Minh*, 185.

that created evil effects for us even today."[12] Phu thus clearly absolved Quoc of any personal responsibility on the matter. The letter did make a specific criticism of Quoc, but this was about his conduct, not his loyalty to the Comintern or his ideological tendency. In particular, the letter asked that Quoc not to be used as a liaison between the ICP and the Comintern "because he is too brief and sometimes he gives us his own opinions without consulting you. Kok [sic] communicates with both the Central Committee and the Northern Regional Committee; he asks for reports from everybody. This situation is terrible. One comrade has even asked us: who is our leader, the Central Committee or Kok [sic]?"[13]

Unlike what Quinn-Judge claims, the tension between Quoc and the Central Committee was bureaucratic but not ideological in nature. As the Comintern representative, Quoc received and responded directly to reports from both the Central and Regional Committees before passing those documents along to the Eastern Bureau of the Comintern in Shanghai. Quoc clearly perceived his role to be a representative, not a liaison. In a letter dated April 20, 1931, for example, Quoc criticized the ICP's regional committees on many issues, from how they convened their meetings to the way they set up the agenda and made their action plans. He chastised them for not following Comintern instructions to change the name of the Party to Indochinese Communist Party. He told them that they all

must discuss Comintern Instruction and the resolution of the ICP Central Committee, then issue their own resolutions about the above Instruction and resolution. Those [locally issued] resolutions must be sent to the Central Committee which would then send them along to the Comintern [for review]. Only when those steps were followed can the skills of party members be raised, can the instructions and resolutions from the Comintern and the Central Committee be implemented; can the thoughts and actions of party members be uniform; can the Comintern monitor the revolutionary skills of party members; and can the communication from party cells to the Central Committee and to the Comintern be thoroughly carried out (that is the wish of the Comintern).[14]

[12] "Thu B.C.H.T.U. Dong Duong," letter from the Central Committee of the ICP to the Comintern dated April 17, 1931, p. 2. Italics added. The Russian version of this letter is from Russian State Archive by courtesy of Quinn-Judge, and the Vietnamese translation is by Lai Nguyen An, with suggestions from Olga Dror. Both the Russian version and the translation are in the author's possession.

[13] Ibid., 10.

[14] "Thu gui Ban Chap hanh Trung uong Dang Cong san Dong duong" [Letter to the Central Committee of the ICP], April 20, 1931. *VKDTT*, v. 3, 133–134.

Quoc's advice to regional committees such as those just mentioned showed that he desired a more centralized Party structure to be fully submitted to the Comintern. Here Quoc was loyally performing the role of a Comintern representative, acting in the interest of the Comintern. Comintern officials would no doubt be happy with what Quoc wrote. For its part, the ICP Central Committee also might have liked Quoc's criticism of insubordinate regional committees, but it was clearly irked by the fact that he was bypassing it and communicating directly with those regional committees. This was why Tran Phu asked the Comintern to confine Quoc to his liaison role.[15]

Quoc's advice for the regional committees also displayed his willingness to implement the Comintern's class war policy made at the Sixth Congress in 1928. Unlike what Quinn-Judge speculates, there is no evidence that Quoc tried to restrain the radical policy against intellectuals and landlords carried out by the Party's regional committee in central Vietnam at the time.[16]

Propaganda work preoccupied the minds of ICP leaders in early 1931 as much as organizational issues.[17] As the Party was still very young, its leaders wanted to build "the foundation of proletarian thought" [*nen tu tuong vo san*] among members and among the "proletarian masses."[18] In their view, propaganda had to be based on the thought and policies of the

[15] Quoc replied by saying that central leaders had earlier agreed with him for the regional committees to send their reports directly to him, that he did not try to impose his personal opinions on them, and that he would refuse to be simply a mailbox. See "Thu gui Ban Chap hanh Trung uong Dang Cong san Dong duong" [Letter to the ICP Central Committee], April 23, 1931. *VKDTT*, v. 3, 135–138.

[16] Quinn-Judge speculates that a directive apparently signed by the Central Committee on May 20, 1931 was in fact written by Nguyen Ai Quoc (Quinn-Judge, *Ho Chi Minh*, 187–190). The "directive" called for a halt to the purges of Party members who did not belong to the working class. Yet my reading of this document (in original Vietnamese) suggests that Quoc could not have been the author because the "directive" used distinctive southern Vietnamese slangs such as "dang vien vo bon, dong chi soc dua," [unstable party members, disloyal comrades] (Quoc came from north-central Vietnam); and because it was so poorly written and self-contradictory. The first part of the document, which criticized radical policies, contradicted its conclusion, which called for striving to strengthen "the essence of the party and its class character" [dang tinh va giai cap tinh]. See "Chi thi cua Trung uong gui Xu uy Trung Ky ve van de thanh Dang Trung Ky" [Central Directive to Trung Ky Committee on the Party purification campaign], May 20, 1931. *VKDTT*, v. 3, 155–158.

[17] The resolution of the Second Plenum devoted as much space to propaganda as to organization.

[18] "Van de co dong tuyen truyen" [The propaganda task], March 1931. *VKDTT*, v. 3, 117–129.

Party; had to be supervised by a specialized organ under the direction of a Party committee member; and had to be aimed at countering "erroneous tendencies," especially those influenced by nationalist, reformist, or collaborationist ideas. Propaganda had to "train Party members and the proletarian masses according to the spirit of Marxism-Leninism and teach them to follow the correct policy of the Comintern and the Party." People had to be persuaded that the Party line was not only correct, but it was *the only* correct path to communism. On propaganda method, repetition was essential: Party members were advised not to worry about people getting bored of hearing the same messages every day. Most importantly, propaganda must be true [*xac thuc*] and must be linked to the masses' everyday struggle. "Marxism-Leninism is a theory for revolutionary action of the proletariat, not a theory for theory's sake [*hu danh*]."[19]

ICP leaders took Marxism-Leninism seriously not as a dogma but as a living theory that guided actions while being embedded in and realized through concrete actions. An examination of how propaganda was organized and how messages were framed yields useful information about the true belief of Vietnamese communist leaders at this point. The revolutionary calendar of the ICP around which their activities were organized contained no dates that tied to Vietnamese culture, history, or people. Instead, the death anniversaries of Lenin, Rosa Luxemburg, and Karl Liebknecht (January 21), International Women's Day (March 8), Paris Commune (March 18), Labor Day (May 1), and the Russian revolution (November 7) served as their occasions for mobilization.[20] These dates were symbolic to the Party's commitments to the international communist movement, and the activities were partially to nurture the internationalist spirit among Party members.

On March 8, 1931, for example, the ICP's Southern Regional Committee distributed a pamphlet about the contrast of women's status between the Soviet Union and capitalist states.[21] Women under capitalism, including those in Indochina, were said to work hard with low pay; to be treated like slaves in their workplaces; to be oppressed by feudal

[19] Ibid., 123.

[20] "Hoi anh chi em tho thuyen dan cay..." [To our brothers and sisters, workers and peasants...], January 1931. *VKDTT*, v. 3, 17–18; "Tieng goi cua Dang Cong San Dong Duong" [The call from the Indochinese Communist Party], January 21, 1931, ibid., 19–21; "Hoi anh chi em tho thuyen dan cay..." [To our brothers and sisters, workers and peasants...], n.d., ibid., 22–23.

[21] "8 thang 3, ngay Quoc te phu nu" [March 8th, the International Women's Day], February 22, 1931. *VKDTT*, v. 3, 59–68.

customs; to be burdened by household chores; and to be abused in their families. In the Soviet Union, in contrast, progressive laws banned female workers from dangerous jobs and guaranteed them good pay and generous vacation time. Women's burdens of child care and household chores were taken away from them with 17,000 child-care centers and "collective canteens" serving 20 million people. Women were educated and well represented in the political system. For example, 312,000 women were members of representative councils of workers and peasants, and 56,000 women were members of workers' councils. They accounted for 20 percent of Party committee membership. The pamphlet concluded that only by overthrowing capitalism could women have freedom and gender equality be achieved.[22]

The pamphlet suggested how Marxism-Leninism was not some abstract ideas but genuinely informed and structured the daily activities of communist activists. There was much truth in the claim that Soviet women enjoyed greater gender equality than their sisters in many traditional and capitalist societies. The overall image of the Soviet Union sounded like a paradise, yet it involved women's everyday concerns: child care, chores, and domestic abuses. The pamphlet inspired women workers to make concrete demands on their employers: no dangerous jobs, good pay, vacation time, child care, and factory canteens. It suggested possible forms of organization for those interested; these were councils of workers and Party committees. The ultimate mission of overthrowing capitalism was not an abstract goal but tied to such everyday issues.

A rare exception to the entirely internationalist calendar of the ICP in 1931 was the first anniversary of the Yen Bai rebellion of February 9, 1931. Of course, the dramatic events on that day and the martyrdom of nationalist leaders greatly impressed all Vietnamese, and ICP leaders wanted to share that popularity. Yet they left no confusion about where their loyalty lay. In a twenty-nine-page pamphlet to instruct cadres about how to organize this event, Party propagandists explained that the date was selected because 1930 was the year when the revolutionary tide in Indochina had reached a historic height, and the Yen Bai rebellion occurred first in that year.[23] However, the pamphlet explained, the selection of that date did not mean that ICP leaders agreed with nationalism [*quoc gia chu nghia*] and totally respected the VNP leaders who had sacrificed their

---

[22] Ibid., 63–64.
[23] "Mot cuoc ky niem" [An anniversary for commemoration], 1931. *VKDTT*, v. 3, 227–258.

lives for that belief. Rather, the occasion was "an appropriate time for communists to explain to the working masses ... that communism and nationalism are like heaven and earth [*mot troi mot vuc*] and the two isms can never accommodate [*dung hop*] each other."[24] The intention was not to commemorate nationalist leaders, but to "use the event to expand the influence of communism so that the Indochinese masses [would] join the fight under the communist flag to overthrow imperialists, feudalists, and landlords, and to form a government of workers-peasants-soldiers." In that struggle, the Indochinese proletariat would not be alone because "the world's proletariat and the oppressed nations in the colonies and semi-colonies were all brothers and not divided by race or nationality."[25]

"THE NIGHT BEFORE ANOTHER REVOLUTIONARY WAVE"

In late April 1931, the French police in Saigon captured Tran Phu, Ngo Duc Tri, and nearly the entire Central Committee of the ICP. Phu died six months later while under arrest, without betraying his comrades.[26] Tri caved in and disclosed to the authorities all his contacts, leading to many more arrests. Nguyen Ai Quoc was arrested in Hong Kong in May and would spend more than a year in jail before being released by British authorities. He then spent some time in hiding in southern China before departing for the Soviet Union in 1934. The ICP had collapsed as an organization, yet communism in Vietnam was kept alive thanks to the faith of those who survived and to the crucial support of the Comintern. By the 1930s, the Comintern network of communist activists and organizations had spread over a large geographic area from Shanghai to Singapore and Saigon, with Western European capitals serving as recruitment centers, training grounds, transit stations, and communication hubs. This network helped Vietnamese communists to rebuild their organizations although, as seen below, reconstructing the organization was a daunting task.

At this point the revolutionary torch was passed on to two new groups of graduates of the University of the Toilers of the East who branched out on two different paths. One group included Tran Dinh Long and Le Hong Phong whose journey back to southern China was told earlier.

[24] Ibid., 232.
[25] Ibid., 255.
[26] Bui Cong Trung who was in prison with Phu at the same time said Phu died of tuberculosis and some other (unclear) infectious disease. See his memoir "Hoi Ky Bui Cong Trung" available in part at http://vanhoanghean.com.vn/van-hoa-va-doi-song27/cuoc-song-quanh-ta46/hoi-ky-bui-cong-trung-ii.

After Phong settled down, he received Ha Huy Tap and other returnees from Moscow. Together this group founded the Overseas Bureau of the ICP [*Ban Chi huy o ngoai*] and tried to direct the communist movement inside Vietnam.[27] The second group involved the duo Nguyen Van Tao and Duong Bach Mai, who came from Cochinchina and who had been college students in Paris before receiving training in Moscow. These were the best-educated Vietnamese communists of their generation. After returning to Saigon via Paris, Tao and Mai collaborated with their Trotskyist friends from Paris days, such as Ta Thu Thau and Phan Van Hum, to run for seats in the Municipal Council.[28] Growing up in Cochinchina, Tao and Mai thrived in the open political environment there, which became even more open after the French Popular Front under Prime Minister Leon Blum came to power in May 1936. While also trained at the same University, Tao and Mai operated legally and independently from the clandestine Comintern bureaucracy that supervised Nguyen Ai Quoc, Tran Phu, and Le Hong Phong.

Shoring up Party members' sagging loyalty after so much loss was a big part of the work by Phong and Tap as new ICP leaders. The Comintern directly coordinated this effort because it also involved the French Communist Party. In early 1932, a letter was sent to the French Communist Party by some group that claimed to be the "Provisional Central Committee" of the ICP. The authors of this letter lamented that French repression was disastrous for the Party, which was now on its death bed [*hap hoi*].[29] Curiously, the letter blamed the failure of the revolutionary high tide during 1930–1931 as much on the ICP as on French brutalities. Backward Indochina had a small and weak proletariat, which meant the great majority of Party members came from peasant and petit bourgeois backgrounds. As the letter recounted, "the Communist Party was born out of the most progressive elements of the Vietnamese Nationalist Party and proletarian and peasant forces."[30] Because of such an impure class composition, it was inevitable that the ICP came to rely on "anarchist methods of struggle." If the ICP was ever to recover from

[27] "Ve cong tac trong ba nam qua va tinh hinh Dang Cong san Dong duong," *VKDTT*, v. 5, 399.

[28] Huynh, *Vietnamese Communism 1925–1945*, 194–198.

[29] "Gui cac dong chi trong Dang Cong san Phap" [To comrades in the French Communist Party]. *VKDTT*, v. 4, 30–37. Editors of *VKDTT* gave the document the date of "April 1932," but based on other documents in the same volume, the letter must have been written in February 1932 at the latest.

[30] Ibid., 31.

the collapse, which the letter said was an uncertain prospect, it would need to be led by "a proletarian core." The Party also must rid itself of nationalist and petit bourgeois elements.

The letter's class line seemed generally correct, and its authors remained loyal to the cause. Its loose use of concepts and its near-desperate tone, however, must have touched a nerve with Comintern officials when they read excerpts of the letter published in the journal *Cahiers du Bolchévisme* of the French Communist Party.[31] At a Moscow meeting of the Eastern Bureau of the Comintern on April 4, 1932, the letter was discussed and a "comrade Vasilieva" was tasked with contacting *Bolchévisme*.[32] The Comintern Bureau then asked Ha Huy Tap (then still in Moscow) to write a rebuttal to be published immediately on *Bolchévisme*. Tap was advised to argue that the defeat was only temporary. The strength of revolutionary movements worldwide, the consolidation of the Chinese communist government, the success of socialist construction in the Soviet Union, the worsening economic crisis and living conditions in Indochina – all indicated that a new revolutionary high tide would soon come.[33]

In his long and eloquent essay, Tap noted that VNP leaders believed in "parochial patriotism" [*chu nghia yeu nuoc hep hoi*], and their failure was predictable.[34] A very small number of VNP members did switch to the ICP after the failed Yen Bai rebellion, and these had fully accepted communist theory and practice. The majority of VNP members, however, kept intact "their petit bourgeois nationalism and their wavering, terrorist, and sectarian behavior."[35] The ICP did not benefit from admitting VNP members; it suffered from the consequences, Tap claimed. He went

---

[31] "Bien ban so 10" [Minute no. 10], April 4, 1932. *VKDTT*, v. 4, 298–299. The Comintern office also learned about the letter from Le Hong Phong. It wrote back and asked what he thought about it but Phong's reply, if he did reply, is not available. "Thu cua Quoc te Cong san gui dong chi Le Hong Phong" [Letter from the Comintern to comrade Le Hong Phong], March 19, 1932. *VKDTT*, v. 4, 278.

[32] Vera Vasilieva ran the Indochina section of the Comintern in Moscow. Quinn-Judge, *Ho Chi Minh*, 199.

[33] "Thu cua Quoc te Cong san gui dong chi Xinhitrokin" [Letter from the Comintern to comrade Sinitrkin], April 14, 1932. *VKDTT*, v. 4, 300–302. "Sinitrkin" was one of Tap's pseudonyms.

[34] The Eastern Bureau sent Tap's essay to *Cahiers du Bolchévisme* with the request to publish it immediately in the next issue. See "Thu cua Dong Phuong Bo Ban Chap uy Quoc te Cong san gui Ban Bien tap Tap chi *Cahiers Du Bolchévisme*" [Letter from the Eastern Bureau of the Comintern to the Editors of *Cahiers Du Bolchévisme*], April 23, 1932. *VKDTT*, v. 4, 303.

[35] "Gui Ban Bien tap Tap chi Bonsovich" [To the Editors of *Cahiers Du Bolchévisme*]. *VKDTT*, v. 4, 255–256. Editors of this document in the collection assumed that this letter was written in February 1932. Given that Ha Huy Tap was responding to the letter

on to dismiss claims that the ICP was on its deathbed, noting that, according to dialectic materialism, revolution did not advance in a straight line. Although he admitted that the ICP had made mistakes and the movement had suffered some losses, the Party was far from being destroyed. Given the protracted economic crisis and intense class struggle in Indochina and elsewhere, now was "the night before another revolutionary wave."

Tap's optimism was not simply to reassure his wavering comrades but may have been grounded in his deep appreciation of historical processes. Before Tap left Moscow for southern China in late 1933, he completed a 300-page history of the Indochinese communist movement that was published in Moscow by the Comintern.[36] The work showcased his intimate knowledge of the movement as an insider from the beginning and his theoretical flair that easily surpassed that of Tran Phu. The study covered the decade from 1923 to 1933, that is, from Thanh Nien to the ICP. It analyzed historical conditions that gave rise to communism, colonial policies that affected the movement, and the theoretical and organizational issues that the movement grappled with. The first chapter on Thanh Nien made succinct observations written in beautiful prose about the origins of Vietnamese communism:

The Indochinese communist movement was a child of the Russian Revolution ... The victory of the working class in a large country like Russia woke up all nations in the world. [When the news of it reached] those in faraway Indochina who were groaning under the yoke of French imperialism, they also joined the struggle of all the oppressed masses in the world to fight against their common enemy, global imperialism. But if the sound of the cannons that October in Russia moved the hearts of the exploited masses in Indochina and brought a fresh wind to them, the Chinese revolution was a guide and a necessary teacher whose fate was inseparable from its Indochinese counterpart.[37]

Because the earliest organizations such as Thanh Nien were deeply influenced by Chinese (nationalist) ideas and methods, Tap argued that "it is unsurprising that their ideology was still unclear, their thinking

---

from the "Provisional Central Committee," the date of his essay must have been between April 14 and 23, 1932.

[36] Hong The Cong (Ha Huy Tap), "So thao lich su phong trao cong san o Dong duong" [Brief history of the Indochinese communist movement], prefaced by André Marty and introduced by Nguyen Quoc Te (Moscow: Revolutionary Movement Library of the Communist Party, 1933). Republished in Ha Huy Tap, *Ha Huy Tap: Mot so tac pham* [Ha Huy Tap's works] (Hanoi: Chinh tri Quoc gia, 2006), 177–482. Nguyen Quoc Te was a pseudonym of Nguyen Khanh Toan.

[37] Hong The Cong, "So thao lich su phong trao cong san o Dong duong," in Ha Huy Tap, *Ha Huy Tap*, 181–182.

muddy, and their views self-contradictory." To him, such a condition also resulted from the class composition of those organizations, which was overwhelmingly petit bourgeois in membership. Members of this class brought with them its ideology, views, and methods such as anarchism, sectarianism, and putschism. However, his long-term perspective allowed Tap to make an overall positive assessment: "Although those early organizations made many errors, they have fulfilled their historic mission. They were the first to introduce new elements into the national liberation movement. They foreshadowed communism."

Although it is well-known that Ha Huy Tap once took issue with Nguyen Ai Quoc's errors during the Thanh Nien and VCP period, his criticisms have been taken out of context.[38] Tap's historical study offered a balanced and detached assessment of Quoc's contributions. The study opened with the following dedication:

In memory: Comrade Nguyen Ai Quoc, the founder of the Indochinese Communist Party, who died on June 26, 1932 in prison in Hong Kong; Comrade Ly Quy [Tran Phu], General Secretary of the Indochinese Communist Party, who died in October 1931 in prison in Saigon; and all those who have sacrificed for the Indochinese revolution.[39]

When he discussed the unification meeting that Quoc oversaw in early 1930, Tap was interested not only in theoretical issues but also in a historical perspective:

The instructions for unifying [the rival communist groups] had been given by the Comintern before the date of the unification meeting. However, because of circumstances beyond their control, many participants at that meeting did not receive those instructions. The late comrade Nguyen Ai Quoc took the initiative to propose and lead the unification. He committed many errors of opportunism that we cannot fail to mention. Yet, his great contribution was to assemble the fragmented communist forces to form a block that would become the revolutionary vanguard [of] Indochinese workers.[40]

Himself being a member of Tan Viet before traveling to the Soviet Union for training, Tap admitted that he could not avoid laughing at his own

---

[38] See for example, Huynh, *Vietnamese Communism*, 184–186; Le Quynh, "Bai hoc tu quan he Viet-Xo" [Lessons from Soviet-Vietnamese relationship], n. d. Accessed at www .bbc.co.uk/vietnamese/specials/170_viet_studies/page3.shtml; Ngo Tran Duc, "Huyen thoai kep Ho Chi Minh: Vinh quang va nhung he luy" [The double myth about Ho Chi Minh: Glory and troubles], April 21, 2011. Accessed at www.viet-studies.info/ NgoTranDuc_HuyenThoaiKepHCM.htm.

[39] Hong The Cong, "So thao lich su phong trao cong san o Dong duong," in Ha Huy Tap, *Ha Huy Tap*, 180. Nguyen Ai Quoc was rumored to have died in Hong Kong at the time.

[40] Ibid., 262–263.

theoretical naiveté in the early days when he and other Tan Viet leaders memorized Nguyen Ai Quoc's "The Revolutionary Path" by heart and "treated it like a Bible."[41] Like Tran Phu before him, Tap did not seek to criticize Quoc personally, and blamed historical circumstances for Quoc's mistakes.

The mid-1930s was not a dead end for the ICP as Huynh Kim Khanh has argued, but not quite the night before the revolution as Tap claimed. The ICP had been provisionally admitted into the Comintern in 1931 and was officially admitted in 1935. The Comintern had trained new cadres for the Party, and among them the finest theoretician to date who was able to formulate clear theoretical lines that kept abreast of the world-wide revolutionary movement. By 1934, the ICP had reemerged in southern China in a new form as the Overseas Bureau of the ICP.[42] This Bureau was formed on the order of the Comintern to prevent another collapse of the Party in case its Central Committee members inside Vietnam were arrested or killed.

Communist organizations inside Indochina were still fragile, however. At the First National Congress of the Party convened in Macao in early 1935 by the newly established Overseas Bureau, most of the thirteen men present hailed from outside Vietnam.[43] No participants had been present at earlier ICP meetings. Despite an entire change of leadership, no significant change of worldview occurred. New ICP leaders did speak of the sharper contrast between the "socialist system" and the "capitalist system" and the more urgent dangers of fascism and world war. The resolution of the Congress took pride in the fact that Stalin's First Five-Year Plan was completed in four years and the Second Five-Year Plan had been making progress in industrialization, in expanding the public ownership of land, and in raising living standards for workers and peasants. Soviet industrial production in 1934 was twice that in 1930, whereas collectivized farms now accounted for 92 percent of total cultivated area.[44] Workers' salary increased from 991 *dong* in 1930 to

[41] This information was from a separate document by Ha Huy Tap titled "Tu lieu bo sung ve nguon goc cac to chuc Cong san o Dong duong" [Supplementary materials on the origins of communist organizations in Indochina]. *VKDTT*, v. 4, 366–368.

[42] "Nghi quyet Hoi nghi Ban Chi huy o ngoai cua Dang Cong san Dong duong va dai dien cac to chuc trong nuoc" [Resolution of the Meeting of the ICP Overseas Bureau and domestic groups], June 16–21, 1934. *VKDTT*, v. 4, 175–176.

[43] For a full list of participants, see Huynh, *Vietnamese Communism 1925–1945* 187.

[44] "Nghi quyet chinh tri cua dai bieu Dai hoi (Congres) lan thu nhat Dang Cong San Dong Duong" [Resolution of the First Congress of the Indochinese Communist Party], March 27–31, 1935. *VKDTT*, v. 5, 2.

1,519 *dong* in 1933.[45] In 1933, collective farmers received 1.6 billion *dong* of funding from the Soviet government while 280 tractor stations were built. These accomplishments were possible thanks particularly to the struggle led by Stalin against opportunism and Trotskyism. Soviet success "opened up the road to liberation for workers and the oppressed people all over the world." It indicated that "socialism [had] become inevitable."[46]

Although the capitalist world had pulled back from the worst of the Great Depression, the resolution quoted Stalin that recovery had resulted from higher tariff barriers, from dumping, from the increased exploitation of the working masses and oppressed nations, from the manipulations of exchange rates and monetary stocks, and from the cutbacks on production.[47] Capitalist economies were far from being stable while people in those societies continued to suffer. That explained the rise of fascism in Europe and the urgent preparations for war among capitalist countries. In contrast, the Soviet Union had done its best to protect world peace by signing mutual nonaggression pacts.

The resolution claimed that the ICP had "generally" reconstructed its domestic organizations and trained new cadres to replace those who had been imprisoned or executed. It called on Party members to focus their recruitment efforts on industrial centers to "turn each factory into a fortress of the Party."[48] Truly committed peasants and intellectuals could become members, but workers must constitute the majority in all executive organs. The resolution noted the growth of the Party in more backward areas of Indochina, including the upland of northern Vietnam, Laos, and Cambodia. Ethnic Tho, Nung, and Chinese had recently joined executive organs of the Party.[49] For the first time, a separate resolution on "the national question" following the Soviet model was discussed and approved at the Congress. This resolution proclaimed that every nation in the future Indochinese Federation should enjoy the right to self-determination. The Party vowed not to impose its will on any minority nations if they insisted on having their own governments, but it would

[45] "Dong" is the Vietnamese unit of currency, but here it appeared to be the translated word for "ruble."
[46] Nghi quyet chinh tri cua dai bieu Dai hoi (Congres) lan thu nhat Dang Cong San Dong Duong," *VKDTT*, v. 5, 2.
[47] Ibid., 3–4.
[48] Ibid., 23.
[49] Ibid., 18–19.

strive to promote the brotherly ties of all Indochinese nations under an Indochina-wide Soviet government.[50]

The Congress elected a new Central Committee of thirteen persons. Among these, one was a peasant and eight had a worker background. Three were former students at the University of Toilers of the East, including Le Hong Phong. Nguyen Ai Quoc, now living in Moscow, was named a "spare" or "candidate" [*du bi*] member.[51] This was not a sign of Quoc's demotion as commonly believed.[52] By assigning Quoc a "spare" status, the Congress may have intended for him to take over the Party if its leadership was arrested or killed. In fact, the Congress appointed (re-appointed?) Quoc to be the ICP representative with the Comintern, and asked him to write a book using his earlier mistakes in Thanh Nien to help the Party fight against the lingering influences of "revolutionary nationalism, reformism, and idealism."[53] Quoc was also asked to translate classified documents. As a sign of trust in Quoc, he was instructed to translate by himself and carefully check the translations by others, including Nguyen Khanh Toan who was a long-time Vietnamese researcher and lecturer at the University.[54]

ENDEARING VISION

Shortly after the First Congress of the ICP, the Seventh Congress of the Comintern opened in Moscow in the summer of 1935. Le Hong Phong and two other Vietnamese communist leaders attended and spoke at

---

[50] "Nghi quyet ve cong tac trong cac dan toc thieu so" [Resolution on work with ethnic minorities]. *VKDTT*, v. 5, 69–75.

[51] "Thu cua Ban Chi huy o ngoai cua Dang Cong san Dong duong (ngay 31-3-35) gui Quoc te Cong san" [Letter from the Overseas Bureau of the ICP to the Comintern], March 31, 1935. *VKDTT*, v. 5, 190–204. The Vietnamese version of this document (likely the original) used the word "du bi."

[52] Huynh, *Vietnamese Communism 1925–1945*, 187–188.

[53] Ibid., 204.

[54] "Thu cua Ban Chi huy o ngoai gui cac dong chi Vasilieva va Lin" [Letter from the Overseas Bureau to comrades Vasilieva and Lin], March 31, 1935. *VKDTT*, v. 5, 188–189. Nguyen Khanh Toan was better educated than most of his comrades, including Nguyen Ai Quoc. He graduated from a pedagogical college in Hanoi and wrote for the anticolonial press in Cochinchina before going to France and then to the Soviet Union in 1929 or 1930. See his memoir included in Pham Xuan Nam, Pham Thi Ha, and Nguyen Ngoc Tuan, eds., *Giao su Vien si Nguyen Khanh Toan: Cuoc doi va su nghiep* [Professor and Academician Nguyen Khanh Toan: His Life and Career] (Hanoi: Chinh tri Quoc gia, 2013), 115–186. Quinn-Judge speculates that Quoc's status at the University of the Toilers of the East was lower than Nguyen Khanh Toan, but the evidence here suggests otherwise. Quinn-Judge, *Ho Chi Minh*, 217–218.

the Congress. Phong was elected to the Executive Committee of the Comintern, its top policymaking organ – the first Vietnamese to have earned that status. The Seventh Congress authorized a major reversal in the tactics of the world communist movement. Instead of waging a class war against the bourgeoisie and their governments, communist parties were now instructed to form broad alliances with nonworking-class groups to isolate and defeat fascism. In Europe, that meant the creation of "people's fronts" between communists and social democrats and trade unionists against fascist governments and parties. In the colonies where the fascist threat was distant, "antiimperialist democratic fronts" were to be founded to unite all the enemies of imperialism, including the indigenous bourgeoisie. The Comintern certainly did not call on communist parties to abandon their communist vision; only the tactics had to be adjusted.

As with the case of the Sixth Comintern Congress in 1928, the new policy of the Seventh Congress took some time to reach Vietnam. Le Hong Phong lingered in the Soviet Union and did not return to China until mid-1936. During that time, the ICP fell into another crisis. Nearly all of its Central Committee members freshly elected at its First National Congress a year earlier were arrested when they returned to Indochina.[55] The ICP practically collapsed again, although this time the situation was not as bleak as in 1931 thanks to the existence of the Overseas Bureau under Ha Huy Tap. Still, gloom pervaded a report Tap sent to the Comintern at the time. Many graduates from the University of Toilers of the East had returned but disappeared without a trace. The Overseas Bureau received a stipend of $2,000 per year from the Comintern, barely enough for sustaining two ICP leaders (Ha Huy Tap and another named K.) who also worked as editors, printers, distributors, translators, and coders and decoders of letters. As Tap lamented,

Money haunts us all the time, affecting our health and activities... [T]his life of voluntary exile is sad because we have no relatives, friends, and others to help us when we need help and when things are not going well. As leaders of the Party, we accept and are ready to sacrifice, but others do not want this kind of life [and have avoided us]. The Overseas Bureau has to work under the most challenging economic and political conditions. Away from our country, lacking staff and money, often being betrayed and provoked [*khieu khich*] in the last 14 months – these things have made it difficult for us to work well or effectively.[56]

---

[55] "Bao cao cua Ban Chi huy o ngoai giua thang 5-1935 va thang 6-1936" [Report by the Overseas Bureau of the ICP for the period between May 1935 and June 1936], July 1, 1936. *VKDTT*, v. 6, 48–49.

[56] Ibid., 53–54.

Fortunately, the election of the Popular Front government in France in May 1936 created a less repressive political environment in Vietnam. Thousands of political prisoners were released, including many ICP members. The Overseas Bureau also began to implement new united front tactics as instructed by the Comintern, calling for other groups, including "the VNP and all nationalist, anti-imperialist, reformist, and reactionary organizations," to join it in an anti-imperialist front for "national liberation."[57] In internal communication, the Overseas Bureau explained the new tactics as follows:

[Our] Communist Party is an uncompromisingly revolutionary party. Given the current situation in our country and in the world, especially in France, the Party believes that, for the time being, we must take advantage of all the conflicts within the imperialist camp and those between indigenous capitalists and their counterparts in [France]. This will help us to unite all the revolutionary and opposition forces to launch a joint struggle against French imperialism.[58]

Party leaders made clear that they remained committed to their communist worldview, and viewed the democratic front simply as one of the "stratagems" or "tricks" [thu doan] to deal with the enemy and to lead the masses to the ultimate goals of the revolution.[59] As Party leaders explained to their members, "[we] believe in internationalism, not nationalism, but in the context of a nation being under two layers of exploitation, we should raise the spirit for national liberation while tying it to the interests of the working masses [that is, we want our struggle to] appear nationalist on the outside but be internationalist inside."

In particular, the goals of the democratic front were "to struggle for the interests of ordinary people and against the inhuman colonial system [in order to] create conditions for the national liberation movement to grow."[60] Translated into tactics, that meant the Party would not raise the slogans of national independence and land redistribution for now. This tactical shift was significant because existing scholarship portrays Le Hong Phong and Ha Huy Tap as "dogmatic" vis-à-vis the "pragmatic"

---

[57] See "Thu ngo cua Ban Trung uong Dang Cong san Dong duong" [Open letter from the ICP Central Committee], c. May 1936. VKDTT, v. 6, 7–25. The original letter in French was filed at the Comintern on June 6, 1936. Despite its title, the letter was actually drafted by the Overseas Bureau, because the ICP Central Committee inside Vietnam would not be restored until October 1936.

[58] "Gui cac to chuc cua Dang" [To (our) Party's organizations], July 26, 1936. VKDTT, v. 6, 77.

[59] "Chung quanh van de chien sach moi" [About the new tactics], October 30, 1936. VKDTT, v. 6, 135.

[60] Ibid., 151–152.

Nguyen Ai Quoc. The decision made at this point by the Overseas Bureau indicated that Phong and Tap were tactically pragmatic while being committed to long-term radical goals. Their policy during 1936–1939, which earned harsh denunciations from Trotskyist groups, was no less pragmatic than the policy of national solidarity under Quoc's leadership during 1941–1945.[61]

Existing scholarship similarly overlooks Quoc and other ICP leaders' absolute loyalty to Stalin, as evidenced in their unanimous and unflinching support for Soviet foreign policy and their vicious polemics against Vietnamese Trotskyists. To counter Trotskyist criticisms of Stalin, ICP leaders went to great lengths to present Soviet policy as befitting a great world power and a generous friend of oppressed people. Although "imperialist" foreign policy was always associated with war, Soviet policy was aimed at peace. When the Soviet Union joined the Non-Intervention Agreement in 1936, Vietnamese Trotskyists criticized this policy for abandoning Spanish Republicans.[62] Ha Huy Tap responded that Soviet policy was based on the calculation that the "democratic people's forces" in Spain without the help of Germany and Italy would quickly defeat General Franco of the Nationalists.[63] Soviet leaders anticipated that fascist Germany and Italy would violate this agreement, but they signed it anyway, in part to show the Soviet desire for peace, and in part to provide the world with concrete evidence on the criminal nature of those regimes. Tap argued that, despite the agreement, the Soviet Union still provided material and mental support to the "heroic workers" of Spain.

To the ICP, the desire for peace was, again, behind Soviet participation in the League of Nations. While imperialist Britain and France were surrendering to Hitler's demands at Munich, the Soviet Union was described in the Vietnamese communist press as trying to use the League to shore up an anti-Fascist coalition.[64] While England and France "conspired" with

---

[61] An example of Trotskyist denunciation is: Tran Van Thach, "Nhom 'Dan Chung' dat quan chung hang phuc De quoc" [The Dan Chung group leads the masses to surrender to imperialism], *Tranh Dau*, March 9, 1939.

[62] This agreement was signed by most Western European powers and was meant to prevent the Spanish Civil War from spreading all over Europe.

[63] Ha Huy Tap (signed as "a group of *La Lutte* readers"), "Thu ngo gui nhom La Lutte" [Open letter to the La Lutte group], *La Lutte*, December 17, 1936. In Ha Huy Tap, *Ha Huy Tap*, 507–508.

[64] H. B., "Phuong phap tranh dau giu vung hoa binh co hieu qua hon het va triet de hon het phai the nao?" [What is the most effective and comprehensive method to struggle for peace?], *Dan Chung* [The People], November 5, 1938. In Vien Bao Tang Cach Mang, *Bao Dan Chung 1938–1939*, v. 2, 14–18. For the Trotskyist account, see No author,

Germany and Italy to isolate the Soviet Union, Moscow wisely and resolutely pursued a policy of collective security. ICP publications were either
silent or defensive about Stalin's purges.[65] Although the ICP offered to
collaborate even with the Constitutionalist Party, which represented the
Francophile wealthy elites in Cochinchina, Tap and his comrades were
hostile to Trotskyists "because Trotskyists opposed the Soviet Union, the
French Communist Party, and the French Popular Front."[66]

While Phong and Tap led the ICP in southern China and later in
Saigon, Nguyen Ai Quoc was back in Moscow. On his arrival in Moscow
in July 1934 after having been released from prison in Hong Kong in
January 1933, Quoc was subject to an investigation by the Comintern for
suspicions related to his unaccounted disappearance following his release
from Hong Kong, and to his relationship with another ICP leader, Lam
Duc Thu, who by then had been discovered to be a spy for the French.[67]
However, the Comintern committee that was set up to investigate Quoc
in February 1936 concluded that "no evidence exists to question [his]
political loyalty." The case was declared closed.[68]

In 1938, Quoc was sent off to Indochina again as a trusted Comintern
agent.[69] He was in China during 1938–1940 as an officer in the People's

"Ban co Au chau dang doi dang" [The European chest game is changing], *Tranh Dau*
[Struggle], October 13, 1938.

[65] See Holcombe, "Stalin, the Moscow Show Trials, and Contesting Visions of Vietnamese
Communism in the late 1930s: A Reappraisal," paper presented at the Workshop on
the Vietnamese Revolution, University of California, Berkeley, November 11–12, 2011;
Nguyen Van Tran (a pseudonym of Ha Huy Tap), *Su that ve vu an o Moscou* [The truth
about the trials in Moscow] (Saigon: Tien Phong tho xa, 1938), reprinted in *Ha Huy
Tap: Mot So Tac Pham* [Ha Huy Tap's works], 687–706.

[66] "Chung quanh van de chien sach moi" [About the new tactics], October 30, 1936.
VKDTT, v. 6, 156–157; "Nghi quyet cua Khoang dai Hoi nghi cua toan the Ban Trung
uong cua Dang Cong san Dong duong" [Resolution of the Plenum of the Central
Committee of the ICP], September 4, 1937. *VKDTT*, v. 6, 288. See also, Ha Huy Tap,
"Su that ve viec chia re trong noi bo nhom La Lutte" [The truth about the split in the
La Lutte group], *En Avant*, no. 3, September 3, 1939, and no. 4, September 10, 1939,
reprinted in *Ha Huy Tap: Mot So Tac Pham* [Ha Huy Tap's works], 641–651; Nguyen
Van Tran (a pseudonym of Ha Huy Tap), *Ai chia re nhom La Lutte?* (Saigon: Le Peuple,
1938), reprinted in *Ha Huy Tap: Mot So Tac Pham* [Ha Huy Tap' works], 657–686.

[67] Ba Ngoc, "Ban tham tra vu viec Nguyen Ai Quoc o Quoc te Cong san," [The Comintern's
committee to investigate the Nguyen Ai Quoc affair], *Xua va Nay* [Past and Present], no.
438 (October 2013), 3–7. This account is based on a letter from the Overseas Bureau to
the Comintern dated April 20, 1935, which is also cited in Quinn-Judge, *Ho Chi Minh*,
205–206.

[68] Ba Ngoc, "Ban tham tra vu viec Nguyen Ai Quoc o Quoc te Cong san," 6. The committee
included Hai An (Le Hong Phong) and two other Comintern officials. Quinn-Judge is not
aware of this committee and its conclusion.

[69] Quinn-Judge, *Ho Chi Minh*, 216–220, 228–233.

Liberation Army, and published many short articles in ICP newspapers inside Vietnam. Available sources suggest that Quoc fully supported specific Comintern instructions for the ICP after the Seventh Congress. On the issue of a democratic front, Quoc conveyed the Comintern's advice to the ICP that the front should try to accommodate "national capitalists" as much as possible, but if not successful, should "isolate them politically." For the Trotskyists, however, "there could not be any compromise, any concession. [The ICP] must do everything to ... eliminate them politically."[70] Quoc minced no words about Trotskyists and praised the Stalin trials in the 1930s for "unmask[ing] the disgusting face of Trotskyism."[71]

Although ICP leadership was united in their loyalty to Moscow, disputes existed on membership policy and on the full legalization of party activities. At first, the ICP created a united front aimed at expanding external links between the ICP and other political parties or groups. In early 1937, membership policy appeared to remain restrictive despite the efforts to form a broad democratic front.[72] "Enthusiastic and honest" peasants as well as people of petit-bourgeois and other class backgrounds were invited to join the Party, but the priority was still given to workers, especially for positions in executive organs.[73] Mass organizations such as the Communist Youth League and Workers' Union were told to utilize all forms of legal and semilegal activism, with clandestine activities reserved for situations in which legal forms were not possible.[74]

At the meeting that would be called the Fourth Plenum of the Central Committee in late August 1937, criticisms began to be voiced about the failure of the Party to expand its membership base into urban groups.[75] The resolution of the meeting also censured those Party members active in the legal sphere who were too independent from the (clandestine) Party. In the Fifth Plenum held in March 1938, the situation apparently

---

[70] "Nhung chi thi ma toi nho va truyen dat" [The instructions I remembered and transmitted]. *VKDTT*, v. 6, 507–508. For an account of a Trotskyist activist at the time, see Ngo Van, *In the Crossfire: Adventures of a Vietnamese Revolutionary*, transl. from French by Helene Fleury et al. (Oakland, CA: AK Press, 2010).

[71] P.C. Line (Ho Chi Minh), "Thu tu Trung quoc" [Letter from China], May 10, 1939. Published in French in *Notre Voix*, June 23, 1939. Translated and reprinted in Pham Quy Thich, *Nha bao Ho Chi Minh o Que Lam* [The journalist Ho Chi Minh in Que Lam] (Hanoi: Cong an nhan dan, 2006), 245–248.

[72] "Thong cao ngay 20-3-1937" [Notice on March 20, 1937]. *VKDTT*, v. 6, 212–213.

[73] "Chu truong to chuc moi cua Dang" [New organizational policy of the Party], March 26, 1937. *VKDTT*, v. 6, 234.

[74] "Thong cao ngay 20-3-1937," *VKDTT*, v. 6, 212.

[75] "Nghi quyet cua Khoang dai Hoi nghi cua toan the Ban Trung uong cua Dang Cong san Dong duong," *VKDTT*, v. 6, 272–273.

worsened. Many clandestine Party organizations "could not direct" the activities of those in the legal sphere because the latter were in most cases newly released political prisoners who were politically seasoned and educated. In contrast, the heads of clandestine organizations were new members with working-class backgrounds and having less experience and education.[76] Ha Huy Tap was criticized at the Plenum for his reluctance to embrace legal activism and was replaced by Nguyen Van Cu, who had never been out of Vietnam but had spent time in Poulo Condore.[77] It is unclear why Tap did not fully endorse legal activism, but the issue soon became irrelevant with the outbreak of World War II in late 1939. A few months later, the colonial government reimposed tight political control and outlawed communism.

Most interestingly, when ICP leaders met for what would later be called the Sixth Plenum, they blamed France and England more than the Axis for the outbreak of war.[78] In their analysis of the world situation at this Plenum, they heaped criticism on "the great conman" Chamberlain, the British Prime Minister, who had appeased Hitler while obstructing Moscow's efforts to make peace.[79] Apparently parroting Soviet propaganda, ICP leaders accused England, France, and their "loyal Polish dog" of starting the war in 1939. The French, British, and Poles did so because they feared the Soviet Union and the world revolutionary movement. Now that war with Germany had started, they had not given up on their anti-Soviet scheme. With help from the United States, Italy, and Japan, they were still trying to turn Germany against the Soviet Union.

The Party did not make any significant policy changes in response to the new situation. Its leaders called for the formation of a new national front to unite "all nations, classes, and political parties to struggle against imperialist wars, fascist aggression, French imperialism, the Annamese royal court, and all their minions."[80] This strategy was based on a new class analysis showing that not only poor peasants and workers, but the indigenous bourgeoisie, small and "middle" landlords, rich farmers, and even the urban petit bourgeois also hated the French because war would

---

[76] "Bao cao sau thang gui Ban Phuong dong Quoc te Cong san" [Six-month report to the Eastern Bureau of the Comintern], April 5, 1938. *VKDTT*, v. 6, 372.

[77] Tap remained in the Central Committee.

[78] Participants at the Plenum included Nguyen Van Cu, the new general secretary, Phan Dang Luu, Le Duan, Vo Van Tan and (likely) Ta Uyen. Quinn-Judge, *Ho Chi Minh*, 236.

[79] "Nghi quyet cua Ban Trung uong Dang" [Resolution of the Central Committee], November 6–8, 1939. *VKDTT*, v. 6, 510–515.

[80] Ibid., 537.

lead to higher taxes, government requisition, low consumer demand, falling prices of agricultural products, rising costs of living, and salary cuts.[81] Party leaders believed that almost all Vietnamese could potentially be their allies. "In the interests of the nation," therefore, they decided that the program of the new anti-imperialist front should not mention land redistribution and the formation of a government based on workers, peasants, and soldiers. Nevertheless, the resolution of the Plenum reiterated that the Party did not give up those goals, only delayed them. If the situation became more favorable, the revolution would and should strive to achieve those goals, and then shift to the proletarian revolution, with violence if necessary.[82]

Party policy on land at this point was nearly identical to the policy platform found in Tran Phu's "Political Thesis discussed earlier," which called for land owned by the church and "traitors" to be confiscated and redistributed. Going even further than Phu's Political Thesis, the resolution of the Sixth Plenum in 1939 made it explicit that no market of land would be allowed. Peasants were to be given "enough land to live," and out of the remaining land the government would create state farms modeled after Soviet *Sovkhoz*.[83]

The Sixth Plenum met when the ICP had been outlawed by the colonial government. Within a few months, nearly all top leaders were nabbed by French police.[84] Nguyen Van Cu and Ha Huy Tap would soon be executed, while Le Hong Phong was sent to Poulo Condore where he died in 1942. Once again, the ICP was on the verge of collapse. The details of what followed remain murky, but the Northern Regional Committee of the Party soon stepped in and claimed to be the new Central Committee.[85] Despite a total change in leadership,[86] the worldview expressed at a meeting in early November 1940, later to be called the Seventh Plenum in official history, remained consistent. If anything, the new leaders were

[81] Ibid., 520–522.
[82] Ibid., 539.
[83] "Nghi quyet cua Ban Trung uong Dang," *VKDTT*, v. 6, 542–543.
[84] Nguyen Van Cu and Le Duan were captured in January 1940, Le Hong Phong in February, Vo Van Tan in April, and Nguyen Huu Tien and Nguyen Thi Minh Khai in July. Tran Giang, *Nam Ky Khoi Nghia: 23 thang 11 nam 1940* [The Southern uprising: November 23, 1940] (Hanoi: Chinh tri Quoc gia, 1996), 52–56.
[85] Quinn-Judge, *Ho Chi Minh*, 237–245.
[86] Participants at this meeting included Truong Chinh, Hoang Quoc Viet, Hoang Van Thu, Phan Dang Luu and perhaps others. Only Phan Dang Luu had been a Central Committee member, but he would soon be captured and executed. (Stein Tønnesson, *Vietnam 1946: How the War Began* [Berkeley: University of California Press, 2010] 115; Marr, *Vietnam 1945*, 160, 167–168).

more radical and their language more bombastic. For example, on the international situation, the resolution of the Seventh Plenum began with a brief but brave announcement: the Plenum would limit its analysis of the war and the world's revolutionary movement to the previous year, "in sum, [to] the basic factors ... that will extinguish the fires of imperialist warfare, destroy the capitalist world and build a new one: the socialist world."[87]

The resolution characterized the Second World War as one over colonies between rising imperialists (Germany, Italy, and Japan) and richer, more established ones (Britain, France, and the United States). The war was described as standing at a critical crossroads: although Germany and Italy now ruled most of continental Europe, they would need time to consolidate their forces before attacking England. With Churchill as the new prime minister, England seemed determined to fight back. ICP leaders dismissed the exiled government of General De Gaulle as "a bunch of slaves without a homeland" [*vong quoc no*] who relied on England but did not abandon their imperial ambitions.[88] They had neither significant forces nor support from their people. More important to England was American assistance. The selfish United States, which had earlier maintained a neutral policy, now helped England not only to cope with the fascist threat but also to wrest control of British military bases and to obtain other economic concessions.

But why did the imperialist gang fight among themselves even though all wanted to attack the Soviet Union to "smother the world's revolutionary oven" [*lo lua*]?[89] ICP leaders imagined that the USSR had become increasingly more powerful, which was why none of the imperialist states wanted to take the responsibility of firing the first shot against it. To prepare for the eventual war with Moscow, they waged a war against each other to consolidate their strength first. Thus, the Second World War could eventually be directed against the Soviet Union. However, because the imperialist states were fighting each other, and the war had spurred widespread uprisings by oppressed peoples, even when imperialist forces were finally able to reunite and attack the Soviet Union, they would then be [easily] defeated by the Red Army and by the revolutionary forces of the world.

[87] "Nghi quyet cua Hoi nghi Trung uong" (Resolution of the Central Committee Plenum), November 6–9, 1940. *VKDTT*, v. 7, 20.
[88] Ibid., 22–23.
[89] Ibid., 24.

The Seventh Plenum also attempted to defend the Molotov-Ribbentrop agreement between Stalin and Hitler. Why did the leader of the revolutionary camp sign a truce with the counterrevolutionary camp? Was it true, as Trotskyists claimed, that the Soviet Union was preoccupied with developing socialism and neglected its responsibility to revolutions elsewhere? The answer was that the Soviet Union had intervened from the beginning to prevent war from spreading; in the process it wisely expanded its influence, "which would help strengthen the world's revolutionary fortress" [*thanh tri*]. Russia did not plot with any imperialist states to rob Poland and the Baltic nations of their independence; rather, it helped to liberate those small nations from the imperialist yoke.[90]

ICP leaders further argued that developing socialism in one country could contribute to world revolution. The success of the Third Five-Year Plan (1938–1941) had made the Soviet Union "the most powerful country on earth"; this changed the balance of force in favor of "the revolutionary camp."[91] The evidence of increased Soviet influence was shown in the fact that the most aggressive and counterrevolutionary imperialist states were now trying to "curry favor with" [*ninh hot*] it. The Soviet Union stood above them all; it had no interest in [*khong them*] helping one imperialist power to fight another. Those who pledged not to attack it were accorded good relations (hence, Molotov-Ribbentrop). The contrast between the two worlds was stark: "Whereas the capitalist world was now full of wails and sobs, of smashed bones and rotten flesh, the socialist world was a humane place where people lived in peace and happiness." This contrast, ICP leaders hoped, would urge the oppressed peoples and classes everywhere to overthrow imperialism and follow Soviet leadership.[92]

On the appropriate revolutionary path for Indochina, new ICP leaders revived Tran Phu's concept of bourgeois democratic revolution, while not mentioning the policy made at the Sixth Plenum that sought an alliance of all classes for forming an anti-imperialist front. Because Indochina was not yet industrialized,

the Indochinese revolution cannot yet be the proletarian or socialist revolution. It can only be the bourgeois democratic revolution. It is not a revolution just to liberate the nation because its mission is to overthrow not only imperialism [but also] feudalism, to carry out land reform in favor of peasants, to develop

---

[90] Ibid., 32.
[91] Ibid., 33.
[92] Ibid., 34.

industries, and to form a democratic government... The anti-imperialist revolution and the land [reform] must walk hand in hand...Although at this time [we may want to] raise the slogan of national liberation higher..., but without land [reform] it would be difficult for the anti-imperialist revolution to succeed.[93]

It was as if Tran Phu had not died in 1931. After a decade of turmoil in world politics and two complete turnovers of leadership, the concept of the "bourgeois democratic revolution" developed by Phu remained endearing to ICP leaders. His theory had become the default program of the Party.

CONCLUSION

In his memoir published online after his death in 2010, Tran Van Giau, a graduate of the University of Toilers of the East in Moscow and an important ICP leader in the 1940s, recounted the time he spent with Ha Huy Tap in the Saigon prison during 1939–1940 prior to the latter's execution.[94] Tap had left his wife and daughter in 1928 to travel to the Soviet Union. They were reunited after his return to Saigon in 1936. While Tap was in prison, his wife who had stuck with him for eight years of exile left him for another man. For many days after receiving the news, Tap could not sleep. His health deteriorated so quickly that he had to be hospitalized. Yet, within a week he was back in jail, completely cured. As Giau whose cell was next to Tap's told us, at the hospital Tap was put in the same room with Ta Thu Thau, a prominent Trotskyist leader mentioned earlier. They immediately engaged in a sharp debate by their hospital beds: Thau accused Stalinists of being Thermidorian reactionaries, and Tap countered by calling Trotskyists anti-Soviet bourgeois vanguards. That vigorous debate, Giau learned, had helped Tap to recover.

The story of Ha Huy Tap not only suggested the power of ideas and ideological belief to revolutionaries but also is instructive for a reassessment of Vietnamese communism in the 1930s. This period has been viewed as the lost decade for Vietnamese communism. Huynh Kim Khanh writes:

[B]y early 1935, the ICP had thus come to an apparent dead end...By sacrificing traditional Vietnamese patriotism to proletarian internationalism, the ICP had of its own volition left the mainstream of Vietnamese politics. As the Party submitted itself totally to the will of the Comintern, ... under the command of

[93] Ibid., 66–68.
[94] Tran Van Giau, *Hoi Ky 1940–1945* [Memoirs]. Available at www.tapchithoidai.org/ThoiDai21/TranVanGiau_HoiKy_ToanBo.pdf.

Moscow-trained left-wing sectarians, the once popular revolutionary movement built by Nguyen Ai Quoc and his comrades in Thanh Nien had become a nonentity among Vietnamese.[95]

The decline of the ICP continued until the end of that decade, Huynh claims. By the eve of the Second World War, by "blindly accepting instructions from the Comintern, lacking a universally accepted leadership and a revolutionary line suitable to Vietnam's conditions, ... the ICP had "foundered in ideological confusion and interfactional disputes."[96] To Huynh, the roots of the problems facing the ICP were the "eclipse" of Nguyen Ai Quoc by those "Moscow-trained professional revolutionaries" like Tap and Phong. Although Quinn-Judge does not make such sweeping claims in her biography of Ho Chi Minh as Huynh does, she describes the period of Quoc's absence as one marked by "fragmentation."[97]

It is true that factional disputes existed between Stalinists and Trotskyists, such as that between Tap and Thau. Nevertheless, those disputes did not bring about ideological confusion. They indicated not fragmentation but polarization. We have seen how Quoc's concept of the Vietnamese revolution evolved during the 1920s and became integrated into world revolution. The disputes between Vietnamese Stalinists and Trotskyists in the 1930s was a sign that the Vietnamese revolution had been fully internationalized and come to reflect fully the polarization within the international communist movement. Rather than generating ideological confusion, polarization radicalized Vietnamese Stalinists like Phong, Tap, and Quoc, deepening their loyalty to Stalin and to the Soviet Union.[98]

Despite two complete turnovers of leadership, continuity and unity within the ICP were far more significant than conventionally believed. ICP leaders were firm in their Marxist-Leninist worldview, which they continued to adjust to changing reality while preserving its core. To them, Marxism-Leninism was not a dogma in the sense of a theory existing in isolation and independent from reality. They were always clear about the distinction between vision and tactics; the latter being flexible but the former not. Significantly, Phong and Tap were not the dogmatic leaders that existing scholarship leads us to believe. Within the leadership, Tran

[95] Huynh, *Vietnamese Communism*, 188.
[96] Ibid., 230–231.
[97] Quinn-Judge, *Ho Chi Minh*, 190.
[98] Both Huynh Kim Khanh and Sophie Quinn-Judge are silent about Quoc's well-documented vicious criticisms of Trotskyists and his admiration for Stalin's show trials.

Phu, Le Hong Phong, and Ha Huy Tap built on the work of Nguyen Ai Quoc and they rarely, if ever, criticized him personally.

A distinct characteristic of the 1930s compared to the previous and following decades was the strong leadership of the Comintern over the ICP. Moscow not only supplied its ICP branch with resources but also with ideas about the world situation. It would have been extremely difficult for ICP leaders to gain an adequate understanding of Marxism-Leninism without the training offered in Moscow. It would have been impossible for them to develop and maintain a global worldview of revolution and counterrevolution without having access to debates in the international communist movement, and often to specific guidelines from the Comintern.

As in the previous decade, ideology was crucial to Vietnamese communists in the 1930s. Ideology helped Tap, Phong, Cu, and their comrades to persevere in extremely difficult situations. It helped them to place the Vietnamese revolution in a world historical context and to interpret the causes and likely consequences of world events such as the Second World War. Based on such interpretations, they were able to devise appropriate strategies for their revolution. Ideology also brought material support from the Soviet Union and its sponsored transnational network of communist and worker movements. This network enabled the Vietnamese movement to recover from near-complete destruction by colonial suppression in 1931. This network also helped Vietnamese revolutionaries to coordinate their strategies with the world communist and worker movement. However, the global movement and transnational network were useful to Vietnamese revolutionaries only at that moment, but did not help them to succeed eventually. If the Soviet Union had lost to Germany, Vietnamese communists would have been doomed. But their bet paid off, as we will see in the next chapter.

3

The Making of a Cold War Outpost
in Indochina, 1940–1951

The 1940s did not open well for Indochinese Communism. Colonial authorities captured nearly the entire central leadership by early 1940. The loss of France to Germany in mid-1940 turned out to be a false opportunity for the Party's Southern Regional Committee to launch an armed revolt in the Mekong Delta in November of that year. The revolt was immediately crushed and the southern base of the Party devastated.[1] By the end of the decade, however, the Party had succeeded in seizing power and creating the Democratic Republic of Vietnam (DRV). Although the French still controlled about half the country, the DRV had achieved significant mass support and was recognized by a dozen states, including the Soviet Union and communist China.

Many factors contributed to the reversal of fortune for the communists. Their northern base survived French repression and formed the nucleus of a new central leadership that included Nguyen Ai Quoc when he returned in 1941. The Japanese coup against the French in March 1945 further weakened colonial control and allowed the Party to spread its influence. Japanese ruthless extraction of resources produced a famine in northern Vietnam in mid-1945. Between one-half and two million deaths were estimated to die of starvation.[2] When Japan surrendered to

---

[1] Tran Giang, *Nam Ky Khoi Nghia: 23 thang 11 nam 1940* [The Southern uprising: November 23, 1940] (Hanoi: Chinh tri Quoc gia, 1996).

[2] Nguyen The Anh, "Japanese Food Policies and the 1945 Great Famine in Indochina," in Paul Kratoska, ed. *Food Supplies and the Japanese Occupation in South-East Asia* (New York: St. Martin's Press, 1998), 208–226; Motoo Furuta and Van Tao, *Nan Doi nam 1945 o Viet Nam: Nhung Chung tich lich su* [The famine of 1945 in Vietnam: Historical evidence] (Hanoi: Khoa hoc Xa hoi, 2005).

the Allies, mass riots and uprisings took place in Vietnam's major towns and cities in an event dubbed "the August Revolution" in Vietnamese history. The communists rode to power on the back of that massive popular discontent and enormous outpouring of nationalism.[3] Yet the French soon returned to reclaim their colony. Despite Ho Chi Minh's repeated appeals, Washington refused to recognize his government, as did Moscow. The victory of Chinese communists on mainland China in late 1949 and subsequent Chinese assistance helped the DRV to break through the stalemate in its war with the French.

One of the most enduring myths of the Vietnam War concerns the "lost opportunity" thesis, which blames the United States for the DRV's decision to join the Soviet camp in 1950.[4] According to this thesis, the Vietnam War could have been avoided if President Truman had offered diplomatic recognition to Ho's government when it was formed in late 1945. A similar myth about America's "lost chance" in China has long been debunked, and the evidence in this chapter hopefully can put its Vietnamese counterpart to rest.[5] In particular, Ho and his comrades displayed loyalty to the Soviet Union and communist China throughout the 1940s even when there was neither contact nor assistance, when Soviet forces were crumbling under German assaults, and when Mao's Red Army was isolated in the northwest corner of China. Left alone by their international brothers in late 1945, they reached out to the United States, and for domestic mobilization they emphasized national unity. Yet their dedication to world revolution remained intact, if now carefully concealed. In their strategic considerations, the United States was a key player but never the only factor. Although anxious to obtain diplomatic recognition from other countries, they cheered Stalin when he

[3] Stein Tønnesson, *The Vietnamese Revolution of 1945* (Newbury Park, CA: SAGE Publications, 1991); Marr, *Vietnam 1945: The Quest for Power* (Berkeley: University of California Press, 1995); Vu, *Paths to Development in Asia: South Korea, Vietnam, China, and Indonesia* (New York: Cambridge University Press, 2008), ch. 5 and 6.

[4] See Bradley, *Imagining Vietnam and America: The Making of Postcolonial Vietnam 1919–1950* (Chapel: University of North Carolina Press, 2000); Robert McNamara, James Blight, and Robert Brigham, *Argument without End* (New York: Public Affairs, 1999); George Kahin, *Intervention: How America Became Involved in Vietnam* (New York: Knopf, 1986). See also the memoir by Archimedes Patti, *Why Vietnam? Prelude to America's Albatross* (Berkeley: University of California Press, 1980).

[5] See Chen Jian, "The Myth of America's 'Lost Chance' in China: A Chinese Perspective in Light of New Evidence," *Diplomatic History* 21:1 (Winter 1997), 77–86; and Chen Jian, *Mao's China and the Cold War* (Chapel Hill: University of North Carolina Press, 2001).

confronted the United States in Berlin. With volatile French politics and with an imminent communist victory in China, they dreamed of a revolutionary front extending from Paris to Indochina via Moscow and Beijing. Thanks to Mao's support, they did everything they could to persuade an uninterested Stalin to admit Vietnam into the Soviet camp. That was how the Soviet Union and communist China were drawn into Indochina. As in Korea, the tail wagged the dog.

Proponents of the lost-opportunity thesis are thus correct that Vietnamese communists were no stooges of Moscow or Beijing. Yet the paradox that is difficult for those scholars to understand is that Vietnamese communist leaders were independently minded but loyal to Moscow at the same time. The solution to the paradox must be found in their view of the world, which was seen in binary, not bipolar, terms. The USSR was the only socialist country on earth before 1945, but a socialist camp emerged following the Second World War. Although Vietnamese communists considered the Soviet Union the center of the socialist camp, Soviet position was viewed as a given historical condition. Soviet leadership did not mean Soviet domination, and Vietnam's junior status in the camp did not imply inferiority or subservience. In fact, Vietnamese national independence and its socialist identity would be mutually reinforcing because the Vietnamese revolution was a component of world revolution. Independent Vietnam was expected to exist and thrive within the family of socialist states, and *only* within that family.

Understanding their binary worldview is essential to explaining why DRV leaders welcomed the Cold War. In fact, the war was precisely what they had looked forward to. It vindicated their beliefs about the fundamental cleavage in international politics between capitalism and communism, between revolutionaries and counterrevolutionaries. It allowed them to proudly display their revolutionary credentials and to work immediately on realizing their radical ambitions. Until then, the revolution had been making empty promises to peasants; the Cold War allowed Vietnamese communists to finally implement their cherished but long delayed land reform.

IMPERIALIST WAR, SOCIALIST PEACE

The Eighth Plenum was convened by Nguyen Ai Quoc in mid-1941, whose name was now "Old Thu" and who would soon adopt still another name: Ho Chi Minh.[6] At this Plenum, Quoc was asked to assume the

---

[6] Truong Chinh, Hoang Quoc Viet, and Hoang Van Thu who attended the Seventh Plenum were present. Besides Quoc, other new participants at the Eighth Plenum included Phung

leadership of the Indochinese Communist Party (ICP) but he declined. According to Truong Chinh, Quoc said that as a Comintern official, he might be transferred to work elsewhere on the Comintern's order and could not serve as the general secretary of the Party.[7] Quoc proposed that Truong Chinh take the position, which he did. As in 1930, Quoc again did not seize the opportunity to personally lead the ICP when he was in a position to do so.

The resolution of this Plenum sounded optimistic about world developments. It was clear by then that the Second World War was on a larger scale and more destructive than the First. To ICP leaders, both were wars among imperialist powers for colonies and markets, but the greater scale of the second one indicated the greater extent of conflict among them. Significantly, the Second World War occurred after the birth of the Soviet Union, "a socialist country of one-sixth of world's area having very important economic and political status and being the pillar of peace and the fatherland of the world's proletariat."[8] In this war, some weak nations such as China had been able to resist fascist aggression. The world's proletariat this time was also much better organized under Comintern leadership. These differences meant that this war would offer an auspicious opportunity for the world revolutionary movement to destroy imperialism. The resolution thus predicted that, if the First World War had given birth to the Soviet Union, the Second would engender many successful revolutions and midwife many more socialist countries.[9]

The war continued to reinforce ICP leaders' view of a bifurcated world. In the Plenum's resolution, the contrast between the Soviet Union and the capitalist world was again described in vivid terms: "while the whole world was drawn by the imperialists into a ferocious massacre, only the Soviet Union enjoyed peace."[10] Thanks to its "wise and determined" policy to pursue peace, the resolution explained, the Soviet Union had been able to expand its border and prevented the war from spreading

---

Chi Kien, Vu Anh, Hoang Van Hoan (some sessions), and two unidentified representatives from central and south Vietnam.

[7] Pham Hong Chuong, Do Dinh Hang, Trieu Quang Tien, et al., eds., *Truong Chinh Tieu Su* [Biography of Truong Chinh] (Hanoi: Chinh tri Quoc gia, 2007), 143, citing a typed document titled "Hoi tuong cua dong chi Truong Chinh" [Reminiscences by Comrade Truong Chinh], archived at Ho Chi Minh Institute in Hanoi. See a similar interpretation in William Duiker, *Ho Chi Minh*, 256 (Duiker does not cite his sources though).

[8] "Trung Uong Hoi Nghi Lan Thu Tam" [The Eighth Central Committee Plenum], May 1941. *VKDTT*, v. 7, 98.

[9] Ibid., 100.

[10] Ibid., 102.

to Eastern Europe. The Soviet Union now had "the most powerful army in the world fully armed with advanced weapons." It was ready to deal with any imperialist aggression and had been selflessly helping "small nations" such as China to combat fascism. On the other hand, in the imperialist camp, the United States was again depicted as cunningly profiteering from the war; it did not fight but sold weapons to both sides so that they could slaughter each other.

The analysis of domestic politics in the resolution appeared more nuanced than its treatment of international affairs. Instead of a simple picture of "the ICP vs. the rest," the analysis counted the ICP as one of the anti-Japanese parties (still the best though), and also discussed briefly pro-Japanese parties.[11] The resolution had a section on "the national issue," pointing out how ethnic groups in Indochina had been divided and turned against each other by the French. To defeat the French and the Japanese, all Indochinese peoples must unite because just one or two groups would not have sufficient strength. As the largest ethnic group, the Vietnamese should lead and help others. Once independence had been achieved, ICP leaders believed that minorities should be offered the right to self-determination.[12]

The class analysis in the resolution showed an appreciation of social and political changes in favor of the revolution. Under Japan's cruel exploitation of resources in Indochina, "the attitudes of various classes" toward revolution had shifted.[13] The working class, peasants, and the petit bourgeois all became more supportive of revolution. Even landlords, rich peasants, and many capitalists had become either neutral or sympathetic rather than hostile. The use of "attitudes" [*thai do*] instead of "interests" [*quyen loi*] indicated a more flexible approach toward class analysis. *Thai do* was manipulable; *quyen loi* was tied to the economic structure and was relatively fixed. Based on this new analysis, the Party authorized the creation of a popular front named League for Independent Vietnam, or Viet Minh, to mobilize support from all classes for national independence.

It was not the first time, as often believed, that the ICP decided to place national interests above those of class. A similar tactical move had been adopted at the Sixth Plenum in late 1939 (see Chapter 2). The new element at the Eighth Plenum was the justifications provided for that move.

---

[11] Ibid., 109–10.
[12] Ibid., 113–114.
[13] Ibid., 115–117.

Specifically, it was argued that national liberation would not necessarily delay the social revolution for two reasons. First, once the ICP had seized the leadership of the movement for national liberation, it could easily direct this movement toward serving the socialist cause. Second, the Indochinese movement was unlikely to be the only one in the world. By the time it succeeded, "the world would be [in turmoil] like a boiling pot." That situation would allow the ICP to leap forward to launch a proletarian revolution and create a socialist Indochina.[14]

After Germany invaded the Soviet Union in late June 1941, supporting the Soviet Union became a main activity on the ICP agenda.[15] The Eighth Plenum resolution explained that supporting the Soviet Union meant working for Indochinese independence, because if the Soviet Union won the war, it would in turn help to liberate Indochina from French and Japanese rule. The Party instructed its members to disseminate propaganda about this issue in order to mobilize mass support for the Soviet Union, to form "Friends of the Soviet Union" groups, and to raise donations for the Soviet Red Army. Indigenous troops under the colonial government also needed to be educated about this issue because one day they might be sent by the Pétain government to fight against the Soviet Union.

In his capacity as editor in chief, main contributor, illustrator, and printing worker of *Viet Nam Doc Lap* (Independent Vietnam), the Viet Minh's weekly newsletter, Nguyen Ai Quoc focused on cultivating national consciousness and anticolonial sentiments among his readers, but he never neglected the Soviet Union.[16] To raise support for Moscow, the newsletter published regular news of the war that exaggerated Soviet success in combat while advertising the Soviet paradise to Vietnamese readers. One account of the war went as follows, "Russia is a revolutionary state. In this country, people enjoy freedom, equality [and] happiness. Externally she does not bully other countries but helps the oppressed nations. Germany is a fascist state, meaning she is extremely cruel and only wants to invade other countries. In this country people live hard

---

[14] Ibid., 120–121.

[15] "Phai ung ho Lien Bang Xo Viet," [We must support the Soviet Union], October 31, 1941. *VKDTT*, v. 7, 203–205. See also "Nghi quyet cua Hoi nghi can bo toan xu Bac ky" [Resolution of the Tonkin Cadre Meeting], September 25–27, 1941. *VKDTT*, v. 7, 189–190.

[16] Quoc founded the newsletter in August 1941 and ran it from then until August 1942 when he left for China. See Bao Tang Cach Mang Viet Nam, *Bao Viet Nam Doc Lap 1941–1945* [The *Viet Nam Doc Lap* newspaper 1941–1945] (Hanoi: Lao Dong, 2000), esp. the introduction by Pham Mai Hung. This volume contains the entire collection of *Viet Nam Doc Lap* held at the Revolutionary Museum in Hanoi.

lives. If Germany wins, the whole of mankind will be enslaved. Only if Russia wins can the world see glorious days."[17] In another article, it was reported that, "[i]n the 5 months since the war began, Germany has suffered 4.5 million casualties, whereas Russia lost only 1.4 million people... In many German cities, most soldiers are only 15 or 16 years old. Officers are only 17 or 18 years old because older officers and soldiers have all been killed or wounded."[18]

In an article entitled "What Kind of Country Is Russia?" we can see a different version of Tran Dinh Long's account in Chapter 1, but this time the story was targeted to uneducated Vietnamese.[19] As this article claimed, Russia was the largest country in the world. Twenty years ago, Russians had been forced to do *corvée* work [*di phu*], paid taxes, and had been "exploited, oppressed, poor and ignorant like [Vietnamese]." Thanks to Russians' "unity and struggle," the emperor was overthrown in 1917, and since then the people had enjoyed "equality, freedom, and happiness." Currently, Russian workers worked only seven hours a day, had a day off for every five days working, had a one-month vacation every year, and "good salaries" on top of those. Peasants had all the land they needed and could borrow plowing and harvesting tractors [*may cay, may gat*] from the state [*nha nuoc*]. A peasant received at least five kilograms of rice [sic] a day; everybody had more clothes and food than he needed. Many women became mandarins [*lam quan*], doctors, and pilots; they enjoyed all the rights men had. Children, regardless of male or female, had to go to school at least up to 16 years of age. Schools were free. The state took care of children and old people, and assigned doctors to treat sick people. The people were free to elect their hamlet chiefs [*ly truong*], village chiefs [*chanh tong*] and the head of the country. If they were not happy with these officials, they could sack them. "No one is oppressed, unlike in our country."

---

[17] "Nga-Duc chien tranh" [Russia-Germany war], *Viet Nam Doc Lap* no. 109, October 21, 1941. The style of this article suggests it was likely to have been written by Nguyen Ai Quoc.

[18] For a sympathetic but realistic account in the colonial press about the Soviet situation, see "Tinh hinh cua Nga tuy nguy ngap nhung Hong quan con du suc khang chien" [Russia in great danger but still able to hold on], *Dien Tin*, October 15, 1941.

[19] B. V. [a pseudonym], "Nga la nuoc the nao?" *Viet Nam Doc Lap* n. 126, July 11, 1942. Nguyen Ai Quoc was likely to be the author of this article. The use of "Nga" (Russia) instead of "Lien Xo" (the Soviet Union) in this context indicated the writer's effort to talk in the language of ordinary people. "Nga" is Vietnamized to a greater extent and more commonly used word than "Lien Xo," which also sounds formal.

Although ICP leaders had long sought to introduce the Soviet paradise to Vietnamese, the significance of this article was its publication at a time when national independence and unity were supposed to be the first priority of the Vietnamese revolution, when German tanks were amassed at the gate of Moscow, and when no contacts existed between the Comintern and the ICP. The article displayed its author's deep commitment to the Soviet Union as well as his talent in targeting propaganda to the uneducated. The extremely high quality of life in the Soviet Union (especially compared to Vietnam) gave the Soviet image a mythical aura; yet the details made it believable. Foreign concepts (*nha nuoc, may cay, may gat*) were interspersed with familiar ones (*di phu, gao, lam quan, ly truong, chanh tong*), making the myth both novel yet accessible to ordinary Vietnamese.

THEORETICAL AND PROPAGANDA CHALLENGES

The attack on Pearl Harbor in December of 1941 suddenly opened up the possibility of an Allied invasion of Indochina. ICP leaders continued to bet Indochina's destiny with the Soviet Union and world revolution.[20] The world was still divided into two camps [*phe*], but these were now overlaid by two fronts [*mat tran*]: the fascist front and the antifascist front. England and the United States were now allies with the Soviet Union in the same antifascist front, but they were not to be fully trusted. ICP leaders called on British and American workers to apply pressure on the capitalists in their countries so that they would fight fascism to the end; otherwise, they might capitulate to the fascists and turn to fight the Soviet Union instead.

Yet the possibility of GMD Chinese, British, and American troops entering Indochina required the ICP to be more accommodating to those governments. To the Guomindang (GMD) government, ICP leaders called for cooperation on an equal status [*binh dang tuong tro*]; the Chinese nationalist government needed to understand that its forces were in Indochina not to conquer it but to help themselves.[21] To the British and Americans, the ICP proposed "conditional concession and alliance" [*nhan nhuong lien hiep co dieu kien*]. If they helped the Indochinese revolution, the Party was willing to grant them certain privileges in Indochina.

---

[20] "Cuoc chien tranh Thai binh duong va trach nhiem can kip cua Dang" [The Pacific War and the urgent tasks facing the Party], December 21, 1941. *VKDTT*, v. 7, 238–253.
[21] Ibid., 243–244.

If they helped De Gaulle to reinstate the colonial system in Indochina, the ICP would denounce them and continue the struggle for independence. The Party warned its members that they should harbor no illusions that those countries would offer Vietnam freedom for free. It also assured its members that collaboration with the British and the Americans did not mean the Party was "serving the interests of imperialism," but that this collaboration was necessary to defeat the fascists.

As the war intensified in 1942, the Soviet-US-British alliance was formally established.[22] In response to the new international situation, top ICP leaders gathered and issued changes in policies.[23] The resolution of this meeting indicated their uneasiness with the new phenomenon that apparently contradicted their binary worldview. At one level, the fundamental cleavage remained the same in their thought: "the socialist system which represented *the new world* was combating the fascist system which was the most corrupt and barbaric part of *the old world*."[24] The same old question still haunted the Party: Why did imperialist America and England ally with the Soviet Union against fascism? Why didn't they help Hitler to destroy the Soviet Union? To these questions the resolution offered two answers. First, American and British capitalists wanted to defeat Germany to retake what the latter had taken from them. Second, the British and American masses protested and demanded their governments to fight fascism.[25] In allying themselves with the Soviet Union, these capitalist governments were primarily motivated by imperialist interests but at the same time had to acknowledge [*nhin nhan*] certain legitimate interests of "the people" in their countries and their colonies. In any case, this was possible because "the bourgeois democratic regimes in these countries still existed and people were struggling to demand greater [democracy]." This fact allowed these countries to be called "democratic" and be part of the antifascist front led by the Soviet Union. Their war against fascism was no longer an imperialist war but a "progressive war."

The resolution insisted that British and American masses should keep struggling until their governments opened a second front in Europe to share the burden with the Soviet Union. At the end of this war, the

---

[22] This was the result of the meeting between Stalin and Churchill in May 1942.

[23] "Nghi quyet cua Ban Thuong vu Trung uong," [Resolution of the Standing Committee of the Central Committee], February 25–28, 1943. *VKDTT*, v. 7, 272–315. The resolution stated that a Central Committee meeting was needed, given the new important developments, but convening such a meeting was not feasible.

[24] Ibid., 275. Italics added.

[25] Ibid., 274.

resolution predicted, "bourgeois democratic England and America" would become very different and much more democratic.[26] They would be willing to collaborate with the Soviet Union to "organize world peace." In any case, if the American and British capitalist ruling class did not keep their promises, they would be overthrown by the Soviet Union and by world revolution.

Overall, this document sounded optimistic about new developments in world politics. ICP leaders could not interpret those developments very well with their ideological tools, but they were ingenious in finding answers without abandoning their two-camp worldview. Significantly, the progressive policies that imperialist countries made were attributed to their people, not to the "ruling classes" or the governments. The "counterrevolutionary nature of imperialist states" remained unchanged.

In contrast with images of British and American governments being driven by imperialist interests but forced to accommodate popular demands, the Soviet Union again appeared as a benevolent world power. The Soviet Union had retreated in the early months following the German blitzkrieg "in part because it did not produce enough weaponry right away and in part because it wanted to prolong the war."[27] It wasn't losing but was only waiting for the consolidation of the international democratic front and also for revolutionary movements in other countries to get ready for the opportunity. In other words, the Soviets were accepting losses to themselves for the sake of world revolution. Among other tasks, ICP leaders called on Party members to do a better job in mobilizing mass support for the Soviet resistance.[28]

In mid-1943, the dissolution of the Comintern posed another theoretical and propaganda challenge to ICP leaders. The Party's claim to leadership in the Indochinese revolution depended in part on its association with the Comintern. The Comintern had also been portrayed as the leader of world revolution. To reassure its ranks who must have wondered why the Comintern dissolved itself at such a critical time of war and revolution, the Party explained that the Soviet Union needed "to join hands with a relatively progressive section of the international bourgeoisie" in their war against fascism.[29] This act was to fend off two possible scenarios. The first involved the United States, England, and the

---

[26] Ibid., 279.
[27] Ibid., 278.
[28] Ibid., 302–304.
[29] "Day manh cuoc chien tranh chong phat xit xam luoc" [Stepping up the fight against the fascists], November 12–13, 1943. *VKDTT*, v. 7, 322–326.

Axis powers forming a joint imperialist front to attack the Soviet Union; and the second involved the United States and England standing by, saving their forces, and dominating the world once the Axis powers and the Soviet Union had destroyed each other. The announcement assured Party members that the ICP still stood firm and called on them to cast off their doubts and to resist criticisms of the Soviet Union by Vietnamese Trotskyists and other groups.

Because an Allies' invasion of Indochina seemed imminent in November 1944, Viet Minh's journal *Cuu Quoc* [Save the Nation] published a special issue on the "overseas problem" [*van de hai ngoai*].[30] This issue was directed to the various exiled Vietnamese groups in southern China; it called for those groups to unite under Viet Minh leadership to welcome Allied forces entering Vietnam to fight the Japanese. In this publication, ICP leaders maintained the same guarded attitude toward GMD China and Western capitalist states as usual. The journal advised its readers not to place their full trust in the promise made at the Moscow conference by England and the United States that all they wanted was to liberate Asian peoples from Japanese domination. If the Vietnamese were not prepared when Allied forces entered Indochina, ICP leaders argued, those forces would not hesitate to carry out their hidden plan of occupying Vietnam. They would set up a puppet regime or help the French resurrect the colonial system.

In mid-1945, however, Party documents showed a friendlier attitude toward Washington and Chongqing. A Party document in April 1945, following the Japanese overthrow of French rule in Indochina, noted the San Francisco Conference and the Hot Springs meeting.[31] The United States and GMD China were praised for taking a "progressive stand" toward former French colonies in contrast to "British hesitancy" and "French stubbornness." China had been "democratized": the Chongqing government had been reformed and the negotiations between the GMD and the CCP had borne some fruits. The Philippines now enjoyed "autonomy" [*quyen tu chu*]. This friendly attitude could have resulted from increased contacts between Ho Chi Minh and the American Office of Strategic Services (OSS) team in southern China at the time. However, when the chips were down, the binary worldview of ICP leaders remained unchanged.

---

[30] *Cuu Quoc*, November 1944, 18 (Copy courtesy of the Revolutionary Museum in Hanoi).
[31] "Nghi quyet Hoi nghi quan su Bac ky" [Resolution of Northern Regional Military Conference], April 15–20, 1945. *VKDTT*, v. 7, 382. It is assumed that the view in this resolution broadly reflected that of central leaders.

On the eve of the Japanese surrender, the resolution of a key Party meeting at Tan Trao, at which Ho presided, offered no lengthy analysis but a brief, bulleted discussion of foreign policy issues.[32] The resolution pointed out that thanks to the war, the Soviet Union expanded its borders and China and other countries were liberated. The fascist states were destroyed, resulting in a weaker world capitalist system. The war did not result in a worldwide socialist revolution but it did create favorable conditions for such a revolution by spreading "new democracies" all over the world.

The document noted two salient aspects of the situation in Indochina. The different attitudes toward the colonies between the United States and GMD China on the one hand, and France and England on the other, would favor the Indochinese revolution. However, because of their antagonism toward the Soviet Union, England and the United States could also allow France to return to Indochina. Why Washington and London must or would be antagonistic toward Moscow (note that at the time they were still cooperating to combat fascism) was left unexplained. What the Soviet Union would have to do with Indochina, or why it would be interested in Indochina was similarly assumed but not explained. Underlying this analysis was the entrenched perception of a divided world and the assumption that Indochinese destiny lay with the Soviet camp even at the height of US-Viet Minh collaboration. The United States, England, and GMD China were subjects of manipulation, never treated as true friends, as the Soviet Union was.

IMPERIALIST LIES, SOCIALIST TRUTHS

After proclaiming independence in September 1945 and establishing a new Democratic Republic of Vietnam (DRV) in Hanoi, Ho's government was soon confronted in the North by GMD Chinese military and their Vietnamese nationalist protégés, and in the South by British occupation forces that brought back thousands of French troops.[33] As president and foreign minister of the new state, Ho pursued a foreign policy that has been labeled as "adding friends and reducing enemies." This policy involved two prongs. One was to send out repeated messages and

---

[32] "Nghi quyet cua Toan quoc Hoi nghi Dang Cong san Dong duong" [Resolution of the All-Nation ICP Conference, August 14–15, 1945. *VKDTT*, v. 7, 423–433.

[33] For accounts of this event, see Tønnesson, *The Vietnamese Revolution of 1945*; Stein Tønnesson, *Vietnam 1946: How the War Began* (Berkeley: University of California Press, 2010).

missions to appeal for international support, especially from Washington and Moscow. Ho's widely quoted declaration of independence that used the language of the American Revolution was part of this strategy. This pragmatic approach involved both existing and new elements: Viet Minh had been courting American and GMD Chinese aid at least since 1944, but secret cables to Stalin marked the first time Vietnamese communist leaders attempted to resume contact with Moscow since Ho left the Soviet Union in late 1938.[34]

The second prong was to negotiate first with the GMD occupation authorities and then with the returning French, if not for Vietnam's full independence, then for some forms of autonomy and the recognition of the Viet Minh government as the sole authority of Vietnam. A key decision was to publicly dissolve the ICP to indicate to both domestic and foreign audiences that his government was not communist (the ICP was in fact not dissolved but went underground, disguised under the name of Association for Marxist Studies). How GMD generals reacted to this event is not known, but this decision, which has been attributed to Ho, would dog him later with internal criticisms and suspicions from his international communist allies.[35] At the same time, it failed to ease the American doubts about Ho's communist ties.

Efforts to "add friends" would continue through 1947 with secret missions to court foreign support. In one such mission, the DRV's representative even offered special trading privileges for American companies in return for American goods and loans.[36] Bradley argues that this gesture signaled the DRV's serious interest in developing "realistic and long-term alliance" with the United States.[37] He acknowledges that sentiments hostile to the United States began to be voiced in ICP documents in late 1945, but dismisses those negative views as "muted" and as merely revealing the tensions among various perspectives held by Vietnamese leaders rather than exposing the lack of "sincerity" in the DRV's diplomatic maneuvers.

Presented as isolated incidents, such expressions of anti-American sentiments indeed may have meant little. However, anti-imperialist

---

[34] Duiker, *Ho Chi Minh*, 282–303; Quinn-Judge, *Ho Chi Minh*, 221–235.

[35] See Christopher Goscha, "Courting Diplomatic Disaster?: The Difficult Integration of Vietnam into the Internationalist Communist Movement (1945–1950)," *Journal of Vietnamese Studies* 1: 1 (2006): 59–103. French historians have also suggested that many leaders such as Truong Chinh and Hoang Quoc Viet were critical of Ho's policy to negotiate with the French. See Phillipe Devillers and Jean Lacouture, *End of a War* (New York: Praeger, 1969), 11.

[36] Bradley, *Imagining Vietnam*, 127–133.

[37] Ibid., 151.

thoughts among ICP members had been deep, systematic, consistent, and longstanding throughout. It is true that the isolated and encircled DRV was serious in obtaining US diplomatic recognition; given the profound attachment of its leaders to social and world revolution, it would be a mistake to infer that ICP leaders now considered the GMD and the United States friends.[38] Next, I will examine the substantial amount of documents and other writings that caution us not to attribute any long-term significance to those diplomatic offers.

Several ICP documents dated in November 1945 displayed strong suspicions of US and GMD motives together with a prophetic vision of a coming Cold War. In its analysis of international conditions, a key document issued by the Central Committee pointed out four main antagonisms [*mau thuan*] in the world.[39] These were (1) the Soviet Union versus the imperialist states, (2) the world's proletariat versus capitalist class, (3) the oppressed peoples versus colonialism, and (4) antagonism among the imperialist states themselves. The Soviet Union was "quietly rebuilding itself and urgently developed advanced machines and weapons to improve the living standards of its people and to defend itself." The Soviet press had acknowledged the legitimacy of the struggles in Indochina and Indonesia for independence. In contrast, England, the United States, and Canada wanted to form "an Anglo-Saxon bloc" directed against the Soviet Union. (But "Soviet calmness and determination overawed them"). The United States did not want to attack the Soviet Union yet, but it had encouraged GMD troops to fire at the Chinese Red Army "to scare the Soviet Union." The United States announced that it was neutral, but, in fact, it was secretly helping France by lending ships to carry French troops to Indochina. On one hand, the United States wanted to compete with England and France for political and economic domination in Southeast Asia; on the other, it also wanted to collaborate with them to encircle the Soviet Union. For this purpose the United States would be ready to sacrifice its own interests in Southeast Asia. The fourth antagonism was thus not sufficient to override the first three, which were simply an extended version of the two-camp view.[40]

---

[38] For a similar view, see Duiker, *Ho Chi Minh*, 573–574.

[39] "Chi thi cua Ban Chap hanh Trung uong ve khang chien kien quoc" [Directive of the Central Committee about resistance and nation-building], November 25, 1945. *VKDTT*, v. 8, 21–34.

[40] In a subsequent instruction issued after the Sino-French agreement to let French troops replace GMD Chinese troops in North Vietnam, it was similarly claimed that England and the United States wanted the French and the Dutch to retake control of Indochina

The ICP had already been predicting the Cold War long before it spread to Asia. The same document noted the tumultuous character of world politics at the time: wars for independence in Southeast Asia, the civil war in China, labor protests in England, and US-Soviet tension over the occupation of Japan.[41] It noted that mankind was experiencing a postwar crisis but this crisis would not lead to a Third World War between the United States and the Soviet Union. Instead, there would be a peaceful and democratizing period before a new era of war and revolution started. War between the United States and the Soviet Union would not start immediately because "the forces for peace" were stronger than "those for war" at that time. Elements of the forces for peace included movements led by the American Communist Party against American policies to increase tension with the Soviet Union and to intervene into China; popular protests against the British government for assisting French and Dutch colonialists; social movements in the West to support independence for India and Indochina; and "new scientific inventions" [read: atomic bombs] in the Soviet Union. War between the imperialist and socialist camps would be inevitable, though which form it would take was not specified. However, ICP leaders did not look forward to a Third World War; they stressed that the struggles for independence in Indochina and Indonesia as well as the civil war in China would not lead to such a war but would lead to more peace.[42] This reasoning implied their lack of interest beyond Indochina. Perhaps they would be satisfied after their Indochinese struggle succeeded; world revolution to overthrow world capitalism (in World War III) would be something of a long-term commitment.

In late 1945 the Viet Minh government under Ho ostensibly focused on the anticolonial struggle while rejecting social revolution. However, a different and thinly veiled face of this government is found in *Su That* [Truth], the biweekly journal of the Association for Marxist Studies in Indochina (the disguised ICP). In the editorial of its debut issue in late 1945 *Su That* bluntly claimed that one of its missions was "to show all fellow Indochinese a basic truth: there was only one way to achieve freedom, peace, and happiness for mankind, for every nation and for the

and Indonesia so that they could devote their efforts to encircling the Soviet Union. "Tinh hinh va chu truong" [The current situation and our policy], March 3, 1946. *VKDTT*, v. 8, 41.
[41] "Chi thi cua Ban Chap hanh Trung uong ve khang chien kien quoc," *VKDTT*, v. 8, 21–22.
[42] Ibid., 21. See also the editorial in *Su That*, January 17–20, 1946.

working class. This way was through the thorough implementation [*thuc hien triet de*] of Marxism."[43]

Despite ongoing diplomatic negotiations with France and overtures to the United States, secret Party documents and fiery articles in *Su That* frequently evoked the two-camp perspective. The "imperialist camp," now led by the United States, was viewed as significantly weaker (compared to before World War II); they needed time to "bandage their wounds" and prepare for an attack on the Soviet Union and nationalist movements in the colonies.[44] The "socialist forces," especially the Soviet Union, had become much stronger, but they were not powerful enough to destroy the capitalist system and establish a proletarian government to rule the world. Indochina had become an important zone of revolution, and Indochina was not alone. Elsewhere in Southeast Asia, England, the United States, and France had collaborated to set up an anticommunist front and suppress national liberation movements.

In discussing the Chinese civil war, an article in *Su That* denounced the United States for favoring the GMD, calling for the Soviet Union to play an equal role in mediation.[45] Although a noncommunist newspaper praised Washington for granting independence to the Philippines in July 1946,[46] *Su That* dismissed the American act as deception to mask American imperialism.[47] This act could hurt the reputation of other imperialist states (because they still wanted to retake their colonies), but it would help the United States achieve world hegemony [*ba quyen the gioi*] and would help consolidate the imperialist camp in their conspiracy against the Soviet Union and "world democratic forces."

Bui Cong Trung, a classmate of Tran Dinh Long in Moscow, argued in *Su That* by quoting Stalin that national liberation was inseparable from world revolution and class struggle.[48] Trung was perhaps responding to an article published earlier in *Chinh Nghia*, the theoretical journal

---

[43] *Su That*, December 5, 1945. As the ICP dissolved itself, it closed *Co Giai Phong* [Liberation Flag], the Party's journal up to then, and started *Su That*. *Su That* was under Truong Chinh's direct supervision. See Quang Dam, *Quang Dam: Nha Bao, Hoc Gia* (Hanoi: Lao Dong, 2002), 29.

[44] "Nghi quyet cua Hoi nghi Can bo Trung uong" [Resolution of the Central Cadre Conference], July 31–August 1, 1946. *VKDTT*, v. 8, 99.

[45] Tran Quoc Bao, "Van de Quoc Cong o Tau va chinh sach My" [The GMD-Communist conflict in China and US policy], *Su That*, July 5, 1946.

[46] *Dan Thanh* [The People's Voice] (Hanoi), July 4, 1946.

[47] Tran Quoc Bao, "Y nghia doc lap cua Phi luat tan" [The meaning of Filipino independence], *Su That*, July 12, 1946, 5.

[48] B. C. T. (Bui Cong Trung), "Thuyet dau tranh giai cap va van de dan toc" [The theory of class struggle and the national issue], *Su That*, July 5 and 12, 1946.

of the Vietnamese Nationalist Party; this article denied the relevance of class struggle for Vietnam where capitalism had not developed and all classes were exploited by the colonial system.[49] To those who argued that advanced capitalist societies had found ways to mitigate class struggle through the mediation between management and labor, Trung gave a stinging denunciation of American society:

No cities match New York as a capitalist paradise! But in April 1935, in the middle of this city full of skyscrapers, there were 600,000 families, a third of its population, living on donations by relief societies. In contrast, about 100 rich families in New York threw their money out the window [*tha ho tieu xai phung phi*]. A child of a millionaire spent on average $40,160 a year while 2,280,000 [poor] children had no money to pay for their schooling. The capitalist paradise has been built on the miseries of the working masses and the exploitation of small nations. We Marxists believe that, to escape from the capitalist hell, the proletariat all over the world must unite.

Although both Washington and Moscow were silent on the DRV's requests for recognition, ICP leaders denounced the United States but continued to find excuses for the Soviet Union. An example is the Moscow conference in January 1946, where Indochina was not even mentioned. An editorial in *Su That* warned its readers not to expect too much from this conference because France and China were not present.[50] But why didn't the Soviet representative bring up Indochina at the meeting? *Su That* speculated that the reason was because the Soviet Union needed British and French support to deal with the American threat. Indochina could still gain, however: the Soviet Union would join the United States in occupying Japan and participating in the Far East committee. "Of course the Soviet Union will raise its voice in matters concerning Indochina" because the Soviet Union was always loyal to the interests of weak nations and because "imperialist crooks are not free to make rains and sow winds [*lam mua lam gio*] in front of the Soviet Union, a first-rate world power with antifascist credentials." It would not be a bad idea, *Su That* argued, if Indochina (like Korea) could be freed from colonialism and temporarily placed under an international trusteeship supervised by the Soviet Union before achieving full independence. Although the Moscow conference had not met Indochinese demands for full independence, it "indirectly

---

[49] To Khanh, "Giai cap tranh dau hay dan toc tranh dau?" [Class struggle or national struggle?], *Chinh Nghia* (Hanoi), June 3, 1946.
[50] "Hoi nghi Mac tu khoa ve van de Dong Duong" [The Moscow conference on Indochina], *Su That*, January 12, 1946.

solved the Indochina problem and opened up the road for Indochina to move ahead."

The ICP view of two opposing camps further sharpened in the next two years and beyond. In this view, the "antidemocratic camp" continued to evolve with the United States being its leader; this camp was keen on encircling the Soviet Union and destroying world revolution. The United States in turn was seen as being dominated by financial cliques who cunningly expanded their power over the entire capitalist world.[51] The Marshall Plan was similarly a means for Washington to colonize Europe.[52] Although French and Dutch imperialists waged wars against anticolonial movements, England and the United States, "the old imperialist foxes," deceived the colonized peoples by granting mere formal independence to India, Burma, and the Philippines.[53] Their moves were to avoid war while hiding behind the "puppet governments" in those countries to continue exploiting and oppressing their peoples.

On the other hand, the "democratic camp" gradually took shape with closer collaboration between Eastern Europe and the Soviet Union, culminating in the formation of the Communist Information Bureau (Cominform) among European communist parties in September 1947. As political conditions in France became volatile in early 1948, ICP leaders were imagining a scenario of civil war in France, the collapse of the French government, and open American intervention in Indochina.[54] The Party realized that this could be a difficult situation for Indochina if the United States, counterrevolutionary France, England, and GMD China allied to fight French communist, Chinese, Indochinese, and Southeast Asian revolutions. The wonderful thing about this scenario was that it offered a good opportunity for the Chinese and Vietnamese revolutions to "harmonize their march forward" [*hoa nhip tien buoc*], and for the weak nations in Asia to build close links and unite with Western European revolutions. This scenario would be favorable for world revolution: the democratic front would have the opportunity to destroy imperialism, their common enemy, once and for all.

---

[51] "Nghi quyet Hoi nghi Can bo Trung uong" [Resolution of Central Cadre Conference], April 3–6, 1947. *VKDTT*, v. 8, 173–175.

[52] "Nghi quyet Hoi nghi Trung uong mo rong" [Resolution of Expanded Central Committee Conference], January 15–17, 1948. *VKDTT*, v. 9, 16.

[53] Truong Chinh, "Chung ta chien dau cho doc lap va dan chu" [We fight for independence and democracy], speech at the Fifth Cadre Conference, August 8–16, 1948 (Ban Chap hanh Lien khu Dang bo Lien khu X, 1948), 15–18.

[54] Ibid., 18–19.

Just as ICP leaders viewed the "antidemocratic camp" as being divided into different (capitalist, fascist, and military authoritarian) regimes, they did not view the "democratic camp" as a monolithic bloc of similar states directed by the Soviet Union.[55] In this view, the Soviet Union was a socialist state with a proletarian dictatorship. Eastern European countries, North Korea, communist-controlled China, and Vietnam were "people's democracies" where "dictatorships of the people are led by the proletariat." Thanks to Soviet help, the revolutionary path toward socialism in these countries might need less violence, but countries in the same camp faced different historical conditions and should pursue their own paths to socialism. ICP leaders did not hide the problems within the "democratic camp"; in response to questions about the Cominform's criticisms of Yugoslavian President Josip Tito, they explained that Tito was only "a straw stuck in the new democratic wheel that was rolling forward."[56] In his own speech, Ho was even blunter, calling Tito "America's running dog" [*cho san cua My*].[57] The case of Tito did not expose the weakness of the democratic camp; on the contrary, it indicated that the camp had "iron discipline" [*ky luat sat*] and would not "condone arrogant militaristic behavior" [*quan phiet, tu man*].[58]

A VOLUNTEER FIGHTER ON THE COLD WAR FRONTLINE

A specific event that marked the beginning of the Cold War in Europe was the dramatic conflict in Berlin between the Soviet Union and Western powers. A report by General Secretary Truong Chinh, worth quoting here at length, described the event with unconcealed pride of the Soviet confrontational stand:

The U.S. flaunted atomic bombs to scare the world and issued new currency notes in West Germany and West Berlin. The Soviet Union reacted strongly: West Berlin was blockaded, no cars allowed in and out, hot air balloons flown above, [and] steel fences as high as six kilometers [sic] were erected. British and American airplanes had to be flown very high to cross those fences in order to transport relief goods into that area. The U.S. tried to coax [*phinh pho*] and threaten [*ham doa*]

---

[55] Ibid., 6–12.

[56] Ibid., 20.

[57] Ho Chi Minh, *Bao cao chanh tri* [Political Report], speech at the Second Party Congress in 1951 (Trung Uong Cuc Mien Nam, 1952), 52. This sentence about Tito together with praises for Mao's thought and guidance that appeared in the original 1951 speech were deleted from the same speech published in *VKDTT*, v. 12, 31.

[58] "Chung ta chien dau cho doc lap va dan chu."

but the Soviet Union was as firm as a big rock [*vung nhu ban thach*]. British and American representatives went to Moscow, requesting to meet with Stalin and Molotov. The conditions of the Soviet Union for the U.S. were .... The U.S. did not comply with them, so "the cold war" continued. This event caused the U.S. and England to lose their faces. It showed the world that the Soviet Union was tough and the U.S. was only bluffing [*doa gia*].[59]

The comment not only lacked seriousness but also showed jubilance; the entire episode appeared like a mildly amusing imperialist farce. Did Vietnamese leaders see any dangers in the new situation? As the fortunes of Chinese communists were rising in China, ICP leaders began to imagine a scenario in which Washington would intervene directly to help the GMD and the French to defeat both Chinese and Vietnamese communists. "We are not afraid," Truong Chinh declared, "because if the U.S. is defeated in China, it shall be defeated in Vietnam." The Vietnamese guerrilla army was ordered to prepare for joint operations with Chinese forces once they reached southern China.[60] Hovering large above this military strategy was the familiar prophetic vision: "A time will come when Chinese and Vietnamese revolutions will merge into a new democracy bloc in the Far East to counter American imperialists and their stooges – French colonialists and Chinese and Vietnamese traitors."

That time arrived around 1949, when Chinese communist forces chased the retreating GMD army to southern China. Since 1946, Ho's government had maintained contacts with and offered assistance to local communist forces in southern China. Chinese Red Army units were allowed to station in Vietnamese territory, and were provided with food, supplies, and medicine.[61] In return, they helped train Vietnamese soldiers. In early 1949, in response to a request from the Chinese, Ho sent several Vietnamese units across the border to help the Red Army to defend their base against Chiang Kai-shek's attacks. Right after the People's Republic of China was founded in October 1949, the DRV sent envoys to Beijing to request diplomatic recognition. Beijing gladly offered it, and thanks to Mao's personal effort to make the case to Stalin, Moscow followed suit.

---

[59] Truong Chinh, "Tich cuc cam cu va chuan bi tong phan cong" [Zealously holding off the enemy and preparing for the general attack phase], January 14, 1949. *VKDTT*, v. 10, 29–30.

[60] Ibid., 36–37, 53.

[61] Nguyen Thi Mai Hoa, *Cac nuoc Xa hoi chu nghia ung ho Viet Nam khang chien chong My, cuu nuoc*, 53–55 [Socialist countries' assistance to Vietnam's resistance against America to save the country] (Hanoi: Chinh tri Quoc gia, 2013); Qiang Zhai, *China and the Vietnam Wars, 1950–1975* (Chapel Hill: University of North Carolina Press, 2000), 11–12.

Clearly China and the Soviet Union had become involved in Indochina not at their own initiatives, but by the persistent and proactive efforts of Ho and his comrades.

Despite having secretly secured Soviet and Chinese recognition, the ICP was careful not to provoke US intervention. This strategy was implemented by making cautious diplomatic announcements and broadcasts designed to manipulate world opinion. These announcements conveyed the impression that, by obtaining diplomatic recognition from new Communist China and the Soviet Union, Vietnam was only seeking national independence and did not intend to join the Soviet bloc. It was not clear whether the idea to proceed cautiously came from the Chinese or was their own idea because the minutes of the ICP Standing Committee meeting mentioned only briefly the steps Vietnamese leaders planned to take:

> Based on suggestions from the Chinese [Communist] central leadership and also due to our need to act fast, [our Party] has recommended [our] government to announce that we would want to establish diplomatic relations with all countries, then a day later to announce that we recognize the People's Republic of China. After the Chinese have responded, we will transmit our announcement to the governments of Siam, Burma, India, and Pakistan.[62]

The reception of Beijing representatives in Vietnam was also to be carried out secretly and as an interparty, not intergovernmental, affair. In a follow-up directive issued a few days later, the Party ordered government *newspapers* to "attack [*cong kich*] American imperialists, showing clearly the plots of U.S. military and financial cliques to directly intervene into Indochina."[63] Government *radio stations*, however, were not allowed to attack the United States directly; they were told to broadcast news of American intention to intervene into Indochina and to declare specifically that "any imperialist powers messing with Indochina would fail as

---

[62] "Quyet nghi cua Ban Thuong vu Trung uong" [The decision of the Standing Committee], January 15–16, 1950. *VKDTT*, v. 11, 11. The DRV's clever arrangement for a long time succeeded to confuse even informed observers. Nearly forty years later, Kahin still argued that "Not having yet received diplomatic recognition from any country, the DRV leaders felt the urgent need to break out of their isolation, and on January 14, 1950, they appealed worldwide to all governments for diplomatic recognition. Four days later, once Hanoi had recognized Mao's government (on the 15th), Peking reciprocated; and on January 30, the Soviet Union followed suit." See George Kahin, *Intervention: How America Became Involved in Vietnam* (New York: Knopf, 1986), 35.

[63] "Chi thi cua Ban Thuong vu Trung uong ve viec tuyen truyen chinh sach ngoai giao cua Chinh phu ta" [Directive of the Standing Committee on propaganda about our foreign policy], January 18, 1950. *VKDTT*, v. 11, 16.

the U.S. did in China." Criticism of Vietnam's neighbors, such as India and Indonesia, was also not permitted. Newspapers were written for and limited to domestic consumption, whereas the Party knew its radio messages would be picked up abroad. The Party wanted the Vietnamese to hate the United States but it was cautious not to provoke Washington into intervention.

Parallel to cautious measures intended for foreign consumption were bolder steps to take full advantage of the opportunity. The same secret document that explained the decision to recognize China also mentioned that the ICP had "proposed to the Chinese Communist Party to allow [more] Vietnamese forces to enter Chinese territory to intercept and destroy fleeing GMD troops."[64] The Party also planned to "propose to the Chinese a common political and military strategy in Southeast Asia and to ask the French Communist Party to coordinate action."[65] Close links with communist parties in Southeast Asia were also sought.[66]

After the DRV established relations with China and the Soviet Union, Ho Chi Minh traveled on foot through Vietnamese jungles for seventeen days to reach Guangxi.[67] From then on, he went to Beijing by train, then waited near the Sino-Soviet border for permission to have a personal meeting with Stalin. In Moscow, Ho asked Stalin for a Soviet-Vietnamese Mutual Defense Treaty similar to the Sino-Soviet Treaty just signed by Stalin and Mao, but his request was denied.[68] Stalin preferred to entrust Mao with the task of assisting the Indochinese revolution.

Ho's arduous trip encapsulated the deep Vietnamese yearning for close relations with the Soviet bloc. The wide range of proposed collaboration between the DRV and China/the Soviet Union went far beyond the need to break out of diplomatic isolation. They can be explained only within the context of ICP leaders' broader ideological conception that had always divided the world into two camps and placed the destiny of Indochina solely with the socialist camp. Three weeks after the DRV had been recognized by the Soviet bloc, the ICP Standing Committee noted that the absolute majority of Vietnamese were "very positive"

---

[64] "Quyet nghi cua Ban Thuong vu Trung uong," *VKDTT*, v. 11, 11.

[65] "Nghi quyet cua Thuong vu Trung uong" [The resolution of the Standing Committee], February 4, 1950. *VKDTT*, v. 11, 223.

[66] "Nghi quyet cua Hoi nghi Toan quoc lan thu ba" [Resolution of the Third All-Nation Party Conference], January 21–February 3, 1950. *VKDTT*, v. 11, 218.

[67] Zhai, *China and the Vietnam Wars*, 16.

[68] Stalin laughed upon hearing Ho's verbal request. See Ilya Gaiduk, *Confronting Vietnam: Soviet Policy toward the Indochina Conflict, 1954–1963* (Washington, DC: Woodrow Wilson Center, 2003), 1–11.

about this event. It also pointed out that there were a few who "worried that Indochina would become a battlefield for the democratic and anti-democratic camps to compete for influence."[69] However, these intellectuals were dismissed as caring only about their selfish interests [*quyen loi rieng*]. The Committee justified its decision as follows:

> After the victory of the Chinese revolution, Indochina has become an outpost [*tien tieu*] in the anti-imperialist front in Southeast Asia. However, the world counterrevolutionary camp is not deterred [*chun*] by the fact that Vietnam has been recognized by [the socialist bloc]; they are even more actively executing their conspiracy to intervene. The issue for us is that we must act faster [*tranh thu thoi gian*]... to move on to the all-out attack phase to liberate our country and also to protect world peace, to protect the Soviet Union, to stall the plot of the warmongers, and to spread revolution to Southeast Asia.[70]

Given the total lack of Chinese and Soviet interest in Indochina during 1945–1949, and the ruthless rivalry between the United States and the Soviet Union in China during that period, DRV leaders should have interpreted the victory of Chinese communists as signaling that French-controlled Indochina would become an outpost on the *imperialist* front in Southeast Asia. After all, imperialist powers had been interested in Indochina as early as 1945, and their defeat in China only raised the geopolitical stakes in Indochina for them. Conceivably the ICP could have tried, as many intellectuals advised it to do, to reassure the imperialist camp that Vietnam would not ally with any bloc. In contrast, what ICP leaders did was to extend the *anti-imperialist* front into Indochina by patiently approaching and persuading Moscow and Beijing that they could play a role in Indochina as well, that they should not abandon Indochina to the imperialist camp, and that Indochina could do its share to help with world revolution.

To be fair to them, open or secret American assistance to the French since 1946 implied that, even if ICP leaders had declared neutrality, the United States might not have believed them and supported them against

---

[69] "Nghi quyet cua Thuong vu Trung uong," 222–223, *VKDTT*, v. 11, 223. In another document, Party leaders also discussed the attitude of "pro-American" intellectuals such as Hoang Xuan Han (a former minister in the Tran Trong Kim government) and Nguyen Manh Ha (the first Minister of Economy in the Viet Minh government in 1945) who wanted the ICP not to ally with any camp for fear of Vietnam becoming the battlefield of a Third World War. "Tinh hinh cac Lien Khu trong ba thang 1, 2, 3 nam 1950" [The situation in the Interzones during the first quarter of 1950], n.d., *VKDTT*, v. 11, 271.

[70] Ibid., 223.

the French. However, nowhere did Party documents consider neutrality as an alternative. Clearly, its leaders and members would not have accepted giving up their ideology. They had not done so when they appeared hopelessly abandoned by the revolutionary camp; why would they do so now that they might be able to finally get support from it? A potential US intervention – the cost of that support – was accepted and believed to be surmountable.

A year later, Truong Chinh would proudly state in his report at the Second Party Congress in 1951, the congress when the ICP reemerged as the Vietnamese Workers' Party (VWP):

Vietnam has become one of the outposts [*tien don*] on the front for peace and democracy against imperialism, and has [also] been viewed by the imperialist powers as a strategic post on their defense line against democracy. *History* has entrusted the Vietnamese working class and people with the duty to defend this outpost. The Vietnamese working class and people are determined not to let down people around the world who have placed their trust in us.[71]

Truong Chinh appeared modest by giving history all the credit for the fact that Vietnam had become an outpost in the coming Cold War. But he may have been trying to dodge the charge that the ICP had dragged Vietnam into the conflict between the superpowers. Regardless of his intention in this statement, there is no doubt that history played a role, but the ICP's active efforts to draw international communist powers into Indochina should not be overlooked.

In any case, the embrace of the Cold War allowed the ICP to accelerate the pace of its *domestic* revolution. Party leaders had always viewed international conditions as closely linked to and, to a critical extent, determining the process of revolution in particular countries.[72] In 1946, at the height of the struggle for national liberation, Truong Chinh continued to argue for not separating the two revolutions:

Now a mistaken view about the stages of the Vietnamese revolution needs to be criticized. Some people believe that our revolution has to go one step at a time: (anti-imperialist) national liberation first, then (antifeudalist) land

---

[71] Truong Chinh, "Hoan thanh giai phong dan toc, phat trien dan chu nhan dan, tien toi chu nghia xa hoi" [Achieving national liberation, developing people's democracy, and marching forward to socialism], speech at the Second Party Congress, February 1951. *VKDTT*, v. 11, 47. Italics added.

[72] An important study of revolutions supports Vietnamese leaders on this point. See Theda Skocpol, *States and Social Revolutions: A Comparative Analysis of France, Russia, and China* (New York: Cambridge University Press, 1979).

revolution, then socialism. This step-by-step view that strictly divides the revolution into three stages is not correct. Externally, the Soviet Union, a socialist country, has emerged victorious and the new democratic movement is growing fast. Internally, the leadership of the revolution is firmly in the hands of the proletariats and the democratic progressive forces are united. Under these historical conditions, our national liberation revolution can accomplish anti-imperialist tasks and fulfill *part of* our antifeudalist responsibilities.[73]

How large a part of antifeudalist responsibilities must be accomplished at any particular time depended on the international and domestic situations at that time. Favorable international conditions were not necessarily synonymous with the availability of external support. Even when there was no forthcoming assistance from the Soviet Union, some ICP leaders, of whom Truong Chinh was the most powerful, still called for land reform measures, albeit moderate ones. At the same time, these ICP leaders held a long-term view of the revolution and always kept their eyes open for new opportunities to leapfrog. By mid-1948 when Chinese Red Armies were pouring into central China after their victories in Manchuria, Truong Chinh began to call for a revived campaign to reduce rents for tenants.[74] Rent reduction policy had been issued in 1945 but had not been seriously implemented. He predicted that, "If the international situation undergoes a great change favorable to the democratic camp, or if the resistance succeeds [within the near future], our Party can take advantage of the new conditions to take the land reform one step higher [than merely rent reduction]."[75] The arrival of the Cold War and the promise of concrete Chinese support would mean a great opportunity to leapfrog. Although Soviet and Chinese pressure may have accelerated the timing of the radical land reform as Christopher Goscha argues, it would be a mistake to underestimate ICP leaders' commitment to land reform.[76] They had showed impatience and sought to implement parts of the revolutionary agenda when no such pressure existed.

---

[73] "Cach mang thang Tam: Trien vong cua Cach mang Viet nam" [The August Revolution: The prospects of Vietnam's revolution]. *Su That*, September 7, 1946. Italics in original.

[74] Tuong Vu, "It's Time for the Indochinese Revolution to Show Its True Colors: The Radical Turn in Vietnamese Politics in 1948," *Journal of Southeast Asian Studies* 40: 3 (October 2009), 519–542.

[75] Truong Chinh, "Chung ta chien dau cho doc lap va dan chu" [We fight for independence and democracy], 80–85.

[76] Goscha, "Courting Diplomatic Disaster?: The Difficult Integration of Vietnam into the International Communist Movement (1945–1950)," *Journal of Vietnamese Studies* 1, no. 1 (2006): 90.

CONCLUSION

Many US-centric studies of the Vietnam War assert that the war was something inconceivable from the vantage point of 1945. As former US Defense Secretary Robert McNamara and his collaborators wonder, "How did these two countries, with little common history and less common knowledge of each other, become during the post-World War II period the bitterest of enemies...? Clearly Ho Chi Minh could not imagine this in September 1945..."[77]

The evidence in this chapter demonstrated that Vietnamese communist leaders, including Ho Chi Minh, may have possessed little *empirical* knowledge about the United States, but they never lacked *theoretical* assumptions about the grave defects of American society and about US behavior as a leading imperialist. These assumptions were informed by their two-camp worldview in which the American capitalist system was unjust and cruel in contrast to the just and progressive Soviet system. In addition, the United States was a clever and dangerous enemy of world revolution, whereas the Soviet Union was its savior; mutually destructive conflict between the two camps was inevitable. Vietnamese communists kept these assumptions long before 1945 and continued to hold them, even during late 1944 and early 1945 when the United States appeared to be on their side.

Although their worldview was not static, ICP leaders throughout the period identified themselves with the revolutionary camp. At the darkest moments when no support was forthcoming from this camp, Vietnamese communists did not cease associating themselves with the Soviet Union in their imagination and displaying their admiration for Lenin's homeland. Even while they were searching frantically for alternative sources of international support, their lack of contact with Moscow did not diminish their ideological loyalty.

The arrival of the Cold War only reaffirmed their binary worldview. Although their nation was small and weak, they were only partially constrained by world events. Viewing the Cold War as a great opportunity, they took advantage of it while being fully aware of the risks of their policy.[78] It was China and the superpowers that decided to send aid,

---

[77] McNamara et al., *Argument without End*, 77. See also Bradley, *Imagining Vietnam & America*, 6.

[78] Vietnamese communists were not alone in seeing the Cold War as a great opportunity. As Westad concludes in his study of Chinese communist foreign policy, "while anticolonial insurgents of the late 19th and early 20th centuries had little hope of forming alliances with a foreign power, the bipolarity and the scope of the Cold War conflict opened the

arms, and men to Vietnam, but Ho and his comrades spared no efforts to make the initially uninterested revolutionary camp admit their small nation into its ranks. In this sense, they and not China or the superpowers brought the Cold War to Vietnam. The Vietnamese leaders were not "drafted"; they volunteered and brought Vietnam into war with them.

Thus, ideology played an even more crucial role during the 1940s in the ways Vietnamese revolutionaries interpreted world events and the policies of foreign powers. Such interpretations may have been correct or incorrect, sophisticated or naïve, but the point here is that ICP leaders would have been at a loss without their ideology. Those interpretations clearly helped them to sustain their vision and to devise their strategies. The strategies were not always correct, and Ho and his comrades would have faced significant difficulties if their Chinese comrades had lost the civil war. Unlike the 1930s, the Vietnamese communist movement in this decade received little or no support from the transnational network of worker and communist movements. Until 1949 or so, ideology did not help them in this respect as it had previously. Ideology did play a central role in their decision to join the Soviet bloc in 1949. If they had been simply nationalists and not also communists, they certainly would not have made that decision.

Chapter 4 will turn to the 1950s as Vietnamese communists began their rule over a divided Vietnam and confronted new challenges to their struggle to build a socialist regime in the North and launch a revolution in the South.

door for Third World rebels to exploit the international great power system for their own purposes." See Odd Arne Westad, *Cold War and Revolution* (New York: Columbia University Press, 1993), 178.

4

Patriotism in the Service of Socialism, 1953–1960

From 1945 to 1949, Ho Chi Minh and his comrades knocked on every door to gain Stalin's attention.[1] Ho wrote several letters to the Soviet leader but these went unanswered. His diplomats approached Soviet representatives in Thailand, France, and Switzerland to no avail. One desperate Party official, Le Hi, tried to initiate unauthorized contacts with Soviet officials while traveling through Moscow; he failed. Another, Tran Ngoc Danh, who was the younger brother of Tran Phu, a graduate of the University of the Toilers of the East, and a high-ranking Party leader, also took the matter in his own hands and sent unauthorized reports directly to Moscow in late 1949. Danh not only requested Soviet assistance for the Vietnamese revolution but also criticized Ho Chi Minh and, to a lesser extent, Truong Chinh for deviating from Marxism-Leninism-Stalinism. In both cases, Hi and Danh acted as if their party were still a branch of the now dissolved Comintern which used to have the authority to appoint, transfer, and discipline leaders of all branches worldwide.[2] Danh's criticisms were clearly unfair to both Ho and Truong Chinh. As seen in the previous chapter, at that very time they were, after so much hard work and with some good luck, about to open a new door to Moscow – via

---

[1] This paragraph is based on Goscha, "Courting Diplomatic Disaster?" 59–103.
[2] In a letter to the Party leadership in 1983, Le Hi claimed that he was influenced by Tran Ngoc Danh and Musso, an Indonesian communist leader, and was motivated by his concern about the Vietnamese revolution falling under the influence of nationalism. Le Hi, "Vai net ve cuoc doi hoat dong cua Tu Lam" [Sketches of Tu Lam's activist career] (Tu Lam was one of Le Hi's pseudonyms). *Talawas*, July 2, 2007. Available at http://www.talawas.org/talaDB/showFile.php?res=10325&rb=11.

Beijing. By the end of January 1950, the DRV had won recognition from both China and the Soviet Union.

Because of their persistent efforts, it was natural that ICP leaders considered Vietnam's acquisition of membership in the Soviet camp a great victory. But membership in the Soviet camp was also a natural development, given the history of the Party. The Party was formed under the guidance of the Comintern and became an official branch of the Comintern in 1935. Since its founding, the Party had espoused social revolution and proletarian internationalism. All its leaders viewed their revolution as a component of world revolution. In Tran Phu's vision, for Indochina to advance to socialism without passing through the capitalist stage, support from other proletarian governments was key.[3] When the DRV was founded in late 1945, isolation from the international communist network in the face of overwhelming French power compelled Party leaders such as Ho and Truong Chinh to be flexible in revolutionary tactics and to seek diplomatic recognition from the United States and India. But it was the socialist camp where their passion really was.[4]

The ICP's decision to join the communist camp brought in enormous support from the Soviet bloc. After the DRV established relations with China, Ho immediately sent several requests for Chinese weapons, Chinese training of Vietnamese troops, Chinese advisers for Vietnamese command centers and at the division level, and Chinese commanders of Vietnamese forces down to regimental and battalion levels.[5] China satisfied all requests from Vietnam except the one for commanders, perhaps out of concern for possible US reactions or for the safety of those commanders. Chinese military assistance was instrumental in a series of communist forces' gains in war against France, culminating in the stunning Vietnamese victory at Dien Bien Phu in May 1954.

[3] Tran Phu, "Luan cuong chanh tri," *VKDTT*, v. 2, 94.
[4] For a sense of how the DRV's membership in the Soviet camp was a natural development, see Appendix A for an interesting letter Ho wrote to Stalin in 1951. Ho's tone and his Russian pseudonym in the letter gave the strong flavor of a comrade, a Comintern agent, and a disciple addressing his comrade, boss, and God, rather than a head of state communicating with another head of state.
[5] Zhai, *China and the Vietnam Wars*, 18–19. According to Stanley Karnow, in early 1946 Ho justified his negotiation for French forces to enter Tonkin to replace Nationalist Chinese troops by saying that "Better to sniff a bit of French shit briefly than eat Chinese shit for the rest of our lives." Karnow, *Vietnam, a History* (New York: Viking, 1983), 111–112. The authenticity of this statement has been questioned by historians; see https://leminhkhai.wordpress.com/2012/09/01/ho-chi-minh-said-what/. Even if Ho did make the statement, the evidence here suggests that *Nationalist* Chinese "shit" smelled differently from *Communist* Chinese "shit" for Ho.

The DRV's joining the Soviet camp also set up a chain of reactions. It alarmed the United States, which, together with its allies, immediately countered by offering diplomatic recognition to the French-backed State of Vietnam's government headed by the former king Bao Dai.[6] This state had, until then, been dismissed as a French creation. Bao Dai gained immediate legitimacy not only externally but also domestically as numerous Vietnamese noncommunist patriots previously rallying to Ho's government now fleeing it to join his government. After the French left, this anticommunist government based in Saigon would be in control of Vietnamese territory south of the seventeenth parallel. With US support, it sought to resist Hanoi's desire to unify Vietnam under communist rule.

The 1950s presented both opportunities and challenges to the Vietnamese revolution. The young revolutionary state was to demonstrate its great ability to overcome the challenges while making contributions to the communist camp to which its fate was now tightly bound.

"CLASS STRUGGLE UNDER THE APPEARANCE OF A NATIONALIST STRUGGLE"

In March 1952, Stalin made a surprising proposal to the West for free elections throughout Germany to create a unified and neutral German state.[7] He published his short book titled *Economic Problems of Socialism* at about the same time. The year also marked the third year of the Korean War in which Allied and communist forces locked in a stalemate. In China, the Chinese communist government had just completed its land reform in 1951 and was poised to take the rural revolution to the next step, collectivization.[8] These events revived the optimism of the DRV government after an unsuccessful military campaign in 1951.

In his speech to open the Fourth Plenum of the Central Committee in January 1953, Ho Chi Minh recounted these developments with pride and joy. After summarizing the contents of Stalin's book, Ho said that

[6] For the shift in diplomatic recognition from Ho Chi Minh's to Bao Dai's government in South and Southeast Asia in 1950, see Christopher Goscha, "Choosing between the Two Vietnams: 1950 and Southeast Asian Shifts in the International System," in Christopher Goscha and Christian Ostermann, eds. *Connecting Histories: Decolonization and the Cold War in Southeast Asia, 1945–1962* (Washington DC: Woodrow Wilson Center Press, 2009), 207–237.
[7] John Lewis Gaddis, *We Now Know: Rethinking Cold War History* (New York: Oxford University Press, 1997), 126–129. The West did not trust Stalin enough to accept this proposal, and Stalin soon abandoned it.
[8] Yang Dali, *Calamity and Reform in China* (Stanford, CA: Stanford University Press, 1996).

the book taught Vietnamese communists "how to assess the future of the world correctly." Now they could be "assured of the ultimate victory waiting them."[9] Ho then turned to China and enthusiastically presented an array of statistics about the success of socialist policies there. For example, the land reform in China was said to have redistributed 700 million acres of land to farmers, raising production by 40 percent in 1952. The percentage of poor farmers fell from 70 percent to around 10 to 20 percent. Between 60 and 80 percent of Chinese farmers were already organized either in mutual aid teams or in collectives. Forty-nine million children of farmers were now enrolled in schools. If real, these statistics were impressive.

In contrast to the great progress made by "the democratic camp" [*phe dan chu*], Ho described the United States, which led "the imperialist camp" [*phe de quoc*], as being "on its last leg" when it used biological weapons in Korea.[10] This act led to "great outbursts" of world opinion against Washington. Because the United States had to concentrate all its forces to prepare for war, the American economy was in shambles and Americans became impoverished. Ho called for continued vigilance against imperialists: "We have to keep in mind that colonizing backward countries and exploiting their peoples are one of the basic characteristics of monopoly capital. French and American imperialists crave our rich reserves of raw materials such as rice, rubber, coal, and tin. They also want to conquer and use our country as a military base to invade China."

Echoing Ho, General Secretary Truong Chinh, who gave the main report at the same Plenum, quoted Stalin at length about the "vast chasm" [*mot troi mot vuc*] between the basic principles of modern capitalism and those of socialism. Whereas the former was characterized by "exploitation," "impoverishment," "enslavement," "profiteering," and "war-making," the latter was said to make "the effort to satisfy to the greatest extent the material and spiritual needs of the whole society by continuously improving production with advanced technology."[11]

What most impressed Truong Chinh was Stalin's "invention" [*phat minh*] of the dialectic logic of the predictable economic crisis in the capitalist camp. According to Stalin, the imperialist countries' economic

---

[9] Ho Chi Minh, "Ve tinh hinh truoc mat va nhiem vu cai cach ruong dat" [On the situation and our task of land reform], January 25, 1953. *VKDTT*, v. 14, 18.

[10] Ibid., 14–19.

[11] "Bao cao cua Tong Bi Thu Truong Chinh" [Report by General Secretary Truong Chinh], *VKDTT*, v. 14, 32.

blockade against the Soviet Union and other "people's democracies" led to the latter forming a market among themselves in which they "collaborated closely and equally and helped each other sincerely."[12] The unified world market that had existed until then was broken into two opposing economic blocs. The socialist camp had grown so rapidly that soon socialist countries would not need goods supplied to date by the capitalist camp. This, Stalin predicted, would shrink the markets for goods from capitalist countries and throw their economies into deep crises. These crises in turn would further weaken world capitalism; capitalist countries would have to cling to their colonies at any cost; the conflict among imperialists would intensify; and war would break out among them.[13] Because of this coming war *within* the imperialist camp, war might not occur *between* the two camps for the time being. As Truong Chinh paraphrased Stalin, the Second World War had shown the imperialist warmongers that attacking the Soviet Union was risky business. Whereas fighting among imperialist states would only affect their relative status within the capitalist camp, war with the Soviet Union now would endanger capitalism itself.

While being vigilant against "imperialist plots," Truong Chinh cited three reasons for Vietnamese communists to support the Soviet policy of protecting peace. First, protecting peace for the time being was necessary for the Soviet bloc to develop its forces while imperialist strength declined. Second, encouraging wars among imperialist armies would not ensure the destruction of imperialism. Imperialism would be destroyed only when people in imperialist countries overthrew their rulers, or when socialist armies liberated them (as the Soviet Union did in Eastern Europe during World War II). Finally, people in imperialist countries would not need imperialist wars to make revolution. Many revolutions in history had occurred in the absence of such wars. Although Truong Chinh believed Stalin's claim that peace was possible, he also quoted the Soviet leader's point that peace was only temporary and war was inevitable in the long run because imperialism still existed.

The significance of this Plenum cannot be exaggerated. First, the analysis of the world situation formed a critical background to the most important decision made at the Plenum, which was to launch a Chinese-style land-reform campaign in 1953. Stalin and Mao may have pressured Vietnamese leaders to undertake this move, and Chinese advisers, in fact,

---

[12] Ibid., 32–34.
[13] For discussion of Stalin's ideas in this book, see Gaddis, *We Now Know*, 195–198.

supervised the campaign at many levels.[14] But that was not the only factor. Party leaders had been vigorously debating this policy since 1946 and the achievements of the socialist camp, especially in China and Korea, clearly inspired them to take this long awaited radical step. The new situation, Truong Chinh argued, made irrelevant the experience of the Chinese Communist Party during 1937–1945 when this party pursued rent reduction but not land redistribution:

> We do not want to apply [that] Chinese experience mechanically. At that time, the Chinese Communist Party was collaborating with Chiang Kai-shek to fight the Japanese. Chiang was the representative of feudal landowning and comprador capitalist classes. He did not want land redistribution and he had a government and an army. Now we are not collaborating with such a powerful partner; so we can make a [bolder] step forward. Also, at that time China was under siege by feudal and imperialist forces. Today, our country has formed one single bloc [*lien mot khoi*] with the socialist and democratic camp and is connected to a great people's democracy which is China.[15]

Truong Chinh's reasoning led him to a concise theoretical formulation that effectively solved the longstanding debate among Vietnamese communists about land reform. As he said, "National democratic revolutions are [essentially] peasant revolutions. Wars of national liberation are essentially peasant wars... Leading peasants to fight feudalism and imperialism is class struggle and national struggle at the same time. It is class struggle within a national struggle and under the appearance of a national struggle."[16] The debate until then had pitted radicals like Truong Chinh against those who feared that land reform would break up the national coalition in the ongoing struggle for independence.[17] Given the favorable international and domestic conditions, Chinh had now succeeded in persuading his cautious comrades to go along. Land reform from then on was viewed as complementing, not contradicting, the goal of independence. Land redistribution assumed an importance equal to national liberation, exactly as Tran Phu had argued in 1930.

Second, with the help of Stalin's book, the Plenum also accepted the theoretical justifications for another key decision to be made later in the year – namely, to negotiate with the French at Geneva. Several factors

---

[14] Nguyen Thi Mai Hoa, *Cac nuoc Xa hoi chu nghia ung ho Viet Nam khang chien chong My, cuu nuoc*, 76–77.
[15] "Bao cao cua Tong Bi Thu Truong Chinh," *VKDTT*, v. 14, 52–53.
[16] Ibid., 53–54.
[17] Vu, *Paths to Development in Asia: South Korea, Vietnam, China, and Indonesia* (New York: Cambridge University Press, 2010), chap. 5.

have been put forward to explain the DRV's acceptance of the Geneva Agreements, including the priority given to reconstructing the North, belief in the legality and practicality of the accords, war fatigue, pressure from the Soviet Union and China, and the prospect of American intervention.[18] Although all these factors played some role, Party documents published in 1953 reviewed here suggested that ideology was also a factor. In particular, their loyalty to the socialist cause and desire to coordinate policy with the Soviet camp led Vietnamese communists at the time to accept uncritically Stalin's policy of preserving peace.[19] No objections were raised at the Plenum concerning Stalin's policy. Party leaders even made an effort to justify the policy in doctrinal terms. Although there was internal dissent about Geneva, top leaders felt proud that they were acting on behalf of the camp in the interest of not just their revolution but also world peace.[20]

"COMRADE STALIN IS NEVER WRONG"

Nguyen Kien Giang is a respected Marxist theorist and historian who had once been a high-ranking Party member and former deputy director of the Party's Publishing House *Su That* before he was imprisoned for allegedly belonging to "the revisionist clique" in the late 1960s. In a paper written in 1995 on the import of Marxism-Leninism into Vietnam, he described the communist bloc from the 1930s to the 1950s as "something similar to a church," with Stalin being the Pope. What Stalin said was considered the final words on *any* matter. Giang then told a personal story: in 1950, he attended some controversial lectures about land reform and military policy at the central Party school where he was a student. The matter was perhaps so important that General Secretary Truong Chinh himself came to class to correct the mistaken points made by the lecturers who were themselves high-ranking Party cadres. But even he failed to stop the debate, and one night Ho Chi Minh showed up with

[18] Nguyen Vu Tung, "Coping with the United States: Hanoi's search for an effective strategy," in *The Vietnam War*, ed. Peter Lowe (London: MacMillan Press, Ltd., 1998): 39; Pierre Asselin, *Hanoi's Road to the Vietnam War* (Berkeley: University of California Press, 2013), 13.

[19] No mention was made in the available documents about Stalin's offer to allow free elections throughout Germany, although that may also have influenced the Party's decision to participate in Geneva.

[20] "Thong tri cua Ban Bi Thu ve loi tuyen bo cua Ho Chu tich voi nha bao Thuy Dien" [Party Secretariat's Circulation on Chairman Ho's talk with Swedish journalist], December 27, 1953. *VKDTT*, v. 14, 555.

an unusual seriousness. He went straight into the controversial issue and said, "I just returned from the Soviet Union where I met comrade Stalin and reported our policy to him. Comrade Stalin listened to me and said that the policy of our Party was correct. When comrade Stalin says something is correct, it must be correct. Comrade Maurice Thorez has said that comrade Stalin is never wrong." According to Giang, at this point the whole class fell silent and was totally convinced.[21]

The Party Constitution, which was issued in 1951 indeed proclaimed that "the Vietnamese Workers' Party considered the doctrine of Marx-Engels-Lenin-Stalin and Mao Zedong's thought, combined with Vietnamese revolutionary experience, as the foundation for the Party's ideology and the compass for all its activities."[22] Veneration of Stalin was part of a Soviet cult that swept over North Vietnam after 1954. The cult was promoted through many state-sponsored activities: publications of pamphlets and newspaper articles, organization of "Friendship Months" [*Thang huu nghi*], and visits of top government officials and intellectuals to the Soviet Union (and China and North Korea along the way).[23] On their return, travelers gave speaking tours around the country to talk about their wonderful experiences.

But how effective was this state propaganda? Were people persuaded? Although popular opinion at the time cannot be assessed with accuracy, the excitement about the Soviet Union among Vietnamese intellectuals appeared genuine for many possible reasons. The trips were the first abroad for most. Militarily, Soviet and Chinese support had just helped DRV troops to score major, almost unthinkable, victories in the battlefield such as Dien Bien Phu. The novelty of the experience, the deep appreciation for Soviet help, and a forming belief in the future of socialism were

---

[21] Thorez was leader of the French Communist Party at the time. Nguyen Kien Giang, "Nhin lai qua trinh du nhap chu nghia Mac-Le nin vao Vietnam" [On the process by which Marxism-Leninism entered Vietnam], 1995. Available at http://viet-studies.info/kinhte/NguyenKienGiang_QuaTrinhDuNhap.htm

[22] "Dieu le Dang Lao Dong Viet Nam" [The Constitution of the Vietnam Workers Party], February 1951. *VKDTT*, v. 12, 444.

[23] See Dang Xa Hoi Viet Nam [Vietnamese Socialist Party], *Thang Huu Nghi Viet-Trung-Xo voi nguoi tri thuc Viet nam* [The Vietnamese-Chinese-Soviet friendship month to Vietnamese intellectuals] (Hanoi: Dang Xa Hoi Viet Nam, 1954); Nguyen Van Thom (perhaps a pseudonym of Ho Chi Minh), *Duong di muon dam* [A journey of ten thousand miles] (Hanoi: Tuyen truyen van nghe, 1954); *Chung toi tham Lien Xo* [Our visit to the Soviet Union] (Hanoi: Van Nghe, 1956); Minh Tranh, *Tham nong thon Lien Xo* [Visiting rural Soviet Union] (Hanoi: Su That, 1956); Tran Luc (Ho Chi Minh), *Lien Xo vi dai* [The great Soviet Union] (Hanoi: Su That, 1957); and Thep Moi, *Nhu anh em mot nha* [Like brothers in the same family] (Hanoi: Van Hoc, 1958).

hard to separate and served to reinforce one another. The blissful sense of Vietnamese on arriving in the communist dreamland was palpable and genuine, as described by the famous poet, novelist, and playwright The Lu while riding the train to Moscow: "So we are now inside the Soviet Union. Since ... we crossed the Sino-Soviet border, we have been truly living ... in a real world that comes from the most beautiful dream ever."[24]

Although the new relationship between communist Vietnam and the USSR/China can be viewed as merely reproducing colonial dependency under a new patron, Vietnamese intellectuals did not show the slightest hint of this view. Tu Mo, a well-known satirical poet who was on the same train with The Lu to Moscow and later to Yerevan in the Armenian Republic, described this Republic as being oppressed and exploited to the extreme by the Tsarist regime.[25] Only after the Bolsheviks helped to overthrow the "bourgeois government" of Armenia in 1920 and provided assistance, was Armenia able to develop economically and culturally. The Soviet Union did not want just itself to be rich but was ready to help others so that communism could be achieved globally. The United States "gave one and took back ten [*giup mot lot muoi*], turned its aid recipients into its "vassals," and enticed them into joining aggressive pacts to sacrifice the blood of their own people for American interests."[26] In contrast, the Soviet Union had no ulterior motives in helping small and backward countries like Armenia to reclaim their independence, freedom, and happiness.

Nguyen Huy Tuong, another playwright, writer, and member of the executive committee of the Soviet-Vietnamese Friendship Association, visited the Soviet Union from October 30 to December 2, 1955, as part of an official delegation of the Association. Nguyen Huy Tuong frankly described his feelings in his personal diary that was made public by his family for the first time in 2006, more than 40 years after his death. Here is what he wrote under the entry for November 16, 1955, after having spent many days sightseeing in Moscow and attending meetings with Soviet people:

Love the Soviet Union. The Soviet Union has experienced so much suffering, so it is sympathetic to other peoples' suffering. Love the efforts of the Soviet Union

[24] The Lu, "Cam tuong dau tien" [The first feelings], July 21, 1955, in *Chung toi tham Lien Xo*, 17.

[25] Tu Mo, "Lien Xo: Dang phuc, dang yeu" [The Soviet Union: To be admired and loved], in *Chung toi tham Lien Xo*, 22–27.

[26] Ibid., 26.

[and] love [its] working people. Feel closer to the Soviet Union. Feel that I have to propagandize [*tuyen truyen*] about the Soviet Union, exalt [*de cao*] the Soviet Union, [and] keep an absolute [*tuyet doi*] belief in the Soviet Union.

Miss wife and children. Miss Thang [and] Hoa. Bought wife a watch and daughter a doll.

Talked to Rima [and] Sergueiev ... about Vietnamese feelings about the Soviet Union... Talking about poverty [*thieu thon*] in [Vietnam], Rima said, *Vous l'aurez* (you will have everything). [She] said: "it was the same [in the Soviet Union] when Lenin was alive. At the time the Soviet Union was all by itself. Now [because] Vietnam has the Soviet Union [as an ally], [Vietnam will] make rapid progress." Feel greater gratitude to the Soviet Union. The more [I came to know] about the Soviet Union, the more understanding, the closer [I] feel...

The whole night [I] cannot sleep [*tran troc*]. Keep thinking about the Soviet Union. Feel [I] must protect the Soviet Union.[27]

This was what Nguyen Huy Tuong wrote to himself. His affection for the Soviet Union was just as real as that for his family. The following is what appeared to be a draft of a speech he delivered at the Red Square during the same visit (under the entry for November 6, 1955):

When I was a little pupil in Hai Phong, in a night on either May 1 or the anniversary of the Russian Revolution in 1930, I was assigned the task of raising a hammer-and-sickle flag on a street lamppost in [the local] *Sat* market. [As I did this,] I was worried about the police while thinking about the Soviet Union at the same time. I knew people over there were having freedom and happiness, but I also thought that, because my country was colonized [no le], I would never have the chance to go there.

Then the Vietnamese people rose up to liberate our country, following the light from the Russian Revolution. The Soviet Union defeated fascist Germany, helping our revolution to succeed in August [1945]. Then our resistance won and the Geneva Agreements, thanks to the support of the Soviet Union that we will never forget, brought peace to our country. After that, Soviet ships brought rice to Vietnam; Soviet specialists came to Hanoi; Vietnamese delegations visited the Soviet Union. Everyday I feel closer to the Soviet Union...

My wish [*uoc vong*] of 20 years has become true. I'm honored to set foot in the Soviet Union... I have visited the tombs of the great Lenin and Stalin... As I walked by the bodies of these two great revolutionaries, solemnly and respectfully like everyone else, I promised them to struggle harder to advance [*tien len*].[28]

There was little difference between Nguyen Huy Tuong's private thoughts and his public speech (although the public speech perhaps required him to dramatize a little). His personal feelings were genuine

---

[27] Nguyen Huy Tuong, *Nhat Ky* [Diary] (preserved by Trinh Thi Uyen and edited by Nguyen Huy Thang), v. 3 (Hanoi: Thanh Nien, 2006), 57–58.
[28] Ibid., 51–52.

and the belief was sincere. As a Party member, he perhaps appreciated the experience more than others. However, available sources suggest that affection for the USSR was broadly shared among the cultural elites.

THE UNDECLARED PROPAGANDA WAR: "CIVILIZED" SOVIETS VERSUS "ODIOUS" AMERICANS

Nguyen Huy Tuong, Tu Mo, and countless other intellectuals in North Vietnam were called "soldiers on the cultural and artistic front" in the DRV. They contributed significantly to instilling the two-camp worldview in Vietnamese people. In this effort to inculcate loyalty to socialism and incite hatred against America and American imperialism, they were assisted by Ho Chi Minh, who played an active role as a satirist and commentator. From 1951 to 1956, he authored nearly 100 short articles under a few pen names (Tran Luc, T.L., C.B., D.X., and Chien Si) published in the Party's newspapers *Nhan Dan* [The People] and *Cuu Quoc* [National Salvation]. Most articles were about five hundred words long and were published during 1953–1955, or about one every other week. They were written in a simple style for ordinary readers, but the language was sharp, concise, and idiomatic. The topics ranged from the story of an ordinary farmer in the Soviet Union to the history of the Soviet Communist Party. In these articles Ho often cited sources from foreign newspapers, presenting himself as a well-read and objective observer who wanted to educate his people about those foreign lands through hard facts (statistics) and interesting vignettes. The stories about the Soviet Union conveyed the happy life, advanced technology, economic success, and progressive society there. In a typical piece, the author wrote the following about a 147-year-old farmer named Aivazov:

"Communist Youth" is the name of a collective farm in Azerbaijan (the Soviet Union). This farm was organized by Mr. Aivazov decades ago, when he was more than 120 years old. He named the farm "Communist Youth" because he considered himself a young man. Indeed, although he is now 147, he is still healthy and likes to do such things as keep sheep, raise chickens, plant crops, do carpentry, and blacksmith...[29]

Although Vietnamese leaders fully supported Stalin's policy of preserving peace, they never underestimated the American threat. They

---

[29] C.B., "147 tuoi ma van thanh nien" [Still a young man despite being 147 years old], *Nhan Dan*, October 17, 1965. Reprinted in C.B. (Ho Chi Minh), *Lien Xo Vi Dai* [The Great Soviet Union] (Hanoi: Nhan Dan, 1956): 26–27.

concluded the Geneva Agreements but were in many ways preparing for war. During and after the Geneva talks, they intensified their propaganda to counter the tendencies of "fearing and admiring America" among Vietnamese. About two-thirds of the articles (67) written by Ho were about the United States; the rest were about the Soviet Union.[30] Most of the pieces about the United States were in satirical form, in which the author adopted a mocking tone to criticize American society, from its decadent culture to its racist practices, from its crime-infested cities to its oppressive government. The author wanted to make the Vietnamese neither admire, trust, nor fear the United States because it was morally, socially, and politically corrupt. A typical piece discussed the hypocrisy of American policy as follows:

America brings money and medicine to help people in other countries. At the same time, how do Americans live? On July 5, the American president admitted, there are 32 million Americans without doctors. Last year more than 1 million Americans died of intestinal diseases. More than 600,000 Americans had mental disorder [dien]; more than 25 million had this or that disease. The great majority of Americans have no money to see doctors or to buy medicine... So you see, the American people live such miserable lives, but American reactionaries are wasting money by providing assistance to French colonizers, [Vietnamese] puppets, Chiang Kai-shek, [and] Rhee Syngman so that they can help spread American "civilization" to Asian people! How crazy. Even crazier are those who admire America, trust America, fear America.[31]

Ho's biting criticism was not limited to American policy or American government, but was as often directed against American leaders as well as against American (capitalist) culture and society. He viewed the struggle in both political and cultural terms. In the following passage, he ostensibly translated for readers materials from American newspapers in mid-August 1954:

Phoenix has 25,000 residents. Casinos, cocaine shops, and brothels open freely. Gangsters can be hired to kill people: the cost to kill a person is 12,000 francs [sic]. A merchant wanted to organize a self-defense group; his house was bombed to the ground the next day. A local paper reported this case; the paper was raided and two correspondents were critically beaten. A judge wanted to investigate the case; his house was also bombed. Another judge declared he would wage war

---

[30] For an incomplete list of these articles, see Appendix B.

[31] D.X., "Mo cha khong khoc, khoc mo moi" [They care about strangers but not their own people; literally, they cried not at their father's grave but at a pile of dirt], *Cuu Quoc*, October 12, 1951. Reprinted in C.B., D.X., T.L. et al. (Ho Chi Minh), *Noi Chuyen My...* [Talking about America] (Hanoi: Quan Doi Nhan Dan, 1972), 31. (This is a collection of articles written by Ho Chi Minh under various pseudonyms such as C.B. and D.X.).

on crimes; he was assassinated a few days later. Criminal gangs control the city. The government and the police are their puppets ... Phoenix is a small city; what about big ones? New York...³²

Ho then asked his readers: "Is [America] a civilized country? Or is it a disgusting and odious place [*hoi tanh ron nguoi*]? Ho's technique was to use an isolated (perhaps true?) story and present it as typical of America:

American capitalist magazine *Tin Tuc Hang Tuan* (January 30, 1956) reported, "Phe-rit [sic], 22, was executed in Oklahoma for killing a policeman. When Phe-rit was 18 months old, his *uncle* was executed for murder. A year later, his *mother* (who had left his father for another man) shot to death her new husband. She was absolved from this case because she was 'defending' herself from her husband who threatened to kill her. Later she killed her third husband and spent 5 years in jail for this crime. Phe-rit's *brother* is serving 10 years for theft. (Another) *uncle* of his received a life sentence for repeated crimes without repentance. Phe-rit's *girlfriend* is serving time in Virginia for stealing a car. Phe-rit's *father* is in a Texas prison because of theft." Father, mother, uncles, brother, and even girlfriend all committed crimes or have been executed. What a "model family" of America!³³

Ho's newspaper articles raise many questions. Their timing is puzzling as even by the late 1950s the DRV ostensibly still sought a political solution to reunify Vietnam under its rule. The radical view in the articles was not conducive to such as goal. Ho's motive of writing is another question. In existing scholarship, which has never examined his (covert) journalistic writings, his public persona has been that of a cosmopolitan man with moderate political views in contrast to his firebrand younger comrades. Under false identities (disguised to outsiders but not to his comrades), however, Ho emerged a very different person. This begets the question of whether the radical worldview expressed in the articles reflected his genuine belief. One theory is that he wrote those articles just to demonstrate his communist loyalty but did not necessarily think so. He had to do so perhaps to refurbish his communist credentials in the face of past criticisms of his alleged "nationalistic" tendencies (by Tran Phu and Ha Huy

³² C.B. (Ho Chi Minh), "My ma: Phong khong thuan, tuc khong my," [America means beautiful but here are its coarse and ugly customs], *Nhan Dan*, September 1, 1954. Reprinted in C.B., D.X., T.L. et al. (Ho Chi Minh), *Noi Chuyen My...*, 50–51.
³³ C.B., "Mot 'gia dinh guong mau' cua My" [A model family of America], *Nhan Dan*, February 16, 1956. Reprinted in C.B., D.X., T.L. et al. (Ho Chi Minh), *Noi Chuyen My...*, 64–65. Italics in original. The magazine's name *Tin Tuc Hang Tuan* in the quote may have been *Newsweek*, but I did not find the story in the *Newsweek* issue published on January 30, 1956. An alternative translation is *Weekly News*, but I could not find any national publication with this title in 1956.

Tap in the 1930s and by Tran Ngoc Danh in the 1940s).[34] This theory would discount the value of the articles as reflecting to some extent Ho's true belief.

Yet Ho's pro-Soviet and anti-American attitude of the 1950s was nothing new. As seen earlier, he already articulated it in the 1920s when he was a young revolutionary apprentice. He continued to do so in the early 1940s on the pages of the Viet Minh's newspaper *Viet Nam Doc Lap*. As I have argued, personal conflicts and power rivalries between Ho and other leaders such as Tran Phu and Ha Huy Tap have been exaggerated. Twice, Ho did not grab the General Secretary post when he had the power to do so (February 1930) or was offered the position (1941). In the Tran Ngoc Danh affair related earlier, Danh criticized not just Ho but also Truong Chinh, and Danh was expelled from the Party for doing so.

By 1951, Ho was well established as founding Father and President of the DRV and the Party and had little reason to fear being removed.[35] Khrushchev's denunciation of Stalin and his cult of personality in February 1956 led to the downfall of several Eastern European leaders but not Ho, attesting to his secure status. As will be seen later in this chapter, no other leaders took the opportunity of Khrushchev's speech to criticize Ho's pervasive cult of personality that he himself had contributed to.[36] Later that year, when Truong Chinh was forced to resign from his position to take responsibility for the disastrous land reform errors, Ho was in fact appointed as acting General Secretary besides holding the Presidency. These facts do not sit well with the speculations about Ho's insecure position or nonentity status in the Party in the 1950s.

The articles themselves demonstrated that Ho was a talented satirist who liked to play with words and to make short verses. In Vietnamese, "America" is called "My" (from Chinese "Mei guo"). "My" also means

[34] For the point about Ho's vulnerability in the 1950s, see Sophie Quinn-Judge, "Rethinking the History of the Vietnamese Communist Party," in Duncan McCargo, ed. *Rethinking Vietnam* (New York: Routledge, 2004), 33.

[35] See the rhapsodic reactions to his speech at the Third Party Congress in 1951 as recorded in "Loi Ho Chu Tich trong Dai hoi toan Dang" [President Ho's words at the (Second) Party Congress], *Hoc Tap* (Nghe An), no. 35 (April 1951), 1–8 (available on http://www.talawas.org/?p=24635). Le Van Hien, the Minister of Finance who witnessed the event, expressed the same sentiment in his diary: *Nhat ky cua mot Bo truong* [Diary of a minister], v. 2 (Da Nang: Da Nang Publishing House, 1995), 503 (entry dated February 14, 1951).

[36] According to Asselin, in 1956 Ho's "image was practically everywhere in Hanoi and [his] every major public utterance was treated as an article of revolutionary faith." Asselin, *Hanoi's Road to the Vietnam War*, 36. See also Olga Dror, "Establishing Ho Chi Minh's

"beauty." Ho pointed this out, warning Vietnamese that the name of the country suggested beauty and goodness but its actions were just the opposite.[37] Another brilliant example is Ho's transliteration of General Douglas McArthur's name into Vietnamese as *Mat-Acte* ("very cruel face!" in Vietnamese).[38] Given that Ho devoted significant time and talent over many years to write those articles, it is unlikely that he wrote them under pressure. Rather, they suggested his enthusiasm and awareness of the need to educate his people about the dark side of America and the greatness of the Soviet Union.

As a cultural entrepreneur, Ho was subtly and skillfully revising the popular image of the United States in Vietnam. The skills he brought to the task, the strong messages the articles conveyed, and the great frequency and long duration in which they appeared suggested possible impact on their readers. At least Ho helped to make the idea of fighting the most powerful but also most corrupt superpower not that daunting and certainly justified.

DEFENDING COMMUNISM AND BUILDING
A PEOPLE'S DEMOCRACY AT HOME

Despite some dissent within their ranks, Vietnamese leaders trusted Stalin's policy to preserve peace and followed Soviet and Chinese advice to sign the Geneva Agreements in July 1954. At the same time, they watched closely every move the Americans made. Even before signing the Agreements, they had noted American efforts to create a new Southeast Asian military alliance. Ho warned his comrades that:

[W]e should not be complacent. Our victory [at Dien Bien Phu] has wakened up the Yankee imperialist. He is adjusting his conspiracy and plans to prolong the war by internationalizing it. [He wants to] wreck the Agreements, expel the French to take over Indochina, enslave Indochinese people, and create more tension in the world.[39]

The DRV's strategy at the time was to exploit the conflict in the imperialist camp between Washington and Paris. By late 1954, after a

Cult: Vietnamese Traditions and Their Transformations," *Journal of Asian Studies* 75: 2 (2016), 433–466.

[37] D.X., "My la xau" [America means ugliness], *Cuu Quoc*, November 3, 1951. Reprinted in C.B., D.X., T.L. et al., *Noi Chuyen My*, 30.

[38] C.B., "Dao duc cua My" [American morality], *Nhan Dan*, June 14, 1951. Reprinted in C.B., D.X., T.L. et al., *Noi Chuyen My*, 97.

[39] Ho Chi Minh, "Bao cao tai Hoi nghi lan thu sau" [Report at the Sixth Central Committee Plenum], July 15, 1954. *VKDTT*, v. 15: 165.

series of successful American moves to consolidate the anticommunist bloc, Vietnamese leaders already sensed that their strategy would fail.[40] This new development created a siege mentality. At the Eighth Plenum in March 1955, the Party's Central Committee reviewed the balance of forces between two camps, and expressed concerns that Vietnam was the weaker outpost of the socialist camp compared to the other three (East Germany, North Korea, and China).[41] The Committee warned about possible US attacks on the Soviet Union, China, and other Southeast Asian countries.[42] They predicted that Washington and Saigon were likely to delay or refuse to carry out elections as proposed in the Geneva Agreements.[43]

On this occasion, Ho Chi Minh and Truong Chinh appeared to differ in their assessment of the world situation. First, Ho viewed the United States and the Soviet Union as more or less equal in force capabilities, but the latter was ultimately stronger because it represented a just cause.[44] Speaking after Ho, Chinh noted that Moscow was helping some "people's democracies" (i.e., China) to build nuclear-fuelled electricity plants. Compared to the United States, which was still trying to test nuclear weapons, he argued that the Soviet Union was clearly superior in nuclear technology and science.[45] Second, Chinh chided the Party propaganda department for praising India and Burma too much; this would mislead people about the political stand of those countries.[46] In contrast, Ho counted India and Indonesia as forces for peace, suggesting that those countries could be allies of the socialist camp.[47] These differences confirmed the well-known fact that Truong Chinh was among the most radical leaders of Vietnamese communism. These differences aside, all Party leaders largely ignored the bustling diplomacy by governments of the emerging nonaligned bloc. The Asian conference to be held in India and the Asia-Africa Conference to be held later in Bandung, Indonesia, were

[40] This refers to the Manila conference (September 3, 1954), the Paris Agreement (October 23, 1954), and the US-Taiwan Relations Act (December 2, 1954).

[41] "Ket luan cuoc thao luan o Hoi nghi Trung uong lan thu bay" [Conclusions to the discussion at the Seventh Plenum], March 3–12, 1955. *VKDTT*, v. 16, 177.

[42] "Tinh hinh hien tai va nhiem vu truoc mat" [Current situation and upcoming tasks], Truong Chinh's report at the Seventh Plenum (March 3–12, 1955). *VKDTT*, v. 16, 97, 128.

[43] Ibid., 184.

[44] "Loi khai mac cua Ho chu tich" [Chairman Ho's opening remarks], March 3, 1954. *VKDTT*, v. 16, 92.

[45] "Tinh hinh hien tai va nhiem vu truoc mat," *VKDTT*, v. 16, 100.

[46] Ibid., 166.

[47] "Loi be mac cua Ho chu tich" [Closing speech of Chairman Ho], March 12, 1955. *VKDTT*, v. 16, 222.

mentioned only once in one sentence.[48] These activities clearly did not fit the Vietnamese leaders' two-camp worldview.

In response to the rising temperature of the Cold War, Vietnamese communists still thought that the need to preserve world peace was more urgent than Vietnam's unification, even though they paid greater attention to the latter now.[49] Thus, the Party wanted to further consolidate Vietnam's "solidarity" with the Soviet bloc through diplomacy and educate the masses at home more about proletarian internationalism.[50] This call for mass indoctrination indicates a consistent pattern of behavior that will be seen again and again. The pattern was that, whenever life became more difficult, the Party would resort to ever more rigorous indoctrination of the masses. The reason was that Party leaders never blamed their doctrine for what went wrong. Marx and Lenin were always right but cadres (including the top leaders themselves) did not understand the masters correctly, which was why more ideological study and training were required.

By late 1955, it became clear to Hanoi that things were not right. Ngo Dinh Diem declared that he would not honor the Geneva Agreements because his government did not sign them, and because elections as stipulated in the Agreements would not be free in North Vietnam under the communist dictatorship. Ngo also organized a referendum to oust Emperor Bao Dai while making himself president of a new Republic of Vietnam. He named communism as one of the three enemies of his regime, together with feudalism and colonialism.[51] In the wake of Ngo's attack on communism, Party leaders decided that not to defend the doctrine was a serious right-leaning mistake.[52] They launched a propaganda campaign designed to showcase to North Vietnamese the superiority of the socialist camp over its imperialist enemy. Party members were mobilized to fight against the "lies and slanders about our regime and the regimes in our socialist brother-countries."[53] The goal was to make "the

---

[48] "Tinh hinh hien tai va nhiem vu truoc mat," *VKDTT*, v. 16, 100. Chinh mentioned these events in his speech; Ho did not.

[49] Ibid., 178. See also Hoang Quoc Viet, "Dau tranh de thong nhat nuoc nha tren co so doc lap va dan chu, bang phuong phap hoa binh" [Struggle to unify the country by peaceful means based on independence and (socialist) democracy], *Hoc Tap* (December 1955), 41–43.

[50] "Tinh hinh hien tai va nhiem vu truoc mat," *VKDTT*, v. 16, 159.

[51] "Bai phong, da thuc, diet cong" (Oppose feudalism, fight colonialism, and destroy communism). See Edward Miller, *Misalliance: Ngo Dinh Diem, the United States, and the Fate of South Vietnam* (Cambridge, MA: Harvard University Press, 2013).

[52] "Thong tri cua Ban Bi Thu so 48-TT/TW" [Party Secretariat's Circulation], July 21, 1955. *VKDTT*, v. 16, 459.

[53] Ibid., 460–461.

people, especially the working people, to enthusiastically support communism and actively defend communists."

This unfavorable international situation revived internal debate among Party leaders about the ongoing land-reform campaign.[54] Some argued that the violent class warfare in the North could alienate the upper classes in South Vietnam, making it more difficult to unify the country. Hoang Quoc Viet, a Politburo member in charge of united front work, asserted that any successful united front must be based on the alliance of workers and peasants and must meet their "basic demands." This essentially meant that class struggle should continue. In his report at the Eighth Central Committee Plenum in August 1955, Truong Chinh advocated sustaining the land reform but nevertheless admitted that calling for rapid socialist industrialization in the current environment was a "left-leaning mistake."[55] He mentioned the word "socialism" only twice in his fifty-nine-page report.

The Plenum resolution reflected some uncertainty, but the radical view adopted since 1953 still held sway. On the one hand, the Party decided that the North was to take "gradual but firm steps toward socialism," and that the political system in the North must *essentially* be a "people's democracy." On the other hand, the regime *in appearance* was allowed to retain certain characteristics of "old-style democracy," and it would be acceptable if the progress of socialism in North Vietnam would be slower than that in other people's democracies.[56] This confusing formulation basically meant that class struggle would continue but must be organized in a way that would not appear harsh from the outside. There were thus different views among Party leadership about the speed of the socialist revolution but not about socialism itself. No Party leaders expressed any reservations about the need to publicly and proudly defend communism.

"NO OTHER WAY OUT BUT REVOLUTION"

Soviet leader Nikita Khrushchev's denunciation of Stalin in early 1956 shocked Hanoi as it did in many Eastern European capitals. In response, Vietnamese leaders accepted Khrushchev's overall argument but denied

[54] Hoang Quoc Viet, "Dau tranh de thong nhat nuoc nha" *Hoc Tap* (December 1955), 40.
[55] "Bao cao cua dong chi Truong Chinh" [Comrade Truong Chinh's report]. *VKDTT*, v. 16, 524.
[56] "Nghi quyet Hoi nghi Trung uong lan thu 8" [Resolution of the Eighth Central Committee Plenum], August 1955. *VKDTT*, v. 16, 577. "Old-style democracy" referred to bourgeois democracy.

its relevance to Vietnam. First, they argued that their Party had been prac-
ticing collective leadership, and "personality cult" was not a big problem in their party.[57] They pledged to strengthen collective leadership, but
also warned about committing right-leaning mistakes, such as "excessive
democracy" and the wholesale refutation of the role of individual leaders in revolution.[58] It was stressed that Ho Chi Minh's role must still be
elevated.

Second, Vietnamese leaders took exception to Khrushchev's calls for
peaceful coexistence between the communist and capitalist camps on two
grounds. Perhaps with South Vietnam in mind, they asserted that, although
it was possible to prevent war, imperialism was war-oriented by its economic nature.[59] Until the day when imperialism was totally destroyed,
the threat of war remained and "people of the world" [*nhan dan the gioi*]
must always be on guard. Also, while it was possible for some countries
to advance to socialism by peaceful means as Khrushchev claimed, in
cases where the capitalist class still controlled the coercive apparatus and
were determined to suppress revolution with force, the proletariat must
be prepared to take up arms if it were to win. Although Hanoi pledged to
continue its peaceful unification policy toward the South, Party leaders
publicly distanced themselves from Khrushchev's stand.

North Vietnam's reactions to Khrushchev's speech cast doubt on the
conventional assumption that Ho was politically vulnerable. Rather than
taking the opportunity to attack Ho, his comrades rallied behind him.
Hanoi's keeping some distance from Khrushchev was similarly puzzling
for those who argue that the DRV had joined the Soviet bloc simply to
obtain material support. If that had been true, one would expect DRV
leaders to dance to Khrushchev's tunes.

Party leaders formulated a clearer assessment of their Southern policy by the end of 1956 as they convened the Tenth Central Committee
Plenum. They noted that the international environment had become more
favorable to the socialist camp.[60] The Soviet Union was at the forefront of
the world's disarmament movement. Soviet-Yugoslavian talks improved

[57] "Bao cao cua Bo Chinh Tri" [Politburo's Report at the Ninth Central Committee
Plenum], April 19–24, 1956. *VKDTT*, v. 17, 158–162.

[58] Ibid., 165–166. The term for "excessive democracy" in Vietnamese is *dan chu cuc doan*,
which literally meant "extreme democracy."

[59] "Nghi quyet cua Hoi nghi Ban chap hanh Trung Uong lan thu chin mo rong" [Resolution
of the expanded 9th Central Committee Plenum]. *VKDTT*, v. 17, 169.

[60] "De cuong bao cao cua Bo Chinh tri tai Hoi nghi Trung uong lan thu 10" [Draft report
of the Politburo at the Tenth Plenum], August 25-October 5, 1956. *VKDTT*, v. 17,
418–419.

unity in the socialist camp, and internal frictions emerged in US-led military alliances in Europe, Asia, and the Middle East. Domestically, the Central Committee agreed that the land-reform and "organizational rectification" campaigns in the North had committed serious errors by the excessive use of violence and the rampant misapplication of quotas for landlords.[61] This admission would lead to the resignation of General Secretary Truong Chinh at the end of the Plenum. Ho was elected to assume Truong Chinh's position until a replacement was appointed.

In South Vietnam, Ngo Dinh Diem had categorically rejected the Geneva Agreements. July, the month when national elections were supposed to take place to unify the country, passed without any such events. This presented Party leaders with the problem of how to explain such a failure to their followers. In this sense, Le Duan's forty-two-page analysis from the South came as a timely blessing (although conventional scholarship views this only as a criticism of central leadership).

Born Le Van Nhuan in 1907 in central Vietnam into the family of a small merchant, Le Duan had only an elementary school education before leaving for work as a clerk in the Indochinese Railroad Agency.[62] He joined the communist movement in the late 1920s and spent two terms of nine years total in Poulo Condor prison before 1945. Duan led the Party in the South during the anti-French war and requested to stay behind in the South to continue the struggle after the Geneva Agreements. In this document, Duan as the third-ranking party leader and the head of the Party office in the South called for a new policy of revolutionary struggle to defeat the Ngo Dinh Diem regime.[63] He presented the harshest

---

[61] A sympathetic account shows that more than 70 percent of rich farmers and landlords were wrongly labeled and persecuted. Dang Phong, ed. *Lich Su Kinh Te Viet Nam 1945–2000* [An Economic History of Vietnam], v. 2, 1955–1975 (Hanoi: Chinh Tri Quoc Gia, 2005), 85.

[62] Dang Van Thai, ed. *Le Duan tieu su* [Biography of Le Duan] (Hanoi: Chinh tri Quoc gia, 2007). He graduated from the only Franco-Vietnamese elementary school in Quang Tri, his home province, in 1923, and did not pass the examination to enter the Quoc Hoc School in Hue for middle school.

[63] Le Duan, "Duong loi cach mang mien Nam" [Revolutionary line in the South], August 1956. *VKDTT*, v. 17, 783–825. Robert Brigham mistakenly wrote that "[in 1956, f] ew in the party recognized Duan as a potential national leader." In fact, Duan had been a Central Committee member in the late 1930s, and was elected to the seven-member Politburo at the Second Congress in 1951, which ranked him third below only Ho and Truong Chinh and above Hoang Quoc Viet, Vo Nguyen Giap, Pham Van Dong, and Nguyen Chi Thanh. See Brigham, "Why the South Won the American War in Vietnam," in Marc Jason Gilbert, *Why the North Won the Vietnam War* (New York: Palgrave, 2002), 101; *VKDTT*, v. 12, 521.

and most doctrinaire analysis of the Saigon regime to date, calling it "a neocolonialist regime under the control of an aggressive imperialist – the United States," and "a cruel and clever fascist dictatorship."[64] He eloquently asserted that revolution was the only way out in the South, pushing central policy toward, if not a more radical, then a sharply clarified position.[65]

Either out of respect for the general policy of the socialist camp or based on a strategic analysis of military balance in the South, Le Duan accepted that the revolution could proceed for the time being as a "political struggle" but not yet an "armed struggle." At the same time, he stressed that political struggle should be based on mass forces in opposition to the Saigon government, not on mere legal or constitutional demands. Here Duan implicitly dismissed as misguided the central policy to demand the implementation of the Geneva Agreements. To Duan, the goal of the struggle from then on must be "revolutionary" – namely, to eventually overthrow the Saigon government and to implement communism.[66] Duan offered a lengthy historical analysis of the Vietnamese revolution to conclude that it must give equal priority to both class struggle and national struggle to be successful.[67] This was exactly how Tran Phu had defined the bourgeois democratic phase of the revolution – in 1930.

Following a well-set pattern, the Tenth Plenum did not blame land-reform mistakes on the doctrine or on Chinese advisers. Instead, the leaders humbly blamed themselves for having failed to apply Marxist-Leninist theories correctly.[68] At the same time, Party leaders were concerned about many post-land-reform developments in the countryside, including "right-leaning" errors and the "revival of capitalism" among upper-middle peasants.[69] In response to the new situation, Party leaders called for more rigorous study of the doctrine (for the leaders) and more systematic indoctrination (for the rank and file).[70] People must study

[64] Le Duan, "Duong loi cach mang mien Nam," *VKDTT*, v. 17, 787–788.
[65] At the Tenth Plenum, which met without Duan who was still in the South, the Politburo claimed that the idea of revolution in the South was not new to them although they admitted to failure in clarifying the idea, in researching the Southern situation, and in pursuing a corresponding policy. "De cuong bao cao cua Bo Chinh tri tai Hoi nghi Trung uong lan thu 10," *VKDTT*, v 17, 423.
[66] "Duong loi cach mang mien Nam," *VKDTT*, v. 17: 805–806.
[67] Ibid., 806–822.
[68] "De cuong bao cao cua Bo Chinh tri tai Hoi nghi Trung uong lan thu 10," *VKDTT*, v. 17, 449.
[69] Ibid., 480–482.
[70] Ibid., 486–498.

harder so that they could unite patriotism and proletarian internationalism harmoniously in their belief system. The idea that Vietnam could be a
neutral country between the two camps must be specifically denounced.
People must believe in the socialist camp led by the Soviet Union and
China, and must work hard to strengthen Vietnam's solidarity with the
socialist brother-countries, friendship with neighboring nations, and support for the peace and democratic movement.[71] Party leaders vowed that,
"regardless of circumstances," North Vietnam must be consolidated to
make "gradual steps toward socialism."

Conventional scholarship discusses socialist development in the North
and national unification as conflicting goals in the thinking of Party
leaders.[72] If this had indeed been the case, it was no longer true by 1956.
Both regions were assigned tasks that together would take Vietnam on
parallel tracks to socialism. This formulation created ideological consis-
tency but it also required clarifying that the upcoming war in the South
was not just a war for national unification but also a step on the long
road to socialism. Le Duan's analysis of the Southern situation in clear
doctrinal terms as a neocolony under imperialist rule was a crucial theoretical move to prepare for new concepts of the war to be developed over
the next two years.

"TO BE PATRIOTIC IS TO DEVELOP SOCIALISM"

Vietnamese communists found innovative discursive formulations to justify
class struggle during the war for independence against France. They translated foreign Marxist-Leninist arguments into concise Vietnamese formulations such as "class struggle within a nationalist struggle." As they launched
an armed struggle in the south, they did not hide but in fact emphasized their
socialist agenda. By 1958, they no longer talked simply about "strengthening the North" but planned for "socialist industrialization." In this section,
I trace the process in which new definitions of *patriotism* were invented to
justify continuing revolution in both North and South.

Prior to 1957, Party leaders talked of "patriotism" [*chu nghia yeu
nuoc*] and "proletarian internationalism" [*tinh than quoc te vo san*] as
two separate things.[73] Patriotism was defined as love for the fatherland.

---

[71] Ibid., 496.
[72] Lien-Hang Nguyen, The War Politburo: North Vietnam's Diplomatic and Political Road
to the Tet Offensive," *Journal of Vietnamese Studies* 1: 1–2 (2006), 5–48.
[73] An example is To Huu's report on thought work [cong tac tu tuong] at the Tenth Plenum
in August 1956. VKDTT, v. 17, 495–497.

Proletarian internationalism meant support for the socialist camp and for the international working-class movement. Party leaders frequently stressed the need to educate their cadres and the masses about these two isms. By 1957, as they debated the approaches to economic development in the North and revolution in the South, a new formulation that tied these two concepts together gradually emerged.

In an article in the Party's theoretical journal *Hoc Tap* [Study], Hoang Xuan Nhi, a professor at the College of Pedagogy, attempted to elaborate on the standard Marxist-Leninist proposition that "the national problem" was reducible to class struggle.[74] He argued that patriotism was a historical phenomenon that had different class contents in each historical period. In feudal times, patriotism was understood as loyalty to the king. In the struggle against feudal classes, capitalists claimed to represent the nation but their nationalism was ultimately made to serve their class interests, not those of the working people. Nhi claimed that, of all classes, workers loved their country the most. Through their [manual] labor, generations of workers produced material goods and created cultures, languages, writing systems, and other national traditions. Although they loved their country, their patriotic sense was spontaneous and easily manipulated. As Nhi argued, only when led by a vanguard party armed with Marxism-Leninism could they develop "genuine patriotism" [*chu nghia yeu nuoc chan chinh*]. Genuine patriotism must unite passionate love for the motherland with class consciousness. Because the Communist Party represented the interests of the working class in North Vietnam, patriotism also meant support for the Party and for its rule in all aspects of society. Although Nhi's theoretical discussion was so blatantly directed to justify the Party's rule, he showed an early effort of Party theorists to find new ideological expressions for the old concept of patriotism.

Throughout 1957, all Party members were required to study Marxism-Leninism. High-ranking cadres studied "Marxist-Leninist theories" while the rest studied the basic concepts of historical materialism.[75] This was the first nationwide, systematic organization of mass study sessions, which aimed to enhance members' theoretical understanding, loyalty to the causes of the proletariat, and belief in the Party and the socialist camp. In the previous year, a series of international and domestic events

---

[74] Hoang Xuan Nhi, "Boi duong chu nghia yeu nuoc, tang cuong chu nghia quoc te vo san trong nhan dan ta [Inculcating patriotism and strengthening proletarian internationalism in our people], *Hoc Tap* (January 1957): 34–45.

[75] See Nguyen Hoi, "Ket qua cua dot hoc tap duy vat lich su vua qua" [Results of the study sessions in historical materialism]. *Hoc Tap* (March 1958), 53–62.

had seriously eroded popular support for the regime.[76] As Party theorists sought to quell heretical ideas within their ranks, they had to clarify their concepts and sharpen their arguments.

According to a report in the Party journal, among the topics for study and criticism was the notion that Vietnam could be reunified faster if it took the neutral path like many Asian and African countries.[77] This notion was denounced as "completely mistaken" for three reasons. First, it was argued that revolutionary victory could result only from a long and difficult class struggle but would never be granted by imperialist powers. Second, "[national] independence and reunification were not abstract concepts but embodied class contents. Independence and reunification meant the liberation of the working people, and for this reason, could be brought about only by the Party of the proletariat." Third, the emergence of neutral countries (such as India) was not a random process but required two essential conditions: the international condition was the rise of the socialist camp, whereas the domestic condition was the power of mass movements in those countries. The Party thus rejected a neutral path between two Cold War blocs for Vietnam. National interests were now publicly associated with those of working classes. The ultimate goal of the Party was publicly laid out, which was revolutionary changes through class struggle, not mere national independence and reunification. A neutral, nonaligned foreign policy would not "fit the bill," so to speak. As the report indicated, the mass study sessions forced not only the students but also their lecturers to grapple with what patriotism should mean in the new era.

It was Pham Van Dong, the Premier and a Politburo member, who produced a succinct formulation that would acquire the status of a new doctrine of patriotism. The formulation was: "to be patriotic is to develop socialism."[78] Dong came to this formulation after a lengthy but eloquent recount of the world revolutionary movement, from its success in Russia in 1917 to its current status in Vietnam in 1958.[79] Boldly declaring that "our era is the era when patriotism joins socialism," Dong depicted the Bolshevik Revolution as "the result of two great struggles: one by Russian workers and peasants led by the Bolshevik party, and the other by the

---

[76] These events included mistakes in the land reform, rural unrest, the surge of intellectual dissent, Khrushchev's denunciation of Stalin, and Hungarian and Polish revolts.

[77] Nguyen Hoi, "Ket qua cua dot hoc tap duy vat lich su vua qua," *Hoc Tap*, 59.

[78] A later variant of this formulation is, "to love your country means to love socialism" [yeu nuoc la yeu chu nghia xa hoi].

[79] Pham Van Dong, "Chu nghia yeu nuoc va chu nghia xa hoi" [Patriotism and Socialism], *Hoc Tap* (August 1958, 6–17.

nations under Czarist rule." The encounter of patriotism with socialism
was a key factor determining the success of that revolution. As he argued
passionately:

The Soviet Union, the product of the October [1917] Revolution, is the first
model image of a state comprising many nations who live together in an equal
and friendly relationship and who together develop socialism. [In this society,] all
nations enjoy the conditions required to develop their capacity to build their happy
lives while contributing to the prosperity of the entire Soviet Union. "The prison
of all nations" has been replaced by "the Fatherland of 100 brother-nations."[80]

   After reviewing the history of the Vietnamese revolution, he made a
similar claim that it was also "the history of the marvellous, inevitable,
and productive encounter between patriotism and socialism." It was the
fusion of patriotic forces with the leadership of a working class's Party.
But, to Dong, this fusion reached its "highest stage" in North Vietnam
only since 1954, when patriotism and socialism came to share the goal of
the revolution: "to be patriotic is to develop socialism; to develop socialism is to be patriotic."[81] In South Vietnam, the "people's struggle ... must
be accompanied by their enthusiastic and determined support for the
socialist North... The South's patriotic movement and the North's construction of socialism [together will represent] that fusion of patriotism
and socialism in the revolutionary process." This fusion, Dong concluded,
would "lead to unification and to the favorable development of *socialism in all of Vietnam*. In our contemporary world, this path is inevitable;
nothing can prevent it from taking place."[82]

   The significance of this formulation is that for the first time Vietnamese
communists raised *socialism* in the *public* discourse to the same level of
patriotism.[83] *Patriotism* was an older and more respected concept than
socialism. No Vietnamese had ever questioned patriotism, but socialism
had always been controversial.[84] As Hanoi leaders debated the revolutionary paths in the North *and* the South, they found a formulation that
placed the two apparently separate paths in each region in one single
phrase that expressed the dialectic relationship between them: to struggle
in the South would contribute to the development of socialism in the
North, and vice versa. For this formulation to make sense, the struggle in

[80] Ibid., 9.
[81] Ibid., 14.
[82] Italics added.
[83] In their *internal* discourse, Vietnamese communists talked far more about socialism than
   about patriotism.
[84] Vu, *Paths to Development in Asia*, chapter 8.

the South must necessarily be viewed as a revolution for socialism, not simply one for reunification. To win the war, the Party must aggressively and publicly promote socialism rather than restrain or hide it under a nationalist appearance as in 1953. The new formulation paved the way for the subsequent revision of the Party Constitution in which the class base of the Party was changed from "the working class and the working people" to "the working class" only. The removal of the fuzzy phrase "the working people" was to align the text strictly with the communist doctrine. This change was followed by a newly inserted phrase pledging "to organize the teaching of Marxist-Leninist principles to Party members and to the people in a broad and systematic way..."[85] The new formulation of patriotism and socialism would later be included in the new national Constitution approved in 1960.[86]

"CAPITALISM IS THE ROAD OF DEATH"

Le Duan's forceful analysis helped secure his appointment as the successor to Truong Chinh around 1957. Existing scholarship credits Duan and other Southerners in the Politburo with winning support for the decision made at the Ninth Plenum in January 1959, which authorized an armed struggle in South Vietnam.[87] This is true, but we should not underestimate the contributions of other leaders from Ho Chi Minh to Pham Van Dong. Ho produced propaganda that readied North Vietnamese for confronting the United States, and Dong formulated a significant concept that advanced revolution in both regions. These leaders played critical albeit less acknowledged roles in the eventual making of that decision.

At the Third Party Congress in September 1960, Le Duan presented a political report of 161 pages that reportedly was a collective work with contributions of ideas from other top leaders.[88] The body of this report included seven parts: The section on the "democratic revolution" in the

[85] Le Duc Tho, "Viec sua doi Dieu le Dang," [Revising the Party Constitution], *Hoc Tap* (May 1960): 23.

[86] The Party leadership discussed and decided to proclaim in the new national Constitution that the North would take the path of socialism. See "De cuong bao cao ve Hien phap sua doi" [Draft report about revising the Constitution], n.d., likely late 1959. *VKDTT*, v. 20: 834–837.

[87] For a discussion of this decision, see Carlyle Thayer, *War by Other Means: National Liberation and Revolution in Vietnam, 1954–1960* (Sydney: Allen & Unwin, 1989).

[88] "Bao cao chinh tri cua Ban Chap hanh Trung uong Dang tai Dai Hoi Dai bieu toan quoc lan thu III" [Political report of the Central Committee at the Third National Party Congress], September 5, 1960. *VKDTT*, v. 21, 495–656.

South was presented first, followed by three sections on the North (the socialist revolution in the North, the First Five-Year Plan, and the building of a "democratic dictatorship"), and the section about the international situation was presented near the end (Part VI). This contrasted with his predecessor's reports, which always began with the international situation as the most important section. The order of the sections suggested that Duan viewed the South with a greater urgency, although he did not downplay the tasks facing the North. By putting the international context at the end, Duan strongly hinted that, regardless of the international situation, he wanted the Vietnamese revolution to move forward to fulfill its historical mission.

The literature on the Vietnam War creates the impression that Hanoi leaders were preoccupied with national reunification. There is some truth in this, but the evidence thus far in this chapter has indicated that those leaders thought of the war in the context of the broader socialist revolution which they had been waging since the 1930s. Winning the war was not just for the sake of reunification, but more importantly to complete one more step on the revolutionary road. In Le Duan's report at the Third Party Congress we see more evidence along the same line. Vietnamese communist leaders did not downplay socialist development in the North when they decided to launch a war for reunification in the South. Rather, they viewed both tasks as complementary, which *together* would take Vietnam further along the road to socialism.[89]

Le Duan offered three reasons that the North would need to develop socialism, and only one of them was because of the South. First, because the North had completed the "people's national democratic revolution" (that is, achievement of independence and land reform, or the bourgeois democratic revolution in Tran Phu's terms), Duan argued that "the North can't stop there, but must go further. The next step of the revolution should be only socialism, not capitalism. Capitalism means exploitation, oppression, privation, suffering... [it] is the road of death ... The revolution in the North should instead take the road of life, to socialism, not the road of death."[90] Second, because the North had become "the rear base for revolution in the entire country," socialist development in the North would allow it to offer greater assistance to the Southern revolution. Third, socialist development in North Vietnam had international significance due to the fact that "the Yankee imperialist and his lackeys

[89] Ibid., 512.
[90] Ibid., 505–506.

are preparing for a new war to seize our country and turn it into a spring-
board for attacking the socialist camp, resisting national liberation movements in Southeast Asia, and wrecking world peace." Duan thus believed
that the stronger the North became as a bastion of socialism, the more
it would contribute to the socialist camp, to Southeast Asian liberation
movements, and to world peace.

The report divided the specific tasks for the revolution in the North
into two: socialist reform [*cai tao xa hoi chu nghia*] and socialist development [*xay dung chu nghia xa hoi*, literally "socialist construction"].[91]
Socialist reform was primarily to replace "capitalist" and "feudal" relations of production with socialist ones, specifically through the nationalization of private enterprises and the collectivization of agriculture and
trade. Duan predicted that socialist reform would be a "difficult" and
"complicated" class struggle. Peasants and traders made a living with
their labor, which was good, but they tended to spontaneously develop
into capitalists [*khuynh huong tu phat tu ban chu nghia*]. To make sure
they would stay in cooperatives, the report called for ideological education and for "appropriate measures to cut off their economic links with
the capitalist class."[92] As for the capitalist class in the North, the report
viewed it as being small and weak, but predicted that capitalists "would
inevitably resist reform by every means at their disposal." They could be
reformed peacefully, but the struggle would be long and would require
determination and persistence. The report warned that socialist reform
would be difficult also because of the opposition from "hostile forces,"
including supporters of the old regime left behind in the North, the "reactionaries under religious disguise," "reactionary capitalists and rich peasants," and those "obstinate" landlords who refused to "be reformed."

On the development of socialism, the report made "socialist industrialization" to be the central task of "the transition period," and called for
prioritizing heavy industries while also creating modern agriculture and
light industries. The scale and structure of the heavy industries must be
suitable to domestic conditions and to the division of labor and cooperation in the socialist camp.[93] The report noted that the economy of each
socialist country had become "an integral part of the world's socialist
economic system" [*he thong kinh te xa hoi chu nghia the gioi*]. Through
the division of labor and cooperation in the socialist system, each member

[91] Ibid., 536–543.
[92] Ibid., 541.
[93] Ibid., 546.

state could develop its own economy, drawing from the great economic strength of the entire system. Because North Vietnam bypassed the capitalist stage to advance directly to socialism, it needed the support of the Soviet bloc. At the same time, the report called for a self-reliant spirit. Although the North must rely on help from more developed "socialist brethren" for capital, equipment, technology, and expertise, the report recommended that the DRV should try to offer the brethren what they needed in return.[94]

But a revolution in the economic sphere would not be sufficient, according to the report. There must be a concomitant revolution launched in the areas of thought [*tu tuong*], culture [*van hoa*], and technology [*ky thuat*].[95] The goal of the thought revolution was "to make the entire people, especially the working classes, believe deeply in socialism. The people should learn to reject traditional worldviews and beliefs and adopt that of Marxism-Leninism." The revolution should aim at "making Marxism-Leninism the hegemonic belief [*chiem uu the tuyet doi*] in the country and in the minds of the entire people who would develop a new ethic" based on the doctrine.[96]

As with the North, Le Duan also viewed the Southern revolution primarily in doctrinal class-struggle terms. He believed that:

[T]o launch the revolution to liberate the South is to solve two fundamental antagonisms in its society today: one is between Southerners and ... the Yankee imperialist and his lackeys; and the other is within Southerners, especially between peasants and the feudalistic landlord class. Only when those two antagonisms have been solved can the Southern people escape their current sufferings and privations, and the Southern society develop progressively and merge with the North into a single unit.

Although reunification appeared to be the end goal of the revolution in Duan's analysis, it was not reunification under any terms, but reunification on the basis of the North annexing the South into its political system following a successful anti-imperialist and class struggle in the South. It was political, not national or even territorial, reunification that was most emphasized.

The report minced no words in its vicious portrayal of life and politics in the South. The region was called "an American colony and a [military]

---

[94] Ibid., 536. The report did not elaborate but the authors probably meant the minerals and agricultural produce that Vietnam could export to its socialist brethren.

[95] Ibid., 548–559.

[96] Ibid., 550.

base for the invasion of Southeast Asia."[97] The United States controlled the Ngo Dinh Diem government; American companies controlled the Southern economy and dumped their surplus stocks there; and the "corrupt" American lifestyle was "poisoning" Southern people, especially the youth. The Ngo Dinh Diem regime drew its power from the pro-American and most reactionary elements among the landlord and comprador classes in the South.

In the South, according to the report, "not a day passed by without the sound of gunshot, without patriots being killed." Southern troops "razed houses to the ground, burned crops, raped women, and tortured and murdered people with barbaric techniques." In urban centers, there was one unemployed person for every eight people, and the economy was near collapse. In the countryside, taxes, corvée labor, and military raids caused even greater sufferings. The government "used coercion and limited economic freedom [*bao vay kinh te*] to force peasants and artisans into cooperatives to rob them of their produce and to exploit their labor." As a result, thousands of Southerners of all classes had risen up to protest.

From the way the Southern situation was described in the report, it did not appear that the division of the country and a sense of anger about that division motivated the call for struggle. If that had been the case, the report would have said something about how Vietnam had always been a unified country and nation, and how miserable for families and friends to be separated from each other. The emotional energy was instead directed toward a raw and bitter hatred for class enemies viewed as reactionary, cruel, and dependent on foreign imperialists. *Social* revolution appeared to be the primary rationale of the struggle in the South, and *national* reunification was merely implied or expected as its by-product.

Although Duan did not assign equal importance to the international situation as his predecessor, the report was optimistic about the strength of the socialist camp and the rise of national liberation movements globally.[98] After comparing the outputs between the two blocs in terms of steel, coal, oil, and electricity, the report asserted, "in the near future the Soviet Union will rank first in the world in terms of output per capita, and the Soviet people will have the highest living standards on earth." China was predicted to catch up with or surpass England in major industrial outputs and to complete the modernization of its industries, agriculture, and science within the next ten years. Czechoslovakia had completed

[97] Ibid., 513–523.
[98] Ibid., 612–613.

socialist development and was about to start the stage of communism. Bulgaria, North Korea, and Albania were "galloping" [*phi nuoc dai*] forward to socialism. The superiority of the socialist bloc was also manifest in the Soviet success in launching manmade satellites and planets [sic], space and intercontinental rockets, and a spaceship carrying an animal to outer space and back.[99]

In sum, Le Duan's report at the Third Party Congress in 1960 unambiguously suggested that Hanoi leaders had more than national reunification in mind when they launched the war in the South. National reunification was a step along the revolutionary path *for both regions* of Vietnam. Their enemies were not just Americans but also social classes *in both regions* that stood to lose from a proletarian revolution. The war was to be as much a civil war and a class struggle as one against imperialism.

CONCLUSION

The Soviet bloc experienced great tumult in the late 1950s as leadership was passed from Stalin to Khrushchev.[100] Yet North Vietnam seemed to buck the trend as its leaders displayed a renewed revolutionary enthusiasm while the communist ideology gained broad support from the cultural elites.

Party leaders were not a monolithic group being of one mind on all ideological matters. Their worldview and strategic understanding of the environment were not fixed, and continued to be debated and clarified during the period examined here. Yet they generally achieved consensus; at the crucial points of 1953 and 1957, the radicals among them won the internal debates. During this period, class struggle was not downplayed although efforts were made to create a moderate appearance to outsiders. Party leaders took pain to construct innovative ideological formulations when confronted with new political challenges. Socialism was promoted, not delayed or denied, after 1956, precisely at the time when a new struggle for national unification was decided. By 1959, Party leaders were no longer reticent about their ultimate goal of making socialism a reality in the whole country, even though they did not expect victory in the South in the near future. In the theoretical formulations that these men finally achieved, patriotism was made to serve socialism, not vice versa.

[99] Ibid., 616.
[100] See Zbigniew Brzezinski, *The Soviet Bloc, Unity and Conflict* (Cambridge, MA: Harvard University Press, 1967), 155–395.

As in previous decades, ideology continued to serve as a guide to Vietnamese communist leaders in this period. It offered explanations of world events and helped North Vietnam to coordinate policies with the transnational network ("our camp") that it belonged to. Their Chinese comrades provided substantial assistance in the war against France and in the land reform that helped the Party extended its control down to the village level. Ideological concepts helped Ho Chi Minh produce effective propaganda attacking the United States and generating popular support for the Soviet bloc. Ideological goals, specifically the desire to create a socialist society, informed and motivated Hanoi's decision to launch the land reform and socialist development in the North and the revolution in the South. Yet ideologically inspired but vague categories of classes when applied to the land reform led to the persecution and deaths of thousands of innocent farmers. The rush to collectivize farming and to eliminate private industry and trade would soon bring agricultural decline, economic stagnation, and chronic hunger to North Vietnamese for the following two decades.

Chapter 5 will turn to events of the late 1950s and early 1960s as the revolution in South Vietnam escalated.

5

From Idealistic to Realistic
Internationalism, 1957–1963

A specter of breakup loomed over the Soviet bloc in the late 1950s. Khrushchev's policies, from the denunciation of Stalin to the reconciliation with Yugoslavia, encountered criticisms and resistance from leaders of other communist states, most notably Albania and China. A conference of twelve communist parties that Moscow convened in 1957 did not improve the situation. By mid-1960, the Sino-Soviet and Albanian-Soviet disputes came out in the open. Following Moscow and Beijing's first direct and public confrontation at the Congress of the Romanian Communist Party in Bucharest in June 1960, all Soviet experts were withdrawn from China a month later.[1]

That was the context of the second Moscow conference later that year. This conference, which has escaped the attention of historians, marked a significant shift in the course of the Vietnamese revolution. It was the first time that top Vietnamese leaders, including Le Duan, Truong Chinh, and Nguyen Chi Thanh, directly engaged in the paramount ideological debate within the Soviet camp at the time.[2] Like Duan and Chinh, Thanh was a Politburo member with a radical reputation. Born in central Vietnam in 1914 as Nguyen Vinh, Thanh came from a poor peasant family and had

[1] Lorenz Luthi, *The Sino-Soviet Split: Cold War in the Communist World* (Princeton, NJ: Princeton University Press, 2008) chapter 5. For the Sino-Soviet conflict, see also Sergey Radchenko, *Two Suns in the Heavens: The Sino-Soviet Struggle for Supremacy, 1962–1967* (Washington, DC: Woodrow Wilson Center, 2009).

[2] Le Duan had attended the first conference on November 14–16, 1957 with Ho Chi Minh and Pham Hung, but that three-day meeting involved little debate. See R. B. Smith, *An International History of the Vietnam War: Revolution versus Containment 1955–1961* (New York: St. Martin's, 1983), 135.

little formal education.[3] According to his official biography, he joined the Party in 1937, became the Party secretary of Thua Thien province, and was imprisoned for several years before 1945. Thanh was promoted over others since 1950 when the Party sought more men and women of working-class backgrounds for leadership positions. He was elected to the Politburo and appointed a four-star General and Head of General Political Department of the People's Army in 1951.[4] In this position Thanh served as the Commissar of the entire military.

Duan, Chinh, and Thanh participated in the preliminary meeting of the Moscow conference during October 1–22, 1960, together with leaders of twenty-six communist parties. In the official phase of the conference from November 10 to December 1, they were joined by Ho Chi Minh, and the number of delegations increased to eighty-one. According to Tran Quynh, who was a confidante of Le Duan, deputy chief of staff of the Party Central Office, and a member of the Vietnamese delegation, the meeting met everyday from 10 A.M. to 9 P.M.[5] The Soviets provided a draft document as the basis for discussion, and participants went over and discussed every sentence and paragraph. The rule of debate was not to achieve a majority vote on any issues, but to discuss them until a consensus had been forged among all delegations. The final statement, which had about 16,000 words, included 6 sections: (1) the characteristics of the present era, (2) the socialist system, (3) war and peace, (4) national liberation movements, (5) the tasks of the communist parties, and (6) the tasks of the communist bloc.[6] These were all fundamental issues worthy of attention for a bloc that ruled one-sixth of the human population and that aspired to conquer the whole world.

The six-week meeting was no academic conference but essentially a long, face-to-face ideological and strategic debate among power holders in the communist brotherhood to flesh out and reconcile differences in the worldviews and strategies of individual communist parties. Within each party, a similar process occurred, since not all members of the same delegation agreed on all issues. In the Vietnamese delegation, Tran Quynh revealed that Truong Chinh generally agreed with the draft statement

[3] Hong Chuong, "Dong chi Nguyen Chi Thanh," in *Dai Tuong Nguyen Chi Thanh* [General Nguyen Chi Thanh], compiled by Vu Nhi Xuyen (Hue: Thuan Hoa, 1997), 307–335.

[4] This made Thanh one of three highest-ranking leaders of the military.

[5] Tran Quynh, "May ky niem ve Le Duan" [Reminiscences about Le Duan], n.d. Unpublished memoir, courtesy of Sophie Quinn-Judge.

[6] The Statement is available at www.marxists.org/history/international/comintern/sino-soviet-split/other/1960statement.htm.

presented by Soviet leaders, whereas Le Duan and Nguyen Chi Thanh generally disagreed with that document and had to persuade Truong Chinh to go along. The intense debate at the conference helped Duan and Thanh clarify a key ambiguity in their thinking up to that point. This ambiguity involved their conflation of the Soviet Union with the entire socialist camp.

This chapter will begin with events in North Vietnam from 1956 to 1960 to provide the background to the new thinking of Duan and Thanh following the Moscow conference in 1960. Their new thinking led directly to a clash between two factions within the Party leadership in 1963, paving the way for a new radical phase of the Vietnamese revolution.

THE CONTROVERSY OVER REVISIONISM

The year 1956 was a taxing one for the Party. Mao's "Hundred Flowers" campaign and Khrushchev's denunciation of Stalin spurred a reform movement among a group of writers and intellectuals in Hanoi. Many in this group were dedicated communists and loyal Party members. They profoundly resented the corruption, mismanagement, and dogmatism that had grown since the communist state took control of North Vietnam following the Geneva Agreements.[7] By late 1956, internal dissent and major incidents of unrest forced the Party to suspend the land-reform campaign and apologize for its "errors."[8] The Polish and Hungarian revolts in June and October, respectively, further emboldened calls for reform in North Vietnam.

Hanoi applauded Soviet intervention to crush the Budapest uprising. Rather than seeing national self-determination at stake in that revolt, Vietnamese leaders read in the event an imperialist conspiracy to break up the socialist camp.[9] By mid-1957, the Party had crushed the protests in Nghe An and cracked down on intellectual dissent, sending many writers to prison or to the countryside for hard labor. Under Ho Chi Minh as

---

[7] Peter Zinoman, "Nhan Van-Giai Pham and Vietnamese 'Reform Communism' in the 1950s: A Revisionist Interpretation," *Journal of Cold War Studies* 13: 1 (2011), 60–100.

[8] In his speech a year later as the newly designated Party leader, Le Duan admitted that unrest was caused by regrouped Southern students and invalid soldiers and by "reactionaries in Quynh Yen [Nghe An]. "Thong nhat tu tuong, doan ket toan Dang day manh hoan thanh nhiem vu cong tac truoc mat" [Unite our thoughts and all Party's actions to fulfill our upcoming responsibilities], report at the Thirteenth Plenum, December 1957. *VKDTT*, v. 18, 768–769.

[9] Ibid., 760–761.

acting General Secretary and later Le Duan as the newly designated first secretary, the Party returned to orthodox Stalinism. As Duan declared at the Thirteenth Central Committee Plenum in late 1957, "[T]o us, comrade Stalin is always a great Marxist-Leninist; his entire revolutionary career was great; his accomplishments dwarfed his mistakes. His works remain in the treasure of Marxism-Leninism."[10] The Vietnamese party was not the only communist party that defended Stalin, yet its defense of a dead leader at the risk of alienating the incumbent is clear evidence that ideological loyalty trumped practical interests.

Although Hanoi leaders warned about the dangers of "dogmatism," their primary ideological enemy was "revisionism," in particular Titoism.[11] As declared by Yugoslavia's President Tito, all socialist countries were equal and each should be able to pursue its own course of development based on its national conditions or interests. His criticism was directed at the Soviet Union for its perceived imperious behavior toward its socialist brothers. Without naming Tito, Vietnamese newspapers accused "revisionists" of adhering to "bourgeois nationalism" and "chauvinism." They claimed that, by nature, the national interests of each socialist country could only be in harmony with those of the entire socialist camp.[12] Both kinds of interests were based on a common foundation – namely, the interests of working classes. In the face of clever subversive plots by the imperialist camp, socialist countries should not quarrel over small differences; instead, they should bind together based on the proletarian spirit.

On the occasion of the fortieth anniversary of the Russian Revolution in 1957, North Vietnam published many books and articles to defend the Soviet Union from revisionist "slanders."[13] In a long essay to argue for Soviet leadership of world revolution, Ho Chi Minh claimed that the Soviet Union "is the most formidable fortress of progress, democracy, and peace. The immeasurable and growing strength of the USSR and its consistent pursuit of peace is the surest guarantee for the independence of all nations large or small."[14] Vietnamese leaders fully concurred with the

---

[10] Ibid., 769–770.

[11] Ibid., 762–763.

[12] Minh Nghia, "Tang cuong doan ket va hop tac trong phe Xa hoi chu nghia" [Enhancing solidarity and collaboration in the socialist camp], *Hoc Tap*, March 1957, 31.

[13] For example, see Tran Luc (Ho Chi Minh), *Lien Xo vi dai* [The Great Soviet Union] (Hanoi: Su That, 1957); Minh Tranh, *Cach mang Nga va Viet nam* [The Russian Revolution and Vietnam] (Hanoi: Su That, 1957).

[14] Ho Chi Minh, "Cach mang thang Muoi va su nghiep giai phong cac dan toc phuong Dong" [the October Revolution and the liberation of Eastern people], *Hoc Tap*, October 1957, 12–21.

1957 Moscow Declaration that formally acknowledged the Soviet Union as the leader of the socialist bloc. In the words of Le Duan, "given the historical conditions and for the need of the world communist movement and the construction of socialism, the Soviet Union should bear the heavy responsibility as the head of the socialist camp."[15]

Vietnamese leaders' denunciation of revisionism was not only for propaganda purposes. We do not have access to internal debates, but available documents suggested it was intense in Central Committee meetings.[16] Different opinions within the top leadership were displayed even in public statements. For example, Ho Chi Minh wrote with strong approval about various Soviet initiatives to achieve peace, including those about collective security and nuclear disarmament.[17] Soviet support for the parliamentary route to socialism in capitalist countries was praised by Nguyen Khanh Toan as a revolutionary idea, not a reformist one along the line of the Second International.[18] In contrast, Le Duan argued about the same issues with strong theoretical reservations and a darker tone. He stressed that parliamentary competition should necessarily be combined with organizing the masses for class struggle outside of parliament. He warned that the nonviolent path to socialism was only one option among others, and that "communists should avoid spreading illusions among the masses and misleading them" about peaceful options.[19] Duan disagreed with Khrushchev on many points but at this time he did not go beyond particular policies. This was to change in late 1960.

"LOYALTY TO THE ENTIRE CAMP IS THE LITMUS TEST OF A COMMUNIST"

The Ninth Central Committee Plenum in December 1963 is conventionally considered a turning point when the Party decided to side with China against the Soviet Union. The focus on 1963 is not without good reasons,

---

[15] Le Duan, "Nhung nhiem vu lich su cua phong trao cong san quoc te," [The historic missions of the international communist movement], *Hoc Tap*, December 1957, 22.

[16] "Thong nhat tu tuong, doan ket toan Dang day manh hoan thanh nhiem vu cong tac truoc mat," *VKDTT*, v. 18, 762–763.

[17] Ho Chi Minh, "Cach mang thang Muoi va su nghiep giai phong cac dan toc phuong Dong," *Hoc Tap*, October 1957, 15.

[18] Nguyen Khanh Toan, "Chuyen chinh vo san, san pham cua Cach mang thang Muoi Nga," [Dictatorship of the proletariat, a product of the Russian revolution], *Hoc Tap*, October 1957, 85.

[19] Le Duan, "Nhung nhiem vu lich su cua phong trao cong san quoc te," *Hoc Tap*, December 1957, 25.

but ideologically speaking 1960 was when the fundamental shift in thinking occurred in a major faction within the leadership. This faction under Le Duan proposed in 1960 that Vietnam break its ideological link with the Soviet Union. I argue that the 1960 shift was far more important in terms of foreign policy thinking, while the 1963 Plenum merely provided the opportunity for Le Duan's faction to defeat its opponents and convert its preferences into Party policy.

What caused the shift in Duan's thinking on foreign policy in 1960? Let us first examine the situation in the two regions of Vietnam. In the South, the plan for the revolution during 1959–1960 was to develop small or medium-sized armed units to carry out assassinations and other terrorist acts in support of the political struggle. Clearly the revolution at this point did not yet need Soviet or Chinese military aid.[20] The spread of mass uprisings in the Mekong Delta and a failed coup against Ngo Dinh Diem in 1960 in fact suggested great potential for revolutionary success even without a large military force.

By contrast, the coup in Iraq, the defeat of Batista in Cuba, and the fall of Rhee Syngman in South Korea conveyed mixed messages to North Vietnamese leaders. These events were encouraging since the overthrown regimes were pro-American. Yet it was unclear to Hanoi why the United States did not intervene to save its clients. Applying class concepts, Party leaders observed that those events were "led by the bourgeoisie both in form and in substance." In South Korea in particular, the leaders of the protests that toppled Rhee Syngman were pro-American elements of the bourgeoisie.[21] The reason for American inaction there must have been because Washington still needed the support of the local bourgeoisie. South Vietnam was different because a communist party led the mass uprisings there; so perhaps American intervention was likelier. On the other hand, Rhee's ouster suggested to Hanoi leaders the great potential of urban political movements, yet the Saigon regime seemed to have firm control over the cities. The Southern branch of the Party was instructed to examine why the student movement in Saigon-Cholon was slow to develop. Given the uncertainties in the Southern revolution, an immediate change in strategy appeared not in the making.

---

[20] Mari Olsen, *Soviet-Vietnam Relations and the Role of China, 1949–64: Changing Alliances* (London: Routledge, 2006), 84–88.

[21] "Dien mat cua Trung uong Dang so 160" [Secret cable from the Party Central Office], April 28, 1960. *VKDTT*, v. 21, 290; "Dien cua Trung uong Dang so 34" [Cable from the Party Central Office], April 30, 1960. *VKDTT*, v. 21, 306.

In the North, the poor harvest in mid-1960 was the most notable event. By the end of June, the amount of paddy procured and collected as debt payment amounted to only 25 percent of the plan.[22] By August, there were reports of hungry villagers abandoning work in cooperatives and roaming around looking for private work in return for food.[23] As hunger spread, those farmers with surplus refused to sell their surplus paddy to the government or to do so only at very high prices.

Party leaders were alarmed by the problem and blamed it on bad weather, inadequate ideological work by cadres, and "acts of sabotage" by the enemy. To the leaders, government control of rural surplus was not simply a food issue but a class struggle in which the working class persuaded the peasantry to adopt the socialist outlook.[24] The Party Secretariat thus instructed cadres to do a better job in educating peasants on ideological matters [*cong tac tu tuong*]. This was clearly the view of Le Duan and his faction, but no alternative views were found at high levels and there seemed to be no significant debate yet at the time.[25] We will see later that economic issues would figure prominently in ideological debates by late 1962, but as late as 1960 there was little sign of that.

Thus, conditions in both South and North Vietnam in 1960 remained relatively stable. The trigger of ideological rethinking was the fractures in the socialist camp, which unfolded at the 1960 Moscow conference that Le Duan, Truong Chinh, and Nguyen Chi Thanh attended. The thrust of the final statement of the Conference was the Soviet call for peaceful coexistence with the imperialist camp in an age when socialism was apparently on a triumphant march. Yet the statement also contained many passages written with a combative tone and inserted at the demand of Asian parties.[26] The change in Le Duan's thinking was expressed in his report drafted right after he had returned from Moscow.

[22] "Chi thi cua Ban Bi thu so 215-CT/TW" [Directive of the Secretariat], June 30, 1960. *VKDTT*, v. 21 (2002), 392.

[23] "Chi thi cua Ban Bi thu so 219-CT/TW" [Directive of the Secretariat], August 12, 1960. *VKDTT*, v. 21 (2002), 425.

[24] "Chi thi cua Ban Bi thu so 205-CT/TW" [Directive of the Secretariat], April 25, 1960. *VKDTT*, v. 21 (2002), 282. See also "Bao cao chinh tri cua Ban Chap hanh Trung uong Dang" at the Third Party Congress in September 1960, *VKDTT*, v. 21, 604–605.

[25] The Secretariat (Ban Bi thu) was led by Le Duan and included Pham Hung, Le Duc Tho, Nguyen Chi Thanh, To Huu, Le Van Luong, Hoang Anh, and Nguyen Van Tran. The first five members are known as sharing the same view with Le Duan on most issues.

[26] For the inputs of the Vietnamese delegation at the conference, see Tran Quynh, "May ky niem ve Le Duan."

In the report, Duan considered the conference a great success in meeting both ideological and organizational challenges.[27] However, by "success" Duan did not appear to mean consensus. He placed much greater emphasis on the radical view of the Asian parties than the Soviet perspective. In particular, Duan claimed that "class struggle on the global scale has intensified and [now] involves the life and death of either imperialist or anti-imperialist forces... For communism to triumph, there is no other way but to wage a class struggle against imperialism... The conditions for accelerating anti-imperialist revolutions today are more favorable than ever."[28] (In contrast, the statement only talked vaguely about "acute conflict within capitalist societies," "decaying tendencies," and "a general crisis in the capitalist system").

Le Duan briefly acknowledged that the dangers of nuclear weapons made the preservation of peace an important task, which was Khrushchev's major argument. But Duan talked much more about the need for communist parties to be on the offensive against imperialism everywhere and on every occasion to destroy it in parts and eventually in whole.[29] Duan further maintained that the communist camp must keep a hard line – namely, not to accept compromises with imperialism on matters of principle, but at the same time it should devise flexible tactics to divide the imperialist camp and isolate the most dangerous imperialist enemy – namely, the United States. Duan completely ignored the second section in the statement that focused on the economic achievements of the socialist camp; that section was central to Khrushchev's call for peaceful competition between the capitalist and socialist blocs. Duan instead highlighted the point in the statement that the struggle for peace was also a class struggle between the two camps.

Discussing the "Sino-Soviet dispute" [*bat dong*] at the Moscow conference, Duan argued that the dispute was rooted not only in two different ideological standpoints, but also in different "national positions" [*vi tri dan toc*].[30] He noted that it was not a coincidence that most "Eastern" communist parties supported Beijing, whereas most "Western" counterparts allied with Moscow in the debate. The Soviet Union and most European socialist countries started out on the basis of relatively developed capitalism, whereas China and other Asian socialist brothers

[27] Le Duan, "Tang cuong doan ket nhat tri, tien toi nhung thang loi moi" [Strengthening solidarity and consensus, achieving new victories], *VKDTT*, v. 22 (2002), 52–56.
[28] Ibid., 60–61.
[29] Ibid., 66–73, 76–79.
[30] Ibid., 96–99.

sought to create a socialist system on "semifeudal" and backward societies. Dissimilar histories, socioeconomic conditions, and geopolitical locations naturally led to different "national positions" within the socialist brotherhood.

To avoid conflict, Duan believed that "each party should always ensure the correct handling of the relationship between national interests and the interests of the world revolutionary movement."[31] For the first time, Duan implicitly acknowledged the possible incompatibility between national interests of individual socialist countries and those of the whole camp. This was a critical departure from the earlier assumption in the Party's documents that all member countries of the brotherhood shared the same class interests.

This new thinking did not mean that Duan had become a nationalist and placed national interests in opposition to or above those of the socialist camp. He went on to say,

Previously, there was only one socialist country, namely the Soviet Union. Therefore the Soviet Union was the representative and the only hope of the entire international communist movement. A [loyal] attitude to the Soviet Union was the litmus test [to determine the credentials of] any communist in the world. Today's circumstances are no longer exactly so. These days socialism has become a worldwide system, so the representative and hope of the communist movement should be the entire socialist camp centered on the Soviet Union. The litmus test of today should be *one's [loyal] attitude toward the entire socialist camp centered on the Soviet Union.*[32]

This key passage indicated that Duan's participation at the second Moscow conference had helped clarify a key ambiguity in his earlier thinking. In particular, he had dissociated the Soviet Union from the socialist camp. Even though the Soviet Union was still the center of the camp, it was not the same as the camp. Duan also implicitly hinted that Soviet interests had diverged from those of the socialist camp, and that all communists, including Vietnamese communists, should align their national interests with those of the camp, not necessarily with those of Moscow.

After Le Duan and his faction had staked out their controversial ideological standpoint, the remaining matter was to persuade the rest of the Party leadership to go along. According to Tran Quynh's memoir, in Moscow Truong Chinh went along with Le Duan and Nguyen Chi Thanh but remained committed to his pro-Soviet position until mid-1963. There

---

[31] Ibid., 98.
[32] Ibid., 98–99. Emphasis in original.

were certainly others in the leadership who disagreed with Duan (more later). His report thus represented the position of his faction but not of the Party leadership as a whole. For this reason, North Vietnam did not yet show any critical attitude toward the Soviet Union in public beyond the now-familiar attacks on revisionism. Duan's speech was published as an article under his name in the Party journal *Hoc Tap* in January 1961 – without the preceding discussion of the Sino-Soviet dispute.

SELF-RELIANT VERSUS INTERDEPENDENT INTERNATIONALISMS

The situation in the South and the economic problems in the North up to 1960 did not yet have a direct bearing on ideological debates in the Party. After 1960, however, those issues became intricately entangled. In fact, the emerging problems in both regions posed a challenge to Le Duan's faction, which had, by 1961, already dismissed the relevance of the Soviet Union for Vietnam. Rather than retreating, Duan and his associates moved forward to propose military and economic solutions that suited their ideological beliefs. In the ensuing debate, they continued to sharpen their ideological arguments not only on global affairs but also on domestic issues. Opposing them were leaders who were no less internationalist in thinking, but who advocated a different course of action for foreign and economic policy.

North Vietnam's economy encountered some problems by 1960, but the situation worsened afterward. Food shortage continued through 1961 and was severe in some months.[33] Conditions improved in 1962 and 1963 but only after the government had lowered plan targets and raised procurement prices.[34] An economic report for the period 1958–1962 showed that paddy output in 1962 was lower than in 1958, whereas the population had grown by more than two million people in the meantime. With North Vietnamese living standards close to subsistence level, the threat of famine loomed, barely two years after agricultural production had been collectivized. The good news was that the government had increased its control over the harvest by one half, but that was still not sufficient to

---

[33] "Chi thi cua Ban Bi thu so 17-CT/TW" [Secretariat's instruction], April 11, 1961. *VKDTT*, v. 22, 300; "Chi thi cua Ban Bi thu so 29-CT/TW" [Secretariat's instruction], October 31, 1961. *VKDTT*, v. 22, 496–502; "Chi thi cua Ban Bi thu so 34-CT/TW" [Secretariat's instruction], December 11, 1961. *VKDTT*, v. 22, 609–615.

[34] "Thong bao cua Ban Bi thu so 21-TB/HN" [Secretariat's Notice], May 29, 1962. *VKDTT*, v. 23, 573–579; "Thong bao cua Ban Bi thu so 37-TB/HN" [Secretariat's Notice], October 22, 1962. *VKDTT*, v. 23, 783–786. These notices summarized the instructions of the Politburo.

meet the needs of about 20 percent of total population who relied on government-subsidized rice.[35]

The road to socialism through a centrally planned economy was similarly bumpy in other areas.[36] Shortage and hoarding had emerged together with the black market, with regards to not only consumer goods but also raw materials and agricultural produce needed for domestic production and exports. Exports thus fell below plans, affecting the imports of equipment needed for industrial plants. Government overspending had created (implicit) inflation. Most key targets of the 1961 state plan were not met despite a rapid increase in government payroll.[37] By 1963, Party leaders came to realize the full extent of problems with the ambitious industrialization plan that had been drafted in the late 1950s. That plan had been based on a large one-time infusion of foreign aid and on optimistic predictions of agricultural production at the time. Despite massive investment, major industrial projects ran into delays while production at most state enterprises was under-capacity.[38] The imports of industrial equipment now relied on foreign aid and loans that amounted to between one-third and one-half of North Vietnam's exports in 1961–1962. Although foreign aid offered by socialist brothers in the late 1950s had been nearly depleted, foreign debt was rapidly accumulating, including some debt to (unnamed) capitalist countries.[39]

The question of how to save enough to finance industrialization [*tich luy*] was hanging in the air as Party leaders directed the increasingly violent revolutionary struggle in the South in the early 1960s. Both Moscow and Beijing provided aid to Hanoi to the tune of half a billion dollars each in the 1950s.[40] As the proportion of foreign aid and loans in the state budget fell from nearly 40 percent in 1957 to about 16 percent in 1960,[41] whether and how industrialization could continue without

---

[35] "Bao cao tai Hoi nghi Trung Uong lan thu tam" [Report at the Eighth Central Committee Plenum], March 26, 1963. *VKDTT*, v. 24, 223–224.

[36] "Chi thi cua Ban Bi thu so 31-CT/TW" [Secretariat's instruction], November 9, 1961. *VKDTT*, v. 22, 512–529.

[37] "Nghi quyet cua Bo Chinh tri so 43-NQ/TW" [Politburo's resolution], February 1, 1962, *VKDTT*, v. 23, 86–87.

[38] "Bao cao tai Hoi nghi Trung Uong lan thu tam" [Report at the Eighth Central Committee Plenum], March 26, 1963. *VKDTT*, v. 24, 244–263.

[39] Ibid., 256–257.

[40] For data on aid from the socialist bloc during 1954–1957, see Nguyen Thi Mai Hoa, *Cac nuoc Xa hoi chu nghia ung ho Viet Nam khang chien chong My, cuu nuoc*, 124–172.

[41] "Bao cao ve nhiem vu va phuong huong xay dung phat trien cong nghiep" [Report on the task and strategy of industrialization], presented at the Seventh Central Committee Plenum, May 26 to April 16, 1962. *VKDTT*, v. 23, 222.

160 Vietnam's Communist Revolution

foreign aid was a critical question. The debate that had divided the Soviet leadership in the late 1920s and the Chinese leadership in the mid-1950s had finally caught up with North Vietnam in the early 1960s.

North Vietnam traded with some capitalist countries (France, Japan, and Hong Kong) in small quantities, but its leaders neither thought of mobilizing capital and technology from capitalist countries nor of trading extensively with them. It is unclear why the idea never even came up. Because even the Soviet Union had traded with the West in its first decade of existence, the idea would not have been inconceivable, or totally unacceptable from an ideological standpoint for Hanoi. In any case, the rejection of broad economic relations with capitalist countries made cooperation with the socialist bloc a necessity; yet Vietnamese leaders disagreed precisely over what those forms of cooperation should be.

One strategy proposed by leaders such as Bui Cong Trung, a Moscow-trained revolutionary whom we met earlier and who was now an alternate Central Committee member and vice chair of the State Commission on Science, was to develop North Vietnam's competitive advantage as one of the only two tropical economies in the socialist bloc. In this strategy of industrialization through trade, North Vietnam would focus more on agriculture and light industries, and stimulate agricultural production with better procurement prices and more abundant consumer products offered to farmers.[42] Close relationship with European communist brothers was central in this strategy as they would be the primary markets for Vietnamese produce. Le Duan and Nguyen Chi Thanh promoted the opposite strategy, which called for building a self-reliant economy based on heavy industries, especially the machine industry. Industrialization could be financed primarily by domestic resources, by agricultural surplus

[42] Bui Tin, *Following Ho Chi Minh* (Honolulu: University of Hawaii Press, 1995), 39. See also Le Xuan Ta [a pseudonym], "Hoi uc ve cuoc khung bo chu nghia xet lai o Viet Nam" [Memoir of anti-revisionist terror in Vietnam], first published in February 1994, available at www.diendan.org/tai-lieu/bao-cu/so-027/khung-bo-xet-lai/. Bui Cong Trung's view on socialist agricultural development (in relation to collectivization) can be found in Bui Cong Trung, "Huong phat trien nong nghiep cua mien Bac" [The course of agricultural development for North Vietnam], *Nhan Dan* [The People], February 7 & 8, 1958; Bui Cong Trung, "Dam bao kinh te phat trien: Day manh san xuat luong thuc" [Increase grain production to ensure economic development], *Nhan Dan*, October 5, 1958; Bui Cong Trung, "Nghi quyet cua Hoi nghi Trung uong lan thu nam soi duong cho chung ta xay dung Chu nghia Xa hoi o nong thon mien Bac" [The Fifth Central Committee Plenum Resolution shows us how to develop socialism in the North], *Nhan Dan*, August 28, 1961; and Bui Cong Trung and Luu Quang Hoa, *Hop Tac Hoa Nong Nghiep o Mien Bac Viet Nam* [Agricultural collectivization in North Vietnam] (Hanoi: Su That, 1959), esp. 37–42.

and by the most efficient division of labor.[43] In this strategy, the socialist bloc was important only for Vietnam's technological needs, not as a primary source of capital.

Both sides were committed to socialist development, industrialization, and cooperation with the socialist bloc. What distinguished the two strategies were the different emphases on the role of agriculture in the process: agriculture was either to be developed into a globally competitive sector that earned hard currencies for industrialization or to be squeezed hard for surplus, which also was to be used for industrialization. The two strategies had different but ambiguous implications for the Southern revolution. The strategy of close trading relationships with the Soviet Union and other European communist states implied keeping the Southern revolution low key so as not to contradict Khrushchev's policy of peaceful coexistence. By contrast, the other strategy did not require deference to Khrushchev; at the same time, it implied that only limited resources could be sent to help the Southern revolution. In addition, the heavy industries to be developed would make any US attacks on *North* Vietnam especially damaging. This strategy required that the possibility of such attacks be minimized.

We do not have archival access to the contents of the economic debates within the Party leadership, and only the arguments made by the winning faction are available in full detail. The debate could have been entirely technical but turned out to be deeply ideological. It percolated from 1958 with the collectivization campaign, became tense around 1962, and climaxed at the Ninth Central Committee Plenum in December 1963. Le Duan and his faction offered several reasons why North Vietnam would need a "self-reliant" economy [*kinh te tu chu*], which they defined as one "based on heavy industries with relatively broad industrial capacity closely linked with a developed agriculture."[44] First, because the population of a reunited Vietnam would be about 30 or 40 million people, the country would need a relatively complete heavy industrial base to meet all its economic needs once reunification had been achieved. Second,

---

[43] See an excerpt from Le Duan's speech at the meeting to publicize the resolution of the Eighth Central Committee Plenum, in May 1963, in Le Duan, *Giai cap vo san voi van de nong dan trong cach mang Viet nam* [The proletariat and the peasant question in the Vietnamese revolution]. Hanoi: Su That, 1965, 316–320.

[44] This paragraph combines Le Duan, "Tao mot chuyen bien manh me ve cong tac tu tuong" [Generating a major change in thought work], speech at the National Conference on Propaganda and Political Education, April 1962. VKDTT, v. 23, 477–489; and Nguyen Chi Thanh, "Nang cao lap truong, tu tuong vo san, doan ket, phan dau gianh thang loi moi" [Uphold proletarian standpoint and thoughts, uniting and striving for new victories]. *Hoc Tap*, October 1963, 1–13.

each socialist country faced different economic conditions and it was not possible for all of them to form a single economic unit, even though all socialist countries were supposed to help each other. An efficient division of labor *within* each economy (as opposed to across countries within the Soviet bloc) would create the conditions for fastest growth. Third, dependence on assistance from socialist brothers was a selfish behavior unworthy of communists. As Duan said, the goods produced by each country should first serve the needs of people in that country. Helping other socialist brothers was laudable but should be limited to difficult times or to the beginning phase of socialist development only.

Thanh added that the egalitarian principle of proletarian internationalism must be built on self-reliant national units. In his opinion, dependence on outside help would contradict Marx's teaching that revolution was the work of the masses. He further argued that "the dialectics of things" required that the creation of a single socialist and communist economy for the entire world must occur through a process by which each national economy and each region developed separately to a certain level before they could be united to form a single unit.

Despite Duan and Thanh's reference to Marx, their economic arguments can be traced directly to Stalin and Mao. The model economy in their view was the Stalinist model, and the absolute emphasis on self-reliance and on the power of the masses is reminiscent of Mao's Great Leap Forward. Significantly, both their view and that of their opponents could fit within the two-camp worldview. Both rejected any substantial form of economic relations with capitalist countries. Le Duan's view followed the Stalinist model of industrialization based on heavy industries and financed by domestic surplus. Duan's emphasis on self-reliant economies interacting on an equal basis with others in the socialist bloc did not suggest disloyalty to the brotherhood.

In contrast, Duan's opponents sought to integrate the Vietnamese economy into that of the bloc, which would result in an internationalized Vietnamese economy in an interdependent relationship with other brother economies. By accepting the division of labor within a unified socialist bloc and coordinating economic policy with the bloc, the proponents of this view believed they were acting in the spirit of proletarian internationalism, not out of a "national inferiority complex" as Duan and Thanh accused them of having done. Hoang Minh Chinh, the director of the Institute for Marxist-Leninist Studies who defended the position of interdependent internationalism at the Ninth Plenum and who would be imprisoned for a decade afterward, reportedly insisted, "It was not the issue of following or not following the Soviet Union. It was the issue of following or not following the international communist movement, following or not following the truth [*le phai*]."[45]

The claims of acting in the spirit of internationalism by men such as Bui Cong Trung and Hoang Minh Chinh were backed up by their distinguished revolutionary careers. Trung, a classmate of Tran Phu and Tran Dinh Long at the University of the Toilers of the East, had impeccable revolutionary credentials with years of imprisonment in Poulo Condore. The much younger Chinh joined the Party in 1939, was imprisoned in colonial prisons for several years, and studied "Marxist-Leninist philosophy" in the Soviet Union in the late 1950s. Others in this faction had similarly stellar records of revolutionary contributions. Duong Bach Mai, member of the Standing Committee of the National Assembly whom we met in Chapter 2, was a former member of the French Communist Party, studied in the University of the Toilers of the East, and was imprisoned in Poulo Condore during World War II.[46] Retired Major General Dang Kim Giang, a Central Committee member and Vice Minister of State Farms, began his revolutionary career in 1928 as a member of Thanh Nien, spent twelve years in colonial prisons, and was best known for his role as Deputy Commander of the PAVN's Supply Corps during the Dien Bien Phu campaign.[47] There were also Ung Van Khiem, a Central Committee member and Minister of Foreign Affairs; retired Major General Le Liem, an alternate Central Committee member and Vice Minister of Education; and others of less prominence.[48] The ideological loyalty of these men was unquestionable. What perhaps distinguished them from their opponents was social background and formal education: they tended to come from wealthy land-owning families (Mai and Khiem) or urban middle class (Trung, Chinh, and Giang), and acquired much more formal education under the French than their opponents. As seen later, Le Duan, who had

[45] Le Xuan Ta, "Hoi uc ve cuoc khung bo chu nghia xet lai o Viet Nam."

[46] This is based on http://datdo.baria-vungtau.gov.vn/web/guest/huyen-dat-do/-/brvt/extAssetPublisher/content/512196/tieu-su-va-qua-trinh-hoat-dong-cua-nha-cach-mang-duong-bach-mai.

[47] See https://vi.wikipedia.org/wiki/%C4%90%E1%BA%B7ng_Kim_Giang. See also www.diendan.org/tai-lieu/bao-cu/so-042/don-khieu-oan-cua-ba-qua-phu-dang-kim-giang. No official biography can be found.

[48] See http://tinhdoan.angiang.gov.vn/wps/portal/!ut/p/c4/04_SB8K8xLLM9MSSzPy8xBz9CPoos3j3oBBLczdTEwOLMAMLAo8Tb6cwN8sgAz9XQ_2CbEdFABQHBaw!/?WCM_GLOBAL_CONTEXT=/wps/wcm/connect/tinhdoan/tinhdoanag/sinhhoatchidoan/thang2/dong+chi+ung+van+khiem; and https://vi.wikipedia.org/wiki/L%C3%AA_Li%C3%AAm. No official biography of Le Liem can be found.

an elementary-school education, and Nguyen Chi Thanh, who was even less educated, would refer to them derisively as "those intellectual Party members" [Dang vien tri thuc] as a way to discredit them.

"PHONY THEORY," "POLITICAL CORPSE," AND "BOURGEOIS NATIONALIST MUD"

By late 1960, Le Duan and his faction had made clear their loyalty was with the camp but not necessarily with Moscow. They continued to stake out their position in public and sharpen it through debates on practical strategies for Northern industrialization, in conflict with viewpoints held by other leaders. The sense of fluidity can also be found in discussions on foreign policy. Divergent views were still expressed in public by late 1962. By mid-1963, however, pro-China and anti-Soviet rhetoric began to dominate the Party journal, signaling a shift favoring Le Duan's faction with its self-reliant yet internationalist worldview.

In late 1961, the Twenty-second Congress of the Communist Party of the Soviet Union (CPSU) met and approved Khrushchev's ambitious plan to make communism a reality in the Soviet Union in twenty years. At that Congress, Khrushchev's public criticism of Albanian leaders for their loyalty to Stalin provoked a strong reaction by the Chinese delegation whose head, Premier Zhou Enlai, walked out in protest. Together with several other Asian parties, the North Vietnamese team led by Ho Chi Minh abstained from criticizing Albania. Yet, Hanoi did not express any anti-Soviet sentiments in public or at internal meetings. The bold Soviet plan to realize communism on earth in a generation was profusely praised in Hanoi media before and after the Congress.[49] Vietnamese leaders seemed to be sincerely encouraged by the prospects of the first communist society to appear on earth, based on Le Duan's report presented at the Sixth Central Committee Plenum upon his return from Moscow.[50] After pages and pages praising the Soviet plan and highlighting its significance for mankind and for Vietnam, the report mentioned the Albanian incident and the CPSU Congress's decision to remove Stalin's embalmed

---

[49] Editorial, "Chu nghia Cong san nhat dinh thang loi o Lien Xo va tren toan the gioi" [Communism will surely win in the Soviet Union and in the world]. *Hoc Tap*, October 1961, 1–3; Editorial, "Cuong linh xay dung Chu nghia Cong san]. *Hoc Tap*, December 1961, 1–12.

[50] "Bao cao cua Doan dai bieu Dang Lao dong Viet nam du Dai hoi lan thu XXII cua Dang Cong san Lien Xo" [Report from the VWP delegation at the Twenty-second Congress of the CPSU], report presented by Le Duan at the VWP's Sixth Central Committee Plenum, November 30-December 2, 1961. *VKDTT*, v. 22, 568–602.

body from the Red Square. Duan explained that the Vietnamese delegation had not been informed in advance about those issues and thus did not comment on them at the Congress. At the same time, he emphasized that Hanoi's position on Stalin had been determined in 1956 and had not changed. He expressed regrets at the Albanian incident and proposed that Vietnam make some efforts to mediate between Albania and the Soviet Union.

After a lull in 1961–1962, the Sino-Soviet conflict flared up again in summer 1962 as Mao launched a new antirevisionist campaign in part to attack Liu Shaoqi and Deng Xiaoping.[51] Sino-Indian tension also increased sharply in mid-1962, culminating in a brief border war in October, at about the same time as the Cuban missile crisis. Hanoi supported Beijing in this war, whereas Moscow was inconsistent but appeared to lean to New Delhi. In North Vietnam, ordinary Vietnamese, who had had access to Beijing Radio programs in the Vietnamese language since 1961, closely followed these events.[52] North Vietnam took China's side against India, but defended the Soviet Union in the missile crisis. In particular, the Indian government was criticized as acting in the interests of the Indian bourgeoisie and receiving bribes from the United States to attack China.[53] Ho Chi Minh reportedly applauded Moscow's decision to withdraw the missiles from Cuba, against the wishes of some of his comrades.[54] His position appeared to be adopted as official policy: a *Hoc Tap* editorial discussed at length the event, blaming Washington for everything and absolving Moscow of any mistakes.[55]

In early 1963, China published the so-called "Nine Polemics" that viciously denounced alleged Soviet deviations from Marxism-Leninism. Beijing sought to enlist support from other communist capitals, including

---

[51] Luthi, *The Sino-Soviet Split*, chapter 7.

[52] Le Xuan Ta, "Hoi uc ve cuoc khung bo chu nghia xet lai o Viet Nam." The Soviet Union did not engage in such activities.

[53] Tien Dung, "Chinh sach cua Tap doan Ken-ne-di hay la con duong be tac cua chu nghia De quoc My" [The policy of the Kennedy clique or the dead end of American imperialism], *Hoc Tap*, September 1962, 71–78.

[54] According to Tran Thu who was a high-ranking military officer in the People's Army and who would later be imprisoned for allegedly supporting revisionism, Ho published an article on the Party daily *Nhan Dan* to defend the Soviet Union on the decision to withdraw the missiles. Tran Thu, *Tu tu xu ly noi bo* [Deathrow prisoners to be disciplined internally]. Westminster, CA: Van Nghe, 1996, 110–111.

[55] "Tiep tuc nang cao tinh than canh giac cach mang, tich cuc ung ho Cu ba chong De quoc My" [Continuing to raise revolutionary vigilance and actively supporting Cuba against American imperialism]. *Hoc Tap*, December 1962, 7–12.

Hanoi, in this dispute.[56] Not only did Mao quickly grant Vietnamese requests for military assistance in 1962, but Chinese leaders also took an active role in promoting collaboration and shaping North Vietnam's war strategy.[57] In May 1963, Liu Shaoqi declared during his official visit to Hanoi that China would stand by North Vietnam if the United States attacked Vietnam. Liu also brought with him large quantities of food aid.[58] As seen later, Duan and his faction supported a strategy to escalate the war to the extent that Washington would agree to negotiate to withdraw. This strategy risked provoking US military intervention not only in the South but also in the North, and Liu's assurance was particularly welcome.

Beijing's generosity failed to persuade Hanoi to trade ideological principles for aid, that is, to accept China as the new center of world revolution. In the summer of 1963, Le Duan, Truong Chinh, and Nguyen Chi Thanh were invited to Beijing to discuss China's proposal to form a new Communist International.[59] Vietnamese leaders contributed several ideas to the twenty-five items in the proposal, but strongly disagreed with their Chinese hosts over two points. One was the statement that the center of revolution had shifted to China because the Soviet Union adhered to revisionism and was on the way to becoming a capitalist country. The other point was China's proposal to form a new Communist International composed of China, North Vietnam, North Korea, Indonesia, and Albania. At this point, Beijing reportedly offered Vietnamese leaders one billion dollars of aid in return for their acceptance of China's proposal, but they declined.

The Beijing visit marked a consequential shift in the thoughts of Truong Chinh and Le Duan. According to Tran Quynh who accompanied Le Duan on the trip, Mao discussed class struggle in China's countryside at his meeting with the Vietnamese guests. Mao told them in particular that landlords in China had gradually regained their dominant position after collectivization. The evidence of this, according to Mao, was the fact that many chairmen of rural cooperatives had married landlords' daughters. Mao found the same problem in the cities, where directors of state enterprises had married into the old capitalist class. Given the situation, Mao

[56] Luthi, *The Sino-Soviet Split*, 233.
[57] Qiang Zhai, *China and the Vietnam Wars*, 116–120.
[58] Hanoians could buy bread made by Chinese wheat, which they called "Uncle Liu's bread," at half price after Liu's visit. See Le Xuan Ta, "Hoi uc ve cuoc khung bo chu nghia xet lai o Viet Nam."
[59] Tran Quynh, "May ky niem ve Le Duan," 19–20.

said he wanted to launch a new revolution to bring workers and peasants back to power. Mao then bragged that he would organize an army of five million poor peasants not only to make another revolution in China, but also to liberate Southeast Asia, including Vietnam, so his Vietnamese comrades would not need to struggle anymore.

Tran Quynh revealed that Mao totally mesmerized Truong Chinh, who later in his private conversation with Quynh praised the Chairman for having "absorbed Marxism-Leninism deep down to his bone and marrow." Interestingly, Le Duan held the opposite view about the exchange. He reportedly told Quynh that what Mao said was simply

... phony theory![60] [Why would] marrying a landlord's daughter turn someone into a landlord? And liberating Southeast Asia? What right does he have to bring his army down to liberate our Southern region? How dare he so blatantly express his Great Han's chauvinism and expansionism in front of us? That's very dangerous.

Le Duan's scorn for Mao would matter down the road, but in late 1963 what mattered most was Truong Chinh's admiration for the Chinese leader. Quynh recalled that until then Truong Chinh had opposed Le Duan's argument that Hanoi should take Beijing's side in the Sino-Soviet dispute. Chinh's about-face after the meeting with Mao ended the disagreement between these two most powerful leaders and enabled the ascendancy of Le Duan's militant line in late 1963.[61] The evidence of this ascendancy can be observed in a wave of vicious denunciations of the Tito clique and thinly veiled criticisms of Khrushchev unleashed in the Party journal *Hoc Tap* at the time. The hard-liners from Hanoi focused as much on Tito's "reactionary" domestic policy as they did on his "traitorous" foreign policy. In particular, Tito was accused of having abandoned the Marxist-Leninist doctrine on class struggle, rejected the leadership role of the proletariat, and denied the necessity of the dictatorship of the proletariat.[62] These accusations involved Belgrade's decision to decollectivize agriculture and its "failure" to nationalize private economy and to

---

[60] In original, "*ly luan lang bang*," which literally meant beating around the bush with theory.

[61] According to Hoang Minh Chinh, Truong Chinh came to agreement with Le Duan by early 1963 to protect his political status. See Lien-Hang Nguyen, "The War Politburo: North Vietnam's Diplomatic and Political Road to the Tet Offensive." *Journal of Vietnamese Studies* 1: 1–2 (2006), 45, fn. 68.

[62] "Qua ban Hien phap moi, bo mat phan boi cua be lu Ti to lai mot lan nua bi phoi tran" [Through the new Constitution the Tito clique again reveals their traitorous nature]. *Hoc Tap*, June 1963, 16–20.

implement central planning. Essentially the "Tito clique" was accused of having allowed capitalism to return to Yugoslavia.

On Tito's foreign policy, *Hoc Tap* called him a "loyal servant of imperialism" whose "revisionist" arguments about peaceful coexistence served only to consolidate the global domination of imperialism.[63] To the Vietnamese, there was no reason to fear a nuclear war with imperialist powers because nuclear weapons could not change the "developmental laws of human history." Tito had argued that there would be no winners in such a war, but *Hoc Tap* countered that such a war would destroy the imperialist camp "because that was objectively determined by the inevitable direction of human history."

In contrast with the Vietnamese ideological campaign against revisionism in 1957 that was accompanied by a defense of the Soviet Union, this time the country defended in *Hoc Tap* was China. The Chinese Communist Party, a "genuine Marxist-Leninist party," was praised for its persistent defense of Marxism-Leninism from revisionist attacks. Khrushchev (without being named) was criticized as "some people who have helped patch up the tattered Marxist-Leninist cloak of the Tito clique and who have breathed new life into that political corpse so that it could again ... sabotage the world's communist movement."[64]

Rather than directly criticizing the Partial Nuclear Test Ban Treaty signed in Moscow in August 1963 by the Soviet Union, the United States, and Great Britain, *Hoc Tap* linked the treaty to their criticisms of Tito and called it "a fraud masterminded by imperialist America to deceive the world's people."[65] Criticized in the same oblique manner was the "support by some people [read: Khruschev] for the reactionary bourgeois government [of India] when that government blatantly attacked a socialist brother."[66] No such soft treatment was given to the Communist Party of India, however; it was directly and sharply accused of "having sunken deeply in the bourgeois nationalist mud" by following and colluding with the Indian bourgeoisie to slander a brother communist party.[67]

[63] "Ten phan boi Ti to lai phun ra noc doc cua chu nghia Xet lai" [The traitor Tito is spitting out the poison of revisionism again]. *Hoc Tap*, July 1963, 9–17.
[64] Trong Nghia, "Hay canh giac truoc am muu pha hoai cua be lu Ti to!" [Beware of the plots of the Tito clique!]. *Hoc Tap*, October 1963, 79.
[65] Ibid., 73.
[66] Editorial, "Kien quyet bao ve nhung nguyen tac cach mang cua hai ban Tuyen bo Mac tu khoa" [Firmly defending the revolutionary principles of the two Moscow declarations]. *Hoc Tap*, November 1963, 1–10.
[67] Hung Son, "Ban ve chu nghia yeu nuoc chan chinh va chu nghia quoc te vo san" [On the genuine patriotism and proletarian internationalism]. *Hoc Tap*, August 1963, 70–75.

Clearly by mid-1963, North Vietnam's foreign policy increasingly reflected the preferences of Le Duan's militant faction. The ideological work by this faction to defeat their opponents was substantial but has not been extensively analyzed. This faction had fundamental ideological issues to settle with revisionism and wanted to block its rise within the socialist brotherhood and inside Vietnam. They certainly believed that they acted to defend and advance Vietnam's "national interests," but these interests were defined by the ideological concepts of the two-camp worldview and conceived in terms of the imperatives of the proletarian revolution in both North and South Vietnam. The Soviet Union was no longer a trusted brother, but there was no question that the militants remained loyal to the socialist camp. Their opponents in this debate were similarly loyal to the camp and opposed to imperialism. The difference was attitude toward the Soviet Union.

BEHIND THE COVER OF PEACE AND NEUTRALISM

As seen earlier, the Southern revolution involved much uncertainty in 1960. This did not prevent the Politburo from authorizing the escalation of both political and armed struggle in January 1961.[68] If the communist policy since 1959 was to use small, armed units for self-defense purposes and to assist the political struggle, now political and armed struggles were to have equal importance. This escalation met immediate reactions from Washington and Saigon. President Kennedy sent thousands of additional military advisers to South Vietnam, whereas Ngo Dinh Diem ordered total mobilization and launched the strategic-hamlet program. The course of the Southern revolution had turned for the worse by late 1961.[69]

---

[68] "Chi thi cua Bo Chinh tri" [Politburo's directive], January 24, 1961. *VKDTT*, v. 22, 158. Note that the decision was made by the Politburo where the militant faction probably dominated. Politburo members at the time included: Ho Chi Minh, Le Duan, Truong Chinh, Pham Van Dong, Pham Hung, Vo Nguyen Giap, Le Duc Tho, Nguyen Chi Thanh, Nguyen Duy Trinh, Le Thanh Nghi, and Hoang Van Hoan. Two alternate members were Tran Quoc Hoan and Van Tien Dung. Identifiable with Duan were Tho, Hung, Thanh, Nghi, T. Q. Hoan, Dung, and likely H. V. Hoan. Chinh was Duan's rival on some issues. Dong and Trinh likely supported Duan, whereas Ho was known to be ambivalent.

[69] "Chi thi cua Ban Bi thu so 26-CT/TW" [Secretariat's instruction], September 15, 1961. *VKDTT*, v. 22, 472. Nghi quyet cua Bo Chinh tri" [Politburo's Resolution], February 27, 1962. *VKDTT*, v. 23, 145. The tone of these documents seems to confirm arguments about the military situation in the South made by Mark Moyar, *Triumph Forsaken: The Vietnam War, 1954–1965* (New York: Cambridge University Press, 2006), chaps 6–7.

This concern was behind Le Duan's letter to the Party's Central Office in South Vietnam (COSVN) in July 1962 to explain his strategy in the new situation.[70] Essentially this strategy was to follow the Laotian model to demand internationally guaranteed neutrality for South Vietnam. Then, communist forces could seize power from the Saigon government by military combined with political means. This strategy was in response, in part, to the difficult realities facing the insurgency on the ground and, in part, to the lack of support from the Soviet camp for a more militant line.[71] Countering those who wanted to abandon political struggle and focus only on armed struggle, Duan argued that political struggle was absolutely necessary because that form of struggle was suitable to "the masses," and it was a powerful form.[72] The high value placed on political struggle reflected Duan's concept of the Southern struggle as a revolution, which by definition was a mass uprising. The emphasis on political struggle naturally lessened the necessity of military aid from the socialist bloc. A Politburo's resolution issued in December 1962 advised that "the Southern revolution should rely primarily on its own resources, with the active assistance [*giup do*] from the North, and with the increasing support [*ung ho*] from the socialist camp and liberation movements and other progressive forces around the world."[73] The term "ung ho" [support] was used for foreign aid, whereas "giup do" [assistance] was used for Northern involvement. The former term in Vietnamese meant more specifically spiritual or moral support than material, whereas the latter meant specifically material support. The resolution also stated that, "we should secure the full support [*ung ho*] from our camp, first of all from the Soviet Union and China, to make [the United States] understand that if it sends troops to fight in the North [*gay chien tranh cuc bo*], it will lose."[74] In other words, in this strategy, support from the socialist camp had merely deterrent value. What appeared to concern Duan the most was the possibility of Washington sending ground troops into the North, not the South. This view on the limited role of foreign aid to the Southern revolution fitted with the aforementioned self-reliant economic strategy advocated by Le Duan's faction.

[70] "Thu cua Dong chi Le Duan gui Trung uong Cuc mien Nam" [Letter from Comrade Le Duan to the Southern Central Office], July 18, 1962. *VKDTT*, v. 23, 705–725.
[71] Ibid., 717.
[72] Ibid., 713.
[73] "Nghi quyet Hoi nghi Bo Chinh tri" [Politbuto Meeting resolution], December 6–10, 1962. *VKDTT*, v. 23, 819.
[74] Ibid., 820.

Ideological concepts figured prominently in Hanoi's assessments of the enemies even though some analyses appeared stretched. In particular, North Vietnamese analysts viewed the Buddhist crisis facing the Ngo Dinh Diem regime in 1963 not as a mistake of Ngo's religious policy or his failure to control the military, but as evidence of revolutionary success that drove a wedge between the regime and its American backer.[75] They likened the relationship between Washington and Saigon to that between a master [*chu*] and a servant [*to*], regardless of what government was in Saigon. Ngo Dinh Diem's consistent rebukes of American pressure to reform his regime did not disconfirm their analysis, because "Diem dreamed big and wanted to be a powerful king [*muu ba do vuong*]. Although he was now an American lackey, Diem could be brave enough to switch to a new master if necessary." The collapse of the Ngo government, if occurring, was not a chance to relax the revolutionary struggle because whoever replaced Ngo Dinh Diem would also be an American lackey. Rather, "the people" should struggle even more tenaciously.

If Diem was an American puppet, the American government, in particular "the Kennedy clique" [*tap doan*], was the puppet of American monopoly capitalists [*tu ban lung doan*]. To them, the Kennedy administration was not different from previous ones except that it was much more cunning and cruel.[76] Kennedy's aggressive moves to confront the socialist camp had brought some small victories for the United States, such as the isolation of Cuba by Latin American countries or a closer US relationship with "capitalist India." Those victories were essentially bought with dollars. But American monopoly capitalists had failed to find a way out for the beleaguered and crisis-ridden US economy. Their attempt to dump the burden of economic crisis on the working classes by new taxes and by issuing bonds only aggravated existing class cleavages and created ripe conditions for a proletarian revolution in the United States.

Hanoi commentators were particularly excited about rising racial conflicts in American society.[77] In their reasoning, because 90 percent of blacks belonged to the proletariat, racial conflicts in the United States

---

[75] Tran Quang, "Che do my-Diem o mien Nam dang khung hoang tram trong" [The US-Diem regime in the South under severe crisis], *Hoc Tap*, October 1963, 56–61.

[76] Tien Dung, "Chinh sach cua Tap doan Ken-ne-di hay la con duong be tac cua chu nghia De quoc My," *Hoc Tap*, September 1962, 71–78.

[77] Nhi Ha, "Nhiet liet ung ho cuoc dau tranh doi tu do, binh dang cua nhan dan My da den" [Warmly supporting the struggle for freedom and equality of black people in the United States], *Hoc Tap*, October 1963, 68–72.

were essentially a class struggle between the absolute majority of blacks and American monopoly capital. Because the American working class movement had been "sabotaged" and divided by trade union collaborators, it was hoped that the struggle of proletarian blacks could push the movement along a revolutionary path to crush the oppression of monopoly capital and bring socialism to America.

Although class struggle was a useful tool for evaluating US strengths and weaknesses, the concept of "antagonisms" was similarly helpful for Hanoi to assess American intentions. The resolution of the Ninth Central Committee Plenum in December 1963 pointed out four antagonisms in the South, including those between the Vietnamese people and the United States and its lackeys, between peasants and feudal landlords, between the socialist camp and the imperialist camp, and between the American imperialist and other imperialist powers, especially the French.[78] Based on those antagonisms, the resolution pointed out that American goals in South Vietnam were threefold, which were: (1) to suppress the liberation movement and implement neocolonialist policy there; (2) to build a military base in preparation for waging war against the socialist camp; and (3) to prevent socialism from spreading to Southeast Asia. The resolution claimed that the third goal was most important for the United States, because Washington wanted to halt the disintegration of the imperialist system in Southeast Asia and elsewhere in the world. Given those US intentions, the resolution claimed, the Party had correctly framed the Southern revolution in public as a "struggle against American imperialism to achieve national independence, democracy, peace, and neutralism," rather than as a communist revolution. The rationale for disguising the revolution was twofold. First, the struggle ostensibly opposed only *American* imperialism; this would exploit anti-American sentiments in many countries, even in US allies such as De Gaulle's France. Second, the goal of the struggle appeared to be merely national independence but not communism, making it sound less threatening to the Americans and to the South Vietnamese bourgeoisie.[79]

Vietnamese leaders and writers consistently interpreted realities and devised revolutionary strategies based in part on the Marxist-Leninist worldview. The fluctuating revolutionary conditions between 1961 and

[78] "Nghi quyet cua Hoi nghi lan thu chin" [Resolution of the Ninth Central Committee Plenum], December 1963. VKDTT, v. 24, 818–819. This was the resolution on the Southern revolution. The Plenum issued another resolution on the Sino-Soviet conflict, which will be discussed later in this chapter.
[79] Ibid., 820–821.

1963 led to the clash between two factions in the Party. This clash climaxed at the Ninth Central Committee Plenum in December 1963, to be discussed in the next section.

"NOT TO MISS OUT ON THE CHANCE TO DEFEAT CAPITALISM"

On November 1, 1963, Ngo Dinh Diem was overthrown and later killed in a coup. Less than three weeks later, Kennedy was assassinated. Some sources revealed that a tense debate occurred at the Ninth Central Committee Plenum between Le Duan's militant faction and his opponents such as Bui Cong Trung and Duong Bach Mai.[80] Le Duan's speech at the Plenum can be read as a manifesto of the self-reliant internationalist faction he led. The speech began by criticizing a small number of "comrades" who were "intellectuals" [dang vien tri thuc] and who believed that "our Party is small and was born in a colonized backward agrarian country," and that "our leaders have had little formal education and are not capable of understanding the Marxist-Leninist science and complex international issues."[81] Duan painstakingly cited all the successes up to then of the Vietnamese revolution to support his point that the Party was capable of correctly understanding Marxism-Leninism.

Because the aims of Marxism-Leninism were not only to understand the world but also to change it, Duan argued that to understand the doctrine required not only theoretical knowledge but also a determination to change the world. Comparing his opponents to Menshevik figures such as Kaustky and Plekhanov, Duan claimed that the ongoing debate in the socialist camp boiled down to two different attitudes on the questions of "whether to make revolution or not, whether to work and fight for working classes and oppressed people or not, and whether having the will to destroy imperialism and capitalism or not." Of course, Duan's answers to those questions were yes, yes, and yes!

Reviewing the revolutionary ideas and "innovations" of Lenin, Stalin, and Mao, Duan asserted that the Chinese revolution marked a new development of proletarian revolutionary theory with a Marxist-Leninist revolution carried out successfully in an agrarian, backward country. In Duan's words, Mao's theory that made peasants the main force of revolution had been tested successfully not only in China but also in Vietnam,

[80] Nguyen Van Tran, *Viet cho me va quoc hoi* [To my mother and the National Assembly] (Westminster, CA: Van nghe, 1996).
[81] Le Duan, "Mot vai van de trong nhiem vu quoc te cua Dang ta" [Some issues in the international duties of our Party]. *Hoc Tap*, February 1964, 1–20.

which made it a "truth" [*chan ly*] and a model applicable to communist movements in Asia, Africa, and Latin America. This was the first time since the mid-1950s when Mao was raised publicly to the level of Lenin and Stalin in Vietnam, signaling Le Duan's support for Mao's claim to be one of the greatest leaders of world revolution.

A key goal of Duan's speech was to criticize Khrushchev's policy of peaceful coexistence and economic competition between the capitalist and socialist camps. Duan rejected the argument that nuclear weapons could shape the course of development in human society. Nuclear weapons in imperialist hands were offensive, whereas, in socialist control, they were for defensive purpose. Without mass support and a correct political line, nuclear weapons could not destroy imperialism. Despite the American monopoly on such weapons before 1949, the Chinese and Vietnamese revolutions still succeeded, thanks to mass support and a correct revolutionary line. To take a defensive posture at a time when the correlation of forces favored socialism was to give up on making revolution.

Duan similarly rejected the notion of peaceful economic competition between the two camps, arguing that socialism had revealed to be superior to capitalism since its birth. This superiority was demonstrated in the speed of Soviet industrialization and the progressive nature of the socialist system in which exploitation and unemployment were eliminated. If communists waited for imperialism to melt away when socialist economies surpassed their capitalist rivals in outputs, they would miss out on the chance to defeat capitalism in an "age of revolutionary storms" [*bao tap cach mang*].

On imperialism, Duan noted that "imperialist economies" were chronically sick with cyclical crises, widening gaps between the rich and the poor, persistent unemployment, and persistent budget deficits and high inflation. Economically imperialist countries were rich but not strong. Their warmongering nature had not changed. What had changed was the form of domination from colonialism to neocolonialism. To Duan, enemies of imperialism thus included not only the remaining 50 million people still living under the old colonialism, but billions of people being oppressed and exploited by neocolonialism.

Although the entire speech was critical of Khrushchev's ideas and policies, Duan called for all to support the unity of the camp and the solidarity between the Soviet Union and China. He recalled that:

In the most difficult time of [our] struggle under the iron heels of colonialism, in the darkest hours in imperialist prison or when walking to the gallows, in the heart of each Vietnamese communist the image of the great Soviet Union was a burning fire, a bright guiding light to help [us] to keep [our] indomitable spirit and firm belief in [our] invincible cause.

The resolution of the Ninth Central Committee Plenum basically affirmed Duan's position, which was now the official position of the Vietnamese Workers' Party (VWP). The document began with noting that the conflict between the socialist and imperialist camps could not be fully solved without the contributions by the working class in capitalist countries and by colonized and oppressed peoples.[82] Given peaceful coexistence between the two camps, the socialist camp could defeat the imperialist camp only through successful revolutions to overthrow bourgeois rule in capitalist countries and imperialist rule in colonized countries. Furthermore, the resolution argued that Asia, Africa, and Latin America were the focal points of all four antagonisms. These regions were also where the imperialist chain of domination was weakest.

The litmus test of communists was loyalty to the entire camp, as Le Duan had argued since 1960.[83] Yet the resolution distinguished between the "revisionist clique" (read: Tito and his followers) and "adherents to revisionism in brother parties" (read: Khrushchev). The former were clearly enemies, whereas the latter were still brothers.[84] The resolution, therefore, did not criticize Khrushchev by name, and in his trip to Moscow to brief Soviet leaders about the Plenum, Le Duan sought to downplay the new policy (in private, however, Khrushchev was sometimes branded a traitor).[85] Soviet-Vietnamese relations did not significantly worsen in 1964, even while Sino-Vietnamese relations became close. Domestically, Le Duan and his associates were not so benign. During 1964, they summoned home all Vietnamese officials and students studying in the Soviet Union. Many officials sought and were granted asylum, including the Deputy Mayor of Hanoi and a Senior Colonel who was editor in chief of the *People's Army Daily*. Bui Cong Trung and Ung Van Khiem lost their positions and would be expelled from the Party. Dang Kim Giang, Hoang Minh Chinh, Le Liem, and numerous others would be arrested in 1967 and imprisoned for many years.

---

[82] "Nghi quyet Hoi nghi lan thu chin," 729–733.
[83] Ibid., 794.
[84] Ibid., 769.
[85] Tran Quynh, "May ky niem ve Le Duan." Khrushchev was mentioned as a "traitor" in "Nghi quyet Hoi nghi Trung uong Cuc lan thu ba" [Resolution of the COSVN's Third Plenum], January 1965. *VKDTT*, v. 26, 670.

CONCLUSION

The worldview of key Vietnamese leaders underwent a significant shift between 1960 and 1963. Through their direct participation in the ideological debate between China and the Soviet Union, a militant faction led by Le Duan developed the notion that Vietnam could remain loyal to the socialist camp while pursuing a policy different from Soviet global policy. By late 1963, Duan's faction succeeded in making its view accepted by the Party leadership despite significant opposition.

If they had been idealistic, Vietnamese leaders were more realistic now. They no longer trusted their socialist brothers absolutely as before. While continuing to promote solidarity in the camp, they asserted an autonomous position for the DRV vis-à-vis its communist brothers. Unlike their earlier willingness to blindly follow the advice of their big brothers, Vietnamese communists now sought to resist such advice and even to manipulate the brothers. Their relationship with their brothers became partly instrumental as a result, but the brothers still belonged to a different category in their imagination and could never be compared to the imperialists.

Recall that ideology had been a source of unity for the communist movement in the face of brutal French suppression. In this period, ideology became a source of conflict. Marxism-Leninism was broad enough to be interpreted in more than one way. Khrushchev was no less a Leninist than Mao. So was Bui Cong Trung versus Le Duan. Ideological debates fostered factionalism between those men and within the global communist movement. On the one hand, Hanoi's ideological disagreement with Moscow annoyed Khrushchev. On the other, loyalty to the camp prevented Hanoi from accepting Beijing's aid on the condition of acknowledging Beijing's leadership of a new bloc. Ideology clearly trumped practical interests in this case. Although Le Duan's faction gained the upper hand and later came to dominate the Party, thanks in part to their radical ideological formulations, their success was not predestined and their genuine belief in those formulations should not be doubted. For the Vietnamese revolution as a whole, it cannot be said that ideology was helpful. As will be clear later, the new militant line incurred severe risks.

Duan and his faction adopted a more realistic attitude after 1960, but that did not mean that they had or would become Titos. Quite the opposite, as this chapter has shown, Vietnamese leaders remained loyal to world revolution and sought to coordinate policy with China and the Soviet bloc as much as they could. They remained as internationalist as ever. Without understanding this fact, it would be hard to explain the vanguard internationalism to be observed in their thinking after 1968. That we will turn to in Chapter 6.

6

The Rise of Vanguard Internationalism, 1964–1975

The key decision made by North Vietnamese leaders at the Ninth Central Committee Plenum was to escalate attacks on the Saigon government in the attempt to achieve a quick victory. However, events after 1963 did not turn out that way, presenting Hanoi with both risks and opportunities.[1] Le Duan had underestimated American commitment to defending South Vietnam.[2] In response to the Gulf of Tonkin incident in August 1964, President Johnson ordered the bombing of North Vietnam for the first time. Operation Rolling Thunder followed in early 1965 with more sustained bombing. Entire units of US Marines soon landed in South Vietnam, beginning to take over some fighting from the Armed Forces of the Republic of Vietnam (ARVN).

But all was not doom and gloom for the communists. To Hanoi's delight, Leonid Brezhnev replaced "the traitor Khrushchev" in October 1964. Although the Brezhnev team did not differ from Khrushchev ideologically, they responded strongly to American intervention by offering whatever military aid North Vietnam requested. In China, Mao was concerned about US aggression in his backyard and acted similarly. At

---

[1] Duan later blamed the disunity of the camp for the "missed opportunity" to win the war in 1964–1965. In particular, if China and the Soviet Union had not split and had fully supported the Vietnamese revolution, Saigon would have been defeated and the United States forced to disengage. See "Bai noi cua dong chi Le Duan tai Hoi nghi Trung uong lan thu 14" [Comrade Le Duan's speech at the Fourteenth Central Committee Plenum], January 1968. *VKDTT*, v. 29, 15–16.

[2] For a different perspective on Duan's decision, see Zachary Shore, *A Sense of the Enemy: The High Stakes History of Reading Your Rival's Mind* (New York: Oxford University Press, 2014), chap 6.

Hanoi's request, Mao sent not only more aid but also hundreds of thousands of Chinese troops to assist with construction and air-defense work.

Despite such brotherly generosity, North Vietnam's relations with both big brothers remained guarded. In mid-1967, hundreds of high-ranking cadres suspected to have pro-Soviet views were arrested. North Vietnamese relations with China similarly deteriorated in 1968. In the early 1970s Hanoi maintained lukewarm relations with both Beijing and Moscow despite the fact that both were forthcoming and generous in supplying North Vietnam with war materiel and other assistance.[3]

As the revolution in Vietnam became a focal point for anti-Americanism around the world in the late 1960s, a specific form of belief, which I call "vanguard internationalism," emerged in Hanoi. Unlike the realistic internationalism of the earlier period that resulted from frustration with the Soviet Union, vanguard internationalism was the product of rising national pride and revolutionary ambitions. Vanguard internationalism profoundly shaped the thinking and policies of Hanoi leaders even though it was not responsible for their victory.

THE ANTIREVISIONIST CAMPAIGN, 1964 TO MID-1965

The Vietnamese leadership was deeply split in late 1963. At the Ninth Central Committee Plenum, the militant faction that had already controlled the Politburo defeated its opponents after a tense debate. After the meeting, the Politburo sought to enforce unity and suppress dissent by ordering a "rectification campaign" in February 1964. The ostensible goal of this campaign was to make all cadres, party members, and ordinary people "strengthen their proletarian worldview, their revolutionary spirit, the spirit of self-reliance, sacrifice and struggle, commitments to organization and discipline, the spirit of socialist collectivism, and proletarian morality."[4] It was hoped that the campaign would raise cadres'

---

[3] According to Soviet and PAVN's archival sources, military aid from the socialist bloc to North Vietnam during 1969–1972, of which about 50 percent was equipment, was nearly half of all such aid from 1954 to 1974. The supply of military equipment from the bloc increased between five and ten times between 1964 and 1973 on average. See Nguyen Thi Mai Hoa, *Cac nuoc Xa hoi chu nghia ung ho Viet Nam khang chien chong My, cuu nuoc*, 356–357. Martin Loicano argues that communist forces in fact enjoyed advantage over Saigon troops in terms of tanks, long-range rockets, and heavy artillery prior to 1972. See Martin Loicano, "The Role of Weapons in the Second Indochina War: Republic of Vietnam Perspectives and Perceptions," *Journal of Vietnamese Studies* 8: 2 (2013), 44.

[4] "Nghi quyet cua Bo Chinh tri so 95-NQ/TW" [The Politburo's Resolution], February 4, 1964. *VKDTT*, v. 25, 63–65.

morale and motivate them to "overcome rightist thoughts and the influences of revisionism, individualism, liberalism, and commandism."

Ho Chi Minh convened an unprecedented meeting named the "Special
Political Conference" in March 1964. Besides Party, state, and other
leaders, participants included more than three hundred socially influential people such as retired revolutionary figures, nonparty intellectuals,
and "hero workers and soldiers."[5] The key event at this conference was
Ho's address, which recounted the success of the revolution, summarized
the official line on domestic and international issues, and called on all
Vietnamese to unite and work harder to cope with the challenges ahead.[6]
Ho did not go into the internal debate on revisionism at the Ninth Plenum,
nor did he come out against either the Soviet Union or China when discussing international politics. It is well known that Ho was ambivalent
about the new militant line, yet his public appearance at a special venue
right after the divisive Ninth Plenum symbolically signaled his willingness to cooperate with Le Duan's faction.[7]

Despite Ho's call for unity, the ideological struggle against revisionism continued unabated throughout 1964 and 1965. In an article for the
Party journal, General Hoang Van Thai, a Central Committee member
and Deputy Chief of General Staff of the PAVN, took as his aim the argument that nuclear weapons had totally changed the nature of warfare.[8]
In Thai's view, war was still the continuation of politics by other means.
For example, he argued, the behavior of American imperialism had not
changed, judged by its military budget, which tripled between 1949 and
1959. The "barbaric and cruel" use of atomic bombs by the United States
in 1945 against Japan was evidence that new weapons in imperialist
hands fanned rather than dampened their ambitions. Washington continued to test nuclear weapons and encircle the socialist bloc with them. The
reason that the United States had not used nuclear bombs since World
War II was not because it was concerned about the destructive power of
nuclear weapons, but "because it feared the strength of the movement
for peace, democracy, and socialism." Didn't American leaders once toy

[5] www.baotanghochiminh.vn/TabId/495/ArticleId/6388/PreTabId/465/Default.aspx.
[6] "Bao cao cua Chu tich Ho Chi Minh tai Hoi nghi Chinh tri dac biet" [President Ho's
  speech at the Special Political Conference], March 27–28, 1964. *VKDTT*, v. 25, 90–108.
[7] For a different interpretation of Ho's speech, see Pierre Asselin, *Hanoi's Road to the
  Vietnam War, 1954–1965* (Berkeley: University of California Press, 2013), 187.
[8] "Nam vung duong loi quan su cua Dang, ngan chan anh huong cua chu nghia xet lai
  trong linh vuc quan su" [Understanding the Party's military policy, blocking the influence
  of revisionism in military affairs]. *Hoc Tap*, April 1964, 17–25.

with the idea of using nuclear bombs in Korea and Indochina? Thai asked rhetorically.

Thai argued that, in the Marxist view, people rather than weapons played the decisive role in warfare. In the Soviet victory over Nazi Germany and Mao's defeat of Chiang Kai-shek, it was people, not weapons, who made a difference since the vanquished had the upper hand in weaponry in the early phase of the war. Marxists valued weapons because they helped to defeat imperialism without too many lives lost, but the strategy and tactics of revolutionary armies should never be based on nuclear weapons. With human beings playing such a central role in warfare, Thai believed that:

Regardless of the circumstances, regardless of the relative balance of military power between U.S. and our army, regardless of conventional or nuclear warfare, the kind of war we fight will be people's war. Our main strength will come from the people. Our most important weapon will be the will of our people [to fight].[9]

Le Thanh Nghi, a Politburo member and Deputy Prime Minister in charge of industry, echoed Thai's view in the economic field.[10] Le Duan had argued that industrialization should be financed by domestic savings rather than through trade with the socialist bloc. The question confronting North Vietnamese leaders then was how low they could go in setting grain procurement prices and workers' wages. The lower the prices and wages, the more domestic savings could be mobilized, but the harder it would be to motivate peasants and workers to work. Nghi rejected using higher wages and prices to stimulate production, predicting that such material incentives would result in an income gap between a small number of people and the majority of the working class. Rewarding skills also was not fair in the sense that the technical skills that an individual possessed was attributable not only to that person's hard work but also to social institutions such as schools. To Nghi, material incentives were important but not as important as ideological education "for the masses to have socialist consciousness, to love labor, and to care for others as much as for themselves." He advocated that:

While enjoying their material lives, workers ought to be considerate toward peasants; intellectuals toward manual workers; and high-ranking and middle-ranking cadres toward the masses, the working class, and low-ranking cadres. As

[9] Ibid., 24.
[10] Le Thanh Nghi, "Giao duc chinh tri, tu tuong va khuyen khich bang loi ich vat chat" [Political and ideological education and material incentives]. *Hoc Tap*, August 1964, 7–15.

adherents to Marxism-Leninism and proletarian internationalism, we ought to be mindful of our duties to world revolution while we are enjoying our material lives.[11]

On cultural policy, officials from the Propaganda and Ideology department of the Party railed against what they labeled the bourgeois notion of humanitarianism [*chu nghia nhan dao tu san*]. In the bourgeois view, class struggle was "inhumane." To the proletariat, in contrast, class struggle was "most humane." Class struggle was absolutely necessary to liberate workers from capitalist domination.[12] Class struggle was no doubt brutal, but this method was essential to overcome capitalists' "ferocious resistance" [*chong cu dien cuong*]. A figure under attack in North Vietnam for his "bourgeois humanitarianism" was Soviet film director Grigori Chukhrai, whose 1956 movie *The Forty-First* won many prizes in the Soviet Union and abroad. The film was about a Red Army female soldier who fell in love with a White Army man who was a prisoner under her guard. He was later shot by her when he rushed to greet his fellow White Army soldiers who came for his rescue. North Vietnamese critics chided the director for his portrayal of the two lovers as human beings, not as a revolutionary and a counterrevolutionary. The antiwar message conveyed by the tragic ending of the film failed to distinguish between just and unjust war.

Encountering the same criticism were many Vietnamese works such as a poem that praised the Eighth World Youth Festival in Helsinki in 1962 for bringing together participants from all over the world. In the poem, the poet Xuan Quynh imagined the scene of a Vietnamese ex-soldier shaking hands with a former French soldier who used to be his enemy at Dien Bien Phu: "Gone is their hatred, gone is the barrier between them / Our world ... is not just guns and swords and violence ..." An official of the Ideological Department charged that the poem "smacked of peaceful coexistence." It implied that class interests could be compromised and that violence was generally a bad thing.[13]

On foreign policy, the ideological battle was more complex and displayed not only antirevisionist and anti-Soviet but also anti-Chinese attitudes. We saw in Chapter 5 that Le Duan was critical of Mao as early

---

[11] Ibid., 15.
[12] Hong Chuong, "Hai quan niem ve chu nghia nhan dao" [Two views on humanitarianism]. *Hoc Tap*, October 1964, 24–35.
[13] Ibid., 35. The title of the poem is "Tieng Hat" [The Singing Voice]. Entire poem is available at www.thivien.net/viewpoem.php?ID=35951 (accessed May 21, 2012).

as mid-1963. After the Ninth Plenum later that year, anti-Soviet sentiments were widespread in North Vietnam.[14] Yet Le Duan was reportedly unhappy about this "Soviet bashing," as he explained to Tran Quynh that the Party was against revisionism but not against the CPSU.[15] Unlike China, which wanted to replace the Soviet Union as the center of world revolution, in Duan's view Vietnam remained deeply thankful for Soviet assistance and only wanted Moscow to abandon its erroneous view and lead the socialist bloc in the fight against imperialism, as in the good old days under Stalin.

Quynh was certainly not an impartial observer and perhaps exaggerated Duan's foresight of China's conflict with Vietnam in the late 1970s. Yet there is no reason to dismiss his entire account. If it is true, Duan held grudges against China not only because he feared its chauvinism but also because he scorned Mao's theoretical ability. Quynh's larger point about Duan's efforts to distinguish Vietnam's standpoint from China's is in fact confirmed in other writings of the time. For example, a mid-1964 editorial in *Hoc Tap* clearly distinguished between an antirevisionist theoretical position, which Vietnam supported, and the clique-forming activities in the socialist bloc, which Vietnam denounced.[16] The article first attacked the activities of some (unnamed) revisionist leaders of brother parties to form a clique [*ket be phai*] within their own parties and within the bloc. Under the claim to fight the personality cult of Stalin, those leaders purged their parties of "genuine Marxist-Leninist comrades" and used all tricks to coax or intimidate leaders of brother parties into submission. These tricks included such despicable acts such as cutting aid, withdrawing experts, and canceling treaties and contracts. Clearly the target of denunciation thus far was Khrushchev.

But the main point of the article was broader, which was to condemn *all* the activities that could lead to a formal split of the bloc. The article warned that "some people with ill will" had lobbied aggressively for the convening of an international conference in order to exclude certain Marxist-Leninist parties from the movement. This warning could apply to Mao as much as to Khrushchev. In Vietnam's view, no one and no party had the right to do so. Hanoi leaders pledged to preserve solidarity within the camp and to prevent the conflict from further escalating.

---

[14] Tran Thu, *Tu tu xu ly noi bo*, 113–114; Tran Quynh, "May ky niem ve Le Duan."
[15] Tran Quynh, "May ky niem ve Le Duan."
[16] "Giu vung doan ket quoc te, chong moi am muu chia re" [Maintaining international solidarity, opposing all plots to divide (us)]. *Hoc Tap*, June 1964, 1–8.

As the article explained, "in recent years, revisionism has weakened the solidarity of the international communist movement and the socialist camp ... Yet even that weakened solidarity is still better than an open split in the movement and the camp, because such a split would only benefit [the] enemy."

Preserving solidarity within the camp at the current level did not mean that Vietnamese leaders were willing to make compromises with revisionism. Rather, doing so was to create conditions for "the truths of Marxism-Leninism to sink deeper into the minds of genuine communists in those parties currently under revisionist influences, so that they would step forward to combat and defeat revisionism ..."[17] This article suggested that Vietnamese leaders were perhaps hoping for Khrushchev to be overthrown.[18] However, the point here is that a crucial difference existed between China's and Vietnam's approach to the Sino-Soviet split. This difference helps explain why China would so quickly fall out of Vietnam's favor by 1968, even while Chinese aid to Vietnam was at its all-time high level.

Through 1964 up to mid-1965, Le Duan's faction continued to consolidate their ideological domination over the Party. Antirevisionist arguments served to apply ideological principles to various policy issues. Although Vietnam was ideologically closer to China and although Soviet bashing was widespread, the official line distinguished Vietnam's international position from China's. In private some unease and even anti-Chinese sentiments existed.

WHAT DOES "BEING INDEPENDENT" MEAN?

The escalation of war in 1965 posed new challenges to Hanoi. To "dialectically thinking" Vietnamese leaders, American escalation was simply a reaction to the success of the Southern revolution.[19] The greater the success was, the "more vicious" the reaction became. Without denying the seriousness of the situation, Party leaders remained optimistic. They mobilized for war while not neglecting the task of developing socialism. They not only rejected US offers for talks but also brushed aside proposals from the Soviet Union and other countries for mediation.

[17] Ibid., 8.
[18] Asselin makes the same point in *Hanoi's Road to the Vietnam War*, 185.
[19] Le Duan, "Xay dung tu tuong lam chu tap the tren lap truong giai cap vo san" [Building the spirit of collective mastery on the standpoint of the proletariat]. *Hoc Tap*, June 1965, 1.

Why such a hard line? Truong Chinh argued that war, however long and painful, was necessary for the Vietnamese revolution to move forward. Revolutionary goals had long been set, which were to "win national independence, establish a people's democracy, then advance to socialism and communism."[20] War should neither change that goal nor disrupt it. In his view, the revolutionary task of socialist development should continue during wartime and not wait for victory. For external propaganda North Vietnamese leaders proclaimed that the goals of the war were to "liberate the South and protect the North." But as Le Duan told his comrades at the Twelfth Central Committee Plenum, the real goals were to "take the whole country on the path to socialism."[21]

But weren't Vietnamese leaders awed at all by American military prowess? In the 1950s, Ho Chi Minh sought to make his people hate America and not fear it. As communist soldiers battled US troops on the ground, Hanoi's assessment of the enemy became more complex:

Assessing imperialist America is not to solve a simple math problem of measuring how strong it is [militarily], nor to make a general statement about its power relative to revolutionary forces worldwide. Rather, one must analyze its power relative to ours in politics, military, and economy, so that we can identify its strengths and weaknesses in each particular region in the world and in each particular historical period.[22]

Le Duan was ready to admit superior American firepower and technological prowess. Yet overall he did not consider the United States strong enough to defeat communist Vietnam. His assessment continued to reflect his worldview through two main concepts: the nature of the United States as a political actor and the trend of the age. As a political actor on the global stage, the United States was "the boss of the imperialist gang" [*de quoc dau so*] and an "international gendarme" [*sen dam quoc te*] described with such adjectives as "counterrevolutionary" [*phan cach mang*], "bellicose" [*hieu chien*], "stubborn" [*ngoan co*], "deceitful" [*lua bip*], "barbaric" [*da man*], and "cruel" [*doc ac*].[23] This evil nature

[20] Truong Chinh, "Nam vung moi quan he giua chien tranh va cach mang o Viet nam de hoan thanh thang loi su nghiep chong My, cuu nuoc" [Correctly understanding the relationship between war and revolution in Vietnam to complete the task of fighting America to save our country]. *Hoc Tap*, September 1965, 20.

[21] "Bai noi cua dong chi Le Duan ... tai Hoi nghi lan thu 12 cua Trung uong" [Comrade Le Duan's speech at the Twelfth Central Committee Plenum], December 1965. *VKDTT*, v. 26, 603.

[22] Ibid., 575.

[23] Ibid., 571, 574, 595, 599.

of the United States made it not just the enemy of Vietnam but also the nemesis of peace, progress, and humanity. Vietnam was thus shedding blood not just to defend itself but on behalf of all humans. In this struggle Vietnam was not alone; the United States was.

In the same vein, "the trend of the age" [*xu huong thoi dai*] since World War II was the decline and crisis of capitalism and imperialism. Although powerful, the United States was countervailed by the socialist camp, nationalist movements, and "global movements for peace and democracy."[24] American power was also constrained by other imperialist countries that had recovered since World War II.[25] Because of that particular correlation of forces, Washington was not free to escalate the war on any scale but would be forced to limit it. The larger the scale it sought to expand the war, Duan predicted, the more isolated it would become. Eventually it would have to accept withdrawal to cut the losses.

While claiming that they were contributing to world revolution, Vietnamese leaders made it clear that they did not seek to defeat the United States on the world stage, only in Vietnam.[26] In Vietnam, their war goal was to crush the Yankee's "will of aggression" [*y chi xam luoc*] and force him to withdraw, rather than "killing to the last G.I or sweeping all of them into the Pacific Ocean."[27] To achieve the latter goal would perhaps require the unnecessary sacrifice of too many Vietnamese lives. Le Duan calculated that the American will would collapse only if the ARVN disintegrated and if a sizable number of US troops were eliminated on the battlefield. When that happened, it would be time for North Vietnam to accept talks with the United States. We will see later that this rough articulation of war aims would be developed into the plan for the *Tet* Offensive in 1968 and would drive Hanoi's war strategy until 1972. For the time being, Hanoi would reject any offers for talks or mediation. Significantly, Duan said that Moscow and Beijing were kept in the dark about the DRV's war aims and about those conditions for talks with Washington.

Dealing with their Soviet and Chinese brothers, in fact, caused as much headache for North Vietnamese leaders as did fighting the Americans. Their relationship with the big brothers continued to evolve as they groped for an appropriate war strategy. Although relieved that

[24] Ibid., 575.
[25] Ibid., 570.
[26] Ibid., 587–588.
[27] Ibid., 588.

the brothers were coming to their assistance, they did not welcome the unsolicited advice and pressure that accompanied the aid. They remained loyal to the bloc, but made deliberate efforts to search for and assert the "Vietnamese way" of doing things.

Recall that Le Duan was privately critical of Mao after the latter said in mid-1963 that he wanted to launch another revolution to liberate China and all of Southeast Asia. By 1965, Moscow's rapprochement with Hanoi and sharply increased Soviet aid to North Vietnam had unsettled Beijing.[28] China reluctantly agreed to let Soviet goods pass through its territory on their way to Vietnam, but still wanted to obstruct Soviet-Vietnamese relations by badmouthing the Soviets in front of the Vietnamese and by creating delays in the transportation of Soviet aid. That was the context when Le Duan announced the shift toward a more balanced position between China and the Soviet Union at the Eleventh Central Committee Plenum in late 1965.[29]

In his political report at the Plenum, Duan explained that Vietnamese thinking about the strategy of the international revolutionary movement differed from Soviet and Chinese thinking.[30] Hanoi believed that the movement should maintain an offensive momentum against imperialism in general and against the United States in particular. This strategy was necessary both for preserving global peace and for overthrowing imperialism step by step and eventually defeating it globally. In contrast, the Soviet brother wanted to preserve "peace at any cost." Duan's point on the difference between China and Vietnam was apparently deleted from the released version of this document, but based on Tran Quynh's memoir, we can surmise that Duan was likely to have said that China wanted to be the center of a new socialist bloc. This Vietnam rejected.

Despite Vietnam's differences with its brothers, Duan argued, it should not distance itself from the international proletarian movement and from the socialist camp.[31] On the contrary, Vietnam should try to maintain solidarity with the Soviet Union and China. Vietnam had always looked to the CPSU as Lenin's party and to the Soviet Union as the first Fatherland for the world's proletariat. At the same time, Vietnam considered relations with China as "lips and teeth that lived and died together" [*song chet co*

---

[28] Lien-Hang Nguyen, "The War Politburo," 23.
[29] "Bai noi cua dong chi Le Duan tai Hoi nghi lan thu 12 cua Trung uong" [Comrade Le Duan's speech at the Twelfth Central Committee Plenum], December 1965. *VKDTT*, v. 26, 609.
[30] Ibid., 610–615.
[31] Ibid., 610.

nhau]. Duan pledged that Vietnam would never deviate from the policies of protecting the Soviet Union and China and keeping solidarity with the entire socialist camp and the international communist movement.

Although Vietnamese communists would forever defer to the CPSU and the CCP as older brothers and continue to learn from their experiences, Duan wanted his Party to maintain an independent mindset [*doc lap tu chu*]. "Independence," he explained, meant "not to mechanically mimic [*rap khuon may moc*] the policy of another party."[32] To Duan this mindset did not deviate from proletarian internationalism; on the contrary, the mindset was necessary precisely for upholding proletarian internationalism. The entire history of the Vietnamese revolution, Duan claimed, demonstrated that success came (only) when the Party could maintain an independent mindset and be creative in its policy. In the late 1930s, for example, his Party did not copy the CCP's experience of forming a people's front. In 1945, his Party built a rural base (like the CCP) but seized the opportunity available in the cities in August to take power (unlike the CCP). Duan claimed that Vietnamese collectivization of agriculture was based on a uniquely Vietnamese theory of three revolutions.[33] Finally, Vietnam decided to launch the Southern revolution in 1959 against the advice of both Moscow and Beijing. These past experiences demonstrated that it paid to be independent.

Duan noted that the lack of that independent mindset was a "grave problem" in the Party. Cadres who had this problem could not maintain firm adherence to central policy. At this point Duan signaled that central policy was changing subtly. The Party's "heavy responsibility" to defeat the United States was not a Vietnamese duty but an international one. For this reason Vietnam wished to strengthen solidarity within the socialist camp and put aside all disputes. As Duan proposed, "We should not keep attacking revisionism all the time.... Although we criticize revisionism for its willingness to compromise with the Americans, we should not isolate ourselves from the socialist brothers. [Beyond revisionism,] other disputes ... should be resolved internally on the basis of comradely consultation."[34] As Duan told the Central Committee, Vietnam was deeply

---

[32] Ibid., 611.

[33] These were the revolutions on relations of production, on science and technology, and on culture and thought, respectively. Duan did not mention the land reform (1953–1956), which not only copied China's experience "mechanically," but was directed in part by Chinese advisers.

[34] "Bai noi cua dong chi Le Duan tai Hoi nghi lan thu 12 cua Trung uong." *VKDTT*, v. 26, 615.

thankful for the brothers' support thus far, and "this is not diplomatic talk but comes deep from our hearts." This statement may have reflected Duan's true appreciation of Soviet aid or his concern about the campaign against revisionism offending Soviet leaders. But Duan and his faction may have discontinued the campaign simply because they felt secure in power.

The worldview of Vietnamese leaders continued to guide their thinking and action in 1965 as the war escalated. They believed that American military might could not overcome the limits imposed by its imperialist nature and by the trend of the age. Their loyalty to the socialist camp was intact even while they increasingly asserted an independent policy against advice otherwise from their big brothers. This resulted in a difficult balancing act: externally they had to deflect the pressure from their quarreling brothers but internally they had to find ways to minimize the influences from those brothers. Existing scholarship equates being independent with being nationalist,[35] but an independent foreign policy for Vietnamese leaders must be understood within their broad commitments to world revolution. In addition, although the conventional scholarship views patriotism or nationalism as the motivating force of the Vietnamese revolution from its beginning, Le Duan's concern about being independent and his pride in *Vietnamese* revolutionary achievements cannot be found in any speeches or documents before the mid-1960s. The emergence of those sentiments, then, must have come from two sources. One was his long experience as a revolutionary, and the other was his interactions with counterparts in the Soviet bloc. Accumulated wisdom from his personal revolutionary experience in the Vietnamese context gave him pride in being a Vietnamese as he rubbed shoulders with other communist leaders around the world.

ROAD TO THE *TET* OFFENSIVE, 1966–1968

As the number of US troops in South Vietnam rose sharply in 1966, Vietnamese leaders became paradoxically emboldened.[36] Although the

---

[35] For example, see W. R. Smyser, *Independent Vietnamese: Vietnamese Communism between Russia and China, 1956–1969* (Athens: Ohio University Center for International Studies, 1980).

[36] "Nghi quyet Bo Chinh tri so 154-NQ/TW" [Politburo resolution], January 27, 1967. *VKDTT*, v. 28, 143. Although the official date of this resolution was January 27, 1967, it had actually been issued by the Politburo in late 1966. The subject of the resolution was "to accelerate military and political struggle in the South (October and November

American commander General William Westmoreland thought he was winning, Hanoi leaders thought it was they who were winning. After engaging American troops in several battles, they thought they had learned how to defeat the US infantry. On the global front, they imagined that "repeated military and political failures in Vietnam had aggravated the financial, economic, political, and military conditions in America." Thinking ahead about the US presidential election in 1968, Vietnamese leaders expected the Johnson administration to escalate the war further in 1967 with a goal of achieving some kind of preelection victory.

Although the Politburo maintained the strategy of protracted warfare, they called for making a big effort to achieve a decisive victory in the South "in a relatively short period of time."[37] This victory could be achieved by causing heavy casualties for US forces, by destroying or causing the disintegration of most units of the Saigon military, and by launching a general attack combined with general popular uprisings in urban centers and rural areas. The goals were to defeat the American will to fight and to set up a new government in the South. Recall that Le Duan first raised this idea a year earlier in late 1965 in his discussion of the preconditions for talks with Washington. The majority of Politburo members now agreed with Duan about the need for a decisive victory for 1967. To ensure that that victory would lead to US withdrawal, the Politburo also approved the tactic of talking while fighting.

The Thirteenth Central Committee Plenum met in January 1967 and, after some discussion, accepted the aforementioned proposal by the Politburo.[38] The presentations by two Politburo members at the Plenum suggested the main motives for what would become the *Tet* Offensive. On the enemy, General Van Tien Dung who was a Politburo member and the People's Army of Vietnam's (PAVN's) Chief of General Staff reported that the American "ruling clique" [*bon thong tri My*] had become divided over their strategy, with some demanding further escalation and others wanting to end the war in a way that would save face for America. At the same time, the United States had become isolated internationally. On the ground, two-thirds of allied forces were tied down by territorial defensive tasks with only one third being mobile. As General Dung described,

---

1966)." This draft resolution was used for discussion at the Thirteenth Central Committee Plenum, January 23–27, 1967, and most of it would become Resolution of the Thirteenth Central Committee Plenum. Ibid., 141, 171–179.

[37] Ibid., 146–147.

[38] "Nghi Quyet Hoi nghi Trung uong lan thu 13 so 155/NQ-TW" [Resolution of the Thirteenth Central Committee Plenum], January 23–27, 1967. *VKDTT*, v. 28, 174.

American infantry soldiers had low morale and were poorly equipped, lacking the ability to defeat us ... [I]n some battles one U.S. battalion or even one regiment failed to break up our forces of one or two companies ... [I]n one particular case, one entire American battalion fled when a platoon of twenty-three [PAVN] soldiers returned their fire.[39]

Militarily, Dung made it appear that the conditions for a decisive victory existed. In a separate report on opening a diplomatic front, Foreign Minister Nguyen Duy Trinh reported that conditions for "talks" were also ripe, based on four observations.[40] First, the momentum on the ground in the South favored the revolution but not the enemy. Second, the United States' will to fight was on the wane as evidenced by its internal division. Third, for the last two years, the DRV had unquestionably demonstrated to the outside world its strong determination to fight the Americans. Although "some socialist brother" [read: China] had opposed such talks, he could be persuaded to change his mind. And finally, world opinion overwhelmingly supported Hanoi but demanded that it show some flexibility in return.

Here we need to understand what Hanoi leaders meant by "talking." In their view, talking meant the opening of a diplomatic front to assist the military efforts. Talking was not to achieve peace but to help achieve overall revolutionary goals. According to Trinh, North Vietnam had two main goals for the diplomatic efforts, including the halt of American bombing in the North and the withdrawal of its forces from the South. Trinh envisioned that the talking process would include at least two phases.[41] In the first phase, North Vietnam would, on the condition that Washington stop the bombing, accept sitting down for talks. This phase was not to solve the war in the South as the Americans wanted, but only to share views. By setting the precondition that the United States stop the bombing campaign, North Vietnam had already achieved part of its first goal, even before any talks actually occurred. The talks in this phase were not a waste of time but would be used effectively to attack the Washington in the court of world opinion. The second phase was aimed at getting the United States to agree to three things, namely, not resuming bombing, talking to the National Liberation Front, and withdrawing its troops from the South. Trinh understood that the success in this phase

[39] Van Tien Dung, "De cuong bao cao" [Draft report], Thirteenth Central Committee Plenum, January 23–27, 1967. *VKDTT*, v. 28, 92–96.
[40] Nguyen Duy Trinh, "De cuong bao cao" [Draft Report], Thirteenth Central Committee Plenum, January 23–27, 1967. *VKDTT*, v. 28, 123–124.
[41] Ibid., 127–128.

would depend heavily on the outcome of the battlefield. Without major military victories, no diplomatic success could be expected.

The Thirteenth Plenum gave Le Duan the green light to prepare a plan for a decisive victory in 1967 or 1968 that was achievable by combining popular uprisings in the cities [*tong khoi nghia*] with a large-scale general military attack [*tong cong kich*]. During the rest of 1967, Duan apparently sought to persuade others in the Politburo and Central Committee to go along with a specific plan for such an ambitious move.[42] To intimidate real or potential opponents to the risky idea of a general offensive, Duan and his supporters, including Le Duc Tho, Van Tien Dung, Tran Quoc Hoan, and To Huu, carried out a secret purge. Hundreds of those earlier known to have revisionist views or suspected of being close to PAVN's Commander in Chief General Vo Nguyen Giap were arrested in mid-1967 and accused of conspiring to overthrow the Politburo with Soviet help.[43] Initiatives for serious peace talks, if any, were apparently nipped in the bud at around the same time.[44]

When Le Duan gave his speech at the Fourteenth Central Committee Plenum in January 1968, on the eve of the *Tet* Offensive, he in fact envisioned a decisive victory to bring an end to the war, not just to force the United States to stop the bombing. The victory was to be based on two components. The military component in Duan's strategy for the *Tet* Offensive was all-out coordinated attacks on major urban centers and in major battlefields in South Vietnam.[45] Duan assured the Central Committee that communist forces were sufficiently prepared to fight for up to a year, with supplies fully guaranteed by China. The other component of the campaign, the popular uprisings, was to unfold not as a single coup as in the Russian revolution of 1917, but as a stage [*giai doan*] spanning months. This stage would end with the establishment of a new government by a new front that would comprise more politically diverse groups than the NLF.[46] Duan said that the flag, program, and personnel of this new front had already been planned.

[42] Merle Pribbenow, "General Vo Nguyen Giap and the Mysterious Evolution of the Plan for the 1968 *Tet* Offensive." *Journal of Vietnamese Studies* 3: 2 (Summer 2008), 12–19.
[43] Sophie Quinn-Judge, "The Ideological Debate in the DRV and the Significance of the Anti-Party Affair, 1967–68." *Cold War History* 5, no. 4 (2005): 479–500.
[44] Ibid.
[45] "Bai noi cua dong chi Le Duan tai Hoi nghi Trung uong lan thu 14" [Comrade Le Duan's speech at the Central Committee Plenum], January 1968. *VKDTT*, v. 29, 25–29.
[46] Ibid., 34–35.

Duan put considerable faith into the masses as agents of history. If enemy control over Saigon collapsed, he envisioned a million people there would rise up and join the fight on the communist side. That by itself would be a powerful force that could transform the whole situation. In case communist forces could not hold the cities against enemy counterattacks, Duan said, they would simply withdraw after a few months – "no problem!" [*khong co chuyen gi*]. Their forces "would suffer no losses but would multiply by two, three times."[47] On the other hand, if a new government were established, and if a million Vietnamese were on the streets demanding an American withdrawal, Duan predicted that Washington would lose its will to fight.

In trying to sell the plan to the Central Committee, Le Duan's analysis of the military balance exaggerated the relative strengths of revolutionary forces and showed his absolute faith in their morale. In enthusiastic and sometimes even bombastic language, he claimed that the military balance had clearly shifted in favor of the revolution. Communist forces had destroyed more than a half million Allied troops, including 60,000 foreign troops, in the last two years. There were 30,000 American casualties in the last three months of 1967 alone, he claimed.[48] If there had been one revolutionary soldier fighting against five enemy ones from 1962 to 1963, the ratio was only one to three by late 1967. If those enemy forces did not include the 600,000 ARVN soldiers that Duan dismissed as not worth counting, the ratio would have been even more. In terms of mobile force alone, Duan believed that the ratio, in fact, favored communist forces, with two revolutionary soldiers fighting every enemy soldier. In terms of ability and morale, communist troops had destroyed entire battalions and armored units of the enemy. In contrast, the enemy had never been able to destroy even one single communist company. The morale of US troops was very low; its soldiers, including those of the famous Twenty-fifth Infantry Division, were depressed and terrified of fighting [*bac nhuoc, so*]. Saigon troops were much worse; they cried and wept during battle.

Duan's assessment of the enemy's intentions was infused with ideological concepts. It is instructive to contrast his thinking to that of General Westmoreland. The American commander was troubled by the question of why his enemy was suffering thousands of casualties every month but did not quit. The answer he came up with was a Vietnamese lack of concern for human lives. With his widely distorted assessment of the military

[47] Ibid., 26, 35.
[48] Ibid., 10–11.

balance on the ground, Duan raised the same but reverse question, which was why the Americans had not yet quit despite losing tens of thousands of their troops in a mere two years.[49] He offered three reasons. First, the United States had not abandoned its ambition to be the international gendarme despite its weakened global position. Second, Southeast Asia was simply too important for it to give up. As early as Yalta, President Roosevelt had wanted to take control of Indochina by proposing that it be placed under an international trusteeship. President Eisenhower also said that losing Southeast Asia was to lose the source of many raw materials. Indochina was located in the middle of three huge markets – namely, India, China, and Indonesia. To capitalist America, there was too much profit to be made from those markets to neglect them. Not only were there raw materials but also people. They could be made to work eight hours a day and could also be exploited as consumers.

The huge stake the Americans had invested in the Indochinese gamble was the third reason why they did not quit yet, Duan argued. The United States had brought to South Vietnam the largest number of troops since World War II. Its loss in Vietnam would not be limited to Vietnam but would mean a significant jolt [*lung lay*] to its entire global military and economic hegemony. Given such a monumental threat, he reasoned, the United States must persist despite massive casualties. Its intention for now, in this election year, was not to lose big. Its leaders wanted to minimize the losses this year; after the election a new president with broad mandate would perhaps think of another strategy.

Duan's version of "domino theory" had a different underlying logic from the US version. The latter focused on the *geopolitical* threats to American interests in Southeast Asia if communists were to win in South Vietnam. In contrast, Duan was convinced that a defeat in Vietnam could badly damage American *global imperialist* domination. The American theory followed a realist's logic, whereas the Vietnamese version was undergirded by ideological precepts.

Duan had earlier called for independent thinking and not mimicking the policies of socialist brothers. On the eve of the *Tet* Offensive, more than ever before, he displayed an unabashed pride in Vietnam's distinctive war and revolutionary strategy. Using many examples, he boasted about the Party's brilliant policies made with an independent mindset (under his leadership of course).[50] In 1959, for example, the strategy of inciting

---

[49] Ibid., 20–23.
[50] Ibid., 6, 7, 9, 16–17, 19.

popular uprisings in Southern villages, instead of building a resistance base, was a bold move. Duan said that even revolutionaries in "some big countries" [read: China] dared not do what Vietnam did. The revolutionary strategy in the South that combined urban political movement with rural mobilization was another distinctive Vietnamese accomplishment. Still another example was that Vietnam did not follow the Chinese strategy of "three stages" but maintained an offensive momentum throughout. As he bragged:

Had we just followed [old foreign models] we would not have won the war [thus far] against half a million American troops. [Our strategy] was different from and even contrary to Chinese and Soviet [models]. It is our distinctive product ... On our tactics, such as launching attacks on the enemy's rear, we destroyed thousands of aircrafts in a manner that the world had never seen before ... This is [also] distinctively Vietnamese. Only Vietnamese people with Vietnamese experience on Vietnamese [soil] can devise and employ [those tactics]. Recently I talked to some Chinese comrades that our units in the delta were no larger than two combined battalions but were able to destroy one American battalion. In one case four of our soldiers attacked nine American warships armed with 100 big guns. Those [Chinese] comrades had no clue ... Four soldiers did the job of a division and suffered no casualties – how strange [it was to them].

Duan credited the offensive spirit of the Vietnamese revolution to both Marxism-Leninism and to Vietnamese national traditions.[51] Significantly, this was the first time he mentioned such traditions in his speech at a Central Committee meeting. As I argued earlier with regard to his call for keeping an "independent mindset," it would be a mistake to take his reflections on national traditions and his national pride at this point as evidence that Vietnamese communists were simply traditional nationalists in disguise. Rather, those thoughts and sentiments surfaced just as Duan discovered the value of Vietnam's accumulated revolutionary experience while interacting with communist leaders in other countries. National pride in this form would make Duan even more internationalist and daring in his revolutionary endeavors – to show other communist leaders how rich the Vietnamese revolutionary experience was.

As will be seen in the next section, that was in fact precisely what happened. Duan's predictions for the *Tet* Offensive turned out to be widely off the mark but fortuitous circumstances made him feel vindicated in his internationalist belief and become even more audacious in his policies.

---

[51] Ibid., 13–14.

RISE OF VANGUARD INTERNATIONALISM, 1968–1973

The bold *Tet* Offensive and subsequent waves of attacks across South Vietnam in 1968 shocked the American public and the Johnson administration, leading to massive antiwar protests in the United States and around the world. Johnson decided to halt the bombing and not to seek reelection. In his speech on the eve of the Offensive, Le Duan had predicted a different kind of victory – namely, success in smashing the Saigon regime and establishing new governments in Southern urban centers. He had predicted that the heavier the blow, the "crazier" imperialist America's reaction would be. Johnson and McNamara turned out to have feeble will: they caved in even though no popular uprisings took place in Saigon. By contrast, the "imperialist army" and the "puppet" ARVN were not as incapable and demoralized as Duan had imagined. After the initial confusion, they counterattacked and inflicted grave losses on communist forces.[52] An estimated 40,000 communist soldiers were slaughtered, as compared to about Allied forces' 5,000 casualties in the first wave only.[53]

Under President Nixon's Vietnamization program that sought to strengthen the ARVN to take over fighting from American troops, Allied forces took advantage of communist losses to greatly expand their control over territory and people. It would take three years for North Vietnamese units to recover momentum on the battlefield, but they never quite regained the territory lost in 1968.[54] During 1970–1971, Hanoi leaders were preoccupied with how to stabilize and mobilize more resources from the Northern economy and society while regaining the military initiative in the South.[55] In March 1972, North Vietnam launched a massive

[52] For a general account of the *Tet* Offensive and subsequent battles in 1968, see William Turley, *The Second Indochina War*, 2nd ed. (New York: Rowman & Littlefield, 2009), 137–158. See also Andrew Wiest, *Vietnam's Forgotten Army: Heroism and Betrayal in the ARVN* (New York: New York University Press, 2008); for detailed summaries of major battles, see Nguyen Duc Phuong, *Chien Tranh Viet Nam toan tap* [A complete account of the Vietnam War] (Ontario, Canada: Lang Van, 2001).
[53] Turley, *The Second Indochina War*, 149.
[54] "Dien cua Bo Chinh tri so 182/B" [Telegram from the Politburo], March 29, 1972. *VKDTT*, v. 33, 226. This telegram admitted that the only effective communist force was its main-force units, not its local forces and political organizations in urban centers.
[55] "Bao cao cua Bo Chinh tri tai Hoi nghi lan thu 18 Ban Chap hanh Trung uong" [The Politburo's report at the Eighteenth Plenum of the Central Committee], January 27, 1970. *VKDTT*, v. 31, 27–92.

military campaign across the South comparable to the *Tet* Offensive of 1968 albeit with less ambition.[56]

War inflicted not just human casualties on North Vietnam. As Party leaders turned their attention to the economy after the bombing halted, they found production had long stagnated.[57] To cope with peasants' resistance, some rural cooperatives had subcontracted land to peasant households, which, in the eyes of many Party leaders, was a dangerous retreat from the principle of collective ownership.[58] During the bombing, labor discipline was low and government control over domestic trade and social life declined.[59] With the cessation of bombing, the black market and other "criminal" activities further spread and challenged the government's ability to maintain social order and economic stability. Le Duan admitted that there were as many as 1,000 child thieves at large on the streets of Hanoi, and that 2 to 3 percent of Party members had become corrupt. As a possible sign of war weariness, the "poisonous culture of imperialism" in the South had somehow spread to Northern youth, causing Party officials to worry about losing the grip of communist morality on society.[60] The massive casualties in 1968 began to cause a shortage of troops by the early 1970s.[61] New campaigns were launched to raise

[56] "Dien so 119" [Telegram no. 119 (from the Politburo to the COSVN)], March 27, 1972. *VKDTT*, v 33, 210–213. This telegram laid out the strategy of the Offensive in 1972 in both military and diplomatic fields. It was claimed in this telegram that the 1972 Offensive set higher goals than the *Tet* Offensive in 1968, but this claim was not supported by the details of the campaign provided by the telegram. For a comparison with 1968, see Turley, *The Second Indochina War*, 185–186.

[57] "Bai noi cua dong chi Le Duan, Bi thu thu nhat Ban Chap hanh Trung uong Dang, tai Hoi nghi Trung uong lan thu 16" [Comrade First Secretary Le Duan's speech at Sixteenth Central Committee Plenum], May 1969. *VKDTT*, v. 30, 160–169.

[58] Ibid., 162.

[59] "Nghi quyet cua Bo Chinh tri so 185-NQ/TW" [Politburo resolution], December 26, 1968. *VKDTT*, v. 29, 568–571; "Bai noi cua dong chi Le Duan … tai Hoi nghi Trung uong lan thu 16," *VKDTT*, v. 30,157–158.

[60] Le Trung Ha, "Nang cao canh giac cach mang, tich cuc dau tranh chong nhung tan du cua van hoa doi truy" [Raising revolutionary vigilance and zealously struggling against corrupt cultural influences]. *Hoc Tap*, May 1969, 67; To Huu, "Phuong huong cong tac tu tuong trong tinh hinh hien nay" [The direction of our thought work in the current situation]. *Hoc Tap*, November 1969, 25.

[61] No direct admission of shortage was made, but the matter was referred to in an oblique comment by Le Duan in "Bai noi cua dong chi Le Duan … tai Hoi nghi Trung uong lan thu 16." *VKDTT*, v. 30, 150. During 1970–1972, there suddenly appeared several articles on recruitment issue in *Hoc Tap*; for example, see Vu Tuoc, "May kinh nghiem ve to chuc 'Phan doi du bi' cua Huyen Ung hoa" [Lessons from organizing 'reserve units' in Ung hoa district]. *Hoc Tap*, December 1970, 68–73.

recruitment; Catholic and ethnic minority communities that hitherto had largely been left alone were now targets for recruitment.[62]

As the war in South Vietnam and politics in the North moved to a different phase after 1968, the international context was also transformed. The socialist bloc faced a major crisis in August 1968 when Czechoslovakia was invaded and occupied by Warsaw Pact troops. China and several European communist parties denounced the invasion. The bloc came under further stress in 1969 when Chinese and Soviet troops clashed along the border. By the early 1970s, Nixon achieved breakthroughs in establishing relations with China and in pursuing détente with the Soviet Union. He failed to coax Moscow and Beijing into reducing aid to North Vietnam, but it was clear that he had some leverage on both communist giants (more on Hanoi's reactions to Nixon's trip in the next chapter).

The worldview of Vietnamese communists displayed strong continuities with some adjustments. As previously, Vietnamese leaders sought to maintain an independent policy while keeping solidarity with the socialist camp. Soviet and Chinese brothers helped but also imposed some constraints on North Vietnam. Hanoi had to deal with pressures from opposite directions: Moscow wanted it to find a negotiated solution for the South, while Beijing demanded the opposite – namely, no talks with the United States.[63] Disunity in the socialist camp was constantly a major concern on the minds of Hanoi leaders. Le Duan blamed that disunity for the failure of the *Tet* Offensive in achieving its goals.[64] Yet he thought their revolution was contributing to world revolution and to the socialist camp in three ways. First, their "victory" had delivered a powerful blow to American hegemony and helped reduce people's fear of American power.[65] Second, given the disunity in the socialist camp, Vietnam became the only issue that could galvanize the brothers and help them to coordinate a unified policy stand. Third, a communist victory that forced an American disengagement from Vietnam could offer

---

[62] On recruitment in Catholic and ethnic minorities, see Nguyen Quyet, "Huong ra tien tuyen, tang cuong xay dung co so nham lam tot cong tac quan su dia phuong va cung co hau phuong vung manh" [Looking to the front, strengthening local recruitment work and building the rear]. *Hoc Tap*, September 1971, 36.

[63] "De cuong bao cao ve tinh hinh va nhiem vu tren Mat tran dau tranh ngoai giao" [Draft report on the situation and our tasks in the diplomatic front] at the Sixteenth Central Committee Plenum, May 1969. *VKDTT*, v. 30, 90.

[64] "Bai noi cua dong chi Le Duan ... tai Hoi nghi Trung uong lan thu 16," *VKDTT*, v. 30, 143.

[65] Ibid., 85, 92.

socialist brothers "real benefits" [*loi ich that su*].[66] This was the first time that practical benefits were mentioned instead of ideology, although it was unclear whether the benefits referred to were economic or security.

As part of their solidarity policy, Hanoi leaders and propagandists continued to communicate positive views of the bloc and write lengthy but eloquent theoretical papers to contribute to Marxism-Leninism. Karl Marx's one-hundred-fiftieth birthday was celebrated in Hanoi in May 1968, followed by Stalin's ninetieth birthday in December 1969, and Lenin's one-hundredth birthday in April 1970.[67] These unprecedented birthday parties for the great communist masters in the middle of an ostensibly patriotic war displayed not only Hanoi's ideological commitments but also its efforts to galvanize the communist bloc in the aftermath of the Soviet invasion of Czechoslovakia in 1968 and the Sino-Soviet border clash in 1969.

In speeches at those public events or at study sessions for cadres, Vietnamese theorists drew out elements of Marxism-Leninism-Stalinism that affirmed the necessity of proletarian dictatorship and revolutionary violence. These long-dead masters offered still useful advice to deal with current challenges such as "the American plot of peaceful evolution" to subvert the socialist regime in Czechoslovakia.[68] Truong Chinh specifically called for vigilance against "the slogan of democratization that sought to destroy the proletarian dictatorship." He also railed against "all forms of bourgeois nationalism … that would isolate our country [from our socialist brothers] and push us into the arms of imperialism."[69]

Given the theoretical disputes within the socialist camp, Vietnamese leaders vowed to work harder to protect the integrity [*su trong sang*, literally, clarity] of Marxism-Leninism.[70] Truong Chinh declared, "We

---

[66] Ibid., 152.
[67] See Truong Chinh, "Doi doi nho on Cac Mac va di con duong Cac Mac da vach ra" [Forever being grateful to Karl Marx and following the path he pointed out]. *Hoc Tap*, September 1968, 1–12 and October 1968, 10–27, 45–52; Editorial, "Cong lao va su nghiep cua Sta-lin vo cung ruc ro!" [Stalin's achievements and career were brilliant!]. *Nhan Dan*, December 21, 1969. Truong Chinh, "Le-nin vi dai song mai trong su nghiep cua chung ta" [The great Lenin lives forever in our cause]. *Hoc Tap*, April 1970, 19–35; Tran Quynh, "Hoc thuyet cua Le-nin ve chu nghia de quoc va chu nghia de quoc trong thoi dai hien nay" [Lenin's theory of imperialism and imperialism in this age]. *Hoc Tap*, June 1970, 58–71.
[68] See Truong Chinh, "Doi doi nho on Cac Mac," 26, 48; also, "Bao cao tai Hoi nghi Ban Chap hanh Trung uong lan thu 15" [Report at the Fifteenth Central Committee Plenum], August 29, 1968. *VKDTT*, v. 29, 382.
[69] Truong Chinh, "Doi doi nho on Cac Mac," 26.
[70] Ibid., 51–52.

communists are determined not to neglect the battleground of theories and ideas, not even for a brief moment." Like Le Duan, he believed that Vietnam's revolutionary experiences had much to contribute to Marx and Lenin's theory of revolution and socialist development. Vietnamese theorists should fight not only against revisionism and dogmatism but also against [European or American leftist] theories that "deviated" from Marxism-Leninism.[71]

Hanoi's assessment of US "nature" and intention did not change. The ambitions of the United States remained to oppose the global revolutionary movement, to weaken the socialist camp, and to be the world's hegemon.[72] Yet there was a new element in American behavior: Vietnamese leaders noted how American leaders were worried about "a second Vietnam" and only timidly intervened into the Middle East after the Six-Day War.[73] They believed the *Tet* Offensive had weakened American determination, as evidenced in its failure to help the Royal Laotian military in Nam Bac, its humiliating concession in the Pueblo affair, and its inability to take a strong action to protest the Warsaw Pact's invasion of Czechoslovakia.

Domestically, they believed that the United States faced a simmering domestic social revolution and appeared to be on the verge of collapse, as evidenced by massive labor strikes and popular protests involving millions of people.[74] Vietnamese analysts heaped scorn on Johnson's Great Society program as a capitalist trick and a fraud that would not work. A *Hoc Tap* article quoted him as saying that "in America there are 33 million poor people ... Life is hard. Social vices are widespread ... Americans only think of how not to die of hunger tomorrow."[75] Yet, "Johnson and the capitalist rulers of the U.S., [who] are the most bloodthirsty and cruel bandits of the twentieth century," did not really care about the American

[71] Ibid. See also, Pham Nhu Cuong, "Ve su thoai hoa va phan boi cua phan tu xet lai Ga-ro-di" [On the degeneration and betrayal of the revisionist Garaudy]. *Hoc Tap*, April 1971, 40–53; Pham Nhu Cuong, "Dau tranh giai cap hay 'doi thoai', 'hoa dong' tren linh vuc he tu tuong" [Class struggle or dialogue and consensus on ideology?]. *Hoc Tap*, August 1972, 33–47.
[72] "De cuong bao cao ve tinh hinh va nhiem vu tren Mat tran dau tranh ngoai giao," *VKDTT*, v. 30, 97.
[73] "Bao cao tai Hoi nghi Ban Chap hanh trung uong lan thu 15." *VKDTT*, v. 29, 336–337.
[74] Nguyen Cong Hoa, "Lo lua cach mang xa hoi chu nghia dang am i trong long cac nuoc tu ban de quoc" [The fire of socialist revolution is simmering inside capitalist imperialist countries]. *Hoc Tap*, May 1969, 74–83.
[75] Tran Thanh Xuan, "Chuong trinh 'Xa hoi vi dai' cua de quoc My da bi pha san nhuc nha" [The Great Society program of the US imperialist has shamefully bankrupted]. *Hoc Tap*, December 1968, 84.

working class; they only offered the Great Society program as "the bait to soothe [people's] anger and their spirit of struggle." That program did nothing for the fundamental causes of poverty and class antagonisms in the United States – namely, monopoly capitalism and racial discrimination. Nguyen Van Kinh, a Central Committee member, echoed the same theme in his sharp analysis of class struggle in America, noting that "the paradise of the free world in the U.S." is actually "a prison," whereas the Great Society program is a "magician's trick."[76] That trick, Kinh argued, would not reduce "the abyss that separated the millionaires living in luxury on the one hand and the absolute majority of Americans who are submerged under hardship on the other."

Given more timid US global policy and its dire domestic situation after the *Tet* Offensive, Hanoi leaders increasingly viewed their own struggle as the driving force of world revolution. Since 1965, they had employed the concept of "three revolutionary tidal waves" [*ba dong thac cach mang*] that referred to the three struggles: the struggle of the socialist camp to defeat the capitalist camp, the struggle of the working-class movements against capital in capitalist countries, and the revolutions in colonies and neocolonies that aimed at overthrowing imperialism.[77] They now imagined that the third tidal wave contained the most revolutionary potential. As world attention was focused on Vietnam during 1968, Hanoi sent envoys around the world trying to create a "global people's front" against the United States.[78] Vietnamese analysts repeatedly described Vietnam as being the "center," "crest," and "frontline" of the revolutionary struggle of the world's people.[79] As Truong Chinh wrote, Vietnam was proud of leading the offensive [*chien si xung kich*] against imperialism. Because the United States was using Vietnam as a laboratory for all its war strategies

---

[76] Nguyen Van Kinh, "Mat tran thu hai chong chu nghia de quoc My da hinh thanh va lon manh trong long nuoc My" [The second front against American imperialism has emerged and grown inside the US]. *Hoc Tap*, October 1968, 78.

[77] Thayer translates the Vietnamese phrase "ba dong thac cach mang" as "three revolutionary currents," but the term "tidal waves" more accurately conveys the meaning in Vietnamese. See Carlyle Thayer, "Vietnamese perspectives on international security: Three revolutionary currents," in Donald McMillen, ed. *Asian Perspectives on International Security* (London: Macmillan, 1984), 57–76.

[78] "Bao cao tai Hoi nghi Ban Chap hanh trung uong lan thu 15." *VKDTT*, v. 29, 369.

[79] In Vietnamese, "trung tam," "dinh cao," and "tuyen dau." See Truong Chinh, "Doi doi nho on Cac Mac va di con duong Cac Mac da vach ra." *Hoc Tap*, October 1968, 48–49; Nguyen Van Kinh, "Mat tran thu hai chong chu nghia de quoc My da hinh thanh va lon manh trong long nuoc My," 78; Nguyen Duy Trinh, "Cong tac ngoai giao phuc vu cuoc khang chien chong My, cuu nuoc" [Diplomatic work to assist the anti-American resistance to save the country]. *Hoc Tap*, October 1971, 15.

and modern weapons, the world's people had much to learn from the Vietnamese about how to defeat those strategies and weapons.[80]

Elements of realist thinking had emerged in the thoughts of Vietnamese leaders since the early 1960s. By the early 1970s, realist concepts started to seep into their discourse, mingling with ideological concepts. For one, they increasingly viewed their relationship with their big brothers in terms of an exchange of interests (as opposed to a shared ideology).[81] Occasionally the correlation of world forces was framed not in terms of opposing ideological camps but in terms of the economic and security power of the "three big countries" [ba nuoc lon], namely the United States, the Soviet Union, and China.[82]

An example of that mixture of ideological and realist elements in their thinking is a (classified) June 1972 telegram from PAVN Generals Song Hao and Le Hien Mai, members of the Central Military Commission, to the commanders of the B5 Region about the central leadership's view of Nixon's recent meetings with Mao and Brezhnev. What is special about this telegram is that it was written in informal style, stripped of any official euphemisms. The language was perhaps closest to the thinking of the authors. In the telegram, China and the Soviet Union were referred to as "our friend" [ban]. China was alternatively referred to as "our Second Brother" [ong anh Hai] and the Soviet Union as "our Eldest Brother" [ong anh Ca]. Nixon was called "no," a pronoun meaning "he" or "it," indicating lack of respect or actual contempt.

[Nixon] in Beijing: he said essentially two things [to Chinese leaders]: [The United States and China] had no conflict of interest over Vietnam. Both could benefit if [they] exchanged thoughts and solved this problem between [them]. [Nixon] wanted to put pressure on us, but he could do so only to some extent. Regardless of what our Second Brother wanted from him, [their collusion] would be limited because:

- [Our brother] is still a socialist country;
- He offered a few things that looked alluring [bo beo, literally "fatty"] but those were only promises but nothing real yet;
- The power and capability of [our Second Brother] in all areas are not that great to offer him any kickbacks [moc ngoac] or to threaten him in the international arena, except [in regard to] the Vietnam issue. But on this issue, he knew very well that we would not let anyone solve the conflict without going through us.

[80] Truong Chinh, "Doi doi nho on Cac Mac va di con duong Cac Mac da vach ra."
[81] "Bai noi cua dong chi Le Duan … tai Hoi nghi Trung uong lan thu 16." VKDTT, v. 30, 152.
[82] "De cuong bao cao ve tinh hinh va nhiem vu tren Mat tran dau tranh ngoai giao," 96.

At the same time, he also wanted to [expand relations with] our other friend [the Soviet Union] who had greater power and capability.

[Nixon to] our Eldest Brother [in Moscow]:
He and this friend of ours also wanted a "deal." If it worked out, both could gain. For example, on economic issues, investment, military budget reduction, technological exchange, the Middle East, European security, India, Pakistan ... This friend of ours had more power and capability [than the other friend, China], so he wanted to maintain a long-term perspective. But even here striking a "deal" would not be that easy because it depended on our attitude and on how our other friend [China] would react. At the same time, [our Eldest Brother could only compromise up to a point] because of [Soviet] domestic and international needs [and] because of [Soviet] prestige in the international revolutionary movement and among people in the world. In our fight against the U.S. and to save the country, our friend ought to play a role and have some obligations. Thus, however badly our friend wanted a "deal," however hard the U.S. tried to coax him, ... [Soviet] support for us may only decline by 10 to 20 percent, if it will indeed decline ...[83]

Although Hanoi leaders were deeply concerned about improving US relations with China and the Soviet Union (more on this in the next chapter), they still looked up to both as their brothers and considered ideological ties an effective constraint on the brothers' possible opportunistic and power-seeking behavior. Remarkably, the Vietnamese still counted on the continuing stream of aid from both regardless of growing Chinese and Soviet interests in relations with the United States. They still thought that their senior brothers could not have settled any matter without consulting them, regardless of North Vietnam's heavy dependence on outside assistance. This telegram, written in everyday language and conveying an intimate conversation, indicated plainly that faith and self-confidence shaped much of Vietnamese leaders' thinking at that point.

VANGUARD INTERNATIONALISM VINDICATED, 1973–1975

The Paris Agreements signed in 1973 were considered a victory by Vietnamese communist leaders. Under the terms of the Agreements, American troops withdrew from South Vietnam, but North Vietnamese forces were not required to do so as the United States had originally

[83] "Than gui: Anh Quang, anh Bac, anh Hai" [To brother Quang, brother Bac, brother Hai], June 18, 1972. In Tong Cuc Chinh Tri [General Political Department], *Cong tac Dang, cong tac chinh tri chien dich trong khang chien chong My, cuu nuoc* [Party work and political work in campaigns during the anti-American resistance to save the country], v. 2 (internal circulation only) (Hanoi: Quan doi nhan dan, 1998), 86–88.

wanted.[84] Although Nixon promised in private letters to South Vietnamese President Nguyen Van Thieu that the United States would come to help in case of a communist attack, Nixon himself was forced to resign in August 1974 following the Watergate scandal.[85] The US Congress subsequently approved substantial cuts in aid to Saigon. Hanoi was correct in calculating that ideological bonds were still strong enough to keep their socialist brothers in line. The Soviet Union and China continued to provide steady political support and military aid, including advanced weapons systems, to North Vietnam.[86] The communist victory in 1975 was the outcome of a purely conventional military campaign.[87]

Already in 1973, Vietnamese communist leaders' pride in themselves had reached a new pitch. Recall how Le Duan mixed a strong belief in internationalism with an unabashed national pride in his speech on the eve of the *Tet* Offensive. This mode of thinking had now become common. An editorial in *Hoc Tap* following the Paris Agreements claimed that "the anti-American resistance to save the country was the most glorious in Vietnam's thousand-year history of national resistance against foreign invasion.[88] "Vietnam's victory over American imperialism," the editorial asserted, would have "profound impacts on the development of world revolution in the remaining decades of the twentieth century."[89] Nguyen Khanh Toan declared that a communist victory in Vietnam demonstrated "the wonderful vigor and the universality of Marxism-Leninism on the one hand, and the energetic nature and revolutionary potential of the Vietnamese people on the other."[90] As displayed in these two examples,

[84] Excellent accounts of this event are Nguyen, *Hanoi's War*; and Larry Berman, *No Peace, No Honor: Nixon, Kissinger, and Betrayal in Vietnam* (New York: The Free Press, 2001).

[85] Gregory Tien Hung Nguyen and Jerrold Schecter, *The Palace File* (New York: Harper and Row, 1986).

[86] Soviet and Chinese military aid did not significantly decrease after 1972 as claimed by William Turley. According to PAVN and Soviet archival sources, Soviet aid was (in ruble) 1.17 billion (1965–1968), 56 million (1971), 150 million (1972), 210 million (1973), 98 million (1974), 76 million (1975). Chinese military aid was (in yuan) 922 million (1965–1968), 250 million (1969), 87 million (1970), 350 million (1971), 1.1 billion (1973), 452 million (1974), and 196 million (1975). In terms of weight, military aid from the entire Warsaw bloc to North Vietnam was 517,383 tons (1965–1968), 1,000,796 tons (1969–1972), and 724,512 tons (1973–1975). Cited in Nguyen Thi Mai Hoa, *Cac nuoc Xa hoi chu nghia ung ho Viet Nam khang chien chong My, cuu nuoc*, 278–283, 290–293, 377; Turley, *The Second Indochina War*, 210–212, 232.

[87] For a recent account of the campaign, see George Veith, *Black April: The Fall of South Vietnam 1973–1975* (New York: Encounter Books, 2012).

[88] Editorial, "Thang loi lich su" [Historic Victory]. *Hoc Tap*, February 1973, 1.

[89] Ibid., 4.

[90] Nguyen Khanh Toan, "Chu nghia yeu nuoc va chu nghia Quoc te vo san" [Patriotism and Proletarian Internationalism]. *Hoc Tap*, August 1973, 18.

national pride was less about Vietnam's historical traditions than about its revolutionary potential and actual revolutionary accomplishments in the modern world historical context.

Hoang Tung, a communist theorist and editor of the Party newspaper *Nhan Dan*, went beyond bombastic rhetoric and presented a modified two-camp worldview that centered on Vietnam. He argued that the clash between the US and Vietnamese communism was not a coincidence but a "historic encounter" and "historical inevitability."[91] The context of the conflict was the confrontation between imperialism and socialism that marked the twentieth century. Vietnam became a focal point of all the major antagonisms of the age because the national liberation movement in Vietnam was aimed at developing socialism and was led by workers in an alliance with peasants. As Tung argued, this complex character of the Vietnamese revolution gave it the highest revolutionary potential, beyond what existed in other "petty bourgeois democratic and patriotic revolutions." Imperialist Yankee was against all revolutions in general, but he selected Vietnam for the fight because of the "explosive" revolutionary potential in Vietnam.[92] The world revolutionary movement also had strategic interests [*nhu cau chien luoc*] invested in Vietnam where revolutionary potential was highest.

Previously Le Duan had criticized Vietnam's big brothers for their erroneous views, but that had almost always been done indirectly, with China and the Soviet Union mentioned obliquely as "some brother parties." In contrast, by April 1974 Le Duan spoke specifically that Vietnamese theorists knew better than their *Soviet* and *Chinese* comrades in assessing the world situation.[93] The targets of Duan's criticism were the speeches made by Boris Ponomarev, a Soviet leader, on the 104th celebration of Lenin's birthday, and by Deng Xiaoping a few months before at the United Nations. The Soviet speech talked about détente as a world trend and gave credit to Soviet efforts for making it happen. In contrast, Deng viewed the world as being in grave disorder, being divided into three contending groups of countries. The first included the two superpowers, which were both imperialist. The second group comprised the industrialized countries of both East and West, both capitalist and socialist.[94] The third included poor developing countries, including China. Deng's worldview

[91] Hoang Tung, "Cuoc dung dau lich su" [The historic clash]. *Hoc Tap*, March 1973, 40.
[92] In original, "co suc cong pha." Ibid., 43.
[93] "Bai noi cua dong chi Le Duan tai Hoi nghi pho bien Nghi quyet cua Quan uy Trung uong" [Comrade Le Duan's speech at the meeting to study the Resolution of the Central Military Commission], April 25, 1974. *VKDTT*, v. 35, 27–51.
[94] Ibid., 28–35.

was thoroughly realist, since the structure of world politics was defined by power differentials between the groups but not by ideology.

As Duan explained, the Vietnamese image of world order was different from those held by the brothers. In this image, the forces of three revolutionary tidal waves against imperialism shaped the world.[95] The socialist camp that represented one tidal wave still played a very important role despite the open split between China and the Soviet Union. Without the socialist camp, Duan argued, socialist Cuba could not exist right next to the United States. Yet the other two tidal waves were equally important. If the socialist camp did not export revolutions to capitalist countries, who then but the workers there would overthrow capitalism, Duan asked. Similarly, revolutionary movements in developing countries, the third tidal wave, played the indispensable part of overturning the colonial system, which was the rear base of imperialism.

On the current correlation of forces, Duan pointed out that American power had weakened in all areas, whereas conflicts between Washington and other capitalist countries were intensifying and the three revolutionary tidal waves were mounting. Facing an unfavorable correlation of forces especially after its withdrawal from Vietnam, Washington was seeking temporary détente with Beijing and Moscow to concentrate its attacks on small revolutionary states. Duan rejected Ponomarev's argument that the détente was caused by some (Soviet) clever schemes to pursue peace. Rather, revolutionary forces taking the offensive strategy long advocated by Hanoi caused it.[96]

Duan believed that Vietnamese communists could make a correct assessment of the world situation, whereas their big brothers failed because the struggle in Vietnam embodied both national and international antagonisms. This was the "objective condition" that permitted him and his comrades to see reality better. In a particular jab at China, Duan said that the Chinese revolution was essentially a *civil* war and did not embody international antagonisms. Referring to the Soviets, Duan complained, "[A]fter every meeting with us, they always said something for the Americans to know that they made the effort to persuade us to 'preserve peace.'" Duan believed that if North Vietnam had listened to its brothers, it would have lost the war to the United States. The Paris Agreements vindicated Vietnamese ability to make sound judgments.[97]

[95] Ibid.
[96] Ibid., 32–33.
[97] Ibid., 39–41.

With their "victory" in 1973, Hanoi leaders began to articulate the belief that they were the revolutionary vanguard in Southeast Asia and that they expected a say in any regional future. As Duan warned:

The U.S. wanted to subject the interests and sovereignty of small countries to the new world order and to the competition between big powers. After the trips of Nixon and (Japanese Prime Minister) Tanaka to China, and after U.S.-Japanese talks, it was declared that "no country shall have control over Southeast Asia." What does the imperialist [gang] want in Southeast Asia?... The truth is that the U.S. and Japan are contending for hegemony over Southeast Asia. But there is another neglected truth, which is that nobody but Southeast Asian people have sovereignty over this region. Our Vietnamese people have kicked the Americans out of Vietnam. Other Southeast Asian countries ... will surely defeat all plots of aggression and expansion by American and other imperialists.[98]

In October 1974, just as Hanoi made a new battle plan for the Southern revolution, Duan's concerns about imperialist powers meddling in Southeast Asia were raised again. This time, China was the cause of concern as much as Japan and the United States, although all likely references to China have been deleted from the published document quoted here:

The U.S. has been collaborating with [other powers] to divide their respective zones of influence. Even though they are rivals, they all are worried that the Vietnamese revolution will become stronger and achieve complete victory. They all consider a unified and independent Vietnam having close relationships with unified and independent Laos and Cambodia to be a great obstacle to their plots (...). Thus they are trying to stop Vietnam's advance, to prolong our country's division, and to make us weak... At this point, in the strategic calculations of those powers (...) which want to invade and compete for hegemony over Southeast Asia, Vietnam represents not only the confrontation between the two camps, but, objectively speaking, also an important opponent to subdue. *Their conspiracy is very dangerous but none of them is yet ready to carry it out.*[99]

---

[98] Ibid. It is unclear whether Duan implicated China in this warning. Just three months before, the Chinese navy had seized the Paracel Islands off the coast of central Vietnam from the ARVN after a brief but bloody battle. Hanoi did not utter a single word of protest to this Chinese move.

[99] "Thu cua dong chi Le Duan gui dong chi Pham Hung ve ket luan cua Bo Chinh tri" [Comrade Le Duan's letter to comrade Pham Hung on the Politburo's decision], October 10, 1974. *VKDTT*, v. 35, 178. Italics in original. The sign "(...)"appears in the published documents and likely contains specific references to China that have been deleted from the published document. In PAVN General Hoang Van Thai's memoir, he also mentioned Le Duan's speech speaking of the "other big powers [together with the United States] which also nurtured hegemonistic aims in the region," clearly referring to Japan and China. Hoang Van Thai, *How South Vietnam Was Liberated*, 2nd ed. (Hanoi: The Gioi Publishers, 1996), 143.

Although Duan emphasized geopolitical interests, the two-camp struggle did not entirely disappear from his thinking. This mixture of ideological and realist thoughts showed up again after the communist victory in April 1975. The Politburo report at the Twenty-Fourth Central Committee Plenum still affirmed the commitment to proletarian internationalism in foreign policy as follows:

> The fundamental line to pursue in our foreign policy is (1) to harmoniously unite genuine patriotism and proletarian internationalism, defend our political independence and national sovereignty, advance rapidly to economic independence, actively build solidarity with socialist and national independence movements against imperialism led by the U.S.; (2) protect the integrity of Marxism-Leninism and our Party's unity, discover and prevent all conspiracies to intervene into our internal affairs, all opportunistic tendencies, all expressions of nationalism; (3) serve the cause of our revolution and world revolution.[100]

At the same time, the report called for establishing economic relations with both the socialist camp and the rest of the world. A new development was the call for trade with the capitalist bloc. Claiming, "the world is now a [single] market," the Politburo wanted Vietnam to obtain economic and technological gains by trading with capitalist economies and "taking advantage of the economic crises in and conflicts between capitalist states." With respect to the United States, Vietnam was willing to consider areas for exchange and normalization of relations, in the process "demanding the U.S. to contribute to the healing of war wounds and to economic recovery as stipulated in the Paris Agreements."[101] Despite its interest in relations with Washington, the Politburo declared, "[T]he people of Southeast Asia are the masters of the region, and American imperialists or any other imperialists will not be permitted to … place the region under their zone of influence."[102] Again, although Vietnamese leaders did not explicitly claim Vietnam's hegemony over Southeast Asia, it is remarkable that they considered it within their right to proclaim a barrier to all outside powers in Southeast Asia on behalf of "all Southeast Asians."

---

[100] "Bao cao cua Bo Chinh tri tai Hoi nghi lan thu 24" [Politburo report at the Twenty-fourth Central Committee Plenum], no date (likely September 1975). *VKDTT*, v. 36, 383. The numbers in parentheses are added to facilitate reading.

[101] Ibid., 388. In a separate resolution, the Politburo authorized the working with foreign, including American, oil companies to explore offshore oil wells, "based on new terms and on the condition that U.S. control would be reduced gradually." See Nghi quyet cua Bo Chinh tri so 244-NQ/TW" [Politburo Resolution], August 9, 1975. *VKDTT*, v. 36, 288.

[102] "Bao cao cua Bo Chinh tri tai Hoi nghi lan thu 24." *VKDTT*, v. 36, 304.

CONCLUSION

During the most intense phase of the war that they called "the resistance against America to save the country," it turned out that Marxist-Leninist tenets and concepts pervaded the thinking of Hanoi leaders, from the way they defined their struggle to the way they assessed enemy intentions. Vietnamese leaders remained committed to an internationalist worldview despite the profound disunity and even violent conflict within the Soviet bloc. In contrast to Deng Xiaoping who completely abandoned the two-camp doctrine and created a new theory of "three worlds," Le Duan came up with the concept of "three revolutionary tidal waves" which was essentially a modified version of the two-camp worldview but now centered on Vietnam.

There were significant changes to Vietnamese thinking, however. These included a self-centered attitude, a rising national pride, and the embrace of realist concepts of world politics. As argued earlier, Hanoi's independent spirit and national sentiments at this point should not be traced back primarily to some patriotic traditions. Nor should they be conflated with the goal of their revolution, which was to be of a communist nature. Such spirit and sentiments were genuine, but they emerged out of Vietnamese leaders' accumulated revolutionary experience and interaction with their counterparts in other revolutionary states. Although realist concepts contradicted Hanoi leaders' internationalist belief, their soaring and glowing national pride may ironically have intensified their commitments to world revolution. That pride was both a source and a main feature of their vanguard internationalism.

As a belief, the communist ideology kept Hanoi leaders focused on the long-term goal of developing socialism in Vietnam and on the need to defeat imperialist enemies. As the glue bonding the Soviet bloc together, ideology offered Vietnamese communists critical support for their revolution. At the same time, ideological disputes in the 1960s deeply divided their party and nearly destroyed the Soviet bloc. Finally, ideological concepts, such as correlation of forces and revolution being the work of the masses, helped Hanoi formulate its war strategies. Without the Leninist concept of correlation of forces, Hanoi might have been deterred by massive American firepower. The concepts did *not* help Hanoi make correct war strategies, as the heavy losses of revolutionary forces and the absence of mass uprisings during the *Tet* Offensive and the Easter Offensive attested. In the end, determination, ambition, and fortuitous circumstances proved to be more important than strategies.

7

From Revolutionary Vanguard
to Soviet Client, 1976–1979

Early on the morning of May 1, 1975, less than twenty-four hours after Saigon fell to communist troops, Boris Chaplin, the Soviet Ambassador in Hanoi, received the message that DRV Prime Minister Pham Van Dong would like to see him right away.[1] On his way out, Chaplin received an urgent telegram from Soviet leader Leonid Brezhnev to convey the Communist Party of the Soviet Union's (CPSU's) congratulations to the Vietnamese Workers' Party on its victory. Not only did this telegram come after the one from the Chinese government, as Chaplin would learn at his meeting with Dong, but it also came with the private note that the congratulations were not to be publicized to avoid offending the vanquished Americans. This was why Brezhnev signed the telegram in his capacity as CPSU's general secretary, not as a representative of the Soviet government. At the meeting, Chaplin handed the overjoyed Dong the telegram but, out of his personal sympathy with the Vietnamese for their victory, did not feel right to deliver the message that the telegram was not to be publicized. The next day it was published in the Vietnamese press together with the Chinese one. The Soviet press did not publish it.

The episode suggests the tension between Hanoi leaders and their Soviet comrades. Although the Vietnamese were on the receiving end in this episode, they soon got the opportunity to pay back the snub. As the *Far Eastern Economic Review* correspondent Nayan Chanda related, at the meeting to celebrate the Russian Revolution on November 6, 1976,

---

[1] Boris Chaplin, "Thang Tu nam 1975 lich su" [The historic April of 1975], in *Lien Xo – Mot tu khong bao gio quen (Hoi ky)* [The Soviet Union – An unforgettable word (Memoirs)] (Hanoi: Chinh tri Quoc gia 2007), 339–341.

at the Soviet Embassy in Hanoi, Pham Van Dong showed up as the chief guest of Boris Chaplin. To the surprise of those who attended, Dong raised a quick toast to his host, then withdrew into a room with the French Ambassador for twenty minutes before coming out to say good-bye to a humiliated Chaplin.[2]

Placed next to each other, the two episodes implied a great change in communist Vietnam's international status after its victory in 1975. Communism now ruled over all of Vietnam with a military that was the world's third largest and that boasted stunning victories against not one but two imperialist giants.[3] Le Duan achieved a feat that Mao Zedong, Kim Ilsung, and Erich Honecker, communist leaders of divided countries, could only envy. The communist victory in Vietnam (as well as Laos and Cambodia) also had ramifications throughout the regional and international order. Vietnam was a major setback for Washington. Following its retreat from Vietnam and the domestic turmoil of Watergate, the United States turned inward to reevaluate its priorities and rebuild its demoralized military. The result was a scaling down of American strategic presence not only in Southeast Asia but also globally. The vacuum caused by America's diminished role was not immediately filled by the Soviet Union. Disarmament talks continued between the two superpowers, while US-China relations went into a lull after Nixon's resignation and the deaths of Zhou Enlai and Mao in 1976.

The world order was thus fluid in the mid-1970s, just when revolutionary Vietnam reached its zenith in terms of military capability and international prestige. If the international structure and military balance dictate or constrain states' foreign policy, never before had the Vietnamese state enjoyed so much freedom of action. At the same time, Vietnam's war-crippled and aid-dependent economy implied a strong imperative for a flexible foreign policy to facilitate rapid economic recovery and development. Hanoi's policy in this period did exhibit some flexibility, as we saw in Pham Van Dong's unusual coziness with the French Ambassador

---

[2] Nayan Chanda, *Brother Enemy: The War after the War* (San Diego: Harcourt Brace Jovanovich, 1986), 170–171.

[3] Douglas Pike ranked the PAVN (perhaps by size) the third largest armed forces in the world, larger than the United States but behind the two militaries of the Soviet Union and China. Douglas Pike, *PAVN: People's Army of Vietnam* (New York: Presidio Press, 1986), 1. Carl Thayer considers the PAVN the fifth largest standing army in the world in 1987 (after the Soviet Union, China, the United States, and India). Carlyle Thayer, "The Economic and Commercial Roles of the Vietnam People's Army," *Asian Perspective* 24: 2 (2000), 87–120.

and as we will see later in Vietnam's efforts to court Western capital and technology.

However, ideology eventually trumped pragmatism. Out of its vanguard internationalism, Hanoi snubbed not only Moscow but also Washington and Beijing. Within a few years after 1975, Vietnam became embroiled in wars with its communist brothers China and Cambodia. As argued later, the failure of Vietnamese leaders to foresee the Sino-Vietnamese conflict and the way they reacted to it indicate the strong role of ideology. A consequence of the wars was Vietnam being isolated by the West and by Southeast Asian countries and becoming an international pariah by the end of the decade. From a revolutionary vanguard leading socialism in Southeast Asia, Vietnam's role was reduced to being a Soviet client by the 1980s.

"USEFUL LAWS OF CAPITALIST DEVELOPMENT"

From 1968 to 1975, North Vietnam tried to pursue its own war strategy while resisting conflicting pressures from its big brothers. Warming American relations with China and the Soviet Union provoked deep anger and worries in Hanoi. Despite such challenges, North Vietnam achieved victory in 1975 while helping Laos and Cambodia to become communist at the same time. These events formed the background to the rise of vanguard internationalism in Vietnam discussed in Chapter 6. This particular version of internationalism relied on the idea that the three revolutionary tidal waves of world politics were centered on and spearheaded by Vietnam. In this worldview, the two-camp struggle receded into the background. Vietnam's vanguard internationalism conveyed a strong national pride and ambition to shape the future of Southeast Asia and to guide world revolution.

Implicit and explicit expressions of vanguard internationalism were widespread in public and internal documents. In his speech at the Twenty-Fifth Central Committee Plenum in late 1976, which opened with a lengthy reflection on Hanoi's victory in the war, Le Duan boasted:

Our victory over imperialist America created conditions for Laotian and Cambodian revolutions to triumph, opening the path to socialism for them. In the history of [world] proletarian revolution, thus far only the Soviet Union could liberate itself and some other countries [in the process]. It is a very special honor for Vietnam today to have performed that deed.[4]

---

[4] "Phat bieu cua dong chi Le Duan tai Hoi nghi lan thu 25 cua Trung uong" [Comrade Le Duan's speech at the Twentieth Central Committee Plenum]. The Plenum took place during September 24–October 24, 1976. *VKDTT*, v. 37, 344.

Duan went on to express his pride in having foreseen the decline of imperialism since World War II and in having maintained an offensive posture for the Vietnamese revolution against Soviet and Chinese counsel:

The world now sees more clearly [what I have long seen], but [some people] still have not fully appreciated [that fact]. The American loss in Vietnam was a military loss (in a conventional war without nuclear weapons). Given this loss, imperialist America can hardly hope for a future victory in [a similar kind of war]. Yet the US with its imperialist nature will rely on counterrevolutionary violence to obstruct movements for independence, democracy, and socialism ... The world situation is still complicated.[5]

Duan's remarks suggested that the war against Saigon and Washington had in fact been seen from Hanoi not simply along the Vietnamese victim-foreign invader dichotomy. His pride in the communist victory of 1975 was not simply a pride for having defeated a "foreign invader" but for having advanced world revolution in Vietnam as well as in other parts of Indochina. The conceptual frame of reference for Duan and his comrades throughout was the history of world socialism against imperialism. That history continued at the time of his speech, with the United States being defeated in one major battle but surviving to plot the next battle elsewhere in the world.

Historically the two-camp worldview had not prevented Vietnamese communists from accommodating the West out of political expediency. In 1945, Ho Chi Minh rode to power in the "August Revolution" by projecting a public image of Viet Minh being supported by the United States and its victorious allies.[6] At the Twentieth Plenum of the Central Committee in late 1975 (see Chapter 6), Duan had intimated that communist Vietnam wanted to trade with the capitalist West to gain those advanced technologies that the socialist bloc could not provide. At the Twenty-Fifth Plenum a year later, he even flirted with the idea that the "laws [*quy luat*] of capitalist development" could be as useful for Vietnam as the "laws of socialist development" drawn from the experiences of the Soviet bloc.[7] This was, he reasoned, because Vietnam was bypassing capitalism and advancing to socialism directly from a backward economy.

---

[5] Ibid., 344–345.

[6] David G. Marr, *Vietnam 1945: The Quest for Power*. See also Dixie Bartholomew-Feis, *The OSS and Ho Chi Minh: Unexpected Allies in the War against Japan* (Lawrence: University Press of Kansas, 2006).

[7] "Phat bieu cua dong chi Le Duan tai Hoi nghi lan thu 25 cua Trung uong," *VKDTT*, v. 37, 350–351, 382–383, 390.

However, Duan did not elaborate on which "capitalist laws" could be useful, nor did he appear to appreciate market competition as the central principle of a capitalist economy.[8] He grudgingly accepted the need to maintain prices and wages under socialism, but noted that "all production, trade and distribution [was] to be done according to [state] plans. The plans would calculate and decide the prices of rice and food, the amounts of rice and food to be consumed by each individual, and his wage and his living standards." Apparently Duan mistook mercantilism for capitalism, for at one point he asked rhetorically, "Japan has no raw materials, but it can produce all kinds of things because it trades with the entire world. Our natural endowments are richer – why can't we trade like Japan?" Duan wanted Vietnam to devote one-third of its labor force to produce for the Soviet bloc, using machines and raw materials to be imported from "Japan, France, or other [capitalist] countries."

Stressing the need to trade with the capitalist camp, Duan criticized his Party's longstanding idea of relying exclusively on help from the socialist camp for Vietnam's industrialization. He admitted that aid from the socialist brothers was still necessary, but repeated what he had said since 1963, that each country should rely first on its own resources.[9] He expressed gratitude for help from those brothers during the war, without which Vietnam could hardly have won, but noted that Vietnam ought to remain self-reliant. In the international order, he believed, "each socialist country has its own position and its own interests [derived from such a position]." Because of that, disagreement was possible even though all were brothers. As in 1963, the Vietnamese concept of self-reliance indicated a realistic attitude despite Hanoi's unwavering loyalty to internationalism. Given Vietnam's deep dependence on foreign assistance, the concept would justify its making better use of its resources and broadening its trade relations to reduce dependence on any particular partners. Yet, as seen below, in Vietnam's general foreign policies and in its particular relations with the big powers, Hanoi's leaders' self-reliant attitude turned out to be ephemeral. It was overshadowed by their rising internationalist commitments and it proved incapable of restraining their vanguard ambitions.

Although Duan acknowledged the limitations of the socialist brotherhood, socialist solidarity against imperialism remained the bedrock of his worldview on which everything else was based. Vietnam wanted to trade

[8] Ibid., 397–398.
[9] Ibid., 350.

with the West, but its socialist identity was not to be compromised. At the Fourth Party Congress in December 1976 – the first such meeting since 1960 – the name of the Party was changed from Vietnamese Workers' Party to Vietnamese Communist Party, to publicly express its ideological loyalty. The name of the country was changed from Democratic Republic of Vietnam to Socialist Republic of Vietnam (SRV) – again, to fully display its ideological character. Vietnamese leaders could have kept their Party's and the country's old names to convey their pragmatism to outsiders, but they did not. Realist thinking may have motivated Duan to maintain an independent policy stance for Vietnam to make sure its national interests would be well served, but that realism was not allowed to rise above his loyalty to international socialism. This doctrinal allegiance was well summarized in the following statement on the direction of Vietnamese foreign policy, read at the Fourth Party Congress:

In this new era, the Party, the government, and our people must take advantage of favorable international conditions to rapidly heal war wounds, to create the material and technological basis for socialism, to strengthen defense, to continue to struggle alongside socialist brothers and other nations in the world for peace, national independence, democracy, and socialism and against imperialism led by imperialist America.[10]

"Taking advantage of favorable conditions" [read: trading with capitalist countries] did not mean pursuing a new path deviating from the international socialist struggle against imperialism. Some of the most remarkable pledges Party leaders made in that Congress were to work for the recovery of unity in the socialist camp, for a "truly neutral Southeast Asia without military bases and soldiers of imperialist armies," for a "new international economic order based on national sovereignty over natural resources," and for the "eventual and complete triumph of socialism" in the world. The pledges indicated that Vietnamese leaders were still committed to the two-camp worldview, even though they had become arrogant enough with their victory to belittle the advice and experiences of their big brothers, and even though the ordeal they had gone through to defeat the United States taught them to be tactically flexible.

It is instructive to revisit the contrast between Hanoi's belief at this time and the theory of "three worlds" proposed by Deng a few years earlier. That theory viewed China as standing with the Third World against the First World (the United States and the Soviet Union) and the Second

---

[10] "Nghi quyet Dai hoi Dai bieu toan quoc lan thu 4" [Resolution of the Fourth National Congress], December 20, 1976. *VKDTT*, v. 37, 1040–1041.

World (the rest). The three worlds were divided by power and wealth disparities, not by ideology. By contrast, Vietnamese leaders admitted that the Soviet Union and China occupied different positions in the world order than Vietnam, but that was not as salient as the fact that all three were socialist. Hanoi did not characterize Moscow and Beijing as imperialist, even though their behavior toward Vietnam was perceived by the Vietnamese to be imperious at times. Vanguard internationalism exerted tremendous influence on Vietnamese foreign policy, as will be seen in separate analyses of Vietnam's relationship with the United States, with China, and with the Soviet Union in the remainder of this chapter.

STILL "THE MOST DANGEROUS ENEMY":
WASHINGTON SEEN FROM HANOI

During 1976–1977, Vietnam was busy establishing relations and expanding trade with "capitalist" countries (mostly Japan and European nations).[11] Meetings with American firms were also arranged to court investment in Vietnam's oil sector. These activities clearly reflected Duan's strategy of taking advantage of capitalist investment and technology. As events would soon demonstrate, the steps taken by Vietnam did not mean important changes in their strategic thinking, let alone in ideological loyalty.

In 1977, a Democratic President came to office in Washington after eight years of Republican administration. Reversing the policy of his predecessor, Jimmy Carter offered diplomatic normalization with Vietnam without any preconditions.[12] To the astonishment and frustration of American officials, Vietnam demanded that the United States pay at least $3.2 billion for war damages, according to the now-defunct 1973 Paris Agreements, before relations could be normalized. For about a year, the Carter administration took several trust-building steps, such as relaxing the trade embargo, offering to open interests sections in Hanoi and Washington (similar to the US offer to China), and supporting Vietnam's

---

[11] Bo Ngoai Giao [Ministry of Foreign Affairs], "Bao cao tinh hinh va cong tac 6 thang dau nam 1976" [Report on the situation and work in the first 6 months of 1976], no. 21/TH, July 1976 [top secret]; and Bo Ngoai Giao [Ministry of Foreign Affairs], "Bao cao tinh hinh va cong tac 6 thang dau nam 1977" [Report on the situation and work in the first 6 months of 1977], no. 150/TH, July 9, 1976 [top secret]. Files no. 9813 and 10160, Phu Thu Tuong [Prime Minister's Office], National Archive III. Both documents are courtesy of Kosal Path.
[12] Chanda, *Brother Enemy*, 136–160.

entry into the United Nations. Those moves could not persuade Hanoi to change its position. Vietnam dropped the demand for war payment only in late 1978 when it faced an imminent war with both Cambodia and China. By that time, Washington had changed its mind, and seventeen years would pass before the two countries normalized relations in 1995.

Why did Hanoi miss the chance to normalize relations with the United States despite its strong interest in capitalist trade, investment, and technology? An internal memo of the Party Secretariat provided some clues to their thinking after receiving the first American delegation led by Leonard Woodcock to visit postwar Vietnam.[13] Basically, Hanoi saw little difference between Carter and his Republican predecessor. The primary goals of Carter's efforts to engage Vietnam, according to the Secretariat, were "to probe Vietnam's foreign policy, to deceive American public opinion," and to devise a new policy "to gain an advantage for American global strategy after its great defeat" in Vietnam.[14] Imperialists were imperialists after all, regardless of who occupied the White House – Party leaders seemed to think.

The Secretariat believed that Carter merely continued Ford's "New Pacific Strategy" that counterattacked socialist countries and other revolutionary forces to shore up the American position in the aftermath of its failure in Vietnam. In Southeast Asia specifically, US goals were to protect its remaining bases, to limit Vietnam's influence in the region, to contain the Soviet Union and China, and to compete for economic advantages with other imperialists. The Secretariat explained that Vietnam's economy was small but its "great international influence and political-military status" could contribute to the growth of socialist and nationalist forces in Southeast Asia at the expense of American imperialism – hence the efforts by the Carter administration to normalize relations.

The Secretariat did note a host of other possible motives of the United States besides imperialist calculations; these included current "economic and political problems" facing the US government, American needs to find outlets for its exports, American firms' interests in doing business with Vietnam especially in offshore oil exploration, and the pressure from "progressive" domestic public opinion.[15] In dealing with the United States, the memo concluded, Vietnam enjoyed the upper hand because it

[13] The Secretariat is chaired by the general secretary and responsible for implementing Politburo's decisions and can be considered the executive arm of the Politburo.
[14] Thong bao cua Ban Bi thu so 07-TB/TW [Memo by the Secretariat], March 15, 1977, signed by Tran Xuan Bach. *VKDTT*, v. 38, 49.
[15] Ibid., 50–51.

represented a just cause [*co chinh nghia*], had great international status and prestige, and knew American strategic interests very well. In other words, the Secretariat believed that Vietnam was in a position to impose preconditions for normalization.

The Woodcock delegation had barely left when Politburo member and Minister of Internal Affairs Tran Quoc Hoan published a lengthy essay in the Party's theoretical journal *Tap Chi Cong San* [Review of Communism], formerly *Hoc Tap*. In the essay, the head of Vietnam's public security apparatus called for strengthening vigilance against foreign and domestic enemies.[16] He warned that imperialist America was still conspiring to encircle and attack the revolution in the Indochinese countries, as evidenced in the recent coup in Thailand that brought "fascists" to power there.[17] He charged that "imperialist spies" were recruiting among Vietnamese refugees to form anticommunist organizations in the United States and elsewhere to fight against Vietnam. They were sending spies into Vietnam to incite revolts. "*Imperialist America, before and now, remained the most dangerous enemy of our people,*" he concluded.[18] Hoan's accusation was ironic because Vietnam also employed spies in the United States, one of whom was discovered and convicted in late 1977.[19]

Vietnam's anti-imperialist rhetoric was not limited to a domestic audience. Delivering his first address at the United Nations Assembly following Vietnam's accession to the organization, Politburo member and Foreign Minister Nguyen Duy Trinh railed against "imperialist and neo-colonialist forces."[20] He accused them of trying to wage wars, attacking revolutionary movements, and deceiving world opinion in order to protect their hegemony. Solidarity with the socialist camp, including the Soviet Union, China, and other socialist states, was named as the first principle of Vietnam's foreign policy platform. Vietnam also expressed support for China to "liberate" Taiwan, and pledged solidarity with

[16] For Tran Quoc Hoan's role in creating the police state in North Vietnam during the war, see Lien-Hang Nguyen, *Hanoi's War*.

[17] Tran Quoc Hoan, "Tang cuong xay dung va quan ly nen trat tu xa hoi xa hoi chu nghia trong giai doan moi" [Building and managing the socialist social order in the new stage]. *Tap Chi Cong San* 5 (1977), 7–8. Hoan was referring to the military coup in October 1976.

[18] Ibid. Italics in original.

[19] Chanda, *Brother Enemy*, 155–156.

[20] See Nguyen Duy Trinh, "Nhan dan Viet-nam quyet gop phan xung dang hon nua vao su nghiep cach mang cua nhan dan the gioi" [The Vietnamese people pledge to contribute more to the revolutionary mission of the world's people]. Reprinted in *Tap Chi Cong San* 10 (1977), 11–14.

independence movements from Palestine to Puerto Rico. Although not naming the United States, Trinh demanded it to withdraw its troops and bases in South Korea and Guantanamo.

Hanoi was particularly vitriolic about Carter's agenda to promote human rights through American foreign policy. Vietnamese commentators immediately linked criticisms of Vietnam's human rights record to the two-camp struggle, denouncing them as a new strategy for the United States to meddle with socialist countries.[21] The long-term goal of the human-rights strategy, they alleged, was to generate "peaceful evolution" in socialist countries – that is, to cause their people to reject socialism and adopt capitalism peacefully. They argued that socialist systems made working people the "masters" of political, economic, cultural, and social life, whereas, under capitalism, workers had no right except to sell their labor. In the Vietnamese view, the United States was, in fact, the worst country in the capitalist camp when it came to human rights. There, working people were heavily exploited and did not even have the "basic right to employment." Activists who demanded their rights were imprisoned and even murdered. "Blacks have been living the last two centuries in blood and tears."[22] While exploiting and oppressing its own people, the American government trampled the human rights of people in other countries by waging wars and killing innocent people as in Vietnam. These Vietnamese criticisms of the United States echoed earlier views expressed by Nguyen Ai Quoc in the 1920s, by Bui Cong Trung in 1946, by Ho Chi Minh in the 1950s, and Nguyen Van Kinh in 1968. Yet Carter's policy in the first two years did not link human rights to normalization with Vietnam.[23] As Steven Hurst points out, Hanoi ignored the fact that Washington was globally more critical of rightist regimes than of leftist ones, and in Southeast Asia more critical of Vietnam's capitalist neighbors than of itself.

Hanoi's crusade against imperialism went beyond a particular hatred of the United States. Following Truong Chinh's earlier advice not to relax the struggle on the theoretical front for even one brief moment (see Chapter 6), Vietnamese theorists actively engaged theoretical debates in the West on the convergence between capitalist and socialist systems and

[21] Nguoi binh luan [The commentator], "Ve cai goi la 'chien dich nhan quyen' cua de quoc My" [On the so-called 'human rights campaign' of imperialist America]. *Tap Chi Cong San* 11 (1977), 51–54.

[22] Ibid.

[23] Steven Hurst, *The Carter Administration and Vietnam* (New York: MacMillan Press, 1996), chap 5.

on the concept of postindustrial societies. On convergence, Vietnamese writers chastised Raymond Aaron and John K. Galbraith, among others, for using the level of technological development to classify societies while ignoring the fundamental difference in the "relations of production" under capitalist and socialist systems.[24] Scientific and technological development could neither reduce class struggle in capitalist societies nor prevent the ultimate death of capitalism. Although capitalist and socialist countries may enjoy the same high level of technological development, they represented opposing models of social order and would never converge. Vietnamese theorists similarly dismissed the concept of postindustrial societies, developed by such Western authors as Alain Tourane, Hermann Kahn, and Daniel Bell, as merely serving to hide capitalist exploitation and oppression in the West and to deceive people into believing that there was a future for capitalism.[25]

Some foreign authors who study the unrealized promises of US-Vietnamese normalization during 1975–1978 lay the ultimate blame on the United States.[26] Others are more balanced.[27] Prominent researchers in Vietnam today admit that rigid ideological belief made Hanoi hostile not only toward the United States but also toward Vietnam's Southeast Asian neighbors, which were simply dismissed as "American vassals."[28] Based on his conversations with diplomats, Chanda identifies elements of Vietnamese thinking that obstructed normalization with its former enemy.[29] One element was the deeply held Vietnamese notion that the Americans had a moral obligation to heal the wounds of war. Another involved the mistaken assumption that postwar Vietnam was still central to American policy. Chanda also notes how the "Marxist" leaders in Hanoi attached significance to the profit motive of capitalist America.

[24] Phong Hien, "Thuyet Hoi Tu: Hoc thuyet lua bip moi cua chu nghia De quoc" [Convergence theory: the new fraudulent theory by imperialism]. *Tap Chi Cong San* 5 (1977), 71–77.
[25] Tran Quoc Tu, "Ve cai goi la 'xa hoi sau cong nghiep' " [On the so-called 'post-industrial societies']. *Tap Chi Cong San* 7 (1977), 68–73.
[26] For example, see Edwin Martini, *Invisible Enemies: The American War on Vietnam, 1975–2000* (Amherst: University of Massachusetts Press, 2007), esp. 38.
[27] Chanda, *Brother Enemy*; Hurst, *The Carter Administration and Vietnam*.
[28] Luu Doan Huynh, "The Paris Peace Agreement and the Vietnamese vision of the future," in Odd Arne Westad and Sophie Quinn-Judge, eds. *The Third Indochina War: Conflict between China, Vietnam and Cambodia, 1972–79* (New York: Routledge, 2006), 87–102; and Nguyen Vu Tung, "The Paris Agreement and Vietnam-ASEAN relations in the 1970s," in Westad and Quinn-Judge, eds. *The Third Indochina War*, 103–125.
[29] Chanda, *Brother Enemy*, 149.

In fact, the various elements of Vietnamese thinking that Chanda describes were systematically interconnected under the vanguard internationalist worldview. That belief consistently identified the United States as an imperialist power and as an enemy of the Vietnamese revolution, regardless of American policy at any particular time. That belief made Vietnamese leaders see American hostilities everywhere (such as in the coup in Thailand), and caused them to exaggerate the importance of Vietnam to the United States. That belief can be viewed as a symptom of paranoia and self-delusion, which suggests its intensity as well as irrationality.[30] Significantly, Vietnamese vanguardism was not simply pride in victory against "foreign invaders," but also pride in leading world revolution against the imperialist camp.

The troubled postwar relationship between victorious Vietnam and vanquished America was a clear case of ideology trumping interests. Vanguard internationalism overrode Vietnamese leaders' pragmatic sense and seriously hampered Hanoi's economic interests. Given that the belief was expressed widely and consistently in various forms of communication, it is doubtful that US-Vietnamese relations would have been smooth even if the United States had granted Vietnam's wish for war reparations. Fred Halliday is right in arguing that it is not inevitable that revolutionary states would come into conflict with the status-quo international order. Vietnam had a good chance of normalizing relations with its "most dangerous enemy" in 1977, but the thinking of its leaders simply did not prepare them for that.[31]

"MARXISM-LENINISM AGAINST MAOISM": THE SINO-VIETNAMESE CONFLICT, 1978–1979

Although postwar Vietnamese relations with the United States experienced a brief phase of hope, those with Cambodia and China experienced an upheaval. Le Duan's condescending view of the Cambodian revolution had long infuriated Cambodian "Khmer Rouge" leaders who launched border raids on Vietnam as soon as they took power in Phnom Penh in April 1975.[32] Border raids led to counterattacks from Vietnam

---

[30] See Stephen J. Morris, *Why Vietnam Invaded Cambodia: Political Culture and the Causes of War* (Stanford, CA: Stanford University Press, 1999).

[31] See Tran Quang Co, "Hoi uc va suy nghi" [Reflections and Thoughts], 7, for a frank acknowledgement of this point. A senior diplomat, Co was involved in the US-Vietnamese negotiation for normalization and would rise to deputy minister of foreign affairs in the late 1980s.

[32] Thomas Englebert and Christopher Goscha, *Falling out of Touch: A Study on Vietnamese Communist Policy toward an Emerging Cambodian Communist Movement, 1930– 1975* (Melbourne, Australia: Monash Asia Institute, Monash University, 1995). For

and the severance of diplomatic relations in late 1977. Hanoi's relations with Beijing also deteriorated with the Vietnamese accusing China of supporting the Khmer Rouge, whereas Beijing denounced Vietnam for its mistreatment of Chinese-Vietnamese.[33]

As hostilities escalated, more than ten Vietnamese divisions invaded Cambodia in December 1978. Within a month, the Vietnamese drove the Khmer Rouge out of Phnom Penh. Hanoi then set up a new Cambodian government under Vietnamese tutelage. Less than two months later, on February 17, 1979, half a million Chinese troops launched a blitzkrieg attack across Vietnam's land border with China. The Chinese withdrew a month later, after having leveled to the ground major cities on the Vietnamese side of the border. The new war in Indochina was shocking because it came so soon on the heels of the previous war in which communist China, Vietnam, and Cambodia united to defeat the United States. What led the brothers to war? Was it nationalism, strategic interests, or something else?

The causes of the Third Indochina War have been the subject of many excellent studies.[34] Due to the lack of new sources on the Cambodian

---

foreign relations of the Khmer Rouge during 1975–1979, see Ben Kiernan, *The Pol Pot Regime: Race, Power, and Genocide in Cambodia under the Khmer Rouge, 1975–79* (New Haven, CT: Yale University Press, 1996), esp. chapter 9.

[33] A recent work that examines the close Sino-Cambodian relations in these years is Andrew Mertha, *Brothers-in-Arms: Chinese Aid to the Khmer Rouge, 1975–1979* (Ithaca, NY: Cornell University Press, 2014). See also, Kosal Path "China's Economic Sanctions against Vietnam, 1975–1978," *China Quarterly* 212 (December 2012), 1040–1058. The mistreatment of ethnic Chinese in Vietnam referred to Hanoi's campaign to persecute Chinese "capitalists" and expropriate their property in southern Vietnam. The Vietnamese government also pressured all ethnic Chinese who had lived in both North and South Vietnam for generations to return to China. For an informative testimony to that policy from a Chinese-Vietnamese physician whose family was forced to leave Vietnam, see Lam Hoang Manh, *Buon vui doi thuyen nhan* [Life of a Boatperson] (Falls Church, VA: Tieng Que Huong, 2011).

[34] David Elliott, *The Third Indochina Conflict* (Boulder, CO: Westview Press, 1981); Chanda, *Brother Enemy*; Anne Gilks, *The Breakdown of the Sino-Vietnamese Alliance, 1970–1979* (Berkeley, CA: Institute of East Asian Studies, University of California, Center for Chinese Studies, 1992); Morris, *Why Vietnam Invaded Cambodia*; Westad and Quinn-Judge, eds. *The Third Indochina War*; Brantly Womack, *China and Vietnam: The Politics of Asymmetry* (Cambridge: Cambridge University Press, 2006); Nicholas Khoo, *Collateral Damage: Sino-Soviet Rivalry and the Termination of the Sino-Vietnamese Alliance* (New York: Columbia University Press, 2011); Kosal Path, "The Sino-Vietnamese Dispute over Territorial Claims, 1974–1978: Vietnamese Nationalism and Its Consequences," *International Journal of Asian Studies* 8: 2 (2011), 189–220; Zhang Xiaoming, *Deng Xiaoping's Long War: The Military Conflict between China and Vietnam, 1979–1991* (Chapel Hill: University of North Carolina Press, 2015).

war, I will examine only the Sino-Vietnamese conflict here. Unlike existing accounts that privilege Vietnamese nationalism or geopolitical factors such as the Sino-Soviet rivalry, I argue that Hanoi leaders' belief in vanguard internationalism played a central, if not exclusive, role in that war. That belief was a major cause of the growing tension in Sino-Vietnamese relations from the late 1960s. That belief was demonstrated in the failure of Vietnamese leaders to anticipate the Chinese attacks, and in the way they viewed the war as a global rather than a regional conflict.

Existing sources indicate that relations between Chinese and Vietnamese communists had gone back half a century prior to the war in 1979. The relationship had been undergirded by a strong, mutually trustful spirit of internationalism. The intimacy began with a young Nguyen Ai Quoc's meeting with Zhou Enlai, Li Fuchun, Cai Chang, Nie Rongzhen, and their fellow Chinese communists in France in the early 1920s. Quoc introduced several of them into the French Communist Party.[35] A few years later they were all working with Soviet advisors in southern China to organize revolution in both countries. After many years on the run, Quoc was reunited with Zhou in Yan 'an in the late 1930s under cover as an officer in the Chinese Red Army. In the last year of the Chinese civil war, from his base in northern Vietnam, Quoc ordered several Vietnamese units into southern China to help Mao's guerrilla forces defend their base against attacks from the Guomindang army. In 1950, Mao and Liu Shaoqi returned the favor by persuading Stalin to grant diplomatic recognition to a struggling DRV. China then sent hundreds of advisors and large quantities of aid to help the DRV to defeat France. Vietnamese admiration for China reached a zenith when Mao Zedong Thought was enshrined in its Party Constitution side by side with the teachings of Marx, Engels, Lenin, and Stalin.

A remarkable feature of the Sino-Vietnamese brotherhood was that revolutionaries in both countries had helped each other to fight their own countrymen. Although communist China's help to communist Vietnam is well known, Vietnam's reciprocity was revealed only recently. In 1958, when China issued a territorial claim that covered the Paracels and Spratlys archipelagos held partly by South Vietnam, North Vietnam

[35] Marilyn Levine, *The Found Generation: Chinese Communists in Europe During the Twenties* (Seattle: University of Washington Press, 1993), 159–160; Nguyen Van Tuan, "Nhung nguoi ban Trung quoc cua chu tich Ho Chi Minh" [President Ho Chi Minh's Chinese friends], *Xua va Nay* [Past and Present], no. 395–396, January 2012. The Chinese communists were Xiao Zizhang, Zhao Shiyan, Wang Ruofei, Chen Yannian, and Chen Qiaonian.

published the (translated) claim on the first page of the Party's newspaper *Nhan Dan*,[36] and Prime Minister Pham Van Dong promptly sent a letter of support (which would be one of the main documents used by China today as evidence of Chinese sovereignty over those islands).[37] In January 1974, Chinese forces seized the western part of the Paracels from Saigon in a brief but bloody naval battle leading to the death of seventy-four South Vietnamese officers and sailors, but Hanoi did not utter a word of protest.[38] These events testified that Chinese and Vietnamese revolutionaries at the time were constrained not so much by national bonds with their compatriots as by perceived internationalist obligations to each other as fellow communists.

Despite the asymmetry in the Sino-Vietnamese relationship, with China being much larger and more helpful to Vietnam, the fraternity went both ways in the sense that the Vietnamese felt themselves having contributed directly to the Chinese revolution. The relationship was, therefore, crucially different from that between the VCP and other fraternal communist parties. To be sure, there were popular memories of historical Chinese domination of Vietnam, but the ideological, organizational, and personal bonds between the Chinese and Vietnamese revolutions were strong enough to overcome any such traditional legacies. Both sides in fact blamed that past on "Chinese feudalism," which was their common enemy.[39]

After war broke out in 1979, Hanoi leaders often claimed that they resented Beijing for selling them short at the Geneva Conference in 1954. They believed that their Dien Bien Phu victory should have earned them

---

[36] "Chinh phu nuoc Cong hoa Nhan dan Trung hoa ra tuyen bo quy dinh hai phan cua Trung quoc" [The government of the People's Republic of China issued a declaration on China's sovereignty over its territorial waters]. *Nhan Dan*, September 6, 1958.

[37] Kosal Path argues that North Vietnamese leaders at the time were forced to accept Chinese claim due to their need for China's support, but he provides no evidence that they were acting under pressure while privately resenting China. "Hà Nội's Responses to Beijing's Renewed Enthusiasm to Aid North Vietnam, 1970–1972," *Journal of Vietnamese Studies* 6: 3 (2011), 194. See the section on Methodology and Sources in the Introduction of this book for evidence that supports my argument here.

[38] Kosal Path makes a factual error in writing that "In February 1974 the Saigon government seized six islands in the Spratly group and Hanoi gave tacit support to Saigon's action by saying nothing." Path, "China's Economic Sanctions against Vietnam, 1975–1978," 1043. For a South Vietnamese account of the battle, see Ho Van Ky-Thoai, "Naval Battle of the Paracels," in K. W. Taylor, ed. *Voices from the Second Republic of South Vietnam (1967–1975)* (Ithaca, NY: Cornell Southeast Asian Program Publications, 2014), 153–158.

[39] Path, "Hà Nội's Responses," 192.

a better deal. Yet there is no evidence to confirm that claim. It is likely that Vietnamese communist leaders at the time accepted the Geneva Agreements as reflecting a fair outcome. Similarly, no evidence exists to indicate North Vietnamese leaders' blaming China for the debacle of the land reform (1953–1956) carried out under the supervision of Chinese advisers.

From existing sources, Vietnamese resentment was most likely to have started with China's advice in the late 1950s against Hanoi's intention to reunify the country by force. The militant group within the Vietnamese communist leadership who wanted to do so must have questioned Mao's wisdom on this issue, and they must have resented his condescending attitude.[40] On the other hand, as shown earlier, Mao's courage to stand up against Khrushchev's compromises with Western imperialism earned him great respect from those same militant Vietnamese leaders who would come to dominate their party in the early 1960s. Any resentment, if existed, must have been mild.

It is true that some Vietnamese leaders, most prominently Le Duan, had been offended by Mao's statement in 1963 that he wanted to take his army south to liberate Southeast Asia.[41] Yet Duan's sentiment can be interpreted not only as reflecting Vietnamese ancient fears of Chinese domination, but also as a sign of rivalry between the two leaders. On the same occasion, as seen in Chapter 5 through the words of Tran Quynh, Duan was scornful of Mao's argument that the landlords were back in power in China by marrying off their daughters to village cadres. Duan also expressed contempt for Chinese communists' theoretical ability and revolutionary experience on other occasions. He repeatedly, if obliquely, belittled Chinese revolutionary experiences in his political reports. He ridiculed the legendary Chinese Long March by calling it the strategy of "running around" [*truong chinh chay quanh*] instead of confronting the enemy.[42] He dismissed Mao's theory of three stages in guerrilla warfare

---

[40] In 1979, Le Duan would disclose this resentment he and Nguyen Chi Thanh had back then. See Cold War International History Project, "Le Duan and the Break with China," *Cold War International History Project Bulletin* 12/13 (Fall/Winter 2001), 284

[41] See Tran Quynh, "May ky niem ve Le Duan." Also, Cold War International History Project, "Le Duan and the Break with China," *Cold War International History Project Bulletin* 12/13 (Fall/Winter 2001), 281.

[42] See "Bai noi cua dong chi Le Duan ... tai Hoi nghi lan thu 12 cua Trung uong" [Comrade Le Duan's speech at the Twelfth Central Committee Plenum], December 1965. *VKDTT*, v. 26, 597. Le Duan would claim in 1979 that Zhou Enlai admitted to him that the Long March was a big mistake in light of the Vietnamese experience. See Cold War International History Project, "Le Duan and the Break with China," 283.

as irrelevant and inferior to his own strategy of "three kinds of forces."[43] These comments suggested Duan's view of himself as the vanguard leader of world revolution. Curiously, no similar contempt was shown for the Soviet experience even though Duan disagreed with Soviet advice as strongly as with Chinese. Thus it was not just policy disagreements and different strategic interests that generated Sino-Vietnamese frictions. Rather, it was Duan's (arrogant) belief that communist Vietnam was the vanguard of world revolution and was second to none but the Soviet Union, the fatherland of world communism.

Available sources do not reveal any other Vietnamese leaders besides Le Duan and Nguyen Chi Thanh who displayed such contempt for Chinese leaders. It is also unclear why Vietnamese leaders did not express support for the Cultural Revolution and whether all of them disapproved of that event. According to an internal report from the Soviet archive cited by Stephen Morris, Duan and other Vietnamese leaders criticized the Cultural Revolution for its leftist radicalism.[44] Mao's Red Guards were one source of tension. These "troublemakers" caused delays for Soviet shipments of aid to the DRV through China, demonstrated in front of Vietnamese consulates in China, and, through the Chinese embassy in Hanoi, distributed Mao's Red Books without permission.[45] Besides, Vietnamese leaders may have been concerned about the way Mao's close comrades were persecuted by the Red Guards at Mao's orders. But it appeared that they held conflicting views about the event.[46] To Huu, a member of the Party's Secretariat who headed its ideological and cultural apparatus, reportedly championed a similar cultural revolution in North Vietnamese universities.[47]

The event that profoundly distressed Hanoi leaders was China's rapprochement with the United States in the early 1970s. Hanoi no doubt

---

[43] This referred to the organization of revolutionary forces in three different terrains: division-level main forces for the mountainous regions, battalion-level forces for the delta, and militias for urban centers.

[44] Morris, *Why Vietnam Invaded Cambodia*, 138–140.

[45] Path, "Hà Nội's Responses," 124.

[46] Interview with Duong Danh Dy, former Vietnamese diplomat to China, Hanoi, July 2010. See also Duong Danh Dy, "Bo mat that cua cac nha lanh dao Trung quoc" [The real face of Chinese leaders], March 26, 2012. Available at http://xuandienhannom .blogspot.com/2012/03/normal-0-false-false-false.html.

[47] See Hoang Huu Yen, "Mot thoi de nho" [A time to remember], July 28, 2008. Hoang Huu Yen was a lecturer in the Department of Literature and Linguistics at the University of Hanoi in the 1960s when the campaign ordered by To Huu took place. Available at www.talawas.org/talaDB/showFile.php?res=14070&rb=0302.

feared that it would lose Beijing's military support, but more than strategic interests were involved here. In a secret speech to military cadres in 1971, Truong Chinh discussed Nixon's upcoming visit to Beijing at China's invitation and China's assurances to North Vietnam that it would continue to support Hanoi's war against the United States Chinh said,

China cannot go back on its promise [*boi uoc*] to Vietnam that it will not normalize relations with the U.S. ... We still have to wait and see if China will reduce its support for our struggle and if China's talks with the U.S. will help or hurt the [anti-American] resistance of Laotian, Cambodian, and Vietnamese peoples. The future will provide the answer.[48] But as a people who are fighting the American invaders, we [are entitled to] ask these questions right now: First, is it a wise thing to invite Nixon to China while he is sending troops to murder our Vietnamese people? And second, is it a good idea to throw Nixon a lifeline while he's trying to dodge the pressure from American and world public opinion demanding a reply to [our] seven-point [peace] proposal?[49]

Chinh's comments suggested that Vietnamese leaders viewed Nixon's upcoming visit *at the time* with deep anger as an act of betrayal. That anger must have grown even stronger when, a month after his visit to Beijing, Nixon ordered massive bombing over North Vietnam and, for the first time, dropping mines in Hai Phong harbor. Both acts of aggression were in response to Hanoi's Easter Offensive in March 1972, but Hanoi did not see them that way. Despite Beijing's denials backed by increased aid to Hanoi, Le Duan quickly concluded that China cooperated in those US attacks.[50]

Hanoi's sharp denunciation of Beijing's invitation for Nixon to visit reflected in part the internationalist spirit that had long bonded the two revolutionary states. As mentioned earlier, this spirit arose out of close personal and organizational ties between the two revolutions going back nearly half a century until that point. Such ties certainly bred a deep-seated trust that, if perceived as being unjustly violated by one party, could have generated violent reactions.

Internationalism not only explained in part the tensions in Sino-Vietnamese relations, it also illuminated the question of why, up to

---

[48] In original, "reality will speak more eloquently than anyone about those issues."

[49] Truong Chinh, "Noi chuyen voi can bo Quan doi lop tap huan," [Talk to military cadres' study session], August 7, 1971. This speech was disclosed and published for the first time, after the breakout of the Sino-Vietnamese war, in Truong Chinh, *May van de quan su trong cach mang Viet-nam* [Some military issues in the Vietnamese revolution] (Hanoi: Quan Doi Nhan Dan, 1983), 204–207.

[50] Cold War International History Project, "Le Duan and the Break with China," 280.

1978, Vietnamese leaders failed to anticipate Chinese attacks a year later.[51] Vietnamese leaders admitted in internal meetings that they did not expect Vietnam's relations with China (and Cambodia) to deteriorate so fast.[52] As Vo Nguyen Giap vented his anger during China's attack on Vietnam in 1979,

> The [Chinese] war is a dirty and coward attack against the people in a social-ist country that has long been fighting by the side of the Chinese revolutionary people. The war violates the independence and sovereignty of a country that has been considered by the entire world to be the symbol of revolutionary heroism, a country that has sacrificed everything for independence and freedom for the Fatherland, for revolution and peace for all the nations in the world, including the Chinese people.[53]

Implicit in Giap's diatribe was the admission that Vietnamese leaders were unprepared for the Chinese invasion because of the close and mutu-ally trustful relationship between the two parties in the past. Even if that relationship were no longer warm in 1975, in Giap's opinion, which held the same belief in vanguard internationalism as those of his comrades, Vietnam's high international prestige would be sufficient to deter China. The thought and pride that Vietnam had selflessly been at the forefront of world revolution made Vietnamese leaders complacent and blind to the blowback that was coming from the north.

The internationalist perspective continued to color the way Vietnamese leaders viewed China after hostilities had erupted. Regardless of whether Vietnamese accusations of China's betrayal were true or not, the charges themselves betrayed Hanoi's internationalist worldview. In his 1979 speech, Le Duan went back to 1954, 1959, and 1972 to make the case that China had always given priority to its national interests at the expense of the Vietnamese revolution.[54] At Geneva in 1954, he alleged, China forced the DRV to accept the division of Vietnam, leading to twenty years of savage struggle for reunification. In 1959, China refused to support an armed struggle in South Vietnam. In the early 1970s, China used Vietnam

[51] Pike, *PAVN: People's Army of Vietnam*, 74.
[52] "Ket luan cua Bo Chinh tri tai Hoi nghi lan thu 10 Ban Chap hanh Trung uong Dang" [Concluding remarks of the Politburo at the Tenth Central Committee Plenum], November 2, 1981. *VKDTT*, v. 42, 413–414.
[53] Vo Nguyen Giap, "Nhan dan Viet-nam nhat dinh thang loi, giac xam luoc Trung quoc nhat dinh that bai" [The Vietnamese people will win [and] the Chinese invaders will lose]. *Tap Chi Cong San* no. 3, 1979, 11.
[54] Ibid., 280.

as a bargaining chip to gain favors from the United States. Truong Chinh made similar accusations for the postwar period:

As early as 1975, after the humiliating defeat of imperialist America in Vietnam, [Chinese leaders] not only denied new requests for aid from Vietnam, but also deliberately delayed work on ongoing projects that had earlier been agreed upon. In July 1978, they abruptly and unilaterally ended all the technical and economic aid to Vietnam and recalled their experts. This was the time when we had to cope with the border war [with Cambodia], with economic problems left by the Americans, and with several natural disasters.[55]

Truong Chinh likened the alliance of China and Cambodia to premodern China's collaboration with its Champa ally to launch a powerful pincer attack on Vietnam.[56] On the whole, however, Chinese policies toward Vietnam were not framed in the historical perspective of premodern relationship, nor being measured against realist standards. What was the basis for Hanoi to demand Beijing to act against its own interests in 1954 or 1959? Why did Vietnamese leaders think China was obligated to offer aid after 1975? Weren't nation-states expected to serve national interests? Wasn't the *Chinese* state expected to care first for *Chinese* interests? Underlying the accusations was the assumption that Sino-Vietnamese relations were special and ought to have stood above narrow, selfish national interests, and that Beijing violated Hanoi's trust by pursuing such interests. Vietnam's blaming act betrayed the internationalist assumptions in the worldview of its leaders.

But could it be possible that the Vietnamese were merely making up those accusations to discredit China as a socialist state? In this case, that would imply that being a socialist state meant something to Hanoi leaders. Alternatively, one may ask whether Hanoi's emphasis on Chinese selfishness was to deny that Vietnam owed China its generous help during the war. This was unlikely because the Vietnamese rarely, even while they were harshly denouncing "the Beijing clique," failed to acknowledge China's help during the war and thanked "the Chinese people" profusely for that help.[57]

---

[55] Truong Chinh, *Ve van de Cam-pu-chia* [On the issue of Cambodia]. Hanoi: Su That, 1979, 15. A standard account that details all Vietnamese accusations is Bo Ngoai Giao [Ministry of Foreign Affairs], *Su that ve quan he Viet nam – Trung quoc trong 30 nam qua* [The truth about Sino-Vietnamese relations in the last thirty years] (Hanoi: Su That, 1979).

[56] Truong Chinh, *Ve van de Cam-pu-chia*, 17.

[57] For example, see Cold War International History Project, "Le Duan and the Break with China," 284–285.

Vanguard internationalism was also implicit in the way Vietnamese leaders viewed Sino-Vietnamese hostilities as a global rather than a regional or local confrontation. Although President Carter took a neutral stand in the conflict, Vietnamese leaders quickly assumed that the United States was behind China.[58] In Truong Chinh's view, the 1979 attack showed that China had joined the imperialist camp against socialist and nationalist movements.[59] He speculated that Chinese leaders hoped to use the attack to impress the imperialist camp so that they would help realize Deng's plan of "four modernizations."[60] Chinh's accusation was based on Deng Xiaoping's visits to the United States and Japan only a short time before the attack and Washington's decision to normalize relations with Beijing in late 1978. Although Deng did discuss China's intention to "teach Vietnam a lesson" with American and Japanese leaders, the ambiguities in Washington's initial reaction to the Chinese invasion did not quite match the Vietnamese assumption that it approved Beijing's policy. If placed in the context of the American proposal to normalize relations with Vietnam without preconditions only a year earlier, that assumption was even less tenable. Truong Chinh's accusation was not a result of strategic thinking because it unnecessarily added an enemy to Vietnam, and a powerful one at that. The assumption that Beijing would not have attacked [or dared to attack] Vietnam without Washington's approval assigned too much power, as well as ill will, to the United States, and too much importance of Vietnam for American policy (in their meeting Carter in fact discouraged Deng from launching the attack[61]). Not prepared for the war with China, Vietnamese leaders now imagined it to be a global rather than a local conflict. Perhaps Hanoi's accusation of American support for Beijing's attack may well have been a legacy of the recent Vietnam War in which the United States was its primary enemy. At the same time, it would be difficult not to see lurking under Hanoi's thinking the internationalist concept of a worldwide US-directed imperialist conspiracy against revolutions. The notion of Vietnam's being the central target of that conspiracy implied an exaggerated sense of self-importance.

Internationalism blinded Vietnamese leaders from seeing the impending conflict with China. Although Chinese invasion aroused Vietnamese traditional patriotism in many Vietnamese, the conflict did not destroy

---

[58] Hurst, *The Carter Administration and Vietnam*.

[59] Truong Chinh, *Ve van de Cam-pu-chia*, 24.

[60] Chinese sources indicated that Deng appeared more interested in American support to counter the Soviet threat; economic motives were secondary. See Zhang, *Deng Xiaoping's Long War*, 54–55.

[61] Ibid., 61.

the Vietnamese belief in internationalism precisely because of the way Chinese moves were interpreted – as an expression of feudalism and bourgeois chauvinism and an act of "betrayal" to the ideals of internationalism. As Truong Chinh vehemently argued in 1982,

> Until today some Westerners still maintain that [the Sino-Vietnamese conflict] was "a war between communist countries," [and that] it is evidence that "conflict over national interests overshadows ideological unity among socialist countries." That's not true![62] The Sino-Vietnamese war in February 1979 was not a conflict between communists, but essentially a fierce struggle between national independence and socialism on the one hand and aggression, expansionism, and hegemonism on the other, between Marxism-Leninism on the one hand and Maoism on the other.[63]

To an outside observer, Vietnam's war with China clearly contradicted the two-camp worldview held by Vietnamese leaders, but my close reading of Vietnamese statements issued in private as well as in public indicated that their belief in internationalism deeply informed their views of China and explained why they failed to anticipate the war and, after it had broken out, viewed it as a global conflict.

FROM THE VANGUARD OF WORLD REVOLUTION
TO A SOVIET CLIENT

Recounting Pham Van Dong's snub of the Soviet Ambassador in 1976, Chanda remarks in his well-researched book that the episode

> was a reminder of how much change had come in Vietnam's relations with Moscow since the 1950s, when the Vietnamese viewed the Soviet Union almost reverentially as the beacon of the Soviet camp. Not only have the Vietnamese lost their ideological naïveté vis-à-vis their Socialist big brothers, but with the dream of reunification realized and with opportunities appearing to open up for a broad-based foreign policy, they were also ready to be more assertive toward Moscow.[64]

During 1975–1977, Vietnamese leaders indeed sought to expand trade with the capitalist West while resisting Soviet overtures for deepening

---

[62] Truong Chinh, "Nhan dan Viet nam kien quyet danh bai moi muu mo xam luoc cua chu nghia banh truong va chu nghia ba quyen Trung Quoc" [The Vietnamese people will resolutely defeat the aggressive plots of China's expansionism and hegemonism], in Tap Chi Cong San, *Chong Chu Nghia Banh Truong Ba Quyen Trung Quoc* [Against Chinese expansionism and hegemonism] (Hanoi: Tap Chi Cong San, 1983), 37. This volume republished articles that had been published earlier in *Tap Chi Cong San* on the topic.

[63] Ibid., 43.

[64] Chanda, *Brother Enemy*, 171.

military and other ties. Yet the internal documents reviewed earlier suggested that Vietnamese "broad-based foreign policy" was not empty of ideological spirit. What Le Duan wanted was not so much to make friends with capitalist countries as to make their checkbook and technology serve socialist development in Vietnam according to the Soviet model. As we have seen through a wide range of Vietnamese documents, victorious Vietnam was bloated with hatred for imperialism and with pride in its revolutionary vanguardism in Southeast Asia.

It is curious that Hanoi was assertive toward Moscow in 1976 while making economic plans based on expectations of substantial aid from the very socialist brother it snubbed. Here again, the concept of vanguard internationalism is essential to understanding Vietnam's apparently self-contradictory behavior. Vanguard internationalism involved much more than an independent and "broad-based" foreign policy. Vanguard internationalism created in the Vietnamese a strong sense of entitlement. They expected to be treated as leaders of an important country on the same level with the Soviet Union and the United States. They expected their enemies to pay tribute and their allies to contribute. Vanguard status was never separate from a belief in internationalism. In fact, that self-proclaimed status was built on the perceived success in pursuing an internationalist mission against a global imperialist power.

The limits to Vietnam's "broad-based foreign policy" were patently clear in internal reports prepared by diplomats and recently made available. According to a "top-secret" Ministry of Foreign Affairs' report in mid-1976, a conference of senior Vietnamese diplomats in early 1976 offered the following analysis of the world situation facing Vietnam at the time:

The three revolutionary tidal waves have surged and raised revolutionary potentials. The world revolutionary movement and the struggle for world peace have reached a very favorable stage. Vietnam has emerged as a potent force with great international status and role especially in Southeast Asia. The overall decline of imperialist America and its diminished international role have become an irreversible trend, causing a crisis in the entire imperialist system.[65]

The professional diplomats in Hanoi viewed the world through the same lens of vanguard internationalism as did their leaders. Through that lens they screened countries and placed them in different categories:

[In the past six months of 1976] we have strengthened and developed all-around relations with the *socialist* countries, with Laos and Cambodia, actively

---

[65] Bo Ngoai Giao, "Bao cao tinh hinh va cong tac 6 thang dau nam 1976," 1.

participated in the preparation of the upcoming Non-Aligned Movement Summit Meeting in Colombo, developed political and economic relations with *nationalist* countries, and developed economic relations with *capitalist* countries.[66]

Countries were grouped in three ideological categories: from "socialist" to "nationalist" to "capitalist." Vietnam's relations with countries in each ideological category differed in importance and scope: all-around, first-order relations for socialist countries; second-order relations limited to political and economic (i.e., not cultural or social) spheres for nationalist countries; and only economic ties were allowed for capitalist countries, which were ranked last in importance. As the language in this report implicitly revealed, "broad-based foreign policy" did not mean that the United States would be treated the same as India, nor was India regarded the same as the Soviet Union. The categories did not mean that Vietnam would reject having anything to do with the capitalist camp, but they imposed narrow boundaries on the scope of, and assigned limited importance to, relationships with countries in that camp.

Diplomatic reports suggest that vanguard internationalism was responsible for the twists and turns of Soviet-Vietnamese relationship. According to the 1976 report cited earlier, Vietnam was able to secure promises of aid from the Soviet Union and Eastern Europe for many projects.[67] There were problems, though: Some unnamed Eastern European brothers had been slow in fulfilling existing aid obligations, in part because "they paid greater attention to their national interests than previously ... and thus demanded relatively high prices for their exports." Another problem was the Soviet desire to exchange more delegations and generally to increase Soviet presence in Vietnam. Twice asking for its ships to make port calls in South Vietnam, complained the report, the Soviet Union "imposed itself on us and created difficulties for us in our relations with other countries." Vietnam was similarly not keen on becoming a member of the Council for Mutual Economic Assistance (COMECON), which was the organization in charge of coordinating economic activities within the Soviet bloc. The report mentioned that Vietnam preferred bilateral negotiations with each individual socialist brother to being a COMECON member. No reasons were given, but this preference may have come from Vietnamese leaders' desire for maximum autonomy or their feelings that they were not an ordinary state in the same league with underdeveloped Mongolia. To give a symbolic nod to the Soviet Union, which had urged Vietnam

[66] Italics added.
[67] Bo Ngoai Giao, "Bao cao tinh hinh va cong tac 6 thang dau nam 1976," 1.

to apply for COMECON membership, Vietnam sent an official to the COMECON with only observer status.

By 1977, it began to dawn on Vietnamese leaders that their socialist brothers did not take seriously their claim to be a vanguard. The Ministry of Foreign Affairs' report in July 1977 complained that the Soviet Union had dragged its feet in delivering on its aid promises for Vietnam's Five-Year Plan (1976–1981).[68] Moscow had refused Vietnam's requests for additional oil shipments on credit and for some other large loans. East Germany had similarly canceled or delayed some aid projects until the next Five-Year Plan. Among the socialist brothers, only Romania had agreed to a loan of 40 million roubles for Vietnam. The report noted that Vietnam's socialist brothers were facing some economic problems of their own, but the main reason for their reluctance to help had to do with their shifts in policy toward Vietnam. This realization was the backdrop of Vietnam's retreat from vanguardism in mid-1977, when Pham Van Dong cut short his planned trip to France and traveled to Moscow for talks with Soviet leaders. Vietnam soon agreed to apply for membership in the COMECON and to comply more readily with Soviet interests. Soviet aid quickly resumed afterward.[69]

If Vietnamese leaders had valued their national independence more than anything else, they must have behaved differently in the face of Soviet pressure in 1977. They must have contemplated making do without Soviet aid. As argued earlier, the world order with respect to the great powers in the mid-1970s was still fluid and Vietnam had ample room for maneuvering. In mid-1977, the United States was ready to normalize relations with Vietnam while tensions with Cambodia and China seemed manageable. Cambodia was a security threat but that should have made Hanoi even more eager for the hand reached out from Washington.

There is simply no evidence that Vietnamese leaders ever considered leaving the Soviet camp. They were pragmatic enough to yield to Soviet pressure in return for aid, but not pragmatic to the extent of imagining a future outside the Soviet bloc. Only when the security situation became grave in 1978 with the prospects of simultaneously fighting both Cambodia and China did Hanoi accept normalization with the United States, but that was too late. Vietnam then had no choice but to join the COMECON and accept a 25-year friendship treaty with the Soviet Union. The revolutionary vanguard of Southeast Asia had abandoned

---

[68] Bo Ngoai Giao, "Bao cao tinh hinh va cong tac 6 thang dau nam 1977."
[69] Chanda, *Brother Enemy*, 187–191.

vanguardism and chosen the fate of a Soviet client state. Hanoi's quick fall back into Moscow's open arms indicated the more powerful pull of ideology compared to the push of the international structure. It is true that the structure of international politics did not favor Vietnam in 1978, but that was not the case during 1975–1977. With a different set of beliefs, Vietnamese leaders might have made a different choice in 1977 and avoided the fate of a Soviet client state, as their top diplomats would wish years later.[70]

CONCLUSION

Even before their victory in 1975, Hanoi leaders had found gratification in the notion that Vietnam was the center of world revolution. They were proud of their military genius and their vanguard position in a revolutionary tidal wave that was poised to sweep imperialism away from Vietnam and Southeast Asia. Their victory was the greatest vindication of their belief in vanguard internationalism. This belief explained why they failed to take advantage of the fluid international order at the time. They rejected the olive branch offered by their vanquished enemy even though they needed investment and trade from that enemy. They did not anticipate attacks from their former allies. In the end, they were forced to accept the status of a client state of the Soviet Union, something they did not desire at first.

The story of the Vietnamese revolution in this period suggests the poverty of international theories that assume the "rational" behavior of states. The foreign policy of the Vietnamese revolutionary state is difficult to explain without understanding the beliefs of its leaders. Their imposition of preconditions on normalization with the United States was not simply a miscalculation. Behind their thinking was their concept of justice and pride in their prestige. Behind their feeling of betrayal by China was the belief in proletarian internationalism and the expectation that socialist China acted according to that belief.

The Vietnamese postwar saga also implies that conflicts need not occur between new revolutionary states and the *status quo* international order. Revolutionary victories could threaten status quo powers, but in this case victory did not quite have that effect. Ironically, it was China rather than the United States that felt threatened by Vietnam after 1975.

---

[70] Tran Quang Co, "Hoi uc va suy nghi"; Luu Doan Huynh, "The Paris Peace Agreement and the Vietnamese vision of the future."

War between Vietnam and China and hostilities between Vietnam and the United States occurred not only because of counterrevolutionary reactions by *status quo* states, but also because of the radical ideology of Vietnamese revolutionaries.

Although ideology explained many events discussed in this chapter, ideology was inimical to the interests of the Vietnamese revolution in this period. Ideology was a source of conflict between Vietnam and other communist states. Ideology guided Vietnamese leaders along the wrong path, creating unnecessary enemies left and right for them. Fortunately, the Vietnamese revolution was rescued by the Soviet Union to limp along for another decade.

8

The Crisis and Death of Utopia, 1980–1991

In the fall of 1975, Le Duan led a delegation to many Eastern European capitals to thank them for supporting Hanoi during the war and to ask for their continuing assistance. The highlight of the trip came at the end with a five-day visit to Moscow. There the Vietnamese delegation met with top Soviet leaders, including Brezhnev, Podgorny, Kosygin, Gromyko, and others. At the meeting, Duan requested a Soviet loan of one billion rubles for many projects. When Soviet leaders expressed their reluctance to fund his grand pet project, a steel plant worth 200 million rubles, Duan told them,

We are poor now, but it'll be different in five or ten years. We won't be this poor in ten years. When we fought the French, we had many difficulties. We never thought we would achieve victory as we have. Now [even] the U.S. has lost [to us]. Previously the Philippines was an American lackey but now its attitude has shifted. The U.S. and Japan [now] want to control [Southeast Asia]. Our country may be small but we will defeat them with Soviet help. In peace we want to make Vietnam into the center of socialism in Southeast Asia. That's the direction of our political and economic policy. Southeast Asia with more than a hundred million people is a large area. In this region, besides Japan, no other country is [as powerful] as Vietnam. I mean socialist Vietnam… We have set the precondition that Thailand and the Philippines must expel the Americans from their countries in order to improve relations with Vietnam…

Duan asserted that Vietnam had fought selflessly for world revolution and, therefore, deserved Soviet help to achieve even more victories for socialism:

Up to now we have said that we were fighting to defend socialism and world peace and we were willing to shoulder all the losses. Now [the world] has peace, but socialism still needs to be defended. We want to achieve economic victory [besides military victory]. Who knows what will happen in 10, 15, 20 years? Perhaps thanks to our influence Burma and India will also change. Previously India supported the American war on Vietnam. Our Foreign Ministry wanted to sever diplomatic relations with India, but I counseled against that. [I said that,] when we achieved victory, India would change its attitude. After we won the war, India [came around] to help us... India thanked us because we had weakened the Americans.[1]

Duan failed to persuade the Soviets to approve his pet plant, but the statement revealed that his ambition was not only to defeat imperialism at war but also to showcase the economic superiority of socialism that could convert gigantic India to the cause.

The story told in Chapter 7 of how vanguard internationalism turned revolutionary Vietnam into a Soviet client state had a similarly dismal domestic parallel. Drunk with pride in their success in war, Vietnamese leaders set highly unrealistic goals and employed draconian tactics in their quest to develop socialism "in 5, 10 years." To their profound distress, the socialist revolution quickly faltered and within only a few years Vietnam was on the verge of a great famine. Although the military threat from Beijing compelled Hanoi to sign a mutual defense and cooperation treaty with the Soviet Union in 1978, the economic crisis at home deepened Hanoi's dependence on Moscow. That dependence would help reformers in Hanoi to promote limited economic liberalization after Mikhail Gorbachev rose to power in the Soviet Union. Under Gorbachev's blessing, notable changes appeared in Vietnamese worldview and foreign policy. Yet these changes were short-lived. In the aftermath of the Soviet bloc's collapse, ideology motivated Vietnamese leaders to ignore reality and cling to their longstanding revolutionary belief.

"THE NATION AND SOCIALISM ARE ONE"

In late 1975, Le Duan toyed with the idea that some "capitalist laws of development" were useful. Yet the Party decided by the end of 1976 "to

[1] "Bien ban Hoi dam giua Doan dai bieu Dang va Chinh phu Viet nam dan chu cong hoa va Doan dai bieu Dang va Chinh phu Lien Xo trong cuoc di tham Lien Xo cua Doan dai bieu Dang va Chinh phu ta tu 27 den 31-10-1975" [Memorandum of the Meeting between the delegation of the Party and government of the DRV and the Party and government of the Soviet Union during the visit to the Soviet Union of our Party and government delegation October 27–31, 1975], 24–25. File 9735, Phu Thu Tuong, National Archive III, Hanoi.

launch a socialist revolution" to start the country on a "fast, firm, and forceful march to socialism."[2] It was explained that:

Socialism is [now] the immediate goal of the Vietnamese revolution and the inevitable evolutionary path for Vietnamese society, in accordance with the [Marxist] law of development of human society during the transition period from capitalism to socialism on a global scale... Since the birth of our Party, we have always raised the two flags of national independence and socialism ... Now that our Fatherland is fully independent, the nation and socialism are one. Only socialism can realize the working people's ancient dream to be forever liberated from oppression, exploitation, poverty, [and] backwardness ... Only socialism can bring the working people their full rights as masters and return genuine dignity to mankind ... Only socialism can bring our Fatherland a modern economy, advanced culture and science, and strong defense, and guarantee our country's lasting independence, freedom, and increasing prosperity.[3]

Guided by those noble missions, the socialist revolution began with a series of violent campaigns to expropriate "capitalist" property in southern cities, accompanied by a campaign to establish rural collectives throughout the South.[4] However, the disruptions to domestic production and trade, together with bad weather, drops in foreign aid, and peasants' resistance to collectivization soon brought the economy to a halt. As Vietnam went to war with China and Cambodia in 1978–1979, its economy was in shambles.

The threat of urban famine was so grave that in April 1978, exactly three years after reunification, the Party Secretariat had to send an urgent telegram that ordered provincial governments in the Red River Delta to mobilize larger supplies of rice to help Hanoi.[5] Since the 1960s, food consumption had been rationed for North Vietnam's urban residents who could buy at government stores only limited amounts of rice (about 30 pounds per month per person on average).[6] A similar ration system was used for almost every essential consumer good, from meat (one pound per month) to kerosene oil (one quart per month) to fabrics for clothing (five yards per year) to bicycle parts (one tire per year).[7] The black market

---

[2] "Bao cao chinh tri cua Ban Chap hanh Trung uong Dang" [Political report of the Central Committee of the Party], read by Le Duan at the Fourth Party Congress, December 14, 1976. *VKDTT*, v. 37, 500.

[3] Ibid., 500–501.

[4] Huy Duc, *Ben Thang Cuoc*, v. 1, 71–98.

[5] "Dien cua Ban Bi thu so 15" [Telegram of the Secretariat no. 15], April 17, 1978, signed by Nguyen Duy Trinh. *VKDTT*, v. 39, 198.

[6] All the quantities of rationed commodities in this paragraph are approximate.

[7] Huy Duc, *Ben Thang Cuoc*, v. 1, 288–292.

existed and offered many goods, but prices were many times higher. When the aforementioned telegram was sent, the government could supply only ten pounds of rice per month, or one-third of the already paltry rice ration for each ordinary Hanoi resident. The rest consisted of substitutes such as potatoes, cassava, and sorghum, deemed inferior food or food for livestock. Residents in other towns fared no better, and perhaps worse.

Once the food shortage had abated, thanks to international food aid, Vietnamese leaders admitted their mistakes and approved some measures to increase material incentives for producers.[8] The goal was to stabilize and improve living conditions for people. Yet the Party did not relent on its efforts to strengthen cooperatives and expand state control over trade and the overall economy.[9] At the Fourth Plenum in June 1983, Le Duan criticized cadres for their neglect of the socialist revolution as evidenced in the recent growth of private trade. He called on the Party to set the goals of eliminating private trade and completing collectivization in the South by 1985.[10] Not only were those goals not achieved but by late 1985 the economy spiraled out of control after a poorly implemented price, wage, and currency reform sent inflation soaring to more than 500 percent. Three million Vietnamese were near starvation and another five million were malnourished in 1988.[11] Angry but powerless, Vietnamese mocked the Party by joking that "*CNXH*," the acronym of socialism [*Chu nghia Xa hoi*] in Vietnamese, really stood for "the country has fallen into a hole" [*Ca nuoc xuong ho*].

Vietnam's bumpy road to socialism was exacerbated by an American trade embargo that most Western countries complied with. At the United Nations, Vietnamese diplomats found out to their humiliation that Vietnam's popularity following its victory against the United States had evaporated. Most countries voted to keep the seat of the deposed Khmer Rouge government at the UN despite Vietnam's pleading them not to. International and domestic failures combined to deflate Hanoi's legitimacy, as evidenced in many incidents of troop desertion and in the

---

[8] "De cuong ket luan Hoi nghi lan thu sau Ban Chap hanh Trung uong Dang" [Draft Conclusion Statement at the Sixth Plenum of the Central Committee], n.d., probably August, 1979. *VKDTT*, v. 40, 332.

[9] "Ket luan cua Bo Chinh tri tai Hoi nghi lan thu 10 Ban Chap hanh Trung uong Dang" [Concluding statement of the Politburo at the Tenth Plenum of the Central Committee], November 2, 1981. *VKDTT*, v. 42, 428–430.

[10] "Bai noi cua dong chi Le Duan tai Hoi nghi Trung uong 4" [Le Duan's speech at the Fourth Central Committee Plenum]. *VKDTT*, v. 44, 143–144.

[11] Russell Heng, "Leadership in Vietnam: Pressures for Reform and Their Limits," *Contemporary Southeast Asia* 15: 1 (June 1993), 98–110.

massive waves of boatpeople trying to flee the country.[12] In addition, although security became less pressing after Vietnamese troops successfully overthrew the Khmer Rouge in Cambodia and fended off the Chinese invasion, Vietnam's enemies continued to force it to station large numbers of troops in Cambodia and along the northern border.

In the conventional view, Soviet-Vietnamese relations in the 1980s were fraught with tension because Hanoi disapproved of Soviet efforts to normalize relations with China, whereas Moscow resented what it felt to be Vietnam's wasteful use of Soviet aid.[13] This view is certainly true but far from complete. Many Soviet foreign policies won strong approval in Hanoi. An example was the Soviet invasion of Afghanistan in April 1979 to prevent the young communist government there from collapse. The Soviet move triggered an outcry not only from the West but also from many Western leftist parties.[14] This was exactly what Vietnam faced after its invasion of Cambodia. In an internal document, the Party Secretariat expressed contempt for the "bourgeois and petit bourgeois nationalism" that existed in the world's communist movement. Adherents to that kind of nationalism "distorted Marxism-Leninism [and] joined the bourgeoisie ... in criticizing the Soviet Union's helping Afghanistan and Vietnam's helping Cambodia."[15] Ostracism not only by the West but also by some fraternal parties placed Hanoi in the same boat with Moscow and made Vietnamese leaders feel greater sympathy with their Soviet counterparts.[16]

---

[12] On troop desertion, see "Chi thi cua Ban Bi thu so 90-CT/TW" [Secretariat's Directive], April 30, 1980. *VKDTT*, v. 41, 106–110. On corruption, see the documents that set up special committees for investigation: "Quyet dinh cua Ban Bi thu no. 69-QD/TW" [Secretariat's Decision], March 20, 1980, and "Quyet dinh cua Ban Bi thu no. 71-QD/TW" [Secretariat's Decision], April 17, 1980. *VKDTT*, v. 41, 44–45 and 82–83, respectively. The corruption identified in the first decision had to do with the scheme by security officials in some Southern provinces to organize illegal trips for people to leave the country by boat, and their involvement in the smuggling of Thai goods through Cambodia into southern Vietnam.

[13] Robert Horn, *Alliance Politics between Comrades: The Dynamics of Soviet-Vietnamese Relations*. Los Angeles: RAND/UCLA Center for the Study of Soviet International Behavior, August 1987, 15–17. Soviet pressure on Vietnam was greater under Andropov and Gorbachev than under Brezhnev and Chernenko.

[14] Clive Christie, "Internationalism and Nationalism: Western Socialism and the Problem of Vietnam." Occasional papers no. 3, Center for South-East Asian Studies, University of Hull, 1982, 23–32.

[15] "Nghi quyet cua Ban Bi thu so. 36-NQ/TW," [The Secretariat's Resolution no. 36-NQ/TW], February 24, 1981. *VKDTT*, v. 42, 89.

[16] On the Soviet side, Beijing inadvertently helped Soviet-Vietnamese relations by making Hanoi's withdrawal from Cambodia *and* Soviet withdrawal from Afghanistan the preconditions for normalization with Moscow. Although Soviet leaders were keen to

Another example of Hanoi's support for Moscow was the latter's nuclear policy. At the Fifth Party Congress in 1982, for example, the Central Committee's Political Report declared that Vietnam fully supported the peace initiatives of the Soviet Union, especially the recent proposal by CPSU General Secretary Leonid Brezhnev for nuclear disarmament.[17] During the war, North Vietnam was against such détente policies, but in the 1980s Hanoi no longer criticized them.

Scholars underestimate Vietnamese willingness to cooperate with the Soviet Union because they neglect the role of ideology. Part of the security problems in the eyes of Vietnamese leaders had little to do with the direct threats posed to them by China and by Khmer Rouge guerrillas. Vietnamese security concerns were refracted to a great extent through the lens of ideological struggle in the world between two ideological camps. That lens scanned the globe and zoomed in on ideological threats that would be marginally related to Vietnam's security. This explains why Vietnamese leaders were so alarmed when President Reagan assumed office in 1981. In the same document cited earlier, the Party Secretariat revealed Hanoi's deep concern that "the imperialist gang and international counterrevolutionaries were hard at work to assemble their forces, to launch an arms race, [and] to resume the Cold War" against socialism. In the wake of such imperialist advances, the Secretariat felt disturbed by the problems facing the revolutionary camp, including the ever deepening Sino-Soviet split and the recent Solidarity protests in Poland.[18] They were anxious that workers and communist movements were gravely divided and threatened by "opportunism." Given a tense world situation, the role of the Soviet Union "for the protection of world peace and for the victory of world revolution" must have become enhanced in Vietnamese eyes.

In the same vein, Le Duan pointed out at the Fourth Plenum in mid-1983 that Vietnam's enemies, especially the United States, wanted it to be weak and exhausted.[19] They also wanted it to be isolated from the Soviet Union and from Laos and Cambodia so that they could defeat

---

improve relations with China, their interest in rapprochement with Beijing must be weighed against not only Soviet interests in Vietnam but also those in Afghanistan.

[17] "Bao cao chinh tri cua Ban Chap hanh Trung uong Dang" [The Central Committee's Political Report], March 27, 1982. *VKDTT*, v. 43, 139.

[18] "Nghi quyet cua Ban Bi thu so. 36-NQ/TW," *VKDTT*, v. 42, 78–79, 89. All specific references to China have been deleted from the released version of the document, but the context suggested China.

[19] "Bai noi cua dong chi Tong bi thu Le Duan tai Hoi nghi lan thu tu Ban Chap hanh Trung uong Dang" [Comrade General Secretary Le Duan's speech at the Fourth Plenum of the Central Committee], June 24, 1983. *VKDTT*, v. 44, 155.

Vietnam – "a link in the socialist chain that they considered to be weak." Duan's view betrayed a strong concern for security but it was not a concept of security that was strictly limited to Hanoi's relations with Washington or that was directly threatened by specific American activities. Rather, the concept was colored by an ideological view that linked conflicts at the global level to the local level along ideological lines. Through that view, the United States was not simply a past and potential "foreign invader" of Vietnam but also leader of the imperialist camp. Vietnam was not simply a small and vulnerable country but a weak revolutionary state in the socialist chain. Obviously those perceptions implied Vietnam's greater need for close relations with Moscow.

Soviet-Vietnamese relations in the 1980s indeed became closer than any previous period except the 1930s when the Indochinese Communist Party (ICP) considered itself a Southeast Asian branch of the Comintern headed by the Soviet Union. Soviet-Vietnamese intimacy had been observed in the late 1970s,[20] but only now started to grow and expand into all areas, including politics, economics, military, science, and technology.[21] A major component of collaboration involved ideological and economic management training; this component was important but has thus far been neglected in the literature. In late 1979, Vietnam began the annual program of sending instructors and researchers of Marxism-Leninism to advanced communist Party schools or social sciences academies in the Soviet bloc.[22] Also, hundreds of high- and middle-ranking officials were sent to the Soviet Union every year, beginning in May 1980, to take short training courses in economic management.[23] Regular semester-long programs taught by Soviet experts were organized each year in Vietnam for 300 officials, including economic ministers and their deputies, general directors of state enterprises, professors of Party schools and universities, and similarly high-ranking cadres.[24] The bustling training activities

[20] Stephen J. Morris, *Why Vietnam Invaded Cambodia: Political Culture and the Causes of War* (Stanford, CA: Stanford University Press, 1999), 208.

[21] "Nghi quyet cua Bo Chinh tri so 23-NQ/TW" [Politburo's Resolution no. 23-NQ/TW], January 19, 1980. *VKDTT*, v. 41, 16.

[22] "Quyet dinh cua Ban Bi thu so. 47-QD/TW" [The Secretariat's Decision no. 47-NQ/TW], September 1, 1979. *VKDTT*, v. 40, 419–420. The number of Vietnamese officials to go for study in 1979 was 70, with 44 going to the Soviet Union.

[23] "Quyet dinh cua Ban Bi thu so. 74-QD/TW" [The Secretariat's Decision no. 74-NQ/TW], May 20, 1980. *VKDTT*, v. 41, 111–112. See also "Thong bao so 24-TB/TW" [Notice no. 24-TB/TW], October 8, 1983. *VKDTT*, v. 44, 292–294.

[24] For the 1979 program, see "Quyet dinh cua Ban Bi thu so. 46-QD/TW" [The Secretariat's Decision no. 46-NQ/TW], September 4, 1979. *VKDTT*, v. 40, 421–422. For 1980, see "Quyet dinh cua Ban Bi thu so. 80-QD/TW" [The Secretariat's Decision no. 80-NQ/TW], September 6, 1980. *VKDTT*, v. 41, 350–351.

suggested that the Vietnamese were interested not only in Soviet rubles and Katyusha rockets but also in Soviet ideas and experiences.

In fact, Vietnamese leaders did not neglect ideological work despite the massive economic problems facing them. An Institute of Marxism-Leninism that was placed under the direct supervision of the Central Committee was formally established in 1982 to conduct research on socialism and communism and to publish the works of Marx, Engels, Lenin, and leaders of other communist parties, including Vietnam. The Institute could have been named the Ministry of Marxism-Leninism since its rank was equivalent to a line ministry in the bureaucracy. In the same year, the Party decided to install a five-meter-tall bronze statue of Lenin in downtown Hanoi.[25] The next year, the Party's Secretariat authorized and made funding available for the translation and publication of a full collection of works by Marx and Engels scheduled to come out over the following decade.[26] Moving in the same direction was the decision to strengthen and systematize the education of Marxism-Leninism in college.[27] Since 1973, Marxism-Leninism had been made a subject required for college graduation examinations, but the Secretariat felt that "instruction of the subject had brought students only knowledge of Marxism-Leninism, but [the doctrine] had yet to become a belief and an ideal that motivated their action and behavior. Knowledge of Party policy and socialist values [among students] remained superficial."[28]

Although initially Hanoi may have had reservations about signing a mutual defense treaty with the Soviet Union, over time Vietnam developed a close relationship with its "eldest brother." Economic and security needs were no doubt a main Vietnamese motive to pursue close relations with the Soviet Union. Clearly, without Soviet economic and military aid, Vietnam would neither have been able to embark on a socialist revolution, nor to withstand the war in Cambodia and the Western embargo.

---

[25] The statue was a gift from the Soviet Union and was open to the public in 1985. See Nguyen Ngoc Tien, "Tuong dai o Hanoi" [Public statues in Hanoi], *Ha Noi Moi*, December 31, 2011. Available at http://hanoimoi.com.vn/Tin-tuc/1000_nam_thang_long/534712/tuong-dai-o-ha-noi-tiep-theo. Outside the Soviet Union and Eastern Europe, Lenin's statues were apparently installed only in Mongolia, Ethiopia, and Vietnam, with only the one in Vietnam still standing today. See http://en.wikipedia.org/wiki/List_of_statues_of_Vladimir_Lenin.

[26] "Quyet dinh cua Ban Bi thu so. 18-QD/TW" [The Secretariat's Decision no. 18-NQ/TW], November 10, 1983. *VKDTT*, v. 44, 317–318.

[27] "Chi thi cua Ban Bi thu so. 25-CT/TW" [The Secretariat's Directive no. 25-CT/TW], October 12, 1983. *VKDTT*, v. 44, 295–305.

[28] Ibid., 296.

Yet ideology also played a significant role. Vietnam's cooperation with the Soviet Union went far beyond security and economic aid. Over time, ideological ties bound Vietnam to the Soviet Union in multiple ways, despite tensions on some issues.

LENIN, GORBACHEV, AND THE ROAD TO ECONOMIC REFORM IN VIETNAM

Studies of economic reform in Vietnam since the late 1980s have downplayed the influence of foreign ideas or models in the event.[29] Although it is true that the Vietnamese reform had many distinctive features, Vietnam's reformist ideas and policies followed closely those in the Soviet Union and at times gained traction thanks to events there.

After Vietnam signed the Treaty of mutual defense and cooperation with the Soviet Union in 1978, teams of Soviet advisers and experts on socialist economics began to stream into Vietnam in 1979. While Soviet advisers advocated greater state centralization and planning, Soviet academics introduced Lenin's New Economic Policy (NEP) ideas to Vietnamese policy makers who attended their classes on economic management.[30] Implemented in the 1920s, NEP was designed to reduce the economic damages caused by earlier policies aimed at sweeping nationalization and centralization of industry and trade.[31] NEP brought significant economic recovery but was reversed in the late 1920s after Stalin achieved domination over the Communist Party of the Soviet Union (CPSU). For decades, NEP was considered taboo and was not even taught in school in the Soviet Union. By the mid-1970s, however, Soviet scholars had begun to study NEP with a new eye in search of possible answers to the stagnation and decline of the Soviet economy. The spread of NEP ideas to Vietnam in the late 1970s and early 1980s coincided with the crisis caused by rash socialism there. Those ideas likely influenced the decisions on economic reform taken by Vietnamese leaders at the Sixth Central Committee Plenum in late 1979. This Plenum admitted the mistakes made by the hasty march to socialism, acknowledged the useful role of the private sector, and granted greater autonomy to local

---

[29] See a criticism along this line in Balazs Szalontai, "The Diplomacy of Economic Reform in Vietnam: The Genesis of Doi Moi, 1986–1989," *The Journal of Asiatic Studies* (a Korean journal) 51: 2 (2008): 199–252.

[30] Huy Duc, *Ben Thang Cuoc*, v. 1, 336–338, 350.

[31] Alec Nove, *An Economic History of the USSR, 1917–1991* (London, England: Penguin Books, 1992), 73–125.

governments.[32] Nevertheless, Party leaders considered these measures a temporary retreat but not permanent policies because they apparently contradicted the Marxist vision of socialism.[33]

Soon ideologues in the Party leadership led by Le Duan became alarmed by the revival of the private sector and sought to reimpose state control. At this juncture, the reform effort ironically found a champion in Truong Chinh, who, as we saw in previous chapters, had been a rigid ideologue throughout his career. Stepping down in 1956 from his position as general secretary following errors committed during the land reform, Chinh remained in the Politburo as the number-two leader after Le Duan. During the early 1980s, Chinh gathered a new team of advisors with fresh ideas and traveled around the country to study economic problems. In the same period, Le Duan's health deteriorated (he was to die in office in 1986 at 79).[34] By the mid-1980s, often he did not deliver the key political reports at Central Committee plenums but let others perform that role. Truong Chinh was instrumental in scaling back the ambitions of Duan and other ideologues to develop socialism as fast as possible. He was also determined to reform Vietnam's moribund economy by using economic incentives, not administrative decrees, to distribute resources more efficiently and to stimulate production.[35] Chinh naturally viewed Gorbachev, who was launching a bold economic reform in the Soviet Union, as an ally.

In his address at the Ninth Plenum of the Central Committee in late 1985, Truong Chinh sharply criticized mistakes made in the price, wage, and currency reform earlier in the year that sent inflation skyrocketing to 500 percent. In support of his argument, he cited the new Draft Program of the CPSU written under Gorbachev that called for "correcting the errors of [relying solely on] one's subjective views and will to change reality."[36] Chinh argued that the transition to socialism in Vietnam must

---

[32] Huy Duc, *Ben Thang Cuoc*, v. 1, 300–302.

[33] Ibid., 337, citing the view of Professor Dao Xuan Sam, a key advisor to Truong Chinh.

[34] He apparently did not participate in the Twelfth Plenum of the Fourth Congress (February 26–March 8, 1982), and the Second Plenum (July 1982) and the Third Plenum (December 1982) of the Fifth Congress due to health reasons. *VKDTT*, v. 43, 20, 464, 704.

[35] Huy Duc, *Ben Thang Cuoc*, v. 1, 338–340.

[36] "Bai phat bieu cua dong chi Truong Chinh tai Hoi nghi lan thu 9 Ban Chap hanh Trung uong Dang" [Speech by comrade Truong Chinh at the Ninth Plenum of the Central Committee], December 11, 1985. *VKDTT*, v. 46, 361–363, 369. The new Draft CPSU Program was the first document since 1961 that aimed at identifying the goals and strategies for achieving socialism in the Soviet Union. It was released in the Fall of 1985 under Gorbachev's leadership and officially adopted in early 1986.

take a long time because Vietnam's starting point was low and its security was under threat. In this period of transition to socialism, policy should aim for developing commodity production through market relations adjusted by state plans. The new Draft Program of the CPSU, Chinh noted, also called for better exploitation of market relations within the framework of socialism. Some of his comrades only wished Moscow to offer more aid, but Chinh assured them that, if Vietnam used existing aid more efficiently and produced better goods for the Soviet market, the Soviet Union would trust Vietnam more and be even more generous.

It is possible to gauge the strong resistance to Chinh's reformist ideas and the real thoughts of Vietnamese leadership about the Soviet Union through the concluding statement made at the Tenth Plenum in June 1986, when the Central Committee discussed the draft political report to be presented at the Sixth Party Congress scheduled later in the year. The Plenum was presided over by Truong Chinh, because Le Duan was sick and would die a month later. The concluding statement summarized the conclusion of the Politburo on controversial issues that had been raised earlier in small-group discussions or in plenary sessions at the Plenum. Despite a broad agreement within the leadership on the need for continuing economic reform, some Central Committee members wanted to go further than the draft report in emphasizing class struggle in economic policy. The Politburo thus agreed to replace the brief comment in the draft report that "exploiting classes have been essentially eliminated" by this lengthy, more specific, statement:

The exploiting classes such as landlords, comprador capitalists, and large capitalists in industry and trade have been eliminated, but besides a small number of [private] industrial producers authorized to operate, trading capitalist forces now still operate under many guises. The exploitation [of poor farmers] by rich farmers in the countryside and some other forms of exploitation still exist.[37]

The revised statement conveyed a strong commitment to continuing policies of class struggle that would eliminate private trade and rural exploitation. It was as if Le Duan had been in the room instead of breathing his last gasps in the hospital.

In the same vein, the Politburo agreed with another suggestion to revise the draft report so as to be more specific about a serious mistake

---

[37] "Ket luan cua Bo Chinh tri tai Hoi nghi lan thu muoi Ban Chap hanh Trung uong Dang ve du thao bao cao chinh tri" [Concluding statement of the Politburo at the Tenth Plenum of the Central Committee on the Draft Political Report], June 5, 1986. *VKDTT*, v. 47, 109.

in past policy, namely, the Party's lack of firm understanding about the dictatorship of the proletariat and its weak leadership over the struggle between the capitalist and socialist roads.[38] The Politburo now declared its commitment to "seize decisive victories" for socialism in that struggle by the year 1990 through "consolidating socialist relations" in industry, agriculture, and trade. This phrase practically meant greater efforts would be made to crack down on illegal private businesses while promoting the state sector. In sum, the way the Politburo responded to suggestions on economic policy in the draft political report indicated that advocates of class struggle still held reformers like Truong Chinh in check as late as mid-1986.

Regarding foreign policy, the Politburo set the strategic tasks of Vietnam in the draft report to be "the construction of socialism and the defense of the socialist homeland." A committee member suggested that a third strategic task be identified, namely, the development of a "close alliance" with Laos and Cambodia and a "strategic alliance" with the Soviet Union, in order to confront the Sino-US alliance.[39] In response, the Politburo agreed that the development of such alliances was indeed a task of "life-and-death importance" for the Vietnamese revolution. Yet, if the task was identified so prominently in the report, the Politburo feared that it would be subject to possible distortions by Vietnam's enemy once the report was made public. It was not explained specifically how the enemy could distort that point. The Politburo was perhaps concerned that the phrasing could make it appear as if Vietnam wanted to dominate Laos and Cambodia, thus playing into Beijing's propaganda. For this reason, the phrasing in the draft report was to be kept intact, but the Politburo agreed to elaborate more on the details of Vietnam's strategic relationships elsewhere in the revised report. The Politburo also pledged to do more to educate the Vietnamese people on the values of proletarian internationalism.

Ideological resistance to reforms within the Party leadership weakened after Le Duan's death in July 1986. Elected as the interim General Secretary until the Sixth Party Congress scheduled for December of the same year, Truong Chinh quickly adjusted Vietnam's foreign and domestic policy to his preferences. In an important speech in late 1986 at a conference where leaders of the People's Army gathered to select representatives to attend the Party Congress, Chinh declared that Vietnam fully supported

[38] Ibid., 112, 117.
[39] Ibid., 114–115.

Gorbachev's speech three months earlier at Vladivostok.[40] While affirming Soviet-Vietnamese ties, he also made an emphatic offer for talks with China to normalize relations. Chinh was not lenient toward the United States, however:

> We are ready to resume negotiation with China anywhere anytime and at any level to find a solution [to our conflict] acceptable to both sides. With our good will, we wait for China to respond positively to our proposal.
>
> At the same time, [we] need to be aware that imperialist America and [other] international reactionaries still want to weaken us so that they could invade our country. Therefore, we need to raise our vigilance ...

Chinh's role in shaping Vietnam's domestic and foreign policy emerged more clearly at the Eleventh Central Committee Plenum a month later. This Plenum reviewed a new draft political report written under Chinh's supervision after Duan's death. The concluding statement of the Plenum read:

> Through discussion in small groups, all our Central Committee members agreed that this new draft of the political report was much improved in both contents and form compared with the previous one. The new draft reflects many suggestions from local party congresses, cadre conferences, and other cadres and people outside the Party, while including the Politburo's new findings on the economy and [our] new views on defense and foreign policy in the new situation ... Central Committee members also were happy that the new draft was highly regarded by Soviet leaders.[41]

Clearly Chinh had worked hard to mobilize his supporters in Vietnam and to sell the new draft to Gorbachev. The last sentence in the quote was not written to flatter Gorbachev. According to Duong Phu Hiep, a professor and advisor to Truong Chinh, resistance to market reform was still strong within the Party leadership in late 1986 at the time of the Eleventh Plenum.[42] Tran Quynh, who we have met and who was now deputy prime minister, had come back from an earlier COMECON meeting in Hungary and quoted the Soviet Premier as saying that the Soviet Union would not approve market reform in Vietnam. Tran Quynh's

---

[40] "Bai noi cua dong chi Truong Chinh" [Comrade Truong Chinh's speech], October 13, 1986. *VKDTT*, v. 47, 262–263. See also his speech at the meetings of Communist Party leaders of the COMECON countries, where he criticized the United States for failing to agree with the Soviet proposal at Reykjavik, and where he supported Gorbachev's initiative to improve relations with China. *VKDTT*, v. 47, 297–301.

[41] "Ket luan cua Bo Chinh tri va Doan Chu tich" [Concluding statement of the Politburo and the Plenum Presidium], November 19, 1986. *VKDTT*, v. 47, 308.

[42] Huy Duc, *Ben Thang Cuoc*, v. 1, 357–358.

words reportedly "frightened" supporters of reform within the leadership. When Truong Chinh learned about that from his advisors, he asked if Quynh had any documented evidence of what the Soviet Premier said. Quynh did not. Chinh then released a memorandum signed by him and Gorbachev at their meeting in Moscow showing that the Soviet leader approved Vietnam's reform. The memorandum calmed the fears of those who supported reform, according to Hiep.

Under Chinh's guidance, the new draft of the political report was more forthcoming in admitting the mistakes in economic policy since 1975.[43] Mistakes occurred in both strategic direction and implementation (but not in the overall, long-term goal of socialist development). The draft report conveyed a more favorable view of the private sector, emphasizing that sector's role in creating jobs and producing goods despite its "exploitative" nature. That new view stemmed from a different concept of economic governance. The draft report stated that it would be easier for the government to control and supervise private businesses if their existence was legally acknowledged. It would be more difficult if they existed illegally. The private sector from now on was to be tolerated rather than eliminated.

On foreign policy, the draft report revealed Hanoi leaders' thinking even though the published document has been edited to leave out one important section on their views of the world situation. As the report indicated, Vietnamese attitude was now much more accommodating to China: "We propose flexible tactics toward China, making our best efforts to solve problems in our bilateral relations. The struggle will be difficult and complicated. We have no illusions about this, but promise to do our best."[44]

A similar flexibility was shown in the way the draft report elaborated on Vietnam's relations with each foreign country, especially important ones. During discussion at the Plenum, a suggestion was made that the report's section on Vietnam's foreign relations should mention only the general principles of Vietnam's foreign policy without going into its relations with any particular countries. In reply, the Politburo defended its country-oriented approach by saying that mentioning Vietnam's specific attitude toward each country was important; if later the attitude of a certain country toward Vietnam changed, Vietnam would adjust its attitude accordingly.[45]

---

[43] Ibid., 311–312, 317–318.
[44] Ibid., 314.
[45] Ibid., 322.

Greater flexibility did not mean less importance attached to the Soviet Union. The Politburo stated that it totally agreed with the suggestion by many at the Plenum that Vietnam must rely fully [*dua han vao*] on the Soviet Union and other brothers in the socialist community.[46] Given what transpired at the COMECON meeting in Moscow that Truong Chinh had just attended, the Politburo now believed that Vietnam's reliance on the Soviet Union must be emphasized more and described in greater details in the political report.

Interestingly, not all Central Committee members present at the Plenum trusted the Politburo's pledge to foster closer relations with Moscow. A member commented that a careful review of actual policies would be needed to see whether Vietnam really relied on the Soviet Union, or whether that pledge was mere talk to express an ideological or moral belief [*noi theo dao ly*]. The Politburo responded that full reliance on the Soviet Union and on the socialist community had always been the Party's strategic principle throughout. "This [has been shown by] actual deeds, not simply words to express an ideological belief," it was declared.[47] The Politburo admitted that some economic contracts with the Soviet Union were not correctly implemented, but promised that the mistakes would be fixed.

This frank exchange at a key meeting of top Vietnamese leaders is instructive on two levels. It indicated important changes under Truong Chinh's leadership that aimed for a more trustful relationship with Vietnam's socialist brothers. More broadly, it indicated the cynicism some leaders felt about ideological talks. It was not that those cynics no longer believed in the ideology or in the Soviet Union; they still did. Their cynicism perhaps had to do with Le Duan who had often criticized Moscow in internal meetings while praising it in public.

The political report read by Truong Chinh a month later at the Sixth Party Congress presented a more realistic approach to socialist building.[48] State investment in heavy industries was reduced and diverted to agriculture to promote growth in that sector. It was declared that economic management from now on was to rely on economic incentives instead of administrative fiat. Private enterprises were to be tolerated for an indefinite time. On international relations, the report demonstrated Vietnam's

[46] Ibid., 322.
[47] Ibid., 322.
[48] Bao cao Chinh tri cua Ban Chap hanh Trung uong tai Dai hoi Dai bieu toan quoc lan thu VI cua Dang" [Political Report of the Central Committee at the Fourth Party Congress], December 15, 1986. *VKDTT*, v. 47, 345.

greater flexibility within the framework of the two-camp struggle. It declared that relationship with the Soviet Union was still the "big rock" [*hon da tang*] on which Vietnam's foreign policy rested.[49] It praised the new CPSU Program and Gorbachev's initiatives for peace, including his proposal to improve Soviet relations with China and his announcement of Soviet troop withdrawals from Afghanistan. In a lengthy paragraph, the report made the strongest appeal to date to China for resuming talks, calling on their past comradeship against imperialism and their shared interests in peace, national independence, and economic development.[50]

The report made a subtle change in policy toward Washington. It attacked the US head-on in a long paragraph, calling American foreign policy "state terrorism." It blamed the tension in Asia on American efforts to establish military alliances similar to NATO, and demanded Washington to negotiate more seriously with Moscow for nuclear disarmament. There was a single short sentence several pages later, hidden in a paragraph about Vietnam's interests in expanding relations with Sweden, Japan, and others, about Vietnam's readiness to discuss with Washington the humanitarian issues left over since the war and to improve bilateral relations "for the sake of peace and stability in Southeast Asia."[51] It was as if the sentence had been sneaked into the document at the last minute to dodge the opposition from ideologues in the leadership. Still, it is clear from the report that Vietnam's loyalty lay with the Soviet bloc even though Hanoi would be more flexible toward Washington. The contrast in Vietnamese attitude toward China and the United States suggested that Beijing was not regarded in the same category as Washington, although both were hostile to Vietnam, and China was still at war with Vietnam.

RISE OF NEW REALIST AND LIBERAL WORLDVIEWS

The Sixth Party Congress in December 1986 called for "new thinking" [*doi moi tu duy*] not only in economic matters but also in the fundamental approach to developing socialism. The sign of change was clearly showed in the retirement of three most senior Party leaders, Truong Chinh, Pham Van Dong, and Le Duc Tho, and the election of Nguyen Van Linh to the position of general secretary. Born Nguyen Van Cuc in 1915, Linh joined a student group organized by Thanh Nien at 14 and was sent to

---

[49] Ibid., 434, 440.
[50] Ibid., 441.
[51] Ibid., 439, 442–443.

Poulo Condore at 15 for distributing anti-government fliers.[52] Linh spent two separate terms of 10 years total in colonial prison. After the Geneva Agreements, Linh stayed behind in the South as a top Party leader of the insurgency against the Saigon government. At the time of his promotion in 1986, Linh was serving as the Party Chief of Ho Chi Minh City and known as a proreform leader.

The leadership's endorsement of Soviet perestroika enabled the introduction of Gorbachev's "new thinking" on foreign affairs into Vietnam together with his ideas for economic reform. This new thinking drew many elements from realist and liberal worldviews. Right after the Congress, articles and analyses with a proreform bent began to appear with increasing frequency in *Tap chi Cong san* [Review of Communism], the Party's theoretical journal. These views appeared in many forms: individually authored articles, translated writings from other socialist countries, and roundtables on critical themes such as "thinking and the new thinking," "subcontracts in cooperatives," "the concept of exploitation," and "what is socialism?" Among foreign voices in the journal, Soviet and Polish authors were uniformly proreform, whereas those from East Germany and Cuba indicated reluctance and skepticism.

Among domestic authors, there was a similar mixture of views although antireform opinions appeared to be in the minority. Domestic reform and foreign policy were the two most important areas under discussion. In an article on "the human factor in economic development," for example, a professor named Dang Thu used United Nations data to show that economic growth in the socialist bloc had been slower than in capitalist countries, whereas national income in the former was only half the size of the latter.[53] One table in the article showed South Korea, Thailand, Indonesia, and India, long either dismissed as "American lackeys" or relegated to the ambiguous "nationalist" category in the official view, to have made more advances in human development than socialist Cuba and Vietnam. Another table ranked Vietnam 161 out of 164 nations in terms of per capita income in 1983. Still another table showed social inequality in the richest capitalist countries such as England and

[52] Linh's official biography is available at www.cpv.org.vn/cpv/Modules/News/NewsDetail .aspx?co_id=o&cn_id=37039.

[53] Dang Thu, "Ve nhan to con nguoi trong phat trien kinh te cua dat nuoc" [On the human factor in the economic development of our country], *Tap chi Cong san.* 2: 1987 (February 1987) 29–34. See also Tran Do, "Con nguoi la von quy nhat" [Men are the most precious asset], *Tap chi Cong san,* 2: 1987 (February 1987), 35–38. Tran Do was a general and Central Committee member.

Sweden to be lower than in developing capitalist ones such as South Korea and India. The table implicitly raised a question about the association of inequality with capitalism. The author then called for greater incentives for people to work through wages that fairly reflected work efforts without too much concern about inequality. He argued that labor productivity, world population, and total world production had so massively increased since the publication of Marx and Engels' *Manifesto of the Communist Party* that classical Marxism-Leninism must be updated and further developed to remain relevant. In his view, socialist countries could grow faster if they avoided dogmatism, as the Soviet Union was attempting to do.

Along the same line, a roundtable of professors of Marxist-Leninist philosophy was organized to debate the new thinking. A major point made by contributors to this roundtable was that Marxism-Leninism had been incorrectly applied in Vietnam. Ho Van Thong, for example, argued that Marxist-Leninist theory must be treated as an ideal built on logical and objective analysis, not as a religion or a set of morals to be blindly complied with.[54] Socialism must come from people and serve people, rather than be implemented as a set of principles to restrict people and their creative potential. Socialism was not simply to eliminate exploitation by men but must above all gear toward the expansion of productive forces. Le Thi agreed with Thong, calling for the application of dialectic materialism as a method of thinking, not as dogma.[55] He chastised his colleagues for parroting the classics, worshipping foreign models, and overall lacking independent and critical thinking. To develop the new thinking, Nguyen Ngoc Long called for democratization in social life, in scientific and philosophical research, and in the quest for truths and the defense of truths.[56] Not all contributors at the roundtable were as enthusiastic about change as those just noted. Dang Xuan Ky, the son of Truong Chinh and the deputy director of the Institute of Marxism-Leninism, admitted that new thinking was needed, but insisted that the process of reform must not mean the search for completely new thinking.[57] Rather,

[54] Ho Van Thong, "Mot so van de ve tu duy va doi moi tu duy hien nay o nuoc ta" [On thinking and new thinking in our country], *Tap chi Cong san* 10: 1987 (October 1987), 32–36.
[55] Le Thi, "Nhung huong tu duy moi" [New directions of thinking], *Tap chi Cong san* 10: 1987 (October 1987), 36–39.
[56] Nguyen Ngoc Long, "Nang luc tu duy ly luan trong qua trinh doi moi tu duy" [Thinking capacity in adopting the new thinking], *Tap chi Cong san* 10:1987 (October 1987), 51.
[57] Dang Xuan Ky, "Vai tro cua doi moi tu duy" [The role of new thinking], *Tap chi Cong san* 12: 1987 (December 1987), 33–35.

correct elements of existing thinking must be preserved. The mistakes made in the past came not from Marxism-Leninism itself, but from the Party straying from it.

The same tension between those who welcomed new thinking and those who were more cautious was observed among Party leaders. At the seventieth anniversary of the Russian Revolution in November 1987, Nguyen Van Linh who had succeeded Truong Chinh as general secretary at the Sixth Party Congress spoke at length about how Gorbachev continued the creative legacy of the revolution with his call for new thinking. Echoing the Soviet leader, Linh called perestroika "a thorough revolution in all fields," and Soviet new thinking a "watershed event":

The new thinking is fully demonstrated in the reassessment and critical analysis of the domestic situation. That analysis is correct and supported by evidence. It contains no distortions, no cover-ups, no exaggerations – everything is transparent ... The new [thinking] gives primacy to people. The all-around and harmonious development of people is made the most important goal ... Encouraged by the CPSU's Twenty-seventh Party Congress and perestroika, Vietnam's Sixth Party Congress has raised the spirit of reform and employed the critical spirit of Marxist philosophy to look squarely at the truth, assess the truth, and speak the truth ...[58]

On the same occasion, Nguyen Duc Binh, a Central Committee member and director of the Advanced Party School for ideological training, was more reserved in his comments.[59] Binh discussed perestroika briefly and focused mainly on the historical achievements of socialism since 1917. His main point about perestroika was that it did not imply any inferiority but rather the superiority of socialism – namely, its ability to reform itself. To Binh, finding solutions within the boundaries of socialism was more important than identifying past mistakes. The country must overcome the problems not by deviating from socialism but by bringing more socialism to the people.

As debates about Marxist-Leninist principles and the missions of socialism continued, elements of realist and liberal worldviews emerged. Here the marks of perestroika and Soviet new thinking in foreign relations were even more noticeable. In his speech at Vladivostok in 1986,

---

[58] Nguyen Van Linh, "Cach mang thang Muoi va cach mang Viet nam" [The October Revolution and the Vietnamese revolution], *Tap chi Cong san* 11: 1987 (November 1987), 3–10.

[59] Nguyen Duc Binh, "Dang cua V.I. Lenin – dang cua nhung cong cuoc doi moi xa hoi vi dai nhat" [Lenin's Party: the party of the greatest social reform], *Tap chi Cong san* 10: 1987 (November 1987), 30–33.

Gorbachev promoted the concept of collective security for the entire Asia-Pacific region modeled after that in Europe.[60] Recall that, in the two-camp worldview, socialist and capitalist countries had fundamentally opposing interests and could not coexist peacefully in the long term. In that worldview, the concept of a geographical area with socialist and capitalist countries sharing collective interest in security would make no sense. Vietnamese leaders and analysts had in fact rejected the concept of an Asia-Pacific community when it was proposed by Washington and Tokyo in the early 1980s, but now accepted it. They still blamed imperialism for past conflicts between Indochinese and ASEAN countries but welcomed peaceful coexistence and cooperation as the new principles governing relationship between the two groupings.[61]

In his speech at the anniversary of the Russian Revolution in 1987 cited earlier, Nguyen Van Linh declared Vietnam's full support for Gorbachev's proposal to make Pacific Asia a peaceful region.[62] Linh called on the mobilization of a worldwide movement to struggle for a comprehensive agreement that included denuclearization, political solutions to armed conflicts, national self-determination, and good neighborly relations. Linh's vision was more limited than Gorbachev's, being preoccupied with solutions to current conflicts rather than with potentials for regional cooperation. In addition, Linh expressed a strong desire to solve the conflicts with Cambodia and China, but made clear that Hanoi wanted no negotiation with the Khmer Rouge.[63]

Phan Doan Nam, a senior Foreign Ministry official, made the most radical effort to explore new concepts. Nam specifically criticized the "two camps/four antagonisms" as "readymade formulas" that Vietnamese foreign policy had often been forced to comply with.[64] He argued that Marxism-Leninism should be treated not as a bible but as a compass for

---

[60] See Mikhail Gorbachev, *Perestroika: New Thinking for our Country and the World* (New York: Harper & Row, 1987), 180–183.

[61] Hoang Hien, "Cung ton tai hoa binh giua hai nhom nuoc ASEAN va Dong Duong" [Peaceful coexistence between the ASEAN and Indochinese groups of nations], *Tap chi Cong san* 3: 1987 (March 1987), 94–98; Kieu Nguyen, "Chau A-Thai binh duong: an ninh va hop tac" [The Asia-Pacific region: Security and cooperation], *Tap chi Cong san* 8: 1987 (August 1987), 75–79.

[62] Nguyen Van Linh, "Cach mang thang Muoi va cach mang Viet nam."

[63] See also Nguyen Co Thach, "Hon da tang trong chinh sach doi ngoai cua Viet nam" [The bedrock of Vietnam's foreign policy], *Tap chi Cong san* 11: 1987 (November 1987), 25–29. Thach was a Politburo member and foreign minister. There was little substantive difference between Thach's and Linh's speeches.

[64] Phan Doan Nam, "Mot vai suy nghi ve doi moi tu duy doi ngoai" [Some thoughts on new thinking in foreign policy], *Tap chi Cong san* 2: 1988 (February 1988), 50–54.

action: "If Lenin were alive today, he would think that war among impe-rialist powers is not inevitable given the presence of the socialist bloc, the interdependence among capitalist economies, and the availability of nuclear weapons." Nam did not deny the existence of conflicts among countries, but emphasized the "internationalization of contemporary world culture, economy, and politics" due to the deepening international division of labor, sophisticated economic cooperation between countries, and growing international exchanges. Those trends created a more uni-fied, interdependent world even while countries retained their indepen-dence and nations their identities.

Echoing Khrushchev without mentioning him, Nam contended that the availability of nuclear weapons and the balance of force between the United States and the Soviet Union had made peaceful competition and negotiation, rather than war, the preferred solution to the fundamental conflict between the two blocs. Because the priority of the contemporary global class struggle was world peace, it would be wrong for any nation to define its enemies without considering other nations' interest in peace. In the same vein, when countries had become interdependent for their existence, it would be nearsighted for any country to define its enemies based on the class character of the governments. Peaceful coexistence among countries would not impede class struggle within each country.

Nam's concepts of interdependence and internationalization suggested elements of realist and liberal thinking. Significantly, contrary opinions to the new thinking were voiced much less often. Two notable articles were authored by, respectively, General Le Duc Anh, the defense minis-ter, and General Mai Chi Tho, minister of public security.[65] Both called for increasing vigilance against unnamed enemies. Anh's article was pub-lished in April 1988, right after a clash in the South China Sea between Chinese and Vietnamese navies led to Vietnam's loss of seventy-nine sail-ors and several islands in the Spratlys. His article appeared to address the Chinese threat, although he did not name China or mention that particular naval battle.

The unrestricted and generally proreform discussions on the pages of the most important Party journal indicated significant enthusiasm about

---

[65] Le Duc Anh, "Nang cao canh giac, cung co quoc phong va an ninh dat nuoc" [Raising vigilance and strengthening defense and security for our country], *Tap chi Cong san* 4: 1988 (April 1988), 5–10; Mai Chi Tho, "May van de cap bach ve cong tac bao ve an ninh, trat tu va xay dung luc luong cong an nhan dan" [Some urgent issues regarding security, public order, and building people's police forces], *Tap chi Cong san.* 12: 1988 (December 1988), 13–19.

Gorbachev's ideas and policies. They revealed the ability and desire of many Vietnamese intellectuals to engage and embrace reformist ideas elsewhere in the socialist bloc. The profound crisis in Vietnam, the split between reformers and ideologues within the Party leadership, and the fast-paced changes emanating from the Soviet Union opened up a liberal moment for new worldviews to appear and mix with existing beliefs in the two-camp, four-antagonism doctrine. A careful examination of the profiles of authors who held proreform views shows that they were, with the exception of General Secretary Nguyen Van Linh and Foreign Minister Nguyen Co Thach, of lower ranks than the ideologues. Dang Xuan Ky and Nguyen Duc Binh held the minority perspective among commentators in the journal but they both occupied leadership positions in the powerful Party propaganda machine. There were also quite a few fence-sitters who added only opaque comments to the discussion.[66]

As will be seen in the next section, loyalists to orthodox Marxism-Leninism in Vietnam were not convinced by Gorbachev that perestroika was in the interest of global communism. Alternatively, they tolerated his ideas as long as those did not threaten their regime and the world communist movement. The dramatic events in 1989, including the student protests at Tiananmen Square and the crumbling of communism in Eastern Europe, led to Hanoi's rejection of the emerging liberal worldview as seen in the article by Phan Doan Nam. Rather than being abandoned, the two-camp worldview would become further entrenched and dominate Vietnamese politics for another two decades.

THE RED SOLUTION AND HANOI'S FUTILE EFFORTS TO SAVE WORLD SOCIALISM

The domestic economic crisis pushed Hanoi to embrace market reform, which was accepted in no small part thanks to the enactment of similar policies in the Soviet Union. Ideological debates on reform were vigorous, resistance to reform was significant, and reformers would not have won the debates without literally Gorbachev's signature of approval. Gorbachev also helped elements of liberal and realist worldviews to emerge in Vietnam to briefly challenge the reigning two-camp doctrine.

[66] Examples are Nguyen Duy Quy, "Nang cao tri thuc khoa hoc – dieu kien quan trong de doi moi tu duy" [Elevating scientific knowledge: an important condition for new thinking], *Tap chi Cong san* 12: 1987 (December 1987), 35–38; Nguyen Phu Trong, "Cong tac xay dung Dang trong dieu kien cai o Lien Xo" [The task of Party building under reform in the Soviet Union], *Tap chi Cong san.* 12: 1988 (December 1988), 69–74.

Vietnam's foreign policy in the mid- to late 1980s was aimed to improve relations with a new Soviet leadership and to break out of international isolation.[67] Truong Chinh supported Soviet initiatives for peace and vowed to use Soviet aid more efficiently. To reduce international isolation, Vietnamese leaders issued a Foreign Investment Law and promised in 1987 to withdraw troops from Cambodia by the end of 1989 as demanded by the United States, China, and their ASEAN allies. Furthermore, Hanoi expressed a willingness to reach a political solution to the Cambodian issue. It also cooperated with the United States on finding American personnel missing in action during the war, and released thousands of South Vietnamese government officials who had been imprisoned in hard-labor camps for more than a decade since the reunification of the country.

By early 1989, however, an ideological backlash began to gather momentum in Hanoi due to rising demands among intellectuals, writers, and veterans for greater freedom, accountability, and even multiparty democracy.[68] At the Sixth Central Committee Plenum in March, a topic of discussion was political pluralism: to what extent would the Party tolerate it?[69] The majority opinion at the Plenum was that political pluralism and opposition parties should not be allowed in Vietnam. As Nguyen Van Linh spoke on the issue of foreign relations in his concluding speech:

We are striving for peace, but that's not the reason for relaxing our vigilance. [We are not] giving up our struggle and our revolution. It is incorrect to see only struggle and miss the opportunities for dialogues. Conversely, it is incorrect to see only détente, "convergence," [and] "living under the same roof" between capitalism and socialism. Our policy is to coexist and struggle between countries having different sociopolitical regimes. Although its form and tactics have changed, the nature of imperialism has not changed. We should continue to support the worker movement in capitalist countries and the movements to achieve democracy, progress, and national independence in all countries.[70]

The Solidarity movement's electoral victory in Poland and the Tiananmen protest in China panicked Vietnamese leaders who gathered

---

[67] "Bao cao tai Hoi nghi lan thu sau Ban Chap hanh Trung uong Dang (Khoa VI)" [Report at the Sixth Central Committee Plenum (term of Sixth Party Congress)]. *VKDTT*, v. 49, 524–528.

[68] Zachary Abuza, *Renovating Politics in Contemporary Vietnam* (Boulder, CO: Lynne Rienner Publishers, 2001).

[69] Huy Duc, *Ben Thang Cuoc*, v. 2, 70.

[70] "Bao cao tai Hoi nghi lan thu sau Ban Chap hanh Trung uong Dang (Khoa VI)." *VKDTT*, v. 49, 655–656.

for the Seventh Plenum in August 1989. A main item on the agenda of the Plenum was to discuss and approve a resolution on ideology. In his opening speech, Nguyen Van Linh spoke about the "hairy hands of those reactionaries" in the unrest in Poland, Hungary, China, and the Soviet Union, and in the surge of "incorrect ideas about democracy and freedom in Vietnam."[71] The Plenum reaffirmed the Party's adherence to Marxism-Leninism and its rejection of political pluralism. The leadership agreed that reform in the Soviet Union had deviated from socialism, but divided over whether Soviet leadership had committed "right-leaning errors," or more seriously, "revisionist" ones.[72] Vietnamese leaders were particularly vitriolic in reaction to President George H. W. Bush's speech at the US Coast Guard Commencement Ceremony in Connecticut on May 24, 1989, in which Bush triumphantly declared that the end of socialism was near.[73] Citing Bush with profound bitterness, Linh responded that the end of socialism was "the 'daydream' of the representatives of those hardcore anticommunists, who would not live under the same sky with us" [*khong doi troi chung*].

Dissent within the leadership was still expressed openly until early 1990. On domestic reform, Politburo member Tran Xuan Bach, a former rival of Nguyen Van Linh for the general secretary position, continued to speak of the need for political reform to accompany market reform.[74] Bach remained loyal to socialism but he believed that Gorbachev was correct to have pursued both political and economic reforms.[75] On foreign relations, Politburo member and Foreign Minister Nguyen Co Thach continued to argue along the line of new realist and liberal concepts first proposed by his subordinate Phan Doan Nam, projecting the image of an interdependent world characterized by international cooperation for

[71] "Bai phat bieu cua dong chi Nguyen Van Linh khai mac Hoi nghi lan thu bay Ban Chap hanh Trung uong Dang (Khoa VI)" [Opening statement by comrade Nguyen Van Linh at the seventh Central Committee Plenum (term of Sixth Party Congress)]. *VKDTT*, v. 49, 714–715.

[72] "Mot so van de trong du thao Nghi quyet Hoi nghi Trung uong 7 de nghi Ban Chap hanh Trung uong Dang bieu quyet vao chieu 24-8-1989" [Some issues in the draft Resolution of the seventh Plenum for the Central Committee to vote on in the afternoon of August 24, 1989]. *VKDTT*, v. 49, 717, 724–725.

[73] "Phat bieu cua dong chi Nguyen Van Linh be mac Hoi nghi 7 cua BCHTUD" [Closing address by General Secretary Nguyen Van Linh at the Seventh Central Committee Plenum], *Tap chi Cong san* 9: 1989 (September 1989), 5. For Bush's speech, see http://bushlibrary.tamu.edu/research/public_papers.php?id=448&year=1989&month=5

[74] Huy Duc, *Ben Thang Cuoc*, v. 2, 77, footnote 131.

[75] Ibid. See also Tran Xuan Bach, "Mot doi dieu suy nghi tren duong doi moi" [A few ideas on the road of reform], *Tap chi Cong san* 1: 1990 (January 1990), 46–51.

peace and development.[76] In an apparent effort to reach out to ideologues in the Party, Thach credited "socialist internationalism" for Vietnam's victory in previous wars, but argued that socialist internationalism now meant Vietnam should support peace and development because that was the desire of people in the world.[77]

Events from late 1989 to late 1990 culminated in the triumph of Marxist-Leninist ideologues in Vietnamese politics. These events also implied Vietnamese leaders' deep loyalty to world revolution and to the socialist camp. In October 1989, Nguyen Van Linh traveled to Berlin, ostensibly to attend the fortieth anniversary of the birth of the German Democratic Republic (East Germany) but, in fact, to propose to communist leaders gathering there that a conference of communist parties and working-class parties worldwide be convened to save socialism.[78] In Berlin, according to his assistant Le Dang Doanh, Linh's proposal for such a meeting was ignored by most delegations except the East German, Romanian, Polish, Mongolian, Cuban, and West German communist leaders. Nicolae Ceauşescu, the Romanian leader, enthusiastically supported Linh's idea, but he and all the others deferred to Gorbachev. Arrangements were finally made for Linh to meet Gorbachev who politely but swiftly shrugged at Linh's suggestion for a conference of communist parties worldwide and at his request for more aid for Vietnam's next Five-Year plan. A week before Linh left for home, Erich Honecker, the East German leader, resigned and was replaced by Egon Krenz. A month after Linh had returned home, communist regimes fell in East Germany, Romania, and Czechoslovakia.

Despite the collapse of Eastern European communism, Linh and the Politburo did not give up the idea of saving world socialism. They now turned to China. Since 1987, after Le Duan's death, Vietnamese leaders had begun to modify their view on China. They did not deny that China was a big power with expansionist ambitions, but at the same time appreciated more the fact that China had a socialist regime.[79] This was a sign of the reascendance of the communist worldview in their thinking toward China. By late 1989, the idea that Vietnam should join forces with China to defend socialism against the US-led imperialist camp began to gain

[76] Nguyen Co Thach, "Tat ca vi hoa binh, doc lap dan toc va phat trien" [All for peace, national independence and development], *Tap chi Cong san* 8: 1989 (August 1989), 1–8.

[77] Ibid., 4–5. Note that Thach avoided the term "proletarian internationalism," which was a more common term.

[78] Huy Duc, *Ben Thang Cuoc*, v. 2, 63–67.

[79] Tran Quang Co, "Hoi uc va suy nghi," 16–17.

currency in the Party leadership.[80] In this context, the Cambodian conflict, a primary cause of the Sino-Vietnamese war, became less important to Hanoi. Vietnamese leaders picked up an earlier proposal first made by Gorbachev in 1987 that the Hanoi-backed Phnom Penh government and the Beijing-sponsored Khmer Rouge sit down and negotiate peace between them. Because both groups were communist, this proposal earned the nickname "the Red Solution." Yet this proposal was rejected by both groups in 1987. When Hanoi returned to it in April 1990, the underlying reasoning was that "Vietnam and China were both socialist states facing the imperialist conspiracy to overthrow socialism. The two countries must join forces against imperialism. Improving Sino-Vietnamese relations is the priority now; other issues (such as Cambodia) can wait."[81]

Despite China's lukewarm reaction to the idea of defending world socialism, Vietnamese leaders continued to sell their idea to Beijing against the advice of their Foreign Ministry staff. In early 1990, Nguyen Van Linh offered to travel to China to meet with its leaders any time at their convenience.[82] Sensing an opportunity to get Hanoi to make concessions on Cambodia, Chinese leaders invited Pham Van Dong, Nguyen Van Linh, and other Vietnamese leaders to meet secretly in Chengdu in September 1990. There the Chinese leadership achieved important concessions from Vietnam on Cambodia while declining to form an alliance with Vietnam to save socialism.[83]

Tran Xuan Bach was stripped of his position at the Eighth Central Committee Plenum in March 1990, where the Party called on all members to "remain loyal to Marxism-Leninism and the socialist path that Uncle Ho, the Party, and the people had wisely opted for."[84] Nguyen Co Thach was not included in the delegation to Chengdu and would soon retire at the Seventh Party Congress in 1991. Vietnam normalized relations with China later in the same year.

CONCLUSION

As Vietnamese leaders faced grave crises at home and abroad in the 1980s, it took them many years to abandon their hopes in the Stalinist

---

[80] Ibid., 32.
[81] Ibid., 35.
[82] Ibid., 39.
[83] Ibid., 53–58.
[84] "Nghi quyet Hoi nghi lan thu tam Ban Chap hanh Trung uong Dang (khoa VI)" [Resolution of the Eighth Central Committee Plenum (term of the Sixth Party Congress)], March 27, 1990. *VKDTT*, v. 50, 73.

model of socialism. Some of them were pragmatic enough to embrace market reform, but few of them ever wanted to abandon socialism. Like Gorbachev whom they looked up to for support, they pursued market reform to have more, not less, socialism. Gorbachev's ideas of glasnost and perestroika were welcome in Vietnam in part because they came from the Soviet Union, which was leader of the socialist camp and Vietnam's patron. Those ideas were popular among some circles because they seemed to address similar problems facing Vietnam's bankrupt economy. Resistance to them was by no means insignificant. In fact, Vietnam did not fully abandon central planning and dissolve rural cooperatives until after the deaths of Le Duan and several leaders of his cohort such as Truong Chinh, Le Duc Tho, and Pham Hung.

Open, lively, and unprecedented debates introduced many new concepts and ideas from Gorbachev that reflected liberal and realist worldviews. The new thinking certainly influenced shifts in Hanoi's policy to normalize relations with China, the United States, and ASEAN countries. Yet this trend came to an abrupt end in the summer and fall of 1989, when Vietnamese leaders watched in panic how close Chinese students at Tiananmen Square came to bringing down communism in China, and how communism actually crumbled in Eastern Europe. These dramatic events galvanized ideologues who reinstated the dominance of the two-camp worldview. The liberal environment in Hanoi was soon shut down, although market reform, which had shown some positive results, was allowed to continue.

The choice made by Hanoi leaders at this point is puzzling from a strategic perspective. Top Vietnamese leaders like Nguyen Van Linh were popular and not tainted by the old socialism. There was support within the leadership and in society at large for political liberalization. If their minds had not been locked within the two-camp worldview, they would have realized the irreversible bankruptcy of socialism as a twentieth-century world movement. Their repeated efforts to save the socialist bloc were the clearest evidence of commitment to the Marxist-Leninist ideology at the very time when it was abandoned in its own homeland and in most of the world. That commitment motivated their rush to make concessions to China at the expense of Vietnam's strategic security interests in Cambodia for which more than 50,000 Vietnamese soldiers had sacrificed their lives over a decade.

As with the 1970s, ideology explained in part Vietnam's growing dependency on the Soviet Union and the decision to restore comradely relations with China. However, ideological belief continued to be a burden for the Vietnamese revolution in this decade. Hanoi leaders' dogmatic belief in the Stalinist model created a severe and prolonged economic crisis. The collapse of the Soviet bloc offered Vietnam an escape from Cold War entanglements, but Hanoi failed to take that route. In retrospect, the breakup of the Soviet Union, the deaths of the first generation of Vietnamese leaders, and the implementation of market reform in Vietnam effectively meant the end of the Vietnamese revolution. In response to the collapse of world communism, the hardliners in Hanoi led by Nguyen Van Linh blocked political reform and suppressed popular demands for political liberalization. Yet their policy was a rearguard move to defend the regime, not an act to sustain the revolution, their denials otherwise.

This revolution came to an end, not by conscious choice nor marked by a big bang, but by the quiet abandonment of its goals and by the gradual disintegration of revolutionary values and institutions. As the quasi-capitalist economy took hold, many children of revolutionaries have morphed into corrupt bureaucrats and red capitalists who grab lands from farmers, sell national resources to foreign investors, and pocket the profits. Nevertheless, the legacies of ideology remain significant, as will be seen in the Chapter 9.

9

Legacies of Ideology, 1991–2010

The Vietnamese Communist Party turned sixty in 1990. The young and daring men and women who were its first members were now in their seventies and eighties. Four of the most senior Party leaders died in the late 1980s (Le Duan, Le Duc Tho, Truong Chinh, and Pham Hung). Nguyen Van Linh, the incumbent General Secretary, was seventy-five. The oldest member of the Politburo (Vo Chi Cong) was seventy-nine, and its youngest (Dao Duy Tung) was sixty-seven. The revolution may have prevailed against the cruel French, the odious Americans, the chauvinist Chinese, and the traitorous Khmer Rouge, but now was slowly succumbing to the Grim Reaper.

Just three years earlier, the Party had issued a call for foreign direct investment. Next was the allocation of collectivized land to farming households who could now grow and sell their own crops freely after having paid a certain amount of taxes in kind or cash. In the cities, prices were gradually liberalized while rations were abolished. The government now tolerated private enterprises and private trade instead of persecuting them. However, just when the market economy was welcome back and Stalinist institutions were dismantled, political turmoil first threatened China and Eastern Europe, and then spread to the Soviet Union. When a group of Soviet leaders launched a coup to depose Gorbachev in August 1991, Hanoi quickly voiced support for it. Vietnamese leaders then watched helplessly as Russian President Boris Yeltsin turned the tide and engineered the implosion of the Soviet Union. By all indications the Vietnamese revolution effectively ended then, with the first generation of revolutionaries dying in droves, with the substitution of dysfunctional central planning and unpopular collective farms by a market economy, and with the stunning disintegration of the mighty Soviet camp. Nevertheless, the revolutionary ideology would take years to fade and is still influential in Vietnam today through complex mechanisms.

In a vastly different postrevolutionary world landscape, ideological concepts still guided the thinking of Vietnamese leaders throughout the 1990s, while elements of liberal or realist worldviews were tolerated (but not incorporated). By the early 2000s, Party documents and military writings in fact indicated a revival of the Marxist-Leninist worldview. Loyalists to this worldview were concerned about American interventions in southern Europe and the Middle East. They were encouraged by rising global criticism of and opposition to those American policies. Up to the mid-2000s the Vietnamese People's Army (PAVN) still considered the United States as Vietnam's strategic enemy despite the normalization of relations between the two countries in 1995 and the signing of a bilateral trade agreement in 2001.

Even though Marxism-Leninism no longer governs the daily management of the Vietnamese state, it retains its influences on the overall orientations of Vietnam's foreign relations through political culture and institutional and informal mechanisms. Ideological reflexes are creating a schizophrenic state in Vietnam as shown in its policy toward the United States and China. The rising of China as a regional hegemon and global power is confronting Hanoi leaders with an existential dilemma and deeply uncertain future.

"A FRIEND OF ALL NATIONS"?

After the Chengdu trip in 1990, Sino-Vietnamese relations were placed on the path to normalization even though Beijing turned down Hanoi's invitation to form an alliance to rescue world socialism. At the same time, Washington had partially relaxed its embargo on Vietnam when Hanoi cooperated on finding American GIs missing in action and on other issues. In June 1991, the Party held its Seventh Party Congress at which a new Program was approved. Nguyen Van Linh's Political Report read at the Congress called for continuing market reform while affirming the Party's unwavering loyalty to the socialist path.[1] Linh stepped down at the Congress and was replaced by Do Muoi, who was only two years

---

[1] "Tiep tuc dua su nghiep doi moi tien len theo con duong Xa hoi chu nghia" [Continue to advance the achievements of reform along the Socialist path]. *Tap Chi Cong San* 7 (1991), 16–17.

younger. Muoi was, according to his official biography, from a peasant household and had worked as a house painter before joining the revolution in 1940.[2] He is known as the Party's henchman for his role in the earlier campaigns to expropriate capitalist enterprises in North Vietnam in the 1950s and again in the South in the 1970s.

The collapse of the Soviet Union in late 1991 shook the new leadership team in Hanoi. An editorial on the Party journal reviewed the history of world and Vietnamese communism since Marx to show that setbacks and challenges had not been rare and had always been overcome.[3] The crucial thing, the editorial argued, was "to firmly keep our faith, [because] if we lose our property and even our honor, we can still earn them back. If we lose our faith, we'll lose everything."

According to the editorial, there were five reasons for maintaining the belief in socialism. First, socialism had emerged in human history following "objective laws" and could not be easily destroyed. Back in the 1920s, the Soviet Union had survived for decades as the only socialist country despite being "encircled by capitalism." The implication was that socialist Vietnam could survive standing alone even as the rest of the communist camp went capitalist. Second, Vietnam had rich natural resources and a large population still loyal to the Party. Third, the Party had realized its earlier mistakes and embarked on reforming the economy and building a more effective organization. Fourth, the government had been making progress toward improving governance and "democracy" while curbing corruption. Finally, Vietnam's foreign relations had expanded, resulting in growing exports and foreign investment.

Those "objective conditions" formed the basis for the editorial to predict that the coming years would be exciting ones for the Vietnamese revolution. Ironically, economic reform, improved governance, and growing foreign investment were anything but revolutionary. The emphasis of the editorial was in fact not on any particular policies but on faith in revolutionary ideals. This turn away from revolution was just as evident in the Party Program approved at the Seventh Party Congress. The Program did not trumpet the march to socialism but highlighted the need to first combat poverty and backwardness.[4] It was admitted that Vietnam had not

---

[2] Huy Duc, *Ben thang cuoc*, v. 2, 257–259.

[3] "Giu vung niem tin di con duong da chon" [Keeping faith in the path that we have chosen], *Tap chi Cong san* 10 (1991), 2–4.

[4] "Cuong linh xay dung dat nuoc trong thoi ky qua do len Chu nghia xa hoi" [Party Program to build the country during the transition period to socialism], *Tap chi Cong san* 7 (1991), 31–34.

yet recovered from the general socioeconomic crisis of the mid-1980s, despite encouraging initial results of market reform.

In public, Hanoi now pledged to be friends of all countries in the world. Vietnam's foreign relations expanded greatly in the early 1990s as a result.[5] Internally, Vietnamese leaders still evaluated foreign relations through an ideological lens. At the special midterm Party Congress in 1994, the Politburo offered the following remarks in response to comments from the Central Committee on its Draft Political Report to be read at the Congress:

In international relations, [our policy] "to be friends of all nations in the world community" is designed to take advantage of shared interests in concrete issues and concrete policy areas with other nations [in this] and other regions, within the framework of "collaborating while struggling."

For the sake of our mission to develop socialism and defend our fatherland, we place friends in different categories, with some closer and others far. By their nature, our long-term allies are the socialist forces (or countries), the communist and worker parties, and movements for national independence and revolutionary and progressive causes. We affirm solidarity and mutual support with those forces and movements through clever and adaptive [*linh hoat*] measures that are suitable to objective conditions and to our own and our friends' subjective capacity.[6]

It is clear from this high-level internal communication that the Politburo still took ideology seriously as a criterion to evaluate who were true friends. In the short term, interests might need to be attended to, but in the long term, ideology defined interests.

Ideological commitments were combined with practical interests in the way Party leaders perceived existential threats to Vietnam. Spelled out at the midterm Congress in 1994 was the formula of "four threats" [*bon nguy co*] to the regime. These included, in this order, economic backwardness, the loss of socialist orientations, corruption, and "peaceful

---

[5] Carlyle Thayer, "Upholding state sovereignty through global integration: Remaking Vietnamese National Security," paper presented at the Workshop, "Vietnam, East Asia, and Beyond," at the Southeast Asia Research Center, City University of Hong Kong, December 2008.

[6] "Y kien cua Bo Chinh tri so 154/TLHN ngay 30/11/1993 ve mot so van de cua Du thao Bao cao chinh tri qua thao luan cua Trung uong" [The Politburo's opinion no. 154/TLHN on November 30, 1993 about some issues in the Draft Political Report raised in the Central Committee discussion]. Photocopy of document is found in Nguyen Dinh Thuc, "Chu truong cua Dang Cong san Viet nam ve quan he doi ngoai voi ASEAN (1967–1995)" [The VCP's policy on Vietnam's relations with ASEAN], unpublished PhD dissertation, Hoc Vien Chinh Tri Quoc Gia [National Institute of Politics] (Ho Chi Minh City, 2001), Appendix 7, 264–265. Available at the Vietnam National Library, Hanoi, call number L7924.

evolution." Of the four, peaceful evolution had been considered a threat at least since the 1970s. Essentially, this term referred to a strategy of the imperialist camp to engineer revolt or regime change in the socialist countries by propaganda and by cultural, economic, and political tactics instead of by military means. As such, peaceful evolution was simply a variation of the two-camp doctrine, a continuation of the Cold War by peaceful means. The formula of "four threats" was a compromise: whereas the first and third represented practical interests, the second and fourth affirmed ideological loyalty. The method of compromise was to add and not to integrate different elements into a unified conceptual framework. This failure to integrate the new into the old (or to replace the old entirely with the new) indicated ideological incongruence and conflict. New concepts were introduced but old ones based on an opposing worldview refused to disappear.[7]

"PARTNERS FOR COOPERATION AND OBJECTS OF STRUGGLE"

By the early 2000s, Vietnam had experienced a decade of gradual economic opening and stunning turnaround. Policy texts from the Eighth Party Congress in 1996 through the Ninth Party Congress in 2001 and the Eighth Central Committee Plenum in 2003 suggested marked changes in Party worldview in response to new developments.[8] Ideological filters played an important role in the way Party leaders interpreted the changes, however. Two examples that follow are sufficient to demonstrate the point.

The resolutions of the Ninth Party Congress and the Eighth Central Committee Plenum discussed extensively two new concepts – namely,

---

[7] For a similar view, see Carlyle Thayer, "Vietnamese Foreign Policy: Multilateralism and the Threat of Peaceful Evolution." In Thayer and Amer, eds., *Vietnam's Foreign Policy*, 2–3; Chu Van Chuc, "Qua trinh doi moi tu duy doi ngoai," *Nghien Cuu Quoc Te* 58 (September 2005), 6.

[8] Dang Cong San Viet Nam, *Van Kien Dai hoi dai bieu toan quoc lan thu VIII* [Documents of the Eighth Party Congress] (Hanoi: Chinh Tri Quoc Gia, 1996); Dang Cong San Viet Nam, *Cac Nghi quyet cua Trung uong Dang 1996–1999* [Central Committee Resolutions during 1996–1999] (Hanoi: Chinh Tri Quoc Gia, 2000); Ban Tu Tuong-Van Hoa Trung Uong, *Tai lieu huong dan nghien cuu can van kien (du thao) trinh Dai Hoi Dang toan quoc lan thu IX cua Dang* [Materials to guide the study of draft documents presented at the Ninth Party Congress] (Hanoi: Chinh Tri Quoc Gia, 2000); Ban Tu Tuong-Van Hoa Trung Uong, *Tai lieu hoc tap Nghi quyet Hoi nghi lan thu tam Ban Chap hanh Trung uong Dang khoa IX* [Materials for the study of the Eighth Central Committee Plenum] (Hanoi: Chinh Tri Quoc Gia, 2004). The Eighth Central Plenum in 2003 was devoted specifically to strategic international issues facing Vietnam and set long-term directions of Vietnam's foreign and defense policy.

the "knowledge economy" [*kinh te tri thuc*] and "globalization" [*toan cau hoa*]. Party theorists believed that the new knowledge economy was a double-edged sword.[9] On the one hand, this economy might enable Vietnam to catch up with the industrialized countries in less time. It was noted that it took England 100 years, the United States and Germany 60 years, and the newly industrialized countries 30 to 40 years to industrialize. Vietnam could industrialize even faster if it knew how to develop the knowledge economy.[10] On the other hand, Party theorists cautioned that "developed capitalist countries and transnational corporations" dominated scientific fields. As a result, scientific achievements might further impoverish and enslave rather than assist developing countries.

The same reservation was displayed in the case of globalization. Party theorists viewed globalization as fostering an integrated world offering many opportunities for countries to collaborate and develop. At the same time, perhaps borrowing some ideas from the antiglobalization movement, they warned about the danger of big "capitalist countries" to dominate developing ones.[11] They also were concerned about the future division of the world into two camps of developed/rich and underdeveloped/poor countries, as a result of globalization.

United States interventions in Kosovo, Afghanistan, and Iraq in the early 2000s reanimated the declining belief in Marxism-Leninism in Vietnam. Hanoi condemned American acts as violating other nations' sovereignty and right to self-determination.[12] It accused the United States of harboring the ambition to be the world's hegemon [*doc ton lanh dao the gioi*] and intervening everywhere to fulfill that ambition to the extent of inciting secessionism and religious and ethnic conflicts around the world. To demonstrate that it meant business, the Vietnamese government canceled meetings earlier scheduled for the US Ambassador. A protest was organized in front of the American Embassy in Hanoi for the same purpose.[13] Deputy Foreign Minister Le Van Bang told the US Ambassador that some Vietnam War veterans, now in senior positions, even vowed to go to Iraq to fight for Saddam Hussein.

[9] Ban Tu Tuong-Van Hoa Trung Uong, *Tai lieu huong dan*, 13.
[10] Ibid., 131.
[11] The document cited the debates at a conference coorganized by the World Bank and the Panos Institute in May 2000 that discussed the negative aspects of globalization (Ibid., 15).
[12] Ban Tu Tuong-Van Hoa Trung Uong, *Tai lieu huong dan*, 18–19; Ban Tu Tuong-Van Hoa Trung Uong, *Tai lieu hoc tap*, 29, 39.
[13] http://wikileaks.org/cable/2003/03/03HANOI785.html

As widespread anti-American protests erupted around the world, Vietnamese theorists revived the 1960s concept of the "world people movement" [*phong trao nhan dan the gioi*]. Lumped together within this movement were "the struggle for peace and national independence," "the movement against globalization," and the protests and insurgencies in US-occupied Afghanistan and Iraq.[14] The rise of the world people movement appeared to give the Party greater optimism in the future of socialism. Unlike the early 1990s when Party leaders lamented about "the waning of world socialism," they now saw in the current situation an opportunity for socialism to renew itself.[15]

Hanoi was less sanguine about regional security, however, noting several "agents of instability," including the rise of terrorism and ethnic conflicts in Southeast Asia, rivalries among "big countries" in the region, and increased US military presence there. Party strategists were worried that "bilateral and multilateral agreements were allowing the United States to intervene more deeply into the region, to incite secessionism, [and] to pull Southeast Asia into its orbit." It was further projected that "outside forces" might be tempted to intervene more blatantly into Cambodia, Laos, and Vietnam to promote "peaceful evolution" and "to sabotage our revolution."

In response to a tense world situation, the Eighth Central Committee Plenum resolution of 2003 proposed a new principle for foreign relations:

Anyone who respects our independence [and] sovereignty and wishes to establish friendly, equally cooperative, and mutually beneficial relationships with Vietnam is our partner for cooperation [*doi tac*]. Any group that conspires to frustrate our goals of building and defending our country is an object of our struggle [*doi tuong dau tranh*]. On the other hand, in the current changing and complicated situation, we need to have a dialectic view of this issue. With the objects of struggle there may be areas for cooperation; with the partners, there may exist areas where their interests are contradictory to ours."[16]

Some have argued that these concepts of partners for cooperation and objects of struggles reflected more pragmatic and less dogmatic thinking.[17] On a closer look, the new principle still echoed the sentiments of the 1970s vanguard internationalism. Back then Hanoi leaders had imagined themselves leading world revolution and having the leverage

[14] Ban Tu Tuong-Van Hoa Trung Uong, *Tai lieu hoc tap*, 40.
[15] Ibid., 42.
[16] Ibid., 46–47.
[17] Carlyle Thayer, "Security Relations and Prospects for Strategic Dialogue between the United States and Vietnam," unpublished paper, 9.

to impose preconditions on the superpowers for doing business with Vietnam. The new principle sounded as if preconditions existed for foreign countries to be Vietnam's partners. The imagination of hostile forces ganging up against Vietnam similarly betrayed an exaggerated sense of self-importance bordering on self-delusion and paranoia.[18] Although the Party called for flexibility in dealing with both partners and objects of struggle, the fundamental and conceptual separation between the two groups remained.

Witnessing the apparent revival of leftist movements around the world, Party leaders now desired to strengthen "friendly and cooperative traditional relationships" [*quan he truyen thong*] with socialist countries and the "Indochinese brothers."[19] Not only would those traditional relationships express Vietnam's "selfless internationalism and clear affirmation of proletarian values," but they also would help to consolidate socialist countries and to advance the "world revolutionary movement."[20] At the same time, the Plenum resolution restated existing policy that "Vietnam wishes to be a friend and trustful partner of other countries in the international community, striving for peace, independence, and development."[21] This time, the new phrase "trustful partner" [*doi tac tin cay*] was added, and it was explained that this phrase was to express more clearly Vietnam's wish to "actively" establish "long-term and effective" relationships with other countries, especially in the economic realm.

As the worldview of Vietnamese leaders evolved in response to developments in the post-Soviet era, Marxism-Leninism continued to influence their thinking to a great extent. While the Party was willing to accept elements of other worldviews, these were held subordinate to long-held views. Old ideological assumptions still acted as filters for new ideas. Next, we will turn to Vietnamese military thinking, which further demonstrates how Marxism-Leninism still wields its influence in a key state institution with the power to shape Vietnam's foreign relations.[22]

[18] This Vietnamese attitude is best treated in Morris, *Why Vietnam Invaded Cambodia*.
[19] "Cuong linh xay dung dat nuoc trong thoi ky qua do len Chu nghia xa hoi" [Party Program to build the country during the transition period to socialism], in Dang Cong San Viet Nam, *Cac Nghi quyet cua Trung uong Dang 1996–1999*, 308.
[20] Ban Tu Tuong-Van Hoa Trung Uong, *Tai lieu huong dan*, 271.
[21] Ibid., 266.
[22] On the role of the military in Vietnam's political system, see Carlyle Thayer and Gerard Hervouet, "The Army as a Political and Economic Actor in Vietnam," in Christopher Goscha and Benoit de Treglode, eds., *Naissance d'un Etat-Parti – Le Viet Nam depuis 1945; The Birth of a Party-State – Vietnam since 1945* (Paris: Les Indes Savantes, 2004), 355–381.

MILITARY PERCEPTION OF THREATS

We saw earlier how Hanoi's attitude toward the Soviet Union and China was reversed during 1989–1990. Gorbachev changed from a trusted comrade to a despicable traitor, and Deng Xiaoping traveled in the opposite direction. Military thinking in Vietnam underwent a similarly significant change in the same period. The Tiananmen event, the collapse of the Soviet bloc, and the US invasion of Panama combined to force the People's Army (PAVN) to reevaluate its strategic thinking. The imperialist/American conspiracy to generate peaceful evolution and regime change in socialist countries now became a new major threat. Calling for "a new thinking," a Vietnamese general in fact restated old concepts in a new context:

[The deep cause of war] in recent decades is the selfish class interests of monopolistic capitalism, the defense-industry complex, international weapon dealers and primarily American imperialism ... Our own experience with cruel and cunning American imperialism tells us that we should hold absolutely no illusion of persuading American monopolistic capitalists to solve international problems by civilized and humane means.[23]

In 1993, the military intelligence agency sponsored the translation of a Chinese book that presented the history of the Cold War since 1945 as the history of American imperialism adjusting its anticommunist strategy from containment to peaceful evolution.[24] Although containment had failed, this book argued that "peaceful evolution" had succeeded in destroying the Soviet bloc. This master narrative helped Vietnamese military leaders to update and consolidate their Marxist-Leninist worldview. The "historical evidence" collected by the Chinese, which included quotes by George Kennan, Ronald Reagan, Richard Nixon, and Bill Clinton, provided the "scientific basis" for the claim that nothing had changed since the height of the Cold War in the 1950s. The world remained deeply divided into two camps.

As the world greeted a new millennium, the PAVN's fear of "peaceful evolution" intensified as a result of US attacks in Kosovo, Iraq, and

[23] Maj. Gen. Prof. Le Hong Quang, "Chien tranh va chinh tri – tu duy moi" [War and politics – new thinking], *Tap Chi Quoc Phong Toan Dan* [All-People Defense Review, hereafter *TCQPTD*], 3: (1990), 41. This is the theoretical journal of the PAVN.
[24] Tong Cuc II [General Department II], *Chien luoc dien bien hoa binh cua My* [The US strategy of peaceful evolution] (Hanoi: Tong Cuc II, 1993). See also, *Ban ve van de chong dien bien hoa binh* [On the problem of battling peaceful evolution] (Hanoi: Chinh Tri Quoc Gia, 1993).

Afghanistan. There was broad and clear consensus within military circles that the greatest external adversaries were the United States and overseas Vietnamese, whereas internal enemies comprised a broader array of forces, including the market economy and Western values and ideologies. As one colonel analyzed, the security threats posed by the market economy and industrialization were threefold.[25] First, industrialization provided the capacity to modernize the military but also promoted the worship of technology [*tu tuong ky tri*], which he viewed as being "foreign to Vietnam's military art." Military professionalism could lead to mistaken personnel policy based on academic degrees and not along class lines. The modernization of the army could also generate contempt for *political* cadres and tasks as opposed to *military* ones. Second, abundant economic opportunities in a market economy could breed "utilitarianism" [*tu tuong thuc dung*], making it difficult for the military to retain its officers or to indoctrinate them in political values. Rising social inequality and a revival of religions might be reflected within the military and eventually weaken solidarity. Finally, the global integration of the Vietnamese economy was viewed as having blurred the distinction between socialism and capitalism in the minds of officers and soldiers. In the case of a global economic downturn, subsequent recession in Vietnam, and an enemy attack, the military could lose control over its men and women to the allure of capitalism.

The key strategy to cope with the negative impacts of the market economy on the military was the strengthening of class-based recruitment and personnel policy together with indoctrination. As Senior General Le Van Dung, the PAVN's Chief of Staff, instructed, "We should not implement 'classism' but also should not neglect the class line in our personnel management."[26] "Classism" alluded to the rigid application of class-based quotas during the Land Reform of the 1950s that led to the killing of thousands of "rich peasants" and "middle peasants" wrongly classified as "landlords." In addition, General Dung advised that each unit analyze the social backgrounds of their soldiers and find out the social class composition of the locality where the unit was stationed. This was to devise

[25] Col. Assoc. Prof. Dr. Nguyen Ngoc Hoi, "May suy nghi ve tang cuong su lanh dao cua Dang doi voi Quan doi truoc nhung bien doi kinh te-xa hoi hien nay" [Thoughts on strengthening Party leadership over the military in response to current socio-economic changes], *TCQPTD* 7 (2002), 71–73.

[26] Sen. Gen. Le Van Dung, *Xay dung Quan Doi Nhan Dan Viet Nam ve chinh tri* [Building the political character of the PAVN] (Hanoi: Quan Doi Nhan Dan, 2004), 188–193.

appropriate measures in thought control and in personnel management to prevent the unit from being negatively impacted by local conditions.

Military leaders were especially wary about calls from overseas for the "depoliticization" of the military or the PAVN's breaking away from Party control. Most professional militaries elsewhere make pledges to be loyal first and foremost to their nations, but for the PAVN, devotion to the Communist Party preceded its loyalty to the Vietnamese nation. PAVN leaders viewed those calls for depoliticization as part of a "plot for peaceful evolution." To preempt such a process, they called for increased Party leadership over the military and, as a first step, to increase the number of Party members in the armed forces. Toward this goal, one division commander proposed that promotion be tied to willingness to join the Party, if other political conditions for Party membership were also met.[27] In his division, for example, soldiers were eligible to join the Party in their second year in the service. Career soldiers and graduates of officers' training schools were not to be promoted or eligible for pay raises if they did not seek membership in the Party in their second or third year.

Military commentators were vitriolic with regard to criticisms of the Marxist-Leninist ideology; they defended the faith as if it were their bunker. Coordinated counterattacks against "hostile views" were launched almost daily in the military newspaper, *Quan Doi Nhan Dan* [People's Army Daily]. Examples of those views were postings on the websites of overseas Vietnamese that demanded multiparty democracy for Vietnam and blamed Marxism-Leninism for Vietnam's backwardness; and *samizdat* materials written and circulated by dissidents that called for the Party to abandon socialism.

As recently as 2005, Vietnam's military strategists appeared to regard the United States as the chief strategic enemy. General Pham Van Tra, a Politburo member and Minister of Defense, wrote in 2004 that "in our future war to defend our Fatherland, the primary enemy would be imperialist armed forces and their allies and lackeys. This enemy would attack us with advanced means and hi-tech weapons."[28] Although the United States was not named, it was clear what "imperialist armed forces" the general was referring to. Based on Kosovo, Afghanistan, and Iraq, it was

---

[27] Party Secretary, Deputy Division Commander Col. Mai Quang Phan, "Cong tac to chuc, cong tac can bo o Su doan Quan Tien Phong" [The personnel tasks at the Quan Tien Phong division], *TCQPTD* 7: (2002), 43–46.

[28] Pham Van Tra, *60 Nam Quan Doi Nhan Dan Viet Nam* [The PAVN at sixty years] (Hanoi: Quan Doi Nhan Dan, 2004), 204, 212.

further imagined that an American invasion of Vietnam would follow the scenario below:

[In the case of war,] it is certain that the enemy would attack us first from the air on a large scale, with guided missiles and advanced aircrafts armed with smart bombs with high destructive capacity. Unlike their previous bombing of our Northern region [during the Vietnam War], the enemy would not increase the intensity of the bombing gradually but would ... strike on a large scale at all targets – first at air defense systems, airports ... then at economic and political targets all over the country, leading to the paralysis of our economy and political instability. Taking advantage of this situation, domestic counterrevolutionary forces would launch an uprising and seize our local governments in strategic locations. The enemy could then move their rapid reactionary forces in to help those domestic rebels to declare a government [*dung ngon co*] and set up a base, then call for international support to overthrow our regime.[29]

The debate at this point on the pages of the PAVN defense journal was not about who the enemy was, but about the appropriate strategy of defense: whether to try to resist the initial attack as much as possible to defend the large population centers, or to withdraw into base areas in the uplands waiting for the opportunity to counterattack.[30] Vietnam had had contradicting experiences in this matter. On the one hand, its experience during the Vietnam War suggested the strategy of people's war using the countryside to surround the cities. On the other hand, its experience in the Sino-Vietnamese war demonstrated its capacity to resist even a strong enemy blitzkrieg.[31] On the one hand, the losses of major population and economic centers could be too much to accept. On the other hand, US forces would be armed with far more advanced weapons than Chinese ones – it would be too risky to engage the Americans on their first strikes. By around 2005, there was no clear consensus yet beyond building up a

[29] Col. Pham Trang, "Nang cao trinh do, kha nang hiep dong tac chien giua cac binh doan chu luc va khu vuc phong thu trong chien tranh bao ve to quoc" [Raising the skills and coordinating capacity for main forces corps and defense zones in war to defend our country], *TCQPTD* 9: (2002), 74–76.
[30] Lt. Gen. Assoc. Prof. Khieu Anh Lan, "May van de ve quan diem phong ngu chien thuat trong chien tranh bao ve to quoc" [On the viewpoints related to tactical defense in war to defend our country], *TCQPTD* 3: (1994), 30–32; Col. Pham Trang, "Xay dung the tran quoc phong toan dan" [Building the battle plan for all-people defense], *TCQPTD* 4: (2002), 35–37.
[31] Maj. Le Thanh, "May suy nghi ve to chuc luc luong va nghe thuat quan su chuan bi cho chien tranh bao ve to quoc" [Thoughts on the organization of forces and on military art in preparation for war to defend our country], *TCQPTD* 11: (1988), 43–47; Lt. Gen. Prof. Pham Hong Son, "Ve cach danh bao ve To quoc" [On the tactics to defend our country], *TCQPTD* 12: (1988), 37–45.

general preparedness in all regions. General Tra apparently supported a compromise, which was the avoidance of the enemy's concentrated strategic attacks in the initial phase of such a war while a limited counterattack by Vietnamese main forces was attempted.[32]

Strategic debates in Vietnamese military circles indicated that the old Marxist-Leninist ideology still dominated military thinking and planning. PAVN leaders were ambivalent about market reform and they were, just as ever, prepared to engage Yankee imperialism in combat. Some observers have characterized Vietnam's security behavior in recent years as "hedging": It avoids alliances and seeks friendly relationships with all the major powers.[33] This characterization underestimates how seriously Vietnamese military leaders perceived the United States as a security threat, as recently as 2005.[34]

THE SCHIZOPHRENIC STATE

The PAVN is no doubt one of the most loyalist institutions in the Vietnamese state today. It was founded as a revolutionary army and throughout its early life was led directly by revolutionaries, some of whom have doubled as professional soldiers. Other loyalist institutions include the Ministry of Public Security and Party agencies involved in political organization, mass mobilization, and propaganda. Because these institutions are overrepresented in the Politburo,[35] the highest policy-making body of the state, and because they control all the media and coercive means, ideology still wields significant power in the public sphere. Even if few people today, including perhaps most Party leaders and members, truly believe in Marxism-Leninism, it would be politically suicidal for

---

[32] Pham Van Tra, *60 Nam Quan Doi Nhan Dan Viet Nam*, 207.

[33] Evelyn Goh, *Meeting the China Challenge: The US in Southeast Asian Regional Security Strategies* (Washington: East-West Center, 2005).

[34] For an astute analysis of US-Vietnamese defense relations from the American perspective, see William Jordan, Lewis Stern and Walter Lohman, "US-Vietnam Defense Relations: Investing in Strategic Alignment," *Backgrounder* 2707(July 18, 2012). Available at http://report.heritage.org/bg2707.

[35] In the 14-member Politburo elected for 2011-2016, for example, representatives from the military, public security, and Party organization and propaganda account for half its membership (Nguyen Phu Trong, Le Hong Anh, Tran Dai Quang, Phung Quang Thanh, To Huy Rua, Ngo Van Du, and Dinh The Huynh). In the incumbent Politburo of 19 members (term 2016-2021), their proportion increased to about two-thirds (Nguyen Phu Trong, Tran Dai Quang, Truong Hoa Binh, Pham Minh Chinh, Dinh The Huynh, Ngo Xuan Lich, To Lam, Truong Thi Mai, Nguyen Thien Nhan, Tong Thi Phong, Vo Van Thuong, and Tran Quoc Vuong).

them to challenge the doctrine on which the Party was founded and which is still revered as the quasi-official religion.

Countering those loyalist institutions are state agencies involved in foreign affairs, trade, economic planning, and other technical fields. In these branches of the state, thinking is governed by realist and liberal worldviews that build on concepts such as national interests and global interdependence. Many younger officials of these ministries have been trained in the West and hardly differ from their counterparts in other countries.[36] Even older officials no longer speak in Marxist-Leninist terms.[37] Unlike the United States, where the Secretary of State is one of the two or three most powerful members of the cabinet, Vietnamese foreign ministers have often been excluded from the Politburo. Some ministers have been made members of that powerful body in the past, but they have not played any significant or active role in shaping foreign policy (and were likely to have been appointed for that very reason).[38] Ministers of economic and technical ministries are in even worse positions – they have never made it to the Politburo level.

The influence of Marxism-Leninism on foreign policy is channeled not only through loyalist institutions but also through Party elders who no longer hold formal power but remain influential. This ex-institutional influence can be observed in the removal of General Secretary Le Kha Phieu from power in 2001 by three "senior advisors" of the VCP. These advisors were Do Muoi, Le Duc Anh, and Vo Van Kiet, who had been the Party's general secretary, state president, and prime minister, respectively, from 1991 to 1998.[39] Given that their entire careers were spent battling

---

[36] For example, see the analyses in Pham Binh Minh, ed. *Dinh huong chien luoc doi ngoai Viet Nam den 2020* [Guiding Vietnam's foreign strategy] (Hanoi: Chinh tri Quoc gia, 2010). A son of former Foreign Minister Nguyen Co Thach whom we have met in Chapter 8, Minh was trained at Tufts University and is currently minister of foreign affairs.

[37] See articles written by Le Cong Phung, "Tinh chat, xu huong thoi dai hien nay" [The nature and trends of the current era], in Hoi Dong Ly Luan Trung Uong [Central Council on Theory], *Nhung van de ly luan va thuc tien moi dat ra trong tinh hinh hien nay* [Emerging theoretical and practical issues in the current situation] (Hanoi: Chinh tri Quoc gia, 2011), 11–63; and by Duong Van Quang, "Nhung dac diem va xu the cua the gioi" [The characteristics and trends of the world], in Hoi Dong Ly Luan Trung Uong [Central Council on Theory], *Nhung van de ly luan va thuc tien moi dat ra trong tinh hinh hien nay* [Emerging theoretical and practical issues in the current situation] (Hanoi: Chinh tri Quoc gia, 2011),108–189. Phung is a former Ambassador to the United States and Quang former Ambassador to Singapore and director of the Diplomatic Academy of Vietnam.

[38] Examples are Nguyen Manh Cam and Pham Gia Khiem.

[39] Huy Duc, *Ben Thang Cuoc*, v. 2, ch. 20.

imperialism, most Party elders are likely to be loyalists. Among the three aforementioned men, for example, Kiet was the only one open to alternative worldviews. Muoi and Anh have sometimes supported pragmatic policies but ideologically they are not known as being "soft."[40]

Marxist-Leninist loyalists such as Muoi and Anh, whether retired or in power, hold enormous influence in contemporary Vietnam in part because of the political culture of the Party that upholds strict loyalty to the doctrine. Throughout the history of the Party, as Vo Van Kiet bitterly noted in a confidential essay written in 2006, leaders who committed serious "left-leaning mistakes" had at most been criticized, and in some cases not even criticized.[41] All they needed to do was to quietly clean up the mess. Even if they lost or retired from their formal positions, they did not lose their authority in the Party because they were considered "loyal to the revolutionary worldview" [*kien dinh lap truong cach mang*]. In contrast, those who embraced new ideas and reform have been particularly vulnerable to accusations such as "having weak loyalty" [*mat lap truong*], "deviating from socialism" [*chech huong, xa roi Chu nghia Xa hoi*], and "having bitten capitalist baits" [*an phai ba tu ban*]. The political career of someone so labeled was often doomed. Kiet, who is known as a reformist leader and who engineered the normalization of Vietnam's relations with the United States in the 1990s, must have spoken from his personal experience.

Institutional, ex-institutional, and cultural factors have resulted in schizophrenic behavior as the case of the US-Vietnamese bilateral trade agreement (BTA) attested. After Vietnam normalized relations with the United States in 1995, then-Prime Minister Vo Van Kiet wanted to start immediate negotiations for a trade agreement with the United States. That agreement would open up access to the huge American market for Vietnamese goods – a path to wealth that Japan, South Korea, Taiwan, Thailand, Singapore, and more recently even China had trodden. The deal was estimated by the World Bank to bring Vietnam $1.5 billion from

---

[40] All three came from very similar social backgrounds, however. All were from poor peasant families and learned how to read and write but did not go to school. Prior to their assumption of central leadership positions, Muoi had been deputy prime minister. Kiet had been the Party secretary of Ho Chi Minh City and Anh had been a general of the PAVN and minister of defense. Ibid., 109–111, 261–262.

[41] Vo Van Kiet, "Dong gop y kien vao Bao cao tong ket ly luan va thuc tien hai muoi nam doi moi" [Comments on the Review of theory and practice during twenty years of reform]. This essay conveyed Kiet's comments on the Party's review of reform and strategy for the future. The essay was leaked and published online at http://www.bbc.com/vietnamese/vietnam/2015/08/150809_vo_van_kiet_gui_bo_chinh_tri.

exports to the US market alone, and would also ease Vietnam's accession to the World Trade Organization (WTO). The practical benefits to Vietnam were abundantly clear but the deal met significant opposition from loyalist institutions and leaders who at one point nearly succeeded in thwarting it.

At the initial discussion in the Politburo about the agreement, then-General Secretary Do Muoi reportedly said, "We have reformed our economy successfully [and] our living standards have improved. Why do we need the Americans now?"[42] Muoi feared that Vietnam would be "crushed" if it signed the BTA and joined the WTO because Vietnam was still poor and its industries weak. Both Muoi and Kiet retired in late 1997 to be replaced by Le Kha Phieu and Phan Van Khai, but their disagreement over the trade deal continued in their role as senior advisors afterward. By mid-1999, bilateral negotiations had successfully cleared most differences between the two countries, and Washington was ready to conclude the deal. American officials proposed to have the agreement signed at the Asia-Pacific Economic Community (APEC) meeting in Auckland, New Zealand, in September 1999, when President Clinton and Vietnamese Prime Minister Khai would both be present. Clinton wanted to have the deal concluded before his planned visit to Vietnam in December 1999 – the first for a sitting American president since the end of the Vietnam War.

What occurred next on the Vietnamese side was revealed only recently. In early September 1999, a Politburo meeting presided over by General Secretary Le Kha Phieu approved the BTA as recommended by Khai. The next day, Phieu met visiting US Secretary of State Madeline Albright who had met Khai and received the news from him about the Politburo's approval of the trade deal. Albright would later be blamed for the collapse of the deal when she asked Phieu bluntly at their meeting, "The world now has only four socialist countries remaining. Do you think [you] can hold on?"[43] Of course, Phieu assured her in no uncertain terms that socialism would win in the end, but Albright's question must have raised Phieu's suspicions of US ulterior motives behind the trade deal.[44] Prior to assuming his position as general secretary of the Party,

---

[42] My account of this event is based entirely on Huy Duc, *Ben Thang Cuoc*, v. 2, 345–354. Huy Duc conducted interviews with many key participants, including former Prime Ministers Kiet and Phan Van Khai, General Secretary Phieu, and former Ministers and their advisers.

[43] Ibid., esp. 348–349.

[44] This is the opinion of Nguyen Dinh Luong who was the chief Vietnamese negotiator of the BTA.

Phieu had been senior general and political commissar of the PAVN. The man is known for being loyalist to the core. A few days later when Khai was about to leave Hanoi for Auckland, Senior Advisor Do Muoi told him that he would oppose signing the deal. Khai and his entourage left for the APEC gathering while the fate of the trade agreement hung in the air.

It is not known what role Albright's question played in the subsequent Politburo meeting to reconsider the issue. Muoi reportedly argued against the agreement just as he had said. Former State President and now Senior Advisor Le Duc Anh, who wanted Vietnam to sign the border agreement with China first, before concluding the trade deal with the United States, joined Muoi. At the same time, the military intelligence agency under the control of Anh's protégés in the PAVN supplied the intelligence that China would strongly oppose Vietnam's concluding a trade deal with the United States. Casting another "nay" vote was Nguyen Duc Binh, the head of the Party's Central Council on Theory and former professor and director of Ho Chi Minh Academy whom we met in Chapter 8. Binh dismissed the trade deal as likely to bring only poverty and hunger to Vietnam. He reportedly declared that, "We do not oppose globalization, but we should participate only in globalization led by the proletariat, not globalization led by the capitalist class like the current one." Nguyen Phu Trong, another Politburo member, then head of the Party's Central Propaganda Commission, and former editor-in-chief of the Party journal *Tap Chi Cong San*, warned others about the dangers of "peaceful evolution." (Trong would rise to become general secretary of the Party since 2011). In the absence of Kiet and Khai, the chief advocates of the BTA, the Politburo voted no. The agreement would be approved and signed only in late 2001, after Beijing's accession to the WTO early that year had perhaps been reassuring to the loyalists in Hanoi.

The drama around the BTA exhibited clear symptoms of a schizophrenic state. The Politburo's reversal of its own, earlier decision, apparently in reaction to a blunt but random question from Albright, suggests the complex and obscure mechanisms by which ideology wields its influence in Vietnamese politics today. Loyalty to Marxist-Leninist thinking still constrains the Vietnamese state in its conduct of foreign affairs through institutional, ex-institutional, and cultural factors. This explains why Vietnam has thus far maintained close relations with Beijing while only cautiously and half-heartedly expanding relations with Washington.

Unlike what the Politburo had feared, the BTA proved to be a great boost to Vietnam's economy. By 2010, the United States had become

Vietnam's largest trading partner and one of its largest aid providers and investors. By that time, Vietnam's trade with China had risen to rival its trade with the United States in value. However, if Vietnam has annually enjoyed billions of dollars in trade surplus with the United States, it has suffered from an equally large trade deficit with China.

RADICAL PAST, UNCERTAIN FUTURE

In January 2005, members of the Chinese Coast Guard operating in the Gulf of Tonkin shot nine Vietnamese fishermen to death and took eight others into custody.[45] Arrests of foreign fishermen for violating territorial waters are common affairs in this contested area, but such bloodshed had been rare. The Vietnamese government was silent about what happened. Five days later, when a local newspaper leaked the news and aroused angry denunciations by many Vietnamese, Hanoi made an official announcement of the killings.[46] Another three days were to pass before Vietnam sent a diplomatic message to China to protest the killings.[47]

At the time, few would have predicted that this tragic event would have lasting significance. It would become clearer later that China had shifted toward an aggressive approach in solving territorial disputes with its neighbors, including Vietnam. Since the Chengdu meeting in 1990, Hanoi has made sincere efforts to build a strong relationship with Beijing. The preamble of Vietnam's Constitution was changed in 1992 to remove those sentences that denounced China for its past hostilities toward Vietnam. No negative mentions of contemporary China were allowed in the press. Public signs and records that reminded the public of the Sino-Vietnamese war between 1979 and 1989 were systematically destroyed. History textbooks, commissioned by the Ministry of Education for use as the sole texts for high school students, contained less than ten lines on that war.[48] Although victories against France and the United States were

---

[45] "Mot tau danh ca cua ngu dan xa Hoa Loc bi Trung Quoc bat giu" [A fishing boat of Hoa Loc commune fishermen is arrested by China], *Tuoi Tre* January 12, 2005; "Tau Trung Quoc tan cong giet hai ngu dan Viet Nam" [Chinese ship attacks and kills Vietnamese fishermen], *Thanh Nien*, January 14, 2005.

[46] "Ve viec tau Trung Quoc tan cong ngu dan Viet Nam: Yeu cau Trung Quoc giai quyet moi hau qua" [On the attack on Vietnamese fishermen by Chinese ship: Request for China to deal with the consequences], *Tuoi Tre*, January 17, 2005.

[47] "Canh sat bien Trung Quoc vi pham nghiem trong luat phap quoc te" [Chinese Coast Guard seriously violated international law], *Tuoi Tre*, January 20, 2005.

[48] "Cuoc chien bao ve bien gioi 1979: nen dua day du vao su sach," *Tuoi Tre*, February 20, 2013. Available at http://tuoitre.vn/Ban-doc/534517/cuoc-chien-bao-ve-bien-gioi-1979-nen-dua-day-du-vao-su-sach.html#ad-image-0.

majestically celebrated almost every year, the war against China was not commemorated. We saw earlier how openly critical of the United States the PAVN's defense journal was. Much ink was spent on planning for future wars with "imperialist armies," whereas no mention can be found of potential security threats from China.

Until 2005, China had seemed to reciprocate Vietnam's good will. Throughout the 1990s, China developed increasingly closer party-to-party, state-to-state, and military-to-military relations with Vietnam.[49] On Le Kha Phieu's visit to Beijing in 1999, Chinese President Jiang Zemin proposed a new formula for Sino-Vietnamese relationship. This was nicely packaged as "Four Goods" (good neighbors, good friends, good comrades, and good partners) and "Sixteen Golden Words" (neighborly friendship, comprehensive cooperation, durable stability, and focus on the future).[50] During Phieu's visit, China and Vietnam successfully concluded a comprehensive land border agreement, which many believe to have benefited China at Vietnam's expense. As mentioned earlier, Phieu was ousted in 2001 by the triumvirate Muoi, Anh, and Kiet. One of the accusations he faced was a secret meeting he had with Jiang during the 1999 trip when, at the Chinese leader's insistence, the Vietnamese foreign minister and another Politburo member accompanying Phieu on the trip were not allowed to sit in while discussion on the land border agreement was conducted.[51]

The events since 2005 have strained Sino-Vietnamese relations. China continues to forcefully assert its sovereignty over contested territorial waters in the South China Sea against claims made by Vietnam and other Southeast Asian countries. In late 2007, China announced that it would make a new administrative district out of the Paracel and Spratly archipelagoes that were partly occupied and claimed by Vietnam. Subsequently China imposed a ban on fishing in the area surrounding those archipelagoes that had traditionally been exploited by Vietnamese fishermen. In 2011 Chinese ships allegedly cut the cables of Vietnamese

[49] See Carlyle Thayer, "The Structure of Vietnam-China Relations, 1991–2008," paper presented at the Third International Conference on Vietnamese Studies, Hanoi, December 4–7, 2008; and Carlyle Thayer, "Background Brief: Vietnam's Military Diplomacy – China and the United States," unpublished paper, March 2010; Alexander Vuving, "Strategy and Evolution of Vietnam's China Policy: A Changing Mixture of Pathways," *Asian Survey* 46: 6 (2006), 805–824.

[50] In Vietnamese, "lang gieng huu nghi, hop tac toan dien, on dinh lau dai, huong toi tuong lai." See Huy Duc, *Ben Thang Cuoc*, v. 2, 335–344.

[51] Ibid., 355–356. General Nguyen Chi Vinh who was deputy chief of the military intelligence agency was allowed to accompany Phieu at the meeting.

vessels conducting seismic tests in the area within Vietnam's 200-nautical mile zone.

Hanoi seemed to have been overtaken by those events. At the VCP's Fourth Central Committee Plenum in early 2007, the Party issued the first ever document on an ocean strategy to better exploit and defend ocean resources and ocean access.[52] Following this Plenum, articles on threats to Vietnam's sovereignty over its territorial waters began to appear in the PAVN's defense journal – for the first time since the late 1980s.[53] Nevertheless, negative coverage of China was still banned in the press (until around 2014). If a Chinese ship attacked Vietnamese fishermen, Vietnamese newspapers would be prohibited from mentioning that the ship belonged to China. The PAVN has publicized its recent purchases of submarines and other ships from Russia while denying that Vietnam is engaged in an arms race. Vietnam has upgraded diplomatic relations to strategic partnerships with regional rivals of China, including India and Japan. Hanoi also has warmed up to Washington, offering more port calls for American ships and more frequent exchange of visits by military leaders of both countries. However, Vietnam still maintains the three-no's policy – namely, no participation in any military pact, no alliance with a foreign country against another, and no acceptance of foreign military bases in Vietnam.[54] A main rationale of these three no's is to appease China. Vietnam's relations with China remain cozy, at least in public.

With the boom of online social media in Vietnam since 2006, the Vietnamese state has encountered great difficulties in controlling information and maintaining public order. Spontaneous anti-China protests erupted for the first time ever in communist Vietnam in 2007. The government immediately suppressed these protests and sent some protesters to jail; yet it failed to prevent another wave of protests in Hanoi in the summer of 2011 that lasted for twelve weeks. This wave was remarkable

---

[52] Ban Tu Tuong-Van Hoa Trung Uong, *Tai lieu nghien cuu cac Nghi quyet Hoi nghi lan thu tu Ban Chap hanh Trung uong Dang khoa X* [Materials for the study of the Fourth Central Committee Plenum] (Hanoi: Chinh Tri Quoc Gia, 2007).

[53] For example, see Senior General Nguyen Huy Hieu, "Chien luoc bien Viet Nam – mot van de trong yeu trong su nghiep xay dung va bao ve to quoc hien nay" [Vietnam's Ocean strategy – A critical issue in the construction and defense of our fatherland], *TCQPTD* 5 (2007), 5–8; Colonel Nguyen Manh Dung, "Xay dung hoat dong cua dan quan tu ve bien – thuc trang va giai phap" [Developing activities for self-defense militias for the sea – current issues and solutions], *TCQPTD* 9 (2007), 73–75.

[54] "Chinh sach ba khong cua quoc phong Viet Nam" [The three-no's policy of Vietnam's defense ministry], August 26, 2010. Available http://vietbao.vn/The-gioi/Chinh-sach-ba-khong-cua-quoc-phong-Viet-Nam/11178409/159/.

for attracting hundreds who made the protests into a weekly ritual despite the government's heavy crackdown. Through street chanting and blog postings, protesters charged the government of cozying up to China at the expense of Vietnam's long-term national interests.[55] Despite government repression, this new nationalist movement has continued to expand and now connects many groups with demands for democracy, human rights, and the right to own property.

As with the case of the US-Vietnam bilateral trade agreement, Hanoi has displayed schizophrenic symptoms in reaction to the looming conflict with China. An example of such symptoms is the conflicting and confusing messages emanating from Party leaders, sometimes from the same official who may say one thing one day to foreigners and an opposite thing another day to Vietnamese. Consider the case of Nguyen Duy Chien, a Vietnamese diplomat who is the vice chair of the Vietnamese government's Borders Commission. Although Chien is by no means a top-level official, his behavior appears to represent a broader pattern.

In a recent interview by *The Atlantic*'s national correspondent Robert Kaplan, the journalist described that Chien filled the hour-long meeting "with a relentlessly detailed PowerPoint presentation that attacks the Chinese position from every conceivable point of view."[56] However, Chien displayed quite a different face in his lecture at about the same time at a local university in front of a selective Vietnamese audience. The lecture was ostensibly to provide Vietnamese educators with information about a recent incident involving Chinese ships cutting seismic cables of Vietnamese vessels in an area claimed by Vietnam. Photographing and recording of the lecture were specifically prohibited, but according to an unauthorized report of the lecture published online, Chien reminded the audience that Vietnam and China shared the same ideology, and that the Vietnamese should not overreact to the incident. To the shock of many in the audience, he portrayed the Sino-Vietnamese tension as one within the family and likened Chinese aggressive acts toward Vietnam to a father's tough love for his child.[57]

---

[55] Tuong Vu, "The Party v. the People: Anti-China Nationalism in Contemporary Vietnam," *Journal of Vietnamese Studies* 9:4 (Fall 2014).

[56] Robert Kaplan, "The Vietnam solution: How a former enemy became a crucial US ally in balancing China's rise." *The Atlantic*, May 21, 2012. Available at http://www.theatlantic .com/magazine/archive/2012/06/the-vietnam-solution/308969/?single_page=true.

[57] Nguoi Quan Sat [a pseudonym], "Mot cuoc thuyet giang cho tri thuc – Vu cat cap tau Binh Minh 2: Yeu con cho don cho vot' " [A lecture for intellectuals on the incident involving the ship Binh Minh 2: A father's tough love for his child], November 17, 2011. Available at http://boxitvn.blogspot.com/2011/11/nguoi-quan-sat-xin-hay-oc-bai-nay-e.html.

Chien's lecture was not an isolated event. In response to rising popular demand for Hanoi to be more assertive on issues of territorial conflict with Beijing, PAVN Colonel Tran Dang Thanh gave another lecture to university administrators and professors on the issue. This time the lecture was secretly recorded and later posted online, in which we can hear the colonel's exact words that, "with respect to the Chinese we cannot forget that they have invaded our country in the past but that they have also shared with us their food and their clothes [during wartime]. We cannot be ungrateful to them... [In contrast,] the Americans have never been kind to us; their [war] crimes are not to be forgiven by heaven and earth."[58]

The contradictory messages by officials like Chien and Thanh are puzzling. Self-conflicting and pathetic government officials exist everywhere, but this case seemed different because all the lectures in front of Vietnamese audiences were delivered in a restricted and closed format, whereas the interviews given to foreign correspondents were also carefully scripted but allowed to be broadcast. The officials' evocation of the father-son relationship between China and Vietnam was striking and went beyond the need to calm public opinion. The massive amount of resources the government has devoted to suppress popular expressions of anti-China sentiments similarly betrays an excessive deference toward China. On the whole, these episodes suggest that Vietnamese leaders may have been disappointed and even infuriated by Chinese aggressive moves on border issues, but they were far from viewing China as an enemy and the United States as a friend or an ally.

CONCLUSION

In 2007, following the Tenth Party Congress, the Party's Central Council on Theory [*Hoi Dong Ly Luan Trung Uong*] convened a group of experts to advise the Party on strategic issues. Duong Van Quang, a former ambassador and director of the prestigious Diplomatic Academy of Vietnam, wrote a study on the situation facing communist and worker parties around the world.[59] In his study, which was made public only

---

[58] Tran Dang Thanh, "Dai ta Tran Dang Thanh giang ve bien Dong cho lanh dao cac truong Dai hoc" [Colonel Tran Dang Thanh lectures on the Eastern Sea to university administrators], December 19, 2012. Available at http://anhbasam.wordpress.com/2012/12/19/1481-dai-ta-tran-dang-thanh-giang-ve-bien-dong-cho-lanh-dao-cac-truong-dai-hoc/#more-86178.

[59] Duong Van Quang, "Nhung dac diem va xu the cua the gioi," 108–189.

recently, Quang reviewed changes in the US-dominated world order since the end of the Cold War, the revival of leftist movements in Europe and Latin America, and the foreign policy of China. The seasoned diplomat Quang acknowledged that the VCP had class commitments but believed that the Party should give primacy to national interests [*loi ich dan toc*]. He proposed that Vietnam develop strong state-to-state and party-to-party relations with all parties and governments in power, regardless of their class base. Quang argued that in the current world order, class interests should be subordinate to national interests. From the perspective of national interests, Vietnam should not seek to challenge *Pax Americana* and should avoid taking part in or creating the false impression that it was still searching for a way to build an anti-imperialist ideological alliance.

This chapter ends here with Quang's wise words. They attested to the durable legacies of ideology in Vietnam today and confirmed my thesis that ideology has played a central role in driving the Vietnamese revolution and in shaping Vietnam's foreign relations. A quarter century after the collapse of the Soviet Union and the effective end of the Vietnamese revolution, Quang still warned Vietnamese leaders not to place real or imagined class interests above those of the nation. He was still concerned that his leaders might do something to give the impression that Vietnam wanted to challenge the capitalist world order. The conclusion will touch on more recent developments, showing that Vietnamese leaders remain ambivalent and unwilling to leave the Party's radical past behind.

Epilogue

Ho Chi Minh's Last Wish

A few days before his official seventy-fifth birthday and two months after the first brigade of American Marines landed on the shore of Da Nang in central Vietnam, President Ho Chi Minh signed his testament in the presence of Party First Secretary Le Duan. Ho would live on for four more years, and would meticulously revise his testament several times, but the version published right after his death on September 2, 1969 still carried the following words in the original draft:

The anti-American resistance may last for some more years .... Regardless of hardship and suffering, our people shall win completely. The imperialist Yankee shall have to leave our country. Our fatherland shall achieve unification. [Our] Northern and Southern compatriots shall live together under one roof. Our small country shall be able to take great pride in having courageously defeated two big imperialist powers; and [in] having contributed significantly to the [world's] national liberation movement.

Regarding the world's communist movement – As a person who has dedicated his entire life to revolution, the prouder I am of the growth of the international communist and worker movement, the sadder I am about the current disputes among [our] brother-parties!

I hope that our PARTY shall strive to effectively assist with rebuilding the solidarity of [our] brother-parties based on Marxism-Leninism and proletarian internationalism, on both reason and sentiments. I'm very confident that the brother-parties and brother-countries shall become united [again].[1]

---

[1] "But tich cac ban thao di chuc cua Chu tich Ho Chi Minh (1965–1969)" [Handwritten versions of President Ho Chi Minh's testament], signed on May 15, 1969 by both Ho and Duan. *VKDTT*, v. 30, images beginning on page 253. Underlined and capitalized words are in original. In the first announcement of Ho's death, the date of his death was changed to September 3rd, and parts of his testament were deleted before the document

As North Vietnam steeled itself to face direct American intervention, Ho voiced both concern and determination in his testament. Next to the anticipated protracted war with the United States, his other major concern was about the world's communist movement, in particular the breakout of open conflict within the communist bloc. During 1965–1969, Hanoi was enjoying the highest-ever level of material support from Moscow and Beijing; so foreign aid must not have been a cause of Ho's distress. Rather, his concern and thus his wish that Vietnam would make the effort to help rebuild the broken communist brotherhood merely reflected his lifelong revolutionary commitment. In fact, other than Le Duan's failure to preserve fraternal relations with China in the late 1970s, which would likely have upset Ho, other top Vietnamese leaders ever since have pursued policies broadly in line with his dying wish.

The story in this book began with a young Ho but extended to four decades after his death when he left behind the solemn words just quoted. We have traced his and his comrades' evolving worldview as they rose to power and led their country through revolution, war, and peaceful development. The eighty-year history of Vietnamese communism demonstrated their intense and resilient commitment to the doctrine. These men and women revered Marx and Lenin, and strove to live up to the teachings of those Masters. Over more than half a century, Vietnamese communists determinedly confronted not only colonial domination but also "imperialism," "class exploitation," and cultural and economic "backwardness." They identified themselves with the communist brotherhood and entrusted the destiny of their nation to communism. In return, the brotherhood nurtured and protected the Vietnamese revolution. Brotherly ties at times experienced intrigues and betrayals, but they remained a treasure to be cherished.

THE POWER OF IDEOLOGY

The worldview of Vietnamese leaders continually evolved throughout the course of the revolution as a result of profound internal debates at crucial points. Although internationalism was the core element in their belief, some did not grasp its logic right away, and most did not maintain a fixed attitude toward it over time. At first, it took time for the founding members of the communist movement to digest the theoretical notion that the

was made public. The Party disclosed the full contents and the various drafts of his testament around 1990.

Vietnamese revolution was an integral component of world revolution. Confronted by the Sino-Soviet dispute of the early 1960s, Party leaders remained committed to internationalism while developing a realistic perspective of the communist brotherhood. In particular, they recognized that members of the group could have different, even conflicting, interests due to their countries' different positions in the global order. By the late 1960s, overblown confidence in their ability gave Hanoi leaders the conceit of being the world's revolutionary vanguard. They challenged not only the United States but also China and the Soviet Union. They dominated Indochina and sought influence throughout Southeast Asia and beyond. As their worldview clashed against reality, the clarification and reinterpretation of key concepts were frequently required, although this took place within certain clear boundaries. For example, the voluntary withdrawal from the brotherhood, as Tito did, was one boundary that no Vietnamese leader ever crossed.

Ideological loyalty did not necessarily mean an inability to compromise. Following master revolutionary strategists such as Lenin, Stalin, and Mao, Hanoi leaders became masters themselves in using "united front" tactics to manipulate the "balance of forces." This was done by isolating their chief enemy while trying to form a political coalition as large as possible without compromising "class interests." When they fought the Japanese and French in the early 1940s, Washington's support was cultivated. When they were at war with the Americans in the 1960s, Paris was courted. These deft maneuvers often confused their enemies, their supporters, and outside observers. Yet they themselves were rarely confused about who must be regarded as their brothers and who not.

The Marxist-Leninist creed played various roles in the Vietnamese revolution and the communist state's foreign relations. It defined what goals to accomplish, established who were friends and who were foes, brought with it a global and domestic brotherhood of individuals, groups, and states with shared goals and common enemies, and served as an effective tool of state building. However, ideology did not determine the success or failure of any particular policy or of the revolution as a whole. In fact, their worldview frequently misled Vietnamese revolutionaries. For example, Le Duan's persistent belief in Marx's teaching that revolution was the work of the masses led to disastrous military outcomes. In the *Tet* Offensive in 1968, and again in the Easter Offensive in 1972, much of his hope for victory was pinned on urban mass uprisings that would force the United States to withdraw. Hanoi lost hundreds of thousands of its best troops in the two campaigns yet those uprisings never materialized.

Even if being misled, it was those very efforts to live up to their convictions that enabled Vietnamese revolutionaries to have significant impacts abroad and at home. Fueled by ardent ideological commitments and a dogged determination, this revolution lent support to anticolonial and anti-imperialist movements around the world, helped install communism in Laos and Cambodia, drew the two communist giants into Southeast Asia, and sucked the United States into a quagmire. Without Hanoi's determination to unify the country under its rule, Vietnam would likely remain divided today, as China and Korea still are. This was no ordinary feat. Not that the great powers were free from blame for war, but the efforts of Vietnamese revolutionaries to confront imperialism and their dedication to utopia were truly extraordinary.

COMMUNIST STRATEGIC THINKING IN THE VIETNAM WAR

The findings of this book question many enduring myths and assumptions about the Vietnam War. Scholarship on this event is heavily American-centric and often exaggerates the role the United States played or could have played in Vietnam.[2] When Hanoi leaders formulated a revolutionary strategy, their thinking, in fact, centered on the world's revolutionary conditions and not on US policies *per se*. If those worldwide conditions were favorable, the revolution was to proceed despite the risks of Washington's intervention. Of course, American policies *around the world* were closely monitored and attempts were made to minimize the US threat without losing sight of long-term revolutionary goals. However, these US policies were to be considered together with the policies of other powers and balanced against global anti-American forces.

Understanding the nature of the Vietnamese revolution and the strategic thinking of its leaders helps dispel the most cherished myth of US-centric scholarship about the American "missed opportunities" in Vietnam.[3] In light of the Vietnamese evidence, no opportunities were missed in the late 1940s for the United States to lure Vietnamese revolutionaries away from communism, nor was there ever any slight chance they could have become Titos. Ho Chi Minh and his comrades continued to harbor their

---

[2] For an extended critique along this line, see Edward Miller and Tuong Vu, "The Vietnam War as a Vietnamese War: Agency and Society in the Study of the Second Indochina War," *Journal of Vietnamese Studies* 4:3 (2009), 1–16.

[3] For a convincing attempt to demolish a similar myth in the study of Sino-American relations, see Chen Jian, "The Myth of America's 'Lost Chance' in China: A Chinese Perspective in Light of New Evidence," *Diplomatic History* 21:1 (Winter 1997), 77–86.

communist belief even though Stalin ignored their repeated appeals for help from 1945 to 1950. During the same period, world revolution was advancing rapidly: the communist camp expanded across Eastern Europe and into Northeast Asia; the French Communist Party appeared poised to take power in France; communist revolts erupted throughout Southeast Asia; and Mao's Red Army emerged triumphantly in the Chinese civil war toward the end of the decade. The Americans were but one consideration among several in that big picture. Where many American scholars today see a "missed opportunity," Vietnamese leaders, at the time, shared with their Chinese comrades the conviction that the world was going their revolutionary way. It is unthinkable, therefore, that Vietnamese communists would have given up their radical ambitions at such an exciting time, even if American policies had been more accommodating.

The failure to appreciate Vietnamese revolutionary ambitions similarly leads US-centric scholarship to portray North Vietnam as a powerless victim of American aggression.[4] There is no question that the United States enjoyed massive military advantage over communist Vietnam. Concerns about American military might were indeed voiced in North Vietnamese documents many years before actual US intervention. Yet Hanoi authorized armed struggle in 1959 despite such concerns. After the overthrow of Ngo Dinh Diem in 1963, their worries about US intervention generated not restraint but aggression as Hanoi leaders believed that they should try to defeat Saigon *before* the United States decided to intervene.[5] It was Hanoi's escalation during 1964–1965 that provoked a hesitant Johnson into authorizing American troops to be sent to Vietnam.[6] Even though Hanoi leaders soon discovered that they had underestimated the Americans, they did not retreat but proceed to launch the suicidal *Tet* Offensive.

---

[4] For example, see Gareth Porter, *Perils of Dominance: Imbalance of Power and the Road to War in Vietnam* (Berkeley: University of California Press, 2005). Porter argues that an "overwhelming imbalance of power" during the Cold War that favored the United States over the Soviet Union and China shaped American decisions on military intervention in Vietnam.

[5] Pierre Asselin, *Hanoi's Road to the Vietnam War, 1954–1965* (Berkeley: University of California Press, 2013), 198–201, also makes this point.

[6] On the debates in the United States over intervention during 1963–1964, see Fredrik Logevall, *Choosing War: The Lost Chance for Peace and the Escalation of War in Vietnam* (Berkeley: University of California, 1999). Writing about the American decision to escalate the conflict in 1964–1965, Logevall appears unaware that Hanoi had already chosen war in late 1963, so there was no "lost chance for peace" regardless of what Lyndon Johnson decided. Logevall also assumes that Hanoi leaders could have followed Tito's path if Washington had not chosen war, an assumption not supported by the evidence here.

Why did Hanoi dare to challenge the most powerful military on earth? North Vietnamese leaders' foreign and military strategies followed the Leninist concept of "correlation of forces," not Hans Morgenthau's balance of power logic. In their imagination of an "Age of Revolution," they saw the overall American posture crumbling under powerful challenges from global socialist and progressive forces (including conscientious American citizens who opposed the war). Hanoi leaders thus calculated that, despite possessing nuclear weapons, the Americans were vulnerable and could be defeated in Vietnam.

AMERICAN BLUNDERS

Regardless of whether one agrees or disagrees with the Vietnam War, it was not unwinnable, nor did the containment of the Vietnamese revolution even require direct US military intervention. There were cracks inside the communist state and wedges in Hanoi's relations with its brothers that, if effectively exploited, could have rendered direct military intervention unnecessary. North Vietnam's economic situation already was in a dire situation in the early 1960s due to poor weather, collectivization, and mismanagement. The leadership was deeply divided over Khrushchev's policies and over the appropriate strategies for socialist development.

In view of such difficulties, North Vietnam did not pose a serious threat to the security of South Vietnam and other American allies in Asia to the extent that direct military intervention was necessary. In fact, Hanoi might not have escalated the war in the absence of major blunders committed by American leaders. Le Duan was not optimistic about any easy victory in the South in 1961–1962, and American concessions at the Geneva conference on Laos were truly encouraging news for Hanoi.[7] The November 1963 coup against South Vietnamese President Ngo Dinh Diem, which President Kennedy connived in, was a game-changing event. Ngo Dinh Diem had a mixed record as a leader, but Saigon had regained the initiative in its war against the insurgency by late 1962, and South Vietnam in 1963 was not in a difficult military situation.[8] American

---

[7] My interpretation of the evidence here agrees with the arguments made by Mark Moyar and Pierre Asselin about the strong performance of the ARVN and the unpromising situation of the Southern insurgency in 1961–1962. Moyar, *Triumph Forsaken*, chapters 6 & 7; Asselin, *Hanoi's Road to the Vietnam War*, chapters 4 & 5, esp. 94, 109–117, 122–125. See also Turley, *The Second Indochina War*, 61, who notes the "soft" American stand in Laos.

[8] Miller, *Misalliance*, 247–253. It is true that communist forces scored some successes against strategic hamlets in 1963 thanks to a new strategy, but their gains by no means

disengagement would have been the more appropriate and legitimate response to the deadlock between Kennedy and Ngo. The coup set in motion a spiral of chaos that lasted for three years and wiped away many achievements under President Ngo; it necessitated subsequent American direct intervention, which further delegitimized the Saigon regime. In hindsight, this was perhaps the worst blunder made by Washington in the entire course of the war. In Hanoi, Le Duan's militant faction seized the moment to rally the Party leadership and set the goal for a quick victory in 1964–1965.

It was with that militant spirit that the North Vietnamese navy attacked the USS Maddox in the Gulf of Tonkin on August 2, 1964. In his announcement of the bombing of North Vietnam in retaliation to that and subsequent alleged attacks on August 4, 1964, President Johnson declared, "the United States intends no rashness and seeks no wider war."[9] Johnson's statement was reassuring to Hanoi leaders, who feared the most a ground invasion by US forces into North Vietnam and who immediately dispatched their main force units to the South following the Maddox affair.[10] If Johnson had left open the option of a wider war, he might well have kept the infiltration of North Vietnamese troops into the South to a level that the Saigon military could have managed without the need of American troops.

Although it was justifiable and conscientious to oppose the US bombing of North Vietnam for moral or other reasons, Johnson's major mistake was to de-escalate in 1968 following the *Tet* Offensive. Having authorized half a million American troops to be sent to Vietnam, the commander-in-chief abandoned the effort just when his enemy was desperate to break the stalemate, went for broke, and suffered massive losses.[11] Johnson thus offered Le Duan and the militant leaders in Hanoi the opportunity to claim victory, practically rescuing them from their colossal blunder in launching the Offensive. As former PAVN colonel

---

endangered the overall security of the RVN. Philip Catton, *Diem's Final Failure: Prelude to America's War in Vietnam* (Lawrence: University Press of Kansas, 2002), 191–192.

[9] North Vietnamese boats did attack the US ship on August 2 but not on August 4. The statement is available at www.pbs.org/wgbh/americanexperience/features/primary-resources/lbj-tonkin/

[10] Bui Tin, *From Enemy to Friend: A North Vietnamese Perspective on the War*, transl. Nguyen Ngoc Bich (Annapolis: Naval Institute Press, 2002), 81–82. Turley notes the immediate dispatch of whole units but believes that it was unrelated to the Tonkin Gulf resolution. Turley, *The Second Indochina War*, 84.

[11] The term "go-for-broke" is from Lien-Hang Nguyen, *Hanoi's War*, 75. For discussion of communist military losses, see Turley, *The Second Indochina War*, 154–156, 170–172.

Bui Tin would say four decades later, "the [*Tet*] Offensive [was a military failure but] caused a disastrous turnabout in US policy that gave Hanoi breathing room at just the moment when we were hardest-pressed in South Vietnam! ... This paradoxical quirk of history ... is clear proof that politics is not always wedded to military victories, and vice versa."[12] After the coup against Ngo Dinh Diem, this was perhaps the second worst blunder in the American conduct of the war.

REVOLUTIONARY AND POSTREVOLUTIONARY POLITICS

Vietnam teaches scholars of revolutions about a fundamental paradox of revolutionary politics. On the one hand, revolutionary ideologies may unleash extraordinary power by motivating people to sacrifice their lives without hesitation. As Ho Chi Minh reportedly told the French in 1946, "You can kill 10 of my men for every one I kill of yours, yet even at those odds, you will lose and I will win."[13] Although the authenticity of this statement cannot be verified, the fact is that North Vietnam suffered about one million battle casualties out of a population of less than 20 million during the Vietnam War. Proportionally, that number would be equivalent to 10 million American deaths.

On the other hand, the same fanaticism that turns revolutionaries into fearless fighters makes them a threat to everyone, including their own people. For all their possibly noble intentions, Vietnamese revolutionaries took their country into three wars with millions of lives lost. Once acquiring power, they turned Vietnam into a giant laboratory for half-baked utopian ideas. Their draconian policies in the late 1970s pushed millions into the ocean in search of an escape, with tens of thousands of those "boatpeople" perishing along the way. Impatience for radical changes, penchant for violence, and ambition to be the vanguard of world revolution turned the three communist brothers Vietnam, Cambodia, and China against each other. Over half a century, revolutionary energies were consumed by such destructive endeavors, which eventually outlived many revolutionary leaders and left behind a country in ruins and a people in destitution. This self-destructive character of revolutions has been played down in many prominent works whose authors are favorably impressed by the ability of revolutionary states in imposing public order, promoting

---

[12] Bui Tin, *From Enemy to Friend*, 64–65.
[13] According to Stanley Karnow who does not cite any sources, Ho said the above to a French visitor. Karnow, *Vietnam*, 197–198.

peasants' interests, expanding political participation, and mobilizing the masses for international war.[14] However, under that impressive ability of revolutionary states lurk their fanaticism and tendency for destructive violence in the name of utopia.

Even though their revolutionary energies had largely burnt out by the late 1980s when Hanoi leaders embarked on market reforms, the revolutionary ideology has lived on in political culture and institutions, and continued to obstruct Vietnam's process of reintegration into the global order. Comparative scholarship suggests that this process is fraught with difficulties that can be overcome only over a long time and under certain conditions. These conditions include leadership changes,[15] the abandonment of the revolutionary doctrine,[16] changes in the political-economic system of the revolutionary state,[17] the reduction of threats to revolutionary regimes from the international environment,[18] and the lessening of hostility from dominant *status-quo* powers, which can be a result of changes in their domestic politics.[19]

All those factors are present in the Vietnamese case, but ideological legacies are arguably the most important one. The deaths in the late 1980s of Le Duan and other senior leaders facilitated initial market reforms, but these reforms were meant to have more, not less, socialism. The new leaders were only a few years younger than their predecessors, and were no less loyal ideologically. They thus viewed the great change in international politics from bipolarity to unipolarity in the early 1990s chiefly through ideological lens. Their swift move to seek Chinese alliance to substitute for the loss of Soviet patronage in 1990 is puzzling without taking ideology into account. Just two years earlier, China had seized from Vietnam some islands in the Spratly archipelago in a naval

---

[14] Examples include Samuel Huntington, *Political Order in Changing Societies* (New Haven, CT: Yale University Press, 1968), chapter 5; Theda Skocpol, *States and Social Revolutions*; Theda Skocpol, "Revolutions and Mass Military Mobilization," *World Politics* 40: 2 (1988), 149; Theda Skocpol, "What Makes Peasants Revolutionary?" *Comparative Politics* 14: 3 (1982), 363.

[15] Wight argues that the great revolutions have "never for long maintained [themselves] against national interest. Doctrinal considerations have always within two generations been overridden by *raison d'etat*." *Power Politics*, in Hedley Bull and Carsten Holbrand, eds. (New York: Holmes & Meier, 1978), 92–93.

[16] Maximilian Terhalle, "Revolutionary Power and Socialization: Explaining Revolutionary Zeal in Iran's Foreign Policy," *Security Studies* 18: 3 (2009), 557–586.

[17] Halliday, *Revolution and World Politics*, 139.

[18] Walt, *Revolution and War* (Ithaca, NY: Cornell University Press, 1996).

[19] Jervis, "Socialization, Revolutionary States and Domestic Politics," *International Politics* 52:5 (2015), 609–616.

battle resulting in sixty-four Vietnamese casualties. However, that conflict was curiously not as alarming to Hanoi as were successful US invasions of Panama in 1989 and of Iraq in 1991 that took place nearly halfway around the globe.

Robust ideological legacies have since ensured that men loyal to Marxism-Leninism are in control of Party leadership and that the communist character of the regime is preserved. This has resulted in a curious situation. On the one hand, the integration of the Vietnamese economy into the global economy continues to diversify Vietnamese society and leadership, and loyalists are increasingly becoming a small minority. On the other hand, close Sino-Vietnamese relations following bilateral normalization in 1991 have significantly altered Vietnam's reintegration path. Vietnam's political, military, and economic ties with China now dwarf those with the United States, Japan, and others.[20] In a sense, Vietnam still has one foot in the old brotherhood.

China's assertive policy since 2005 to enforce its sovereignty claims in the South China Sea against Vietnam's rival claims has further isolated but not yet dislodged the loyalists from power.[21] At the same time, US policy since 2012 to "pivot" to East Asia, which can be interpreted as a strategy to counter China's rising influence in the region, has translated into greater American willingness to accommodate Vietnam on various issues from trade to weapon sales to human rights. This was symbolized most clearly by the visit to Washington in 2015 by Party leader Nguyen Phu Trong and by the new Trans-Pacific Partnership trade agreements that will expand access to the US market for many Vietnamese goods.[22] Trong, whom we met previously, had just journeyed to Cuba three years earlier to lecture about the evils of capitalism and the merits of socialism.

[20] See Carlyle Thayer, "Background Brief: Vietnam's Military Diplomacy – China and the United States," unpublished paper (March 2010). China was Vietnam's largest trade partner in 2014, with total Sino-Vietnamese trade revenues being $63.7 billion. The United States was Vietnam's second largest trade partner in the same year, with total revenues being $35 billion. See "China-US political contest could aid Vietnam, *Oxford Analytica Daily Brief*, October 22, 2015; data on US-Vietnamese trade is available at www.state.gov/r/pa/ei/bgn/4130.htm.
[21] A key event was China's move to place a giant oil rig within 200 nautical miles from Vietnam's coast in 2014 that spurred violent protests in Vietnam. Kate Hodal and Jonathan Kaiman, "At least 21 dead in Vietnam's anti-China protests over oil rig," *The Guardian*, May 15, 2014, www.theguardian.com/world/2014/may/15/vietnam-anti-china-protests-oil-rig-dead-injured.
[22] www.channelnewsasia.com/news/world/obama-vietnam-party-boss/1967904.html

It is possible that China has threatened Vietnam's geopolitical interests and pushed Hanoi closer to the United States and its allies. President Obama's pivot policy may also have pulled Hanoi further away from Beijing's orbit by reassuring the Vietnamese and offering them practical rewards for cooperation. However, those changes in the international environment are yet to fully overcome ideological legacies. There has been no drastic reorientation of Vietnam's foreign policy to the United States, even after Trong's trip to Washington.[23] Hanoi's conflicting responses to Chinese moves and US overtures continue to baffle analysts. As Party leaders vie for power and fight over the legacies of the revolution, it remains to be seen if and when President Ho's death wish will finally be forgotten.

---

[23] Among other signs, prior to Trong's visit to Washington, he went first to Beijing to inform the Chinese about the trip. Relationship between Chinese and Vietnamese militaries and public security ministries remains close. See http://news.xinhuanet.com/english/2015-04/07/c_134131246.htm.

APPENDIX A

Ho Chi Minh's Letter to Stalin, October 14, 1950

Below is the full text of a handwritten letter in English Ho Chi Minh wrote and sent to Stalin to report the Vietnamese victory in the Border campaign of 1950.[1] Ho's tone and his Russian pseudonym in the letter gave the strong flavor of a comrade, a Comintern agent, and a disciple addressing his comrade, boss, and God, rather than a head of state communicating with another head of state.

Beloved Comrade Stalin,

I am happy to send you the following reports. Thanks to the great help given by you & by the Chinese Comparty [sic], the first phase of our Border counter-offensive has been successfully concluded.

The Caobăng – Dôngkhe – Thâtkhê [sic] front is about 70 kilometers long, very mountainous.

Our force:[2] 25,500 regular army men,

970 local army men,

18,000 villagers, men and women in transport work, each person working 10 days.

Enemy force: 6,000 soldiers (about 2,700 white, 2,600 Nord-Africains, 700 Vietnameses [sic]).

Fighting phases: (1) Đông Khê post, from 16 to 20 September. Enemy force: 350 soldiers. They have been totaly [sic] annihilated. We took Đông Khê.

(2) Enemy troops evacuated Caobăng, trying to get to Thâtkhê, with 1,850 soldiers (Oct. 3). But when near Dôngkhê, they were destroyed by us. Their commander Colonel Charton & his staff surrendered.

---

[1] This document was copied from Russian archive and published in Ban Tuyen Giao Trung Uong & Bao Tang Ho Chi Minh [Central Party Commission on Propaganda and Education & Ho Chi Minh Museum], *Chu tich Ho Chi Minh voi nuoc Nga* [President Ho Chi Minh and Russia] (Hanoi: Chinh Tri Quoc Gia, 2013), 141.

[2] All the underlining in the letter, likely by Ho Chi Minh, was done in red color.

(3) Other enemy troops of about 2,000 soldiers being sent from Thatkhe to meet Charton group. Arrived near Đôngkhê and separated from Charton only 1 kilometer, they were also destroyed by us. Their commander Colonel Lepage, his staff and Colonel Doctor Durif surrendered.

The figthing [sic] started on Oct. 3, and ended Oct. 11.

The result: We liberated Caobang, Dôngkhê, Thatkhê. We took a relatively large quantity of war booty. We killed about 2,300 enemies, and captured some 2500 war prisoners, (3 colonels, 1 commandant, 5 captains, 20 lieutnants [sic]. These figures are not yet totally completed).

According to recent report, the ennemy [sic] left also Thainguyên province on Oct. 11. When occupied that province only 10 days ago (Oct 1st), they called it "capitale [sic] of Ho chi Minh," and made much noise about it.

Another important result: For the first time we fought a big fight, we learned many experiences, and we see more clearly our shortcomings. These shortcomings, we will, with the help of our Chinese comrades and following the Leninist-Stalinist teaching, do our best to overcome.

Our advisers: I have to inform you that the C.C. of the C.C.P. has sent some of its best cadres to serve as our advisers, and they render us very valuable services.[3] We are making ready to fight the next battle when our troops have had some rest. We promise you to try to fight still better.

Dear Comrade Stalin, am I right to consider this our success, small though it be relatively, is part of the great victory of the revolutionary Internationalism for which you are our most valliant [sic] & beloved leader?

* *

About December next, we shall have our National Congress to inaugurate our new Party: The Vietnam Labour Party [sic]. Our first task is to "reform" a party with half a million members relatively educated, in Marx-Lenin theory. (Now, we have over 750,000 members, but many of them will have to be cleansed out).[4]

I hope to receive the Books [sic] you have promised to write especially for us. I will translate them myself. That will be the most precious gift you make to our young party.

I beg you to convey my brotherly greetings to our comrades of the Politburo.

I heartily kiss you and wish you best health and long, long life!

Caobăng Oct. 14th 1950   Yours loving

(signed in Russian) DIN

---

[3] C.C. of the C.C.P. stands for the Central Committee of the Chinese Communist Party.

[4] Ho Chi Minh was referring to the planned "organizational rectification" campaign soon to be carried out under Chinese supervision and in combination with the land reform in most provinces. During these two campaigns, hundreds of thousands of loyal Party members were expelled simply for having "bad" class backgrounds. Tens of thousands were tortured and executed. See Vu, *Paths to Development in Asia*, ch. 5.

APPENDIX B

Anti-American Articles Penned
by Ho Chi Minh, 1951–1955

Below is a (likely incomplete) list of sixty anti-American articles written by Ho Chi Minh but published under various pseudonyms during 1951–1955.[1]

Date	Title of article
06/14/1951	American morality [Dao duc cua My]
07/28/1951	Life in the US [Doi song o My]
08/06/1951	American justice [Cong ly cua My]
08/08/1951	The Yankee Satan [Quy su My]
10/12/1951	They care about strangers but not their own people [Mo cha khong khoc, khoc mo moi]
11/03/1951	America means ugliness [My la xau]
11/05/1951	Foul-smelling society and decadent culture [Xa hoi hoi thoi, Van hoa suy doi]
11/12/1951	American humanism [Nhan dao cua My]
11/14/1951	Ku Klux Klan [Ku-Klux-Klan]
12/14/1951	American-style freedom and peace [Tu do va hoa binh kieu My]
02/18/1952	"American lifestyle" ["Sinh hoat kieu My"]
03/13/1952	American allies [Dong minh cua My]
04/18/1952	Black, White [Den, trang]
06/21/1952	The Americans are afraid of peace [My so hoa binh]
07/25/1952	Brainwashing warfare [Chien tranh nhoi so]
08/22/1952	Kill 9 people for 65 dollars [Giet 9 nguoi lay 65 dong bac]
11/04/1952	Money cannot buy everything [Khong chac "co tien mua tien cung duoc"]
11/06/1952	America dealt several blows [My lai bi them may vo]
11/13/1952	Die in dishonor [Chet ma chua het nhuc]

(continued)

1 The list is likely incomplete as there might have been other articles not included in the collection. C.B., D.X., T.L. et al. (Ho Chi Minh), *Noi Chuyen My...* [Talking about America] (Hanoi: Quan Doi Nhan Dan, 1972). This volume contained sixty-two other articles on the same subject but were published in later years, with the last piece published in June 1968.

Table (*continued*)

Date	Title of article
11/06/1953	American civilization: Men worth less than dogs [Van minh My: Nguoi khong bang cho]
11/20/1953	Japanese against America [Dan Nhat chong My]
02/19/1954	American plot to "use Asians to fight Asians" [Am muu My "dung nguoi A danh nguoi A"]
03/10/1954	Guatemala [Goa-te-ma-la]
03/22/1954	24 dollars, 19 lives [24 do la, 19 mang nguoi]
03/31/1954	American civilization and American humanism [Van minh My va nhan dao My]
04/05/1954	American-style "civilization" ["Van minh" kieu My]
04/15/1954	Who plots war? [Ai am muu gay chien?]
04/19 to 05/21/1954 (15 installments)	American spies [Mat tham My]
07/15/1954	America calculates [My tinh toan]
08/09/1954	American "morality" [Dao duc My]
09/01/1954	America: Coarse and ugly customs [My ma: Phong khong thuan, tuc khong my]
11/20/1954	American political morality [Dao duc chinh tri My]
12/12/1954	"The best of the world" [Nhat tren the gioi]
12/20/1954	Imperialist America has intervened in the war of aggression in Indochina since the beginning [Tu ngay dan ta bat dau khang chien, De quoc My da nhung tay vao chien tranh xam luoc Dong duong
12/21/1954	Imperialist America tried hard to wreck the Geneva Conference but they have failed in disgrace [De quoc My rao riet pha Hoi nghi Gio-ne-vo nhung chung da that bai nhuc nha]
01/12/1955	The Bangkok meeting is a new plot of Imperialist America to destroy peace in Indochina and Asia [Hoi nghi Bang Coc la mot am muu moi cua De quoc My de tien them mot buoc trong viec pha hoai hoa binh o Dong duong va Dong Nam A]
02/18/1955	Need to be vigilant [Canh giac de phong]
02/19/1955	Matthew Show (?) [Ma-tu-so]
03/03/1955	Dulles spits poison in South Vietnam [Da-let phun noc doc o mien Nam Viet Nam]
03/13/1955	War-mongering Dulles's threats only increase animosity among Indochinese and Asians [Nhung loi doa dam cua ten cuong chien Da-let chi tang them long cam phan cua nhan dan Dong duong va nhan dan toan chau A]
04/08/1955	9 million insane people [9 trieu nguoi dien]
04/23/1955	Lynching [Lynch]
07/01/1955	7,000 tons of poison [7.000 tan thuoc doc]
09/24/1955	An American boy killed by other Americans [Mot em be My bi nguoi My giet]
11/29/1955	Poor American children! [Toi nghiep cho tre con My]
12/28/1955	"American lifestyle" again [Lai "doi song kieu My"]

Bibliography

Archival Sources

Thu Vien Quoc Gia (National Library), Hanoi.
Trung Tam Luu Tru Quoc Gia III (National Archive III), Hanoi.
Vien Bao Tang Cach Mang (Museum of the Revolution), Hanoi.

Newspapers and Periodicals

Canh Nong Tap San (Hanoi), 1946 [Ministry of Agriculture journal]
Chinh Nghia (Hanoi), 1946 [Vietnamese Nationalist Party journal]
Co Giai Phong (Ha Dong?), 1944–1945 [Communist Party; predecessor of *Su That*]
Cong Luan (Saigon), 1936–1937
Cuu Quoc (Ha Dong?/Hanoi), 1944–1946 [Communist Party]
Dan Chung (Saigon), 1938–1939 [Stalinist group in the Communist Party]
Dan Thanh (Hanoi), 1946 [non-party]
Dat Moi (Hanoi), 1956 [student publication]
Dien Tin (Saigon), 1940–1941
Doc Lap (Hanoi/Viet Bac), 1945–1953 [Democratic Party]
Du Luan (Hanoi), 1946 [non-party]
Dung Day (Saigon/Ho Chi Minh City), 1975–1980
Giai Pham (Hanoi), 1956 [private]
Ha Noi Hang Ngay (Hanoi), 1955–1957 [private daily]
Hinh Su Cong Bao (Hanoi), 1946 [Ministry of Interior]
Hoc Tap (Hanoi), 1956–1976 [Communist Party journal]
Hoc Tap (Nghe An), 1948-1951 [Interzone 4 Communist Party]

Lang Son Thong Tin (Lang Son), 1949–1954 [Communist Party, Lang Son province]

Lien Hiep (Hanoi), 1945–1946 [Vietnamese Revolutionary League]

Nam Phong, 1917–1918

Ngo Bao (Hanoi), 1933–1935

Nhan Dan (Viet Bac/Hanoi), 1951–1961

Nhan Van (Hanoi), 1956 [private]

Nhut Tan (Saigon), 1924

Su That (Hanoi/Viet Bac), 1945–1950 [Communist Party; predecessor of *Nhan Dan*]

Tap Chi Cong San (Hanoi), 1977–1990 [successor of *Hoc Tap*]

Tap Chi Quoc Phong Toan Dan (Hanoi), 1990–2009

Tap San Cong Thuong (Viet Bac), 1952–1954 [Ministry of Economy journal]

Thanh Nghi (Hanoi), 1943–1945

Thanh Nien (Ho Chi Minh City), various years

Thoi Moi (Hanoi), 1955–1957 [private]

Thoi The (Hanoi), 1950

Thoi Vu (Hanoi), 1939

Thong Nhat (Hanoi), 1957–1958

Tien (Thanh Hoa), 1945 [Viet Minh]

Tien Manh (Viet Bac), 1950 [Communist Party; Viet Bac Interzone branch]

Tien Phong (Hanoi), 1945–1946 [Viet Minh writers]

Tin Cai Cach Ruong Dat (Thanh Hoa, Phu Tho, Bac Giang-Bac Ninh), 1954–1955

Tin Noi Bo (Bac Giang), 1950–1951 [Internal local Communist Party newsletter]

Tin Noi Bo (Cao Bang), 1950 [Internal local Communist Party newsletter]

Tin Sang (Saigon/Ho Chi Minh City), 1975–1981

To Quoc (Hanoi) 1956–1957 [Socialist Party]

Tram Hoa (Hanoi), 1956–1957 [private]

Trang An (Hue), 1939–1942

Tranh Dau (Saigon), 1938-1939 [Trotskyists]

Truyen Thanh (Vinh), 1946 [Communist Party/Viet Minh]

Tuoi Tre (Ho Chi Minh City), various years

Van (Hanoi), 1957 [Writers' Association journal]

Van Hoc (Hanoi), 1958–1959 [Writers' Association journal]

Van Nghe (Viet Bac), 1948–1954 [Writers' Association newspaper]

Viet Dan (Saigon), 1933–1937
Viet Nam (Hanoi), 1945–1946 [Vietnamese Nationalist Party daily]
Viet Nam Doc Lap (Cao Bang), 1941–1945, 1951–1954 [Viet Minh/ Communist Party]
Xua va Nay (Hanoi), various years
Y Dan (Hanoi), 1945–1946 [Catholic]

Collections of Party Documents

Dang Cong San Viet Nam, *Van Kien Dai hoi dai bieu toan quoc lan thu VIII* [Documents of the Eighth Party Congress] (Hanoi: Chinh Tri Quoc Gia, 1996).
   Cac Nghi quyet cua Trung uong Dang 1996–1999 [Central Committee Resolutions 1996–1999] (Hanoi: Chinh Tri Quoc Gia, 2000).
   Van Kien Dang Toan Tap [Collected Party documents], 54 vols. (Hanoi: Chinh Tri Quoc Gia, 1999–2007).

Collected Works and Reprinted Newspapers

Bao Tang Cach Mang Viet Nam, *Bao Viet Nam Doc Lap 1941–1945* [The *Viet Nam Doc Lap* newspaper 1941–1945] (Hanoi: Lao Dong, 2000).
Bao Tang Cach Mang Viet Nam, *Bao Dan Chung 1938-1939* [The *Dan Chung* newspaper 1938-1939], 2 vols. (Hanoi: Lao Dong, 2000).
Chuong Thau, ed., *Phan Boi Chau Toan Tap* [Complete works by Phan Boi Chau], 10 vols. (Hanoi: Trung Tam Van Hoa Ngon Ngu Dong Tay, 2001).
Chuong Thau, Duong Trung Quoc, and Le Thi Kinh, eds., *Phan Chau Trinh Toan Tap* [Complete works by Phan Chau Trinh], 3 vols. (Da Nang: Da Nang Publishing House, 2005).
Ha Huy Tap, *Ha Huy Tap: Mot So Tac Pham* [Ha Huy Tap's works] (Hanoi: Chinh tri Quoc gia, 2006).
Ho Chi Minh, *Ho Chi Minh Toan Tap* [Complete works by Ho Chi Minh], 2nd ed. (Hanoi: Su That, 1995).

Memoirs, Diaries, and Occasional Documents

Bui Cong Trung, "Hoi ky Bui Cong Trung," available at http://vanhoanghean .com.vn/van-hoa-va-doi-song27/cuoc-song-quanh-ta46/hoi-ky-bui-cong-trung-ii.
Bui Tin, *Following Ho Chi Minh* (Honolulu: University of Hawaii Press, 1995).
Chaplin, Boris. "Thang Tu nam 1975 lich su" [The historic April 1975], in *Lien Xo – Mot tu khong bao gio quen (Hoi ky)* [The Soviet Union – An unforgettable word (Memoirs)] (Hanoi: Chinh tri Quoc gia, 2007).
Dang Lao Dong Viet Nam [Vietnamese Workers' Party], "Politburo's Directive Issued on May 4, 1953, on Some Special Issues regarding Mass Mobilization," transl. by Tuong Vu. *Journal of Vietnamese Studies* 5:2 (Summer 2010), 243–247.

Dang Kim Tram, ed., *Nhat ky Dang Thuy Tram* [Diary of Dang Thuy Tram] (Hanoi: Nha Nam, 2005).

Dang Vuong Hung, ed., *Mai mai tuoi hai muoi: Nhat ky cua liet si Nguyen Van Thac* [Forever twenty: Diary of martyr Nguyen Van Thac] (Hanoi: Thanh Nien, 2005).

ed., *Tro ve trong giac mo: Nhat ky cua liet si Tran Minh Tien* [Return in a dream: Diary of martyr Tran Minh Tien] (Hanoi: Hoi Nha Van, 2005).

Dao Duy Anh, *Nho Nghi Chieu Hom* [Memoirs and afternoon thoughts] (Ho Chi Minh City: Tre, 1989).

Do Ha Thai and Nguyen Tien Hai, eds., *Nhat Ky Vu Xuan* [Diary of Vu Xuan] (Hanoi: Quan Doi Nhan Dan, 2005).

Ho Anh Dung, Tran Phu Thuyet, Le Tien Hoan et al., eds., *Lon Len Giua Mac Tu Khoa* [Growing up in Moscow] (Hanoi: The Gioi, 2004).

Hoang Huu Yen. "Mot thoi de nho" [A time to remember], July 28, 2008 at www.talawas.org/talaDB/showFile.php?res=14070&rb=0302.

Hoang Quoc Viet, "Tinh than Pham Hong Thai" [The spirit of Pham Hong Thai], in *Hoi Ky Cach Mang tuyen chon* [Selected memoirs about the revolution] (Hanoi: Hoi Nha Van, 1995).

Le Thanh Hien, ed., *Tuyen Tap Tran Dinh Long* [Tran Dinh Long's selected works] (Hanoi: Van Hoc, 2000).

Le Van Hien, *Nhat ky cua mot bo truong* [Diary of a minister], 2 vols. (Da Nang: Da Nang Publishing House, 1995).

Le Xuan Ta [a pseudonym], "Hoi uc ve cuoc khung bo chu nghia xet lai o Viet Nam" [Reminiscences of antirevisionist terror in Vietnam], February 1994. Available at www.diendan.org/tai-lieu/bao-cu/so-027/khung-bo-xet-lai/.

Ma Van Khang, *Nam Thang Nhoc Nhan, Nam Thang Nho Thuong – Hoi Ky* [Years of hardship and loving memories–memoirs] (Hanoi: Hoi Nha Van, 2009).

Nguyen Huy Tuong, *Nhat Ky* [Diary], preserved by Trinh Thi Uyen and edited by Nguyen Huy Thang, 3 vols. (Hanoi: Thanh Nien, 2006).

Nguyen Kien Giang, "Nhin lai qua trinh du nhap chu nghia Mac-Le nin vao Vietnam" [On the process by which Marxism-Leninism entered Vietnam], 1995. Available at http://viet-studies.info/kinhte/NguyenKienGiang_QuaTrinhDuNhap.htm.

Nguyen Van Tran, *Viet cho me va quoc hoi* [To my mother and the National Assembly] (Westminster, CA: Van nghe, 1996).

Tran Cung and Trinh Dinh Cuu, "Mot vai net ve chi bo dau tien cua Dang va ve Dong Duong Cong San Dang" [On the first party cell and the Indochinese Communist Party], in *Hoi Ky Cach Mang tuyen chon* [Selected memoirs about the revolution] (Hanoi: Hoi Nha Van, 1995), 55–64.

Tran Dan Tien, *Nhung mau chuyen ve doi hoat dong cua Ho Chu tich* [Stories about the life and career of President Ho] (Hanoi: Su That, 1976).

Tran Dinh, *Den Cu: So phan Viet Nam duoi che do Cong san-Tu truyen cua nguoi tung viet tieu su Ho Chi Minh*, 2 vols. [Revolving Lamp: Vietnam's fate under communism – Autobiography of a writer of Ho Chi Minh's biography] (Westminster, CA: Nguoi Viet Books, 2014).

Tran Quang Co, *Hoi uc va suy nghi* [Memories and thoughts] (July 2005). Published online; available at www.diendan.org/tai-lieu/ho-so/hoi-ky-tran-quang-co.

Tran Quynh, "May ky niem ve Le Duan," [Reminiscences about Le Duan], n.d. Unpublished memoir.

Tran Thu, *Tu tu xu ly noi bo* [Deathrow prisoners to be disciplined internally] (Westminster, CA: Van Nghe, 1996).

Tran Van Giau, *Hoi Ky 1940–1945* [Memoirs 1940–1945]. Available at www .tapchithoidai.org/ThoiDai21/TranVanGiau_HoiKy_ToanBo.pdf.

Tran Van Thuy, *Nhat ky Thanh Nien Xung Phong Truong Son, 1965–1969* [Diary of a Youth Assault Brigade volunteer in Truong Son] (Ho Chi Minh City: Van Hoa Van Nghe, 2011).

Other Vietnamese-Language Publications

Ban Tu Tuong-Van Hoa Trung Uong, *Tai lieu hoc tap Nghi quyet Hoi nghi lan thu tam Ban Chap hanh Trung uong Dang khoa IX* [Materials for the study of the Eighth Central Committee Plenum of the Ninth Party Congress] (Hanoi: Chinh Tri Quoc Gia, 2004).

Tai lieu huong dan nghien cuu cac van kien (du thao) trinh Dai Hoi Dang toan quoc lan thu IX cua Dang [Materials to guide the study of draft documents presented at the Ninth Party Congress] (Hanoi: Chinh Tri Quoc Gia, 2000).

Tai lieu nghien cuu cac Nghi quyet Hoi nghi lan thu tu Ban Chap hanh Trung uong Dang khoa X [Materials for the study of the Fourth Central Committee Plenum of the Tenth Party Congress] (Hanoi: Chinh Tri Quoc Gia, 2007).

Ban Tuyen Giao Trung Uong & Bao Tang Ho Chi Minh [Central Party Commission on Propaganda and Education & Ho Chi Minh Museum], *Chu tich Ho Chi Minh voi nuoc Nga* [President Ho Chi Minh and Russia] (Hanoi: Chinh Tri Quoc Gia, 2013).

Bo Ngoai Giao [Ministry of Foreign Affairs], *Su that ve quan he Viet nam – Trung quoc trong 30 nam qua* [The truth about Sino-Vietnamese relations in the last thirty years] (Hanoi: Su That, 1979).

Bui Cong Trung and Luu Quang Hoa, *Hop Tac Hoa Nong Nghiep o Mien Bac Viet Nam* [Agricultural collectivization in North Vietnam] (Hanoi: Su That, 1959).

Cao Huy Thuan, "Cong ham Pham Van Dong: Gop y ve viec giai thich" [Pham Van Dong's Diplomatic Note: How to Interpret it], *Thời Đại Mới* [New Era], July 31, 2014), www.tapchithoidai.org/ThoiDai31/201431_CaoHuyThuan .pdf.

C.B. (Ho Chi Minh), *Lien Xo Vi Dai* [The great Soviet Union] (Hanoi: Nhan Dan, 1956).

C.B., D.X., T.L., et al. (Ho Chi Minh), *Noi Chuyen My...* [Talking about America] (Hanoi: Quan Doi Nhan Dan, 1972).

Chu Van Chuc, "Qua trinh doi moi tu duy doi ngoai," *Nghien Cuu Quoc Te* 58 (September 2005), 1–8.

Dang Phong. ed. *Lich Su Kinh Te Viet Nam 1945–2000* [An Economic History of Vietnam 1945–2000], vol. 2: 1955–1975 (Hanoi: Chinh Tri Quoc Gia, 2005).

Dang Van Thai, ed. *Le Duan tieu su* [Biography of Le Duan] (Hanoi: Chinh tri Quoc gia, 2007).

Dang Xa Hoi Viet Nam [Vietnamese Socialist Party], *Thang Huu Nghi Viet-Trung-Xo voi nguoi tri thuc Viet nam* [The Vietnamese-Chinese-Soviet friendship month to Vietnamese intellectuals] (Hanoi: Dang Xa Hoi Viet Nam, 1954).

Dinh Tran Duong, *Tan Viet Cach Mang Dang trong cuoc van dong thanh lap Dang Cong San Viet Nam* [Tan Viet Revolutionary Party's role in the effort to form the Vietnamese Communist Party] (Hanoi: Chinh tri Quoc gia, 2006).

Duong Van Quang. "Nhung dac diem va xu the cua the gioi" [The characteristics and trends of the world], in Hoi Dong Ly Luan Trung Uong [Central Council on Theory], *Nhung van de ly luan va thuc tien moi dat ra trong tinh hinh hien nay* [Emerging theoretical and practical issues about the current situation] (Hanoi: Chinh tri Quoc gia, 2011), 108–189.

Duong Danh Dy, "Bo mat that cua cac nha lanh dao Trung quoc" [The real face of Chinese leaders], March 26, 2012. Available at http://xuandienhannom .blogspot.com/2012/03/normal-o-false-false-false.html.

Furuta, Motoo and Van Tao. *Nan Doi nam 1945 o Viet Nam: Nhung chung tich lich su* [The famine of 1945 in Vietnam: Historical evidence] (Hanoi: Khoa hoc Xa hoi, 2005).

Ho Chi Minh. *Bao cao chanh tri* [Political Report], speech at the Second Party Congress in 1951 (Trung Uong Cuc Mien Nam, 1952).

Ho Chi Minh, *Ket hop chat che long yeu nuoc voi tinh than quoc te vo san* [Unity of patriotism and proletarian internationalism] (Hanoi: Su That, 1976).

Hong Chuong, "Dong chi Nguyen Chi Thanh," in *Dai Tuong Nguyen Chi Thanh* [General Nguyen Chi Thanh], compiled by Vu Nhi Xuyen (Hue: Thuan Hoa, 1997), 307–335.

Huy Duc, *Ben Thang Cuoc* [The winners], 2 vols. (Los Angeles: Osinbook 2012).

Lam Hoang Manh. *Buon vui doi thuyen nhan* [Life of a boatperson] (Falls Church, VA: Tieng Que Huong, 2011).

Le Cong Phung. "Tinh chat, xu huong thoi dai hien nay" [The nature and trends of the current era], in Hoi Dong Ly Luan Trung Uong [Central Council on Theory], *Nhung van de ly luan va thuc tien moi dat ra trong tinh hinh hien nay* [Emerging theoretical and practical issues about the current situation] (Hanoi: Chinh tri Quoc gia, 2011), 11–63.

Le Duan, *Giai cap vo san voi van de nong dan trong cach mang Viet nam* [The proletariat and the peasant question in the Vietnamese revolution] (Hanoi: Su That, 1965).

Le Hi. "Vai net ve cuoc doi hoat dong cua Tu Lam" [Sketches of Tu Lam's activist career] (Tu Lam was one of Le Hi's pseudonyms). *Talawas*, July 2, 2007. Available at http://www.talawas.org/talaDB/showFile.php?res=10325 &rb=11.

Le Quynh, "Bai hoc tu quan he Viet-Xo" [Lessons from Soviet-Vietnamese relationship], n. d. Accessed at www.bbc.co.uk/vietnamese/specials/170_viet_studies/page3.shtml.

Le Van Dung, *Xay dung Quan Doi Nhan Dan Viet Nam ve chinh tri* [Developing the political character of the PAVN] (Hanoi: Quan Doi Nhan Dan, 2004).

Luong Van Dong, Tan Trong Can, Vuong Trieu Van, et al., *Chien luoc dien bien hoa binh cua My* [The US strategy of peaceful evolution], transl. from Chinese (Hanoi: Tong Cuc II, 1993).

Minh Tranh, *Tham nong thon Lien Xo* [Visiting rural Soviet Union] (Hanoi: Su That, 1956).

Cach mang Nga va Viet nam [The Russian Revolution and Vietnam] (Hanoi: Su That, 1957).

Chung run so truoc anh huong cua Cach mang Thang Muoi toi Viet Nam [They trembled at the influence of the Russian Revolution in Vietnam] (Hanoi: Su That, 1958).

Ngo Tran Duc, "Huyen thoai kep Ho Chi Minh: Vinh quang va nhung he luy" [The double myth about Ho Chi Minh: Glory and troubles], April 21, 2011. Accessed at www.viet-studies.info/NgoTranDuc_HuyenThoaiKepHCM.htm.

Nguoi Quan Sat [a pseudonym], "Mot cuoc thuyet giang cho tri thuc – Vu cat cap tau Binh Minh 2: Yeu con cho don cho vot' " [A lecture for intellectuals on the incident involving the ship Binh Minh 2: A father's tough love for his child], November 17, 2011. Available at http://boxitvn.blogspot.com/2011/11/nguoi-quan-sat-xin-hay-oc-bai-nay-e.html.

Nguyen Anh Lan (Maj. Gen.), ed. *Chien luoc dien bien hoa binh* cua De quoc My va cac the luc phan dong quoc te chong Chu nghia Xa hoi va chong Viet Nam Xa hoi Chu nghia [The strategy of peaceful evolution of the United States and other international reactionary forces against socialism and socialist Vietnam] (top secret, internal circulation only) (Hanoi: Chinh Tri Quoc Gia , 1993).

Nguyen Anh Lan (Maj. Gen.), ed. *Chien luoc dien bien hoa binh* De quoc My va cac the luc phan dong quoc te chong Chu nghia Xa hoi va chong Viet Nam Xa hoi Chu nghia [The strategy of peaceful evolution of the United States and other international reactionary forces against socialism and socialist Vietnam] (top secret, internal circulation only) (Hanoi: Chinh Tri Quoc Gia, 1993).

Nguyen Dinh Thuc, "*Chu truong cua Dang Cong san Viet nam ve quan he doi ngoai voi ASEAN (1967–1995)*" [The VCP's policy on Vietnam's relations with ASEAN], unpublished PhD dissertation (Ho Chi Minh City: Hoc Vien Chinh Tri Quoc Gia [National Institute of Politics], 2001).

Nguyen Duc Phuong. *Chien Tranh Viet Nam toan tap* [A complete account of the Vietnam War] (Ontario, Canada: Lang Van, 2001).

Nguyen Ngoc Tien, "Tuong dai o Hanoi" [Public statues in Hanoi], *Ha Noi Moi*, December 31, 2011. Available at http://hanoimoi.com.vn/Tin-tuc/1000_nam_thang_long/534712/tuong-dai-o-ha-noi-tiep-theo.

Nguyen Quoc Thu and Nguyen Van Chi, eds. *Nguyen Van Nguyen: Nha hoat dong chinh tri, nha bao, nha van hoa* [Nguyen Van Nguyen: Politician, journalist and cultural activist] (Ho Chi Minh City: Tong Hop, 2006).

Nguyen Thi Mai Hoa. *Cac nuoc Xa hoi chu nghia ung ho Viet Nam khang chien chong My, cuu nuoc* [Socialist countries' assistance to Vietnam's resistance against America to save the country] *(Hanoi: Chinh tri Quoc gia, 2013)*.

Nguyen Tuan, The Lu, Tu Mo, et al. *Chung toi tham Lien Xo* [Our visit to the Soviet Union] (Hanoi: Van Nghe, 1956).

Nguyen Van Thom (a pseudonym), *Duong di muon dam* [A very long, long journey] (Hanoi: Tuyen truyen van nghe, 1954).

Nguyen Van Tuan, "Nhung nguoi ban Trung quoc cua chu tich Ho Chi Minh" [President Ho Chi Minh's Chinese friends], *Xua va Nay* [Past and Present], no. 395–396, January 2012.

Nhan Dich Khanh and Chu Quang Ky, *Dia ly the gioi* [World Geography], transl. Nguyen Duoc and Nguyen An (Hanoi: Bo Giao Duc, 1955).

Pham Binh Minh, ed. *Dinh huong chien luoc doi ngoai Viet Nam den 2020* [Guideposts for Vietnam's foreign policy strategy in 2020] (Hanoi: Chinh tri Quoc gia, 2010).

Pham Hong Chuong, Do Dinh Hang, Trieu Quang Tien, et al., eds. *Truong Chinh Tieu Su* [Biography of Truong Chinh] (Hanoi: Chinh tri Quoc gia, 2007).

Pham Quang Tuan, "Co can phai thong cam cho ong Pham Van Dong?" [Should we have sympathy for Mr. Pham Van Dong?], *Bauxite Vietnam*, June 15, 2014, http://boxitvn.blogspot.com/2014/06/co-can-phai-thong-cam-cho-ong-pham-van.html.

Pham Quy Thich, *Nha bao Ho Chi Minh o Que Lam* [The journalist Ho Chi Minh in Que Lam] (Hanoi: Cong an nhan dan, 2006).

Pham Van Tra, *60 Nam Quan Doi Nhan Dan Viet Nam* [The PAVN at sixty years] (Hanoi: Quan Doi Nhan Dan, 2004).

Pham Xuan Nam, Pham Thi Ha, and Nguyen Ngoc Tuan, eds., *Giao su Vien si Nguyen Khanh Toan: Cuoc doi va su nghiep* [Professor and Academician Nguyen Khanh Toan: His life and career] (Hanoi: Chinh tri Quoc gia, 2013).

Quang Dam, *Quang Dam: Nha Bao, Hoc Gia* [Quang Dam: Editor and scholar] (Hanoi: Lao Dong, 2002).

Tap Chi Cong San, *Chong Chu Nghia Banh Truong Ba Quyen Trung Quoc* [Against Chinese expansionism and hegemonism] (Hanoi: Tap Chi Cong San, 1983).

Thep Moi, *Nhu anh em mot nha* [Like brothers in the same family] (Hanoi: Van Hoc, 1958).

Thuy Khue, *Nhan Van Giai Pham va Van de Nguyen Ai Quoc* [Nhan Van-Giai Pham and the issues concerning Nguyen Ai Quoc] (Online publication, 2011), 595–597. Available at http://thuykhue.free.fr/stt/n/nhanvan15-2.html.

Tong Cuc Chinh Tri [General Political Department], *Cong tac Dang, cong tac chinh tri chien dich trong khang chien chong My, cuu nuoc* [Party work and political work in military campaigns during the anti-American resistance to save the country], v. 2 (internal circulation only) (Hanoi: Quan doi nhan dan, 1998).

Tran Dang Thanh, "Dai ta Tran Dang Thanh giang ve bien Dong cho lanh dao cac truong Dai hoc" [Colonel Tran Dang Thanh lectures on the Eastern Sea to university administrators], December 19, 2012. Available at http://anhbasam.wordpress.com/2012/12/19/1481-dai-ta-tran-dang-thanh-giang-ve-bien-dong-cho-lanh-dao-cac-truong-dai-hoc/#more-86178.

Tran Giang. *Nam Ky Khoi Nghia: 23 thang 11 nam 1940* [The Southern uprising: November 23, 1940] (Hanoi: Chinh tri Quoc gia, 1996).

Tran Luc (Ho Chi Minh), *Lien Xo vi dai* [The great Soviet Union] (Hanoi: Su That, 1957).

Truong Chinh, *Ve van de Cam-pu-chia* [On the issue of Cambodia]. Hanoi: Su That, 1979.

"Nhan dan Viet nam kien quyet danh bai moi muu mo xam luoc cua chu nghia banh truong va chu nghia ba quyen Trung Quoc" [The Vietnamese people will resolutely defeat the aggressive plots of China's expansionism and hegemonism], in Tap Chi Cong San, *Chong Chu Nghia Banh Truong Ba Quyen Trung Quoc* [Against Chinese expansionism and hegemonism] (Hanoi: Tap Chi Cong San, 1983).

"Noi chuyen voi can bo Quan doi lop tap huan," [Talk to military cadres' study session], August 7, 1971. In Truong Chinh, *May van de quan su trong cach mang Viet-nam* [Some military issues in the Vietnamese revolution] (Hanoi: Quan Doi Nhan Dan, 1983).

"*Chung ta chien dau cho doc lap va dan chu*" [We fight for independence and democracy], speech at the Fifth Cadre Conference, August 8–16, 1948. (Ban Chap hanh Lien khu Dang bo Lien khu X, 1948).

Books and Articles in English

Abuza, Zachary. *Renovating Politics in Contemporary Vietnam* (Boulder, CO: Lynne Rienner Publishers, 2001).

Adler, Emanuel. "Constructivism in International Relations: Sources, Contributions, and Debates," in Walter Carlsnaes, Thomas Risse, and Beth Simmons, eds. *Handbook of International Relations*, 2nd ed. (New York: Sage, 2013), 112–144.

Anderson, Benedict. *Imagined Communities* (London: Verso, 1991).

Anderson, David and John Ernst, eds. *The War That Never Ends: New Perspectives on the Vietnam War* (Lexington: University Press of Kentucky, 2007).

Ang, Cheng Guan. *Ending the Vietnam War: The Vietnamese Communists' Perspective* (New York: RoutledgeCurzon, 2003).

Armstrong, J. D. *Revolution and World Order: The Revolutionary State in International Society* (Oxford, UK: Clarendon Press, 1993).

Arrighi, Giovanni, Terence Hopkins, and Immanuel Wallerstein. *Antisystemic Movements* (London: Verso, 1989).

Asselin, Pierre. *Hanoi's Road to the Vietnam War, 1954–1965* (Berkeley: University of California Press, 2013).

Baldanza, Kathlene. *Ming China and Vietnam: Negotiating Borders in Early Modern Asia* (New York: Cambridge University Press, 2016).

Bartholomew-Feis, Dixie. *The OSS and Ho Chi Minh: Unexpected Allies in the War against Japan* (Lawrence: University Press of Kansas, 2006).

Berman, Larry. *No Peace, No Honor: Nixon, Kissinger, and Betrayal in Vietnam* (New York: The Free Press, 2001).

Bradley, Mark. *Imagining Vietnam & America: The Making of Postcolonial Vietnam 1919–1950* (Chapel Hill: University of North Carolina Press, 2000).

Brandenberger, David. *National Bolshevism: Stalinist Mass Culture and the Formation of Modern Russian National Identity, 1931–1956* (Cambridge, MA: Harvard University Press, 2002).

Brigham, Robert. "Why the South Won the American War in Vietnam," in Marc Jason Gilbert, ed. *Why the North Won the Vietnam War* (New York: Palgrave, 2002).

Brocheux, Pierre. *Ho Chi Minh: A Biography*, transl. Claire Duiker (New York: Cambridge University Press, 2007).

Brocheux, Pierre and Daniel Hemery. *Indochina: An Ambiguous Colonization 1858–1954*, transl. Ly-Lan Dill-Klein (Berkeley: University of California Press, 2009).

Brzezinski, Zbigniew. *The Soviet Bloc, Unity and Conflict* (Cambridge, MA: Harvard University Press, 1967).

Bui Tin. *From Enemy to Friend: A North Vietnamese Perspective on the War*, transl. Nguyen Ngoc Bich (Annapolis, MD: Naval Institute Press, 2002).

Calvert, Peter. *Politics, Power, and Revolution: An Introduction to Comparative Politics* (Brighton, Sussex: Wheatsheaf Books, 1983).

Catton, Philip. *Diem's Final Failure: Prelude to America's War in Vietnam* (Lawrence: University Press of Kansas, 2002).

Chanda, Nayan. *Brother Enemy: The War after the War* (San Diego: Harcourt Brace Jovanovich, 1986).

Christie, Clive. "*Internationalism and Nationalism: Western Socialism and the Problem of Vietnam.*" Occasional papers no. 3, Center for South-East Asian Studies, University of Hull, 1982.
   Ideology and Revolution in Southeast Asia 1900–1980: Political Ideas of the Anti-Colonial Era (Richmond, Surrey: Curzon Press, 2001).

Cold War International History Project, "Le Duan and the Break with China." *Cold War International History Project Bulletin* 12:13 (Fall/Winter 2001).

Conge, Patrick. *From Revolution to War: State Relations in a World of Change* (Ann Arbor: University of Michigan Press, 1996).

de Tréglodé, Benoît. *Heroes and Revolution in Vietnam*, transl. Claire Duiker (Singapore: NUS Press in association with IRASEC, 2012).

Devillers, Phillipe and Jean Lacouture. *End of a War* (New York: Praeger, 1969).

Dror, Olga. "Establishing Ho Chi Minh's Cult: Vietnamese Traditions and Their Transformations," *Journal of Asian Studies* 75: 2 (2016), 433–466.

Duiker, William. *The Rise of Nationalism in Vietnam, 1900–1941* (Ithaca, NY: Cornell University Press, 1976).
   Ho Chi Minh: A Life (New York: Hyperion, 2000).

Dutton, George. "Cach Mang, Révolution: The Early History of 'Revolution' in Vietnam," *Journal of Southeast Asian Studies* 46: 1 (2015), 4–31.

Elliott, David, ed. *The Third Indochina Conflict* (Boulder, CO: Westview Press, 1981).

Elliott, David. *The Vietnamese War: Revolution and Social Change in the Mekong Delta 1930–1975* (New York: Armonk, 2003).
   Changing Worlds: Vietnam's Transition from Cold War to Globalization (New York: Oxford University Press, 2012).

Englebert, Thomas and Christopher Goscha. *Falling out of Touch: A Study on Vietnamese Communist Policy toward an Emerging Cambodian Communist Movement, 1930–1975* (Melbourne: Monash Asia Institute, Monash University, 1995).

FitzGerald, Frances. *Fire in the Lake: The Vietnamese and the Americans in Vietnam* (Boston: Little & Brown, 1972).

Fitzpatrick, Sheila. "Cultural Revolution as Class War," in Sheila Fitzpatrick, ed. *Cultural Revolution in Russia, 1928–1931* (Bloomington: Indiana University Press, 1978).

Fulbright, William. *The Arrogance of Power* (New York: Random House, 1966).

Fulbright, William with Seth Tillman. *The Price of Empire* (New York: Pantheon Books, 1989).

Gaddis, John. *We Now Know: Rethinking Cold War History* (New York: Oxford University Press, 1997).

Gaiduk, Ilya. *The Soviet Union and the Vietnam War* (Chicago: Ivan Dee, 1996). *Confronting Vietnam: Soviet Policy toward the Indochina Conflict, 1954–1963* (Washington, DC: Woodrow Wilson Center, 2003).

George, Alexander L. "The "Operational Code": A Neglected Approach to the Study of Political Leaders and Decision-Making," *International Studies Quarterly* 13: 2 (1969): 190–222.

Gerring, John. "Ideology: a Definitional Analysis," *Political Research Quarterly* 50, no. 4 (1997): 957–994.

Gettleman, Marvin, Jane Franklin, Marilyn Young, eds. *Vietnam and America: The Most Comprehensive Documented History of the Vietnam War*, 2nd ed. (New York: Grove Press, 1995).

Gibbons, William. *The U.S. Government and the Vietnam War: Executive and Legislative Roles and Relationships: Part I: 1945–1960* (Princeton, NJ: Princeton University Press, 1986).

Gilks, Anne. *The Breakdown of the Sino-Vietnamese Alliance, 1970–1979* (Berkeley: Institute of East Asian Studies, University of California, 1992).

Goh, Evelyn. *Meeting the China Challenge: The U.S. in Southeast Asian Regional Security Strategies* (Washington, DC: East-West Center, 2005).

Goldstein, Judith and Robert O. Keohane, *Ideas and Foreign Policy: Beliefs, Institutions, and Political Change* (Ithaca, NY: Cornell University Press, 1993).

Goldstone, Jack. "Comparative Historical Analysis and Knowledge Accumulation in the Study of Revolutions," in James Mahoney and Dietrich Rueschemeyer, eds. *Comparative Historical Analysis in the Social Sciences* (New York: Cambridge University Press, 2003).

Goodwin, Jeff. *No Other Way Out: States and Revolutionary Movements, 1945–1991* (New York: Cambridge University Press, 2001).

"Revolutions and Revolutionary Movements," in Thomas Janoski, Robert Alford, Alexander Hicks, et al., eds., *The Handbook of Political Sociology* (New York: Cambridge University Press, 2005).

Gorbachev, Mikhail. *Perestroika: New Thinking for Our Country and the World* (New York: Harper & Row, 1987).

Goscha, Christopher. *Vietnam: A State Born of War, 1945–1954* (unpublished manuscript).

"Courting Diplomatic Disaster?: The Difficult Integration of Vietnam into the Internationalist Communist Movement (1945–1950)," *Journal of Vietnamese Studies* 1: 1 (2006): 59–103.

"Choosing between the Two Vietnams: 1950 and Southeast Asian Shifts in the International System," in Christopher Goscha and Christian Ostermann, eds. *Connecting Histories: Decolonization and the Cold War in Southeast Asia, 1945–1962* (Washington, DC: Woodrow Wilson Center Press, 2009), 207–237.

Going Indochinese: Contesting Concepts of Space and Place in French Indochina (Copenhagen: NIAS, 2012).

Gould-Davies, Nigel. "Rethinking the Role of Ideology in International Politics during the Cold War," *Journal of Cold War Studies* 1: 1 (1999).

Halliday, Fred. *Revolution and World Politics: The Rise and Fall of the Sixth Great Power* (Durham, NC: Duke University Press, 1999).

Hellbeck, Jochen. *Revolution on My Mind: Writing a Diary under Stalin* (Cambridge, MA: Harvard University Press, 2006).

Heng, Russell. "Leadership in Vietnam: Pressures for Reform and Their Limits," *Contemporary Southeast Asia* 15: 1 (June 1993), 98–110.

Herring, George. "America and Vietnam: The Debate Continues," *The American Historical Review* 92: 2 (April 1987).

America's Longest War, 4th ed. (New York: Mc Graw-Hill, 2002).

"The War that Never Seems to Go Away," in David Anderson and John Ernst, eds. *The War that Never Ends: New Perspectives on the Vietnam War* (Lexington: University Press of Kentucky, 2007).

Ho Chi Minh, "The path that led me to Leninism," in Prasenjit Duara, ed. *Decolonization: Perspectives from Now and Then* (New York: Routledge, 2004), 31.

Ho Van Ky-Thoai. "Naval Battle of the Paracels," in K. W. Taylor, ed. *Voices from the Second Republic of South Vietnam (1967–1975)* (Ithaca, NY: Cornell Southeast Asian Program Publications, 2014), 153–158.

Hoang Van Thai. *How South Vietnam Was Liberated*, 2nd ed. (Hanoi: The Gioi Publishers, 1996).

Hodal, Kate and Jonathan Kaiman, "At least 21 dead in Vietnam's anti-China protests over oil rig," *The Guardian*, May 15, 2014. Available at www.theguardian.com/world/2014/may/15/vietnam-anti-china-protests-oil-rig-dead-injured.

Holcombe, Alex. "Stalin, the Moscow Show Trials, and Contesting Visions of Vietnamese Communism in the late 1930s: A Reappraisal," paper presented at the Workshop on the Vietnamese Revolution, University of California, Berkeley, November 11–12, 2011.

Horn, Robert. *Alliance Politics between Comrades: The Dynamics of Soviet-Vietnamese Relations* (Los Angeles: RAND/UCLA Center for the Study of Soviet International Behavior, August 1987).

Hui, Victoria Tin-bor, "Why War Both Made and Unmade State? A Synthetic perspective of State formation and the Chinese Case." Unpublished paper, 2014.

Hunt, Michael. *Ideology and US Foreign Policy* (New Haven, CT: Yale University Press, 1987).
The Genesis of Chinese Communist Foreign Policy (New York: Columbia University Press, 1996).
Huntington, Samuel. *Political Order in Changing Societies* (New Haven, CT: Yale University Press, 1968).
Hurst, Steven. *The Carter Administration and Vietnam* (New York: MacMillan Press, 1996).
Huynh, Kim Khanh. *Vietnamese Communism 1925–1945* (Ithaca, NY: Cornell University Press, 1982).
Jervis, Robert. "Socialization, Revolutionary States and Domestic Politics," *International Politics* 52: 5 (2015), 609–616.
Jian, Chen. "The Myth of America's 'Lost Chance' in China: A Chinese Perspective in Light of New Evidence," *Diplomatic History* 21:1 (Winter 1997), 77–86.
Mao's China and the Cold War (Chapel Hill: University of North Carolina Press, 2001).
Johnson, Lyndon. "Lyndon B. Johnson Explains Why Americans Fight in Vietnam, 1965," in Robert McMahon, ed. *Major Problems in the History of the Vietnam War: Documents and Essays*, 2nd ed. (Lexington, MA: D. C. Heath, 1995), 210–211.
Jordan, William, Lewis Stern and Walter Lohman, "US-Vietnam Defense Relations: Investing in Strategic Alignment," *Backgrounder* 2707 (July 18, 2012). Available at http://report.heritage.org/bg2707.
Kahin, George. *Intervention: How America Became Involved in Vietnam* (New York: Knopf, 1986).
Kahin, George and John Lewis. *The United States in Vietnam*, 2nd ed. (New York: Delta, 1969).
Kaplan, Robert. "The Vietnam solution: How a former enemy became a crucial US ally in balancing China's rise," *The Atlantic*, May 21, 2012. Available at http://www.theatlantic.com/magazine/archive/2012/06/the-vietnam-solution/308969/?single_page=true.
Karnow, Stanley. *Vietnam, a History* (New York: Viking Press, 1983).
Katz, Mark. *Revolutions and Revolutionary Waves* (London: Macmillan, 1997).
Kelley, Liam. *Beyond the Bronze Pillars: Envoy Poetry and the Sino-Vietnamese Relationship* (Honolulu: University of Hawaii Press, 2005).
Kerkvliet, Benedict J. *The Power of Everyday Politics: How Vietnamese Peasants Transformed National Policy* (Ithaca, NY: Cornell University Press, 2005).
Khoo, Nicholas. *Collateral Damage: Sino-Soviet Rivalry and the Termination of the Sino-Vietnamese Alliance* (New York: Columbia University Press, 2011).
Kiernan, Ben. *The Pol Pot Regime: Race, Power, and Genocide in Cambodia under the Khmer Rouge, 1975–79* (New Haven, CT: Yale University Press, 1996)
Kim, Kyung-won. *Revolution and the International System* (New York: New York University Press, 1970).
King, Martin Luther, Jr. "Declaration of Independence from the War in Vietnam," April 1967. In Marvin Gettleman, Jane Franklin, Marilyn Young, et al., eds.

Vietnam and America: The Most Comprehensive Documented History of the Vietnam War, 2nd ed. (New York: Grove Press, 1995), 313.

Kotkin, Stephen. *Magnetic Mountain: Stalinism as a Civilization* (Berkeley: University of California Press, 1995).

Lenin, V. I. "On the Tasks of the Proletariat in the Present Revolution," April 7, 1917. In V. I. Lenin, *Selected Works* (Moscow: Foreign Languages Publishing House, 1952), v.2, book 2, 13–17.

The National-Liberation Movement in the East, 2nd impression, transl. by M. Levin (Moscow: Foreign Languages Publishing House, 1962).

Levin, M. "Society, State, and Ideology during the First Five-Year Plan," in Sheila Fitzpatrick, ed. *Cultural Revolution in Russia, 1928–1931* (Bloomington: Indiana University Press, 1978).

Levine, Marilyn. *The Found Generation: Chinese Communists in Europe during the Twenties* (Seattle: University of Washington Press, 1993), 159–160.

Levy, David W. *The Debate over Vietnam*, 2nd ed. (Baltimore: The Johns Hopkins University Press, 1995).

Little, Richard and Steve Smith. *Belief Systems and International Relations* (Oxford, UK: Blackwell, 1988).

Logevall, Fredrik. *Choosing War: The Lost Chance for Peace and the Escalation of War in Vietnam* (Berkeley: University of California, 1999).

Embers of War: The Fall of an Empire and the Making of America's Vietnam (New York: Random House, 2012).

Loicano, Martin. "The Role of Weapons in the Second Indochina War: Republic of Vietnam Perspectives and Perceptions," *Journal of Vietnamese Studies* 8: 2 (2013).

Luthi, Lorenz. *The Sino-Soviet Split: Cold War in the Communist World* (Princeton, NJ: Princeton University Press, 2008).

Luu, Doan Huynh. "The Paris Peace Agreement and the Vietnamese vision of the future," in Odd Arne Westad and Sophie Quinn-Judge, eds. *The Third Indochina War: Conflict between China, Vietnam and Cambodia, 1972–79* (New York: Routledge, 2006), 87–102.

Maley, William. "Interpreting the Taliban," in William Maley, ed. *Fundamentalism Reborn? Afghanistan and the Taliban* (New York: New York University Press, 1998), 1–28.

Marr, David G. *Vietnamese Anticolonialism, 1885–1925* (Berkeley: University of California Press, 1971).

Vietnamese Tradition on Trial, 1920–1945 (Berkeley: University of California Press, 1981).

Vietnam 1945: The Quest for Power (Berkeley: University of California Press, 1995).

Vietnam: State, War, and Revolution, 1945–1946 (Berkeley: University of California Press, 2013).

Martin, Terry. *The Affirmative-Action Empire: Nations and Nationalisms in the Soviet Union, 1923–1939* (Ithaca, NY: Cornell University Press, 2001).

Martini, Edwin. *Invisible Enemies: The American War on Vietnam, 1975–2000* (Amherst: University of Massachusetts Press, 2007).

McMahon, Robert, ed. *Major Problems in the History of the Vietnam War: Documents and Essays*, 2nd ed. (Lexington, MA: D. C. Heath, 1995).

McNamara, Robert, James Blight, and Robert Brigham. *Argument without End* (New York: Public Affairs, 1999).

McVey, Ruth. *The Rise of Indonesian Communism* (Ithaca, NY: Cornell University Press, 1965).

Mertha, Andrew. *Brothers-in-Arms: Chinese Aid to the Khmer Rouge, 1975–1979* (Ithaca, NY: Cornell University Press, 2014).

Mevius, Martin. "Reappraising Communism and Nationalism," *Nationalities Papers* 37: 4 (2009).

Miller, Edward. *Misalliance: Ngo Dinh Diem, the United States, and the Fate of South Vietnam* (Cambridge, MA: Harvard University Press, 2013).

Miller, Edward and Tuong Vu, "The Vietnam War as a Vietnamese War: Agency and Society in the Study of the Second Indochina War," *Journal of Vietnamese Studies* 4:3 (2009), 1–16.

Morris, Stephen J. *Why Vietnam Invaded Cambodia: Political Culture and the Causes of War* (Stanford, CA: Stanford University Press, 1999).

Moyar, Mark. *Triumph Forsaken: The Vietnam War, 1954–1965* (New York: Cambridge University Press, 2006).

Ngo, Van. *In the Crossfire: Adventures of a Vietnamese Revolutionary*, transl. from French by Helene Fleury et al. (Oakland, CA: AK Press, 2010).

Nguyen, Gregory Tien Hung and Jerrold Schecter. *The Palace File* (New York: Harper and Row, 1986).

Nguyen, Lien-Hang. "The War Politburo: North Vietnam's Diplomatic and Political Road to the Tet Offensive." *Journal of Vietnamese Studies* 1: 1–2 (2006).

Hanoi's War: An International History of the War for Peace in Vietnam (Chapel Hill: University of North Carolina Press, 2012).

Nguyen, The Anh. "Japanese Food Policies and the 1945 Great Famine in Indochina," in Paul Kratoska, ed. *Food Supplies and the Japanese Occupation in South-East Asia* (New York: St. Martin's, 1998), 208–226.

Nguyen, Vu Tung. "Coping with the United States: Hanoi's search for an effective strategy," in Peter Lowe, ed. *The Vietnam War* (London: MacMillan Press, Ltd., 1998).

"The Paris Agreement and Vietnam-ASEAN relations in the 1970s," in Odd Arne Westad and Sophie Quinn-Judge, eds. *The Third Indochina War: Conflict between China, Vietnam and Cambodia, 1972–79* (New York: Routledge, 2006), 103–125.

Nincic, Miroslav. *Renegade Regimes: Confronting Deviant Behavior in World Politics* (New York: Columbia University Press, 2005).

Ninh, Kim. *A World Transformed: The Politics of Culture in Revolutionary Vietnam, 1945–1965* (Ann Arbor: University of Michigan Press, 2002).

Nove, Alec. *An Economic History of the USSR, 1917–1991* (London: Penguin, 1992)

Olsen, Mari. *Soviet-Vietnam Relations and the Role of China, 1949–64: Changing Alliances* (London: Routledge, 2006).

Owen, John M. *The Clash of Ideas in World Politics: Transnational Networks, States, and Regime Change, 1510–2010* (Princeton, NJ: Princeton University Press, 2010).

Path, Kosal. "Hà Nội's Responses to Beijing's Renewed Enthusiasm to Aid North Vietnam, 1970–1972," *Journal of Vietnamese Studies* 6, no. 3 (2011).

"The Sino-Vietnamese Dispute over Territorial Claims, 1974–1978: Vietnamese Nationalism and Its Consequences," *International Journal of Asian Studies* 8: 2 (2011), 189–220

"China's Economic Sanctions against Vietnam, 1975–1978," *China Quarterly* 212 (December 2012), 1040–1058.

Patti, Archimedes. *Why Vietnam? Prelude to America's Albatross* (Berkeley: University of California Press, 1980).

Pelley, Patricia. *Postcolonial Vietnam: New Histories of the National Past* (Durham, NC: Duke University Press, 2002).

Peycam, Philippe. *The Birth of Vietnamese Political Journalism: Saigon, 1916–1930* (New York: Columbia University Press, 2012).

Pike, Douglas. *PAVN: People's Army of Vietnam* (New York: Presidio Press, 1986).

Porter, Gareth. *Perils of Dominance: Imbalance of Power and the Road to War in Vietnam* (Berkeley: University of California Press, 2005).

Pribbenow, Merle. "General Vo Nguyen Giap and the Mysterious Evolution of the Plan for the 1968 *Tet* Offensive." *Journal of Vietnamese Studies* 3: 2 (Summer 2008).

"Vietnam Covertly Supplied Weapons to Revolutionaries in Algeria and Latin America." Cold War History Project e-Dossier No. 25, n.d. Available at www.wilsoncenter.org/publication/e-dossier-no-25-vietnam-covertly-supplied-weapons-to-revolutionaries-algeria-and-latin

"Vietnam Trained Commando Forces in Southeast Asia and Latin America." Cold War History Project E-dossier no. 27, January 2012. Available at www.wilsoncenter.org/publication/e-dossier-no-27-vietnam-trained-commando-forces-southeast-asia-and-latin-america.

Quinn-Judge, Sophie. *Ho Chi Minh: The Missing Years 1919–1941* (Berkeley: University of California Press, 2002).

"Rethinking the History of the Vietnamese Communist Party," in Duncan McCargo, ed. *Rethinking Vietnam* (New York: Routledge, 2004), 27–39.

"The Ideological Debate in the DRV and the Significance of the Anti-Party Affair, 1967–68." *Cold War History* 5, no. 4 (2005).

Radchenko, Sergey. *Two Suns in the Heavens: The Sino-Soviet Struggle for Supremacy, 1962–1967* (Washington, DC: Woodrow Wilson Center, 2009).

Renshon, Jonathan. "Stability and Change in Belief Systems: the Operational Code of George W. Bush," *The Journal of Conflict Resolution* 52, no.6 (2008): 821–828.

Rosecrance, Richard. *Action and Reaction in World Politics; International Systems in Perspective* (Boston: Little, Brown, 1963).

Rosenau, James. *International Aspects of Civil Strife* (Princeton, NJ: Princeton University Press, 1964).

Rotter, Andrew. "Chronicle of a War Foretold: The United States and Vietnam, 1945–1954," in Mark Lawrence and Fredrik Logevall, eds. *The First Vietnam War: Colonial Conflict and Cold War Crisis* (Cambridge, MA: Harvard University Press, 2007), 282–308.

Sartori, Giovanni. "Politics, Ideology, and Belief Systems," *The American Political Science Review* 63, no. 2 (1969): 398–411.

Sheehan, Neil. *A Bright Shining Light: John Paul Vann and America in Vietnam* (New York: Random House, 1988).

Shore, Zachary. *A Sense of the Enemy: The High Stakes History of Reading Your Rival's Mind* (New York: Oxford University Press, 2014).

Skocpol, Theda. *States and Social Revolutions: A Comparative Analysis of France, Russia, and China* (New York: Cambridge University Press, 1979).

"What Makes Peasants Revolutionary?" *Comparative Politics* 14: 3 (1982), 351–375.

"Revolutions and Mass Military Mobilization," *World Politics* 40: 2 (1988), 147–168.

Smith, R. B. *An International History of the Vietnam War*, v. 2 (New York: St. Martin's, 1983).

Smith, S. A. *Revolution and the People in Russia and China: A Comparative History* (New York: Cambridge University Press, 2008).

Smyser, W. R. *Independent Vietnamese: Vietnamese Communism between Russia and China, 1956–1969* (Athens: Ohio University Center for International Studies, 1980).

Snyder, Robert S. "The U.S. and Third World Revolutionary States: Understanding the Breakdown in Relations," *International Studies Quarterly* 43: 2 (1999): 265–290.

Szalontai, Balazs. "The Diplomacy of Economic Reform in Vietnam: The Genesis of Doi Moi, 1986–1989," 아세아연구 *(The Journal of Asiatic Studies)*. 51, no. 2 (2008): 199–252.

Tannenwald, Nina. "Ideas and Explanation: Advancing the Theoretical Agenda," *Journal of Cold War Studies* 7: 2 (2005).

Taylor, Keith. "The Vietnamese Civil War of 1955–1975 in Historical Perspective." In Andrew Wiest and Michael Doidge, eds. *Triumph Revisited: Historians Battle for the Vietnam War* (Hoboken, NJ: Taylor & Francis, 2010).

Terhalle, Maximilian. "Revolutionary Power and Socialization: Explaining Revolutionary Zeal in Iran's Foreign Policy," *Security Studies* 18: 3 (2009), 557–586.

Thayer, Carlyle. "Security Relations and Prospects for Strategic Dialogue between the United States and Vietnam." Unpublished paper.

"Vietnamese Perspectives on International Security: Three Revolutionary Currents," in Donald McMillen, ed. *Asian Perspectives on International Security* (London: Macmillan, 1984), 57–76.

War by Other Means: National Liberation and Revolution in Vietnam, 1954–1960 (Sydney: Allen & Unwin, 1989).

"Vietnamese Foreign Policy: Multilateralism and the Threat of Peaceful Evolution." Carlyle Thayer and Ramses Amer, eds., *Vietnam's Foreign Policy in Transition* (Singapore: Institute of Southeast Asian Studies, 1999), 1–24.

"The Economic and Commercial Roles of the Vietnam People's Army," *Asian Perspective* 24: 2 (2000), 87–120.

"The Structure of Vietnam-China Relations, 1991–2008," paper presented at the Third International Conference on Vietnamese Studies, Hanoi, December 4–7, 2008.

"Upholding state sovereignty through global integration: Remaking Vietnamese National Security," paper presented at the Workshop, "Vietnam, East Asia, and Beyond," at the Southeast Asia Research Center, City University of Hong Kong, December 2008.

"Background Brief: Vietnam's Military Diplomacy – China and the United States." Unpublished paper (March 2010).

Thayer, Carlyle and Gerard Hervouet, "The Army as a Political and Economic Actor in Vietnam," in Christopher Goscha and Benoit de Treglode, eds., *Naissance d'un Etat-Parti – Le Viet Nam depuis 1945* [The birth of a party-state – Vietnam since 1945] (Paris: Les Indes Savantes, 2004), 355–381.

Tønnesson, Stein. *The Vietnamese Revolution of 1945* (Newbury Park, CA: SAGE Publications, 1991).

Vietnam 1946: How the War Began (Berkeley: University of California Press, 2010).

Turley, William. *The Second Indochina War*, 2nd ed. (New York: Rowman & Littlefield, 2009)

Veith, George. *Black April: The Fall of South Vietnam 1973–1975* (New York: Encounter Books, 2012).

Vickerman, Andrew. *The Fate of the Peasantry: Premature "Transition to Socialism" in the Democratic Republic of Vietnam* (New Haven, CT: Yale University Southeast Asia Studies, Yale Center for International and Area Studies, 1986).

Vo, Nhan Tri. *Vietnam's Economic Policy Since 1975* (Singapore: ASEAN Economic Research Unit, Institute of Southeast Asian Studies, 1990).

Vu, Tuong. "It's Time for the Indochinese Revolution to Show Its True Colors: The Radical Turn in Vietnamese Politics in 1948," *Journal of Southeast Asian Studies* 40: 3 (October 2009).

Paths to Development in Asia: South Korea, Vietnam, China, and Indonesia (New York: Cambridge University Press, 2010).

"Van Kien Dang Toan Tap: The Regime's Gamble and Researchers' Gains," *Journal of Vietnamese Studies* 5:2 (Summer 2010), 183–194.

"The Party v. the People: Anti-China Nationalism in Contemporary Vietnam," *Journal of Vietnamese Studies* 9:4 (Fall 2014).

"State Formation on China's Southern Frontier: Vietnam as a Shadow Empire and Hegemon," *HumaNetten*, forthcoming.

Vuving, Alexander. "Strategy and Evolution of Vietnam's China Policy: A Changing Mixture of Pathways," *Asian Survey* 46: 6 (2006), 805–824.

"Vietnam: A Tale of Four Players," *Southeast Asian Affairs* 2010: 1, 366–391.

Walt, Stephen. *Revolution and War* (Ithaca, NY: Cornell University Press, 1996).

Weathersby, Kathryn. "Soviet Aims in Korea and the Origins of the Korean War, 1945–1950: New Evidence from Russian Archives," in Christian Ostermann, ed. Cold War International History Project Working Paper 8 (Washington, DC: Woodrow Wilson Center for Scholars, 1993).

Westad, Odd Arne. *Cold War and Revolution* (New York: Columbia University Press, 1993).

The Global Cold War: Third World Interventions and the Making of Our Times (Cambridge, UK: Cambridge University Press, 2005).

Westad, Odd Arne and Sophie Quinn-Judge, eds. *The Third Indochina War: Conflict between China, Vietnam and Cambodia, 1972–79* (New York: Routledge, 2006).

Wiest, Andrew. *Vietnam's Forgotten Army: Heroism and Betrayal in the ARVN* (New York: New York University Press, 2008).

Wiest, Andrew, ed. *America and the Vietnam War* (London and New York: Taylor & Francis, 2009).

Wight, Martin. *Power Politics*, in Hedley Bull and Carsten Holbraad, eds. (New York: Holmes & Meier, 1978), 81–94.

Womack, Brantly. *China and Vietnam: The Politics of Asymmetry* (Cambridge: Cambridge University Press, 2006).

Yang, Dali. *Calamity and Reform in China* (Stanford, CA: Stanford University Press, 1996).

Young, Marilyn. *The Vietnam Wars, 1945–1990* (New York: HarperPerennial, 1990)

Zhang, Xiaoming. *Deng Xiaoping's Long War: The Military Conflict between China and Vietnam, 1979–1991* (Chapel Hill: University of North Carolina Press, 2015).

Zhai, Qiang. *China and the Vietnam Wars, 1950–1975* (Chapel Hill: University of North Carolina Press, 2000).

Zinoman, Peter. *The Colonial Bastille: A History of Imprisonment in Vietnam, 1862–1940* (Berkeley: University of California Press, 2001).

"Nhan Van-Giai Pham and Vietnamese 'Reform Communism' in the 1950s: A Revisionist Interpretation," *Journal of Cold War Studies* 13: 1 (2011), 60–100.

Index

conflict over, 133–134, 136–138, 224–231

DRV acceptance of, 22–23, 122–123, 127–128

Germany
Cold War politics in, 119–120
ICP view of, 83, 85, 95–97
labor unrest in, 64
Soviet Union and, 181

Giang, Dang Kim, 163, 175

Giang, Nguyen Kien, 29, 123–124

Giap, Vo Nguyen, 192, 228

Giau, Tran Van, 28–29, 87–89

globalization
Vietnamese economic reforms and, 270–272
Vietnamese schizophrenia concerning, 280–282

GMD. *See* Chinese Nationalist Party (Guomindang or GMD)

Gorbachev, Mikhail, 9–10, 23–24, 238, 245–252, 253–259, 261–263, 265, 273

Goscha, Christopher, 114

government documents, as research source, 29–30

Great Britain
ICP and, 97–101
postwar occupation of Vietnam by, 101–108
Vietnamese relations with, 85

Great Depression, world politics and, 63–64, 75–77

Great Leap Forward (People's Republic of China), 162

Gromyko, Andrei, 237

Guantanamo, U.S. military in, 219

Gulf of Tonkin
Chinese attack on Vietnamese fishermen in, 282–286
Vietnam War and, 178, 294–295

Ha, Nguyen Manh, 112n.69

Hai Phong harbor, mining of, 227

Halliday, Fred, 12–13, 221

Han, Hoang Xuan, 112n.69

harmonious world, Confucian concept of, 39n.32

Hi, Le, 117

Hien, Le Van, 30

Hiep, Duong Phu, 249–250

Hitler, Adolf, 86–87

Hoan, Tran Quoc, 192, 218

Ho Chi Minh
absence in interwar period of, 87–89
American perceptions of, 6–8
anti-American articles by, 301–302
antirevisionist campaign and, 180
armed struggle for South Vietnam and, 142–147
arrest of, 52, 63, 70
"August Revolution" and, 213
China and, 101–108, 118n.5, 120, 223–224
Comintern investigation of, 81
Comintern ties with, 47–51, 80–81
conversion to Leninism by, 31–32
criticism of, 47, 50, 65–66, 74–75, 89, 102, 129–130
Cuban missile crisis and, 165
cult of, 37n.28
Dong Duong Communist Party leaders and, 44–45
early education of, 31n.2
foreign policy of, 101–108
French colonialists and, 295
Ha Huy Tap and, 74–75, 79–80
ICP purges and, 67n.16
ICP structure and, 45, 67–69, 92–93, 130
interest in Bolshevism of, 34–35
Khrushchev and, 135–136
lack of interest in leading ICP, 45, 92–93, 130
newspaper articles written by, 127–131
Office of Strategic Services (OSS) and, 100–101
path to revolution of, 32–40
propaganda skills of, 127–131, 148
return to Vietnam of, 23, 90
Soviet and Chinese recognition of DRV and, 109–114
Soviet political upheaval and, 150–153
in Soviet Union, 16–17, 35–38, 44, 77, 81–82
Stalin and, 80, 88–89, 91–92, 117–120, 118n.4, 123–124, 299–300
support for class struggle, 67, 300n.4
testimony of, 288–289
Tran Phu and, 47–58, 50–51, 60–61, 65–66
Trotskyists and, 80–82